THE LAST EMPIRE

THE LAST EMPIRE

Nationality and the Soviet Future

Edited by
ROBERT CONQUEST

HOOVER INSTITUTION PRESS

Stanford University, Stanford, California

Hoover Press Publication 325

Copyright 1986 by the Board of Trustees of the
Leland Stanford Junior University

First printing, 1986
Manufactured in the United States of America
90 89 88 87 86   9 8 7 6 5 4 3 2 1

Library of Congress Cataloging in Publication Data
Main entry under title:

The Last Empire.
1. Soviet Union—Ethnic relations—Addresses, essays, lectures. I. Conquest, Robert.
DK33.L347 1986   327.47   85-27225
ISBN 0-8179-8251-5

Design by P. Kelley Baker

Contents

Editor's Foreword

Robert Conquest

Of the various forces that will in one way or another determine the Soviet future, it is widely recognized that those of nationality, in its broadest sense, are among the most crucial.

The intention of this book is to add to the stock of both information and thinking on the matter.

The names of the contributors, which include many of the most brilliant and respected in modern European and American Sovietology, will be enough to validate the claim that this collection is an important contribution to sound study, and so to policy.

The problems are complex and multifarious, and we do not here attempt some final and systematic display of answers. All major aspects of the subject are indeed covered. The opinions of contributors on certain points differ in certain ways. More important, this book, rather than spuriously systematizing a field in which there are so many imponderables, seeks to cast illumination on the whole matter from a number of directions, sometimes by new research, sometimes by the distillation of experienced judgment. Some contributions truly give a fresh illumination; in others the peripheral, the speculative, the newly discovered provide (the reader may think) a further perspective or extra angle of view.

Not that the book was in any sense unplanned, as will be evident from the central core of essays which develop the main themes from all the key perspectives, or cover the main regional problems. It was originally commissioned as a collection. When its contents became known, the Hoover Institution on War, Revolution and Peace of Stanford University, with financial support from the United States Information Agency, sponsored a conference, which was held under my chairmanship at Stanford on April 13–16, 1983. Most of the contributors were able to attend, and most of these essays were presented as papers and debated by an impressive cross-section of academic and governmental experts in the field. Nevertheless, it was originally conceived as a book and is not a collection of conference papers in the ordinary sense.

Generally speaking, the essays speak for themselves and need no further introduction. That is to say, on the national question in general, and on minority aspirations, while many fresh insights and much new information emerge here, the picture of a Moscow in continual difficulties with the minority nations is a familiar one. What has perhaps been more neglected, and is here treated in a number of contributions, is the question of the national feelings of the Russians themselves.

It seems often to be assumed that, since the minority nations in the Soviet empire are denied normal national rights, Russian national feeling is ipso facto "nationalist," in a negative sense. Alexander Solzhenitsyn has long since shown that this is not so: though himself an exemplar of the deepest national feeling, he has urged freedom of secession for the peripheral nations; and though he sees himself as speaking for "the Russians and Ukrainians"—and he has elsewhere added the Belorussians—he puts his hopes for an eventual free union of the East Slav nations second to the fulfillment of their own will to liberty and statehood.

It is surely reasonable to admit that Russian patriotism, even if it has been perverted as other patriotisms have also been, can be a force for good. And, when it comes to Western policies, we should certainly support the liberties of the Soviet subject nations. But we should never neglect appeal to the true Russian national feeling—which has been both exploited and repressed under the present regime.

There are subjects in this field on which our knowledge is imperfect; and which yet need to be discussed. There are themes on which very different views may be held; and I have not in this book excluded some very controversial writing, which may yet develop insights or turn our attention in directions otherwise neglected. For instance, few would probably take the detail of Dr. Agursky's particular Kremlinology as more than speculation: but it is clear that something of that nature has been going on in high party circles. The fact that the "country" writers, whose work is a massive and often overt condemnation of modernization and even of collectivization (which they depict as ruining that rural culture in which they see the true source of the national spirit), have been published and have even received high awards, can only be explained by protection from high party circles; as, indeed, is true of the public patronage of the painter Glazunov of which Dr. Krasnov writes. It is equally clear that a number of influential people and journals oppose them and that since 1983 they have lost ground. None of this is to say that even their party defenders share their views: indeed, it may be that such party figures have no clear and explicit notion of any conscious "National Bolshevism." But it does show a trend or tendency—even if it proves abortive—which it would be unprofessional to ignore.

Only so much can be covered in a single book. This one is restricted, in general, to the problems and perspectives arising within the USSR itself, not dealing with the Soviet-dominated areas outside it. Nevertheless, it would have been absurd not to refer at all to the large and heavily populated countries where Moscow's sway is exerted in a manner different from the direct rule seen at home; and we are fortunate to have a general essay on the region by one of Eastern Europe's most distinguished citizens, Milovan Djilas.

It is sad to record the death, since their contributions were written, of two of the world's most distinguished scholars in the Soviet field—Leonard Schapiro and Hugh Seton-Watson.

Contributors

Mikhail Agursky is a Fellow of the Soviet and East European Research Centre at the Hebrew University of Jerusalem. He was a contributor to *Under The Rubble*.

Frederick C. Barghoorn is Professor Emeritus at Yale University and the author of many books, including *Soviet Russian Nationalism*.

Alexandre Bennigsen is Directeur Emeritus d'Etudes at the Ecole des Hautes Etudes en Sciences Sociales in Paris. He is the author of *Islam in the Soviet Union* and other works.

Mikhail S. Bernstam is a Senior Research Fellow at the Hoover Institution, Stanford University, and has written widely on Soviet demography and other fields.

Alain Besançon is Directeur d'Etudes at the Ecole des Hautes Etudes in Paris. He is the author of *The Intellectual Origins of Leninism* and other works.

Robert Conquest is a Senior Research Fellow and Scholar-Curator of the Russian and East European Collection at the Hoover Institution. He is the author of a number of works on Soviet affairs.

Milovan Djilas is a former Secretary of the Central Committee of the Yugoslav Communist Party and the author of a number of books, including *The New Class.*

John B. Dunlop is Associate Director and Senior Fellow at the Hoover Institution. He is the author of *The Faces of Contemporary Russian Nationalism* (1983) and *The New Russian Nationalism* (1985).

Vladislav Krasnov is Associate Professor and Head of Russian Studies at the Monterey Institute of International Studies. He is the author of *Solzhenitsyn and Dostoevsky.*

Teresa Rakowska-Harmstone is Professor of Political Science at Carleton University in Ottawa, Canada, and the author of *The Warsaw Pact* and other works.

The late **Leonard Schapiro** was Professor of Political Science at the London School of Economics and author of *The Communist Party of the Soviet Union* and other books.

Gertrude E. Schroeder is Professor of Economics at the University of Virginia, specializing in the sphere of the Soviet economy and society.

The late **Hugh Seton-Watson** was Professor of Russian History at the School of Slavonic Studies, London University, and the author of *Nationalism and Communism* and other works.

Alexander Shtromas is a Reader in Politics and Contemporary History at the University of Salford and the author of *Political Change and Social Development: The Case of the Soviet Union* and other works.

Roman Szporluk is Professor of History at the University of Michigan, Ann Arbor, and the author of works on Russian, Ukrainian, and other East European themes.

Donald W. Treadgold is Professor of History at the University of Washington, Seattle, and the author of many works, including *Twentieth Century Russia.*

S. Enders Wimbush is Director of the Society for Central Asian Studies, Oxford, England, and joint author with Alexandre Bennigsen of *Muslim National Communism in the Soviet Union.*

THE LAST EMPIRE

Nationalism and Bolshevism in the USSR

Alain Besançon

Communism is a jealous god. It tolerates nothing at its own level. Where it reigns in absolute triumph, there is room for nothing else—no classes, no religions, no wealth, no culture, no language, no law, no common morality, and no nation. Yet its triumph requires accepting the presence of, seeking out an alliance with, and sometimes even creating these classes, this culture, this morality, and these nations. For the sixty-eight years during which Leninism has taken root and spread across the earth, there is no force it has found as indispensable or as frightening to it as nationalism.

In Russia, the concepts of nation and people jointly sprang from the concept of *narod*. The narod is neither the *plebs* nor the *populus*—both concepts that sprang from an urban political life, absent in Russia. *Narod* has a religious connotation and evokes a community gathered in the same faith, like the Jewish *kahal* or the Greek *laos*. *Narodnost'* carries with it a sense of romantic exaltation, as in *Volkstum*, that gave support to the official nationalism of the tsars of St. Petersburg, the utopia of the Slavophiles, and also that of the populists. It legitimized both that part of the tsarist political system most opposed to the modern world (even to the enlightened tradition of St. Petersburg) and also the revolt that sought to strike down the tsars. The magic word *narod*, ambiguous since it was first coined, was brandished by both sides, and ended up with two accepted (and opposite) uses: it means nation, which from the official point of view encompasses the frontiers of imperial Russia, and from the non-Russian nationalities' point of view strengthens the emancipation movement; and it means people, as opposed to westernized classes and the state. Used in these two senses, *narod* retains the magical qualities that made it the supreme value to which all were invited to devote their lives.

Lenin saw that both interpretations of *narod* could be summed up in an overall theory that the party would put into practice. Insofar as it is a social concept, Lenin saw the concept of people as confused and requiring translation in the light of Marxism; it had to be seen through the perspective of the class struggle. In his first work, his massive study of the development of capitalism in Russia, Lenin took the concept of people out of the village, the very spot where populism had placed it. Instead of the people, he saw an array of classes—or "social levels," if they did not deserve to be called classes—that were, or should be, subordinated to the class par excellence, the proletariat. Insofar as *narod* refers to the nation, he naturally subordinated the concept of people to the class struggle. The role of the people, in both of the word's accepted uses, was to be a source of energy for the revolution. But it was the proletariat, and the party as representative of the proletariat, that was to use this energy. "The bourgeoisie of the oppressed nations will call upon the proletariat to give unlimited support to its aspirations. The most practical response would be for the proletariat to say openly 'Yes' for the liberation of its particular country and 'No' to the right of self-determination of all [other] nations . . . [But] the proletariat recognizes equality of rights and an equal right [for all] to constitute a national state. It gives highest value to the alliance of proletariats from all countries, and it is from the point of view of the class struggle of workers that it evaluates all nationalist demands and national separatist movements."[1]

The nation thus became part of general Marxist theory, which relegated each thing to its place. Lenin's nation is a social entity made up in part by class. Which class? The bourgeoisie. According to Lenin, one must make a "strict distinction" between two periods of capitalism, which "differ radically." In the first period, there is society and a "democratic bourgeois" state, and national movements become mass movements that involve all classes. In the second period, "the eve of the collapse of capitalism," hostility between the proletariat and the bourgeoisie is the dominant feature.[2] Stalin summed all this up with his usual clarity: "On occasion the bourgeoisie is able to get the proletariat involved in the national movement, and on these occasions the national struggle assumes the *guise* of a 'general popular' movement."[3] But the essential nature of this movement remains bourgeois, advancing the interests of and sought principally by the bourgeoisie.

This theory points out the key role of class beneath the trappings of the nation. It "unmasks" the false unanimity of national movements, which are essentially class movements. The proletariat is instructed to redirect the energies of such conflicts toward its own goals and to support national struggles to the extent that it can use them. The proletariat is depicted as international in scope because it has lost its countries to bourgeois usurpation. But, without losing sight of its transnational goal, the proletariat must reconquer the nation, which belongs to it by right. When the revolutionary struggle has ended, when all the people are united behind the proletariat and the entire country is subjugated to it, then the tension between the two senses of the term *narod* will disappear. It will mean indistinguishably both people and nation.

Such is the Leninist perspective. Nation is subordinate to class, and class is subordinate to party, which is its essence. The party represents the working class by virtue of the self-legitimizing nature given it by ideology. In practical terms, therefore, the party decides, according to its overall policies, whether to employ the nationalist forces of political struggle or the class forces, or it may combine the two. Classes and nations are no longer natural realities, entities that have autonomy and the capacity to organize themselves. They are instead abstract notions that exist only in an overall theory, in the wooden language of ideology. Their role is to be used in the changing lines and political positions taken by the party.

These very basic considerations suffice to sketch sixty-eight years of Soviet policy with regard to the national problem.

THE GREAT RUSSIANS

Lenin's problem in the first months after the October putsch was to establish the Bolshevik party as the core around which the state could be reconstituted. So, after a period in which the party sought the disintegration of the state and voiced anarchist slogans, there followed, without the least transition, a period in which the goal was to rally to the party a large part of the traditional military and administrative framework. These officers and functionaries had several motives for joining the Bolsheviks: (1) a desire for order and a wish to make life endurable by ending the anarchy and re-establishing a minimum of legality; (2) patriotism and fear of losing several centuries of constructive efforts in a new "time of troubles"; and (3) nationalism and the hope of saving the one and indivisible Russia, the Russian empire.

The nature of Bolshevik power gave reason to the last motive. But the order that Bolshevism brought was no more acceptable than anarchy, and the systematic destruction of all Russian and human values could only offend patriotism. Bolshevik power, however, was capable of restoring the domination of a single state over most of the territories of the old empire. This result was enough to satisfy the proponents of nationalism in its lowest form. According to Custine, "the slave on his knees dreams of world empire." This is how the alliance between Bolshevism and Great Russian nationalism was formed; that alliance has been the principal moral force of the Soviet regime for its entire history, and it remains so even today.

The Bolshevik–Great Russian alliance was quick to attract non-Bolshevik theorists, often from the extreme right, like Nikolai Ustrialov. But I do not think that this alliance was between equals, nor that there was a progressive fusion between nationalism and Bolshevism in the Stalinist synthesis, as Agursky tries to show.[4] In fact, the party remained the master of this alliance and knew how to maintain the subordinate relationship that Lenin had established: party-class-nation. The revolutionary goal, which was utopian and ideological, was not abandoned for the sake of the nationalist goal: extension or maintenance of the empire. The problem for the party was to keep the party-class-nation hierarchy in the correct order.

For several years it appeared necessary to fight actively not only against Russian patriotism—an obvious necessity—but also against nationalism itself. This was done by waging antichauvinist and even anti-Russian campaigns. But these had only pedagogical value and only served to keep in line allies that might compromise the party. Then, beginning in the 1930s, Russian nationalism was progressively integrated into the ideology. Russian cultural and historical heritages were worked into a stockpile from which the party could select items of nationalistic value that would serve the dynamics of the Soviet state. Peter the Great, for instance, served as a historical example of the military and modernization program of the Soviet state, and a few years later Ivan the Terrible provided a precedent for the permanent purge. The paintings of the Peredvizhniki, in which populism and nationalism were inextricably intertwined, became the formal model for socialist realism. The regime found a socialist use for the classical novel, particularly when, as in the case of Tolstoy, it depicted military glory and scorn for the West. But anything in this same heritage that had universal value and could only be appreciated in a transnational context (religious thought, modern art, Dostoevsky, and so forth) was censored and banned.

If one makes a distinction between patriotism—one's ties to a natural community—and nationalism, in which resentment of the nation's weaknesses and hatred of things foreign play a role, patriots were suspect because they were bound to a former reality that was doomed to destruction along with religion, the family, and social classes, all the targets of persecution. Nationalism was encouraged because it fostered destructive hatred toward what was external to the communist world, which the revolutionary project planned to annihilate. Authentic patriotism was thus stigmatized as "bourgeois nationalism." But the most chauvinistic Russian nationalism was praised as "Soviet patriotism." Even better, this Soviet patriotism was the principal force that supported communism's world project, so that chauvinistic nationalism, by following a carefully marked "dialectical" detour, was put in the service of "proletarian internationalism." Thus the state formed a necessary alliance with nationalism and used it to implant the Soviet state within the old frontiers of the Russian empire; it then used this same instrument to extend its form and domination beyond its frontiers. Proletarian internationalism was the external expression of Russian nationalism, an assistance in and a motivating force for communization. It was for this reason that all advances of communism were accompanied by advances of Russianism. In Poland or in Czechoslovakia, this meant the obligatory study of Russian in school; a revamping of history to underscore the ties between these peoples and the Russian people; a premium given to Russian art, music, and literature; and a corresponding de-emphasis of Western art.

THE NON-RUSSIAN NATIONALITIES

Lenin's use of the nationalist demands of the non-Russian nationalities came even earlier than his call to Russian nationalism. Indeed, the latter was used for the construction of the Soviet state whereas the former was the most efficient engine for the decomposition of the tsarist empire. By March 1921, however, when Georgia was retaken, all of the non-Russian nationalities were under Soviet control. Was this a contradiction? Not at all. "In any bourgeois nationalism in an oppressed nation," Lenin wrote in 1914, "there is a general democratic content that is focused against oppression; and it is this content that we support without reserve, while rigorously isolating it from the tendency toward national exclusivism."[5] Once the "general democratic content" has spent its energies, the task of the party is to struggle against "nationalist exclusivism," which works against the working class, represented by its party. As Stalin noted beginning in May 1918: "Autonomy is a form. Soviet power is not against autonomy; it is for autonomy, but only for an autonomy where all the power is in the hands of the workers and peasants, where the bourgeoisie of all nationalities is not only deprived of power but also of participation in elections for the governing bodies.'"[6] So the Georgians had the right to separatism, but the place of the Georgian Mensheviks was in prison, as was the case for all Mensheviks. The fact that they represented the vast majority of Georgians did not in the least mean that they had the right to represent their country. This right of representation belonged legitimately to the weak Bolshevik minority, solely by virtue of the fact that they were Bolsheviks. If this minority was put in power by the Red Army, did not demand separatism, and on the contrary developed "friendship between peoples," it had the complete right to do so.

Nevertheless, integrating the communist project with the demands of the non-Russian nationalities remained a problem. Bolshevism had triumphed as the "emancipator of peoples." How could it keep that title? Here we encounter the most essential component of the Bolshevik art of governing: compromise.[7] In Bolshevik ideology, a compromise is a temporary concession to practical considerations. It is imposed in order to allow the ideology to retain power while awaiting the opportunity for complete victory when conditions permit the withdrawal of concessions. An example of a political compromise was NEP, the new economic policy that ended War Communism but saved the state and prepared the way for collectivization. Brest-Litovsk is an example in foreign policy; great amounts of territory were abandoned in 1918 to save the state and allow eventual reconquest. In religious policy, one compromise was the re-establishment during World War II of the patriarchate, which, at the beginning of the war, had placed the existing resources of the Orthodox church at the service of the state. In economic policy, Soviet compromises included tolerance of the private lots, the kolkhoz market, the black market, and corruption. A compromise must be agreed to in such a manner that it brings to the party an extra boost of force. This allows the party to remain master of the terms of the compromises and able to revoke them whenever it deems appropriate. To describe nationalities policy, therefore, is to describe the compromise that was effected in this essential domain.

One can distinguish between the general pan-Soviet clauses of compromise and the local clauses that applied to the particular conditions of each nationality. The nationalities do have frontiers. It is easy to see in this fact only a symbolic satisfaction, but in nationality matters symbols have importance. One can say the same of administrative autonomy and the facade of self-government, with Supreme Soviets, Presidiums, Councils of Ministers, and Supreme Courts in each republic. Although these provisions appear merely decorative, they are not entirely so. They were the subject of a conflict between Communists who advocated centralized power and called themselves internationalists—their opponents called them Luxemburgists—and Communists who claimed strict adherence to the autonomist provisions. This conflict continues even today. It was apparent when Brezhnev redrew the Soviet constitution. One version sought to wipe out national frontiers and replace them with "economic regions." It was vainly defended as a progressive step in the construction of communism, but it did not see the light of day.

The other major area of compromise is culture and national language. Stalin had already indicated the limits: "Proletarian culture, whose content is socialist, takes on different forms and manners of expression with each of the different peoples who participate in the work of building socialism, according to differences in language, style of life, etc. Proletarian in its content, national in its form: such is the universal human culture toward which socialism is advancing."[8] So above all there is the same *diamat* (dialetical materialism), but for each national region it is appropriate to allow something of the former cultural structure to subsist.

The Soviet system retained the local classics, which mixed with Russian classics and were deemed compatible with Soviet ideology. This strategy did not cause problems with the medieval epics of the Caucasus or Central Asia, but it created delicate problems with the works of Shevchenko. What would be cut and what would be retained was subject to compromise, and the party decided which way to go. Generally, it was the higher level of culture that was most closely scrutinized, and often repressed, on the grounds that it could furnish the basis of a bourgeois nationalist movement; lower levels of culture, it was held, were neutral and posed no threat. In consequence, national culture moved toward folklore. In theaters throughout the Soviet Union, functionaries costumed as Cossacks, Circassian mountain people, or medieval Uzbeks dance and sing melodies collected and arranged by the ideologized folklorists of the past century or the present one. Performances of these traditional works serve as a substitute for the cultural life of these nations, replacing what for some time now has been wiped away by the dreary drabness of the cities and of local dress and by the pan-Soviet uniformity of the wooden language. Folklore serves to remind these nations of their past cultural life—through the prism of a falsified history—and to make them see socialism's promised convergence of people and nation into the eschatological *narod*.

Besides these major areas of compromise, there are also special compromises involving each nation; we cannot explore the details here. In some cases only minimal concessions to the characteristics of the nationality are necessary. The Ukraine falls into this category. For three centuries, control over the Ukraine made the Russian empire a great power. It is out of the question to give the Ukraine hope of independence. It is too populous, too rich, and too strong to allow the creation of a viable, balanced compromise; the nation would instead move toward independence. The Ukraine was struck by two great famines in 1921 and 1933; it underwent several purges; and after destruction by the Nazis it was destroyed again by a new wave of repression and another famine. It has lost its elites, its vital forces. The Ukrainian language has been eliminated from the cities and reduced to a rural dialect. The Baltic countries have been treated in much the same manner, but for another reason: they were too weak. The imbalance of forces did not necessitate the granting of concessions.

There has, however, been maximum compromise with the Turkish nationalities. They were at first terribly decimated (the Kazakh people in particular), Balkanized, and Russified. But for the past twenty years the terms of the compromise have been reversed. These nations have maintained their coherence, thanks to the role played by Islam. Their demographic growth has progressively pushed out the Russian element. They recall their illustrious history of independence and dominance. They know that time works in their favor. This trend makes of the compromise a medium-term alliance. These nations are developing in the shelter of the Soviet system, which perhaps offers less threat of destruction than does contact with the West. They furnish great services to the Soviet state through their loyalty in matters regarding foreign policy. Meanwhile they wait for circumstances to become more favorable to a radical restructuring of their relations with the Soviet state. Confident that this moment will arrive, they are content to let things develop naturally.[9]

Finally, other nations have worked out special arrangements. This was the case for Georgia, which has undergone several ups and downs. It was also the case for the Jews. Their majority support was one of the causes of the Bolshevik success. They had no reason to support the old regime, and the new one promised emancipation and free access to secondary and higher education, which had always been one of the deepest aspirations of the Russian Jews. The situation of the Jews rapidly worsened, to the point where it was almost a question of a "final solution" in 1953; in recent years there has been a slow and inexorable pressure on them, marked by increasing restrictions on their access to higher education. They have, however, precariously obtained an exorbitant privilege—the possibility of emigration. The Armenian people has been perhaps the only non-Russian nationality to collaborate openly and continuously with Soviet communism; in the aftermath of genocide, the survival of the nation was at stake. Armenia has suffered in turn from Bolshevism, but it—as well as its diaspora—has obtained significant advantages, the most recent of which has been the opportunity to fill some of the posts of Jews who have been dismissed.

The overall balance sheet of Soviet nationalities policy, now in its seventh decade, is certainly positive, because the Soviet system endures. It does seem, however, that the difficulty of holding together is increasing.

The sum of Soviet concessions to the non-Russian nationalities has had a quasi-geographic result that all observers have noticed. The border areas of the USSR that are inhabited by the non-Russian nationalities are better cultivated, cleaner, more decent, and benefit from higher living standards than the core Russian area. In many areas the compromise has been carried so far that the kolkhozes have almost become agricultural production cooperatives, which they do not have the right to be in Russia, except in theory. The existence of the parallel economy has caused the growth of a veritable civil society, which threatens to absorb or to influence the local Communist parties. Decisions by the courts and actions by the police benefit the interests of the new elite, and it might not be long before political decisions themselves can be influenced by private interests—and this would mark the end of Bolshevism. The accumulation of privileges dulls the edge of the nationality question and makes the Soviet framework endurable. The movement for national independence is thus corrupted at the same time that it is repressed. It is not suppressed, however. Should there be a vacuum of authority, as there was in 1917, the USSR would disintegrate as rapidly as did the old empire of the tsars.

From the point of view of the Russian nationality, the erosion of the relative weight of Russia brings uneasiness. The alliance with Bolshevism that brought so much satisfaction to Russian nationalism—the pleasure of domination, the accomplishment of Slavophile messianic prophecies, the extension of the language, and so on—has also produced an extraordinary diminution of the Russian nation. Because it has served as an instrument of Bolshevism and has remained closest to the center of power, it has been exposed more than other nationalities to the destructive aspects of the regime. Central, Muscovite Russia, the historical heart of the nation, displays, as far as the eye can see, ruined villages, fallow fields, gloomy towns, and miserable people, destroyed by alcoholism and morally crippled. The essential biological supports of life appear stricken—the birthrate is in decline, the mortality rate on the rise, and there is a frightening lack of good sanitary conditions. As for the condition of culture and language, it is better not to talk of them. Because of all these changes, the Bolshevik-Russian alliance might not be as solid as it used to be. To document this observation, we have not only the protests of Solzhenitsyn, which draw their inspiration from the purest sort of patriotism, but also a semiofficial or tolerated literature (such as the "peasant" literature of Valentin Rasputin), which evaluates this alliance and quietly condemns its monstrous cost. And there is also what remains, or is being revived, of the old Orthodox religious culture. The state's propaganda explains the condition of the Great Russians as best it can: as the result of the millenarian idealism and disinterested devotion of the Russian people to the happiness of humanity, which will of course be a socialist happiness.

The leaders of the people are aware of the malaise. But can they turn their backs on these compromises that represent the painstaking work of sixty-eight years? From the Bolshevik point of view, there are only two possible alternatives.

The first possibility would be a return to strict Leninism, which is what Stalin dreamed of accomplishing in his last years. Such a policy would entail the destruction of the nationalities, which would be mixed together in the magma of Sovietism—with a Russian flavor, no doubt, but even the Russian nation would lose its sharp definition. The current regime apparently does not have the strength to try such a policy. It would bring troubles and difficulties that would weaken the power of the state at the very moment when it most needs its power for foreign policy. It is no longer conceivable, at present, to do what Stalin dreamed of doing: to deport all the Jews and the entire Ukrainian nation. And yet such actions would be necessary to resolve this question completely.

The second alternative policy would be to increase Russian privileges and to strengthen the Russian-Bolshevik alliance by abandoning the compromises reached with the non-Russian nationalities. The practical effect of this step would be to restore officially the Russian empire and to abandon the fiction of a Soviet Union—which would not be very united and would have no Soviets. In order to gauge the full extent of such a move, it is first necessary to abandon the commonly held view that this change has taken place already. Most Western statesmen see the USSR as a prolongation of the Russian empire with a thin coating of socialist phraseology. If this were the case, abandoning Soviet ideology would be a simple matter. This is why so many experts hold that the technocrats and the military men are going to seize power at any moment, if they have not already done so. But power in the USSR is the pendant of ideology, which is its legitimizing support. If the ideology were withdrawn, power would dissipate. The USSR is not an empire. To have an empire, one must have a privileged people, an essentially military means of conquest, and limited goals. These were the characteristics of the Roman, Spanish, English, and French empires. The Russian people has no privilege. It has "advantages," certainly, as the surest ally of communism, and party leaders are often drawn from its ranks, even in the national republics. But these advantages are not rights. Moreover, they are compensated for by heavier obligations, exemption from which is considered by the Russians to be a privilege of the non-Russian nationalities. A Russian who enjoys privileges as a Communist owes his privileges to his communism, not to his Russianness. In theory he holds his loyalty to communism or to the Soviet Union, not specifically to Russia. Finally, the socialist scheme is unlimited in scope and intensity: it strives to transform the entire world, based on the initial communist model of the USSR, insofar as its ideology dictates and its self-occupation strategy permits.

There would be significant and immediate advantages to making official a pan-Russian military and police empire. Many advantages would flow from the suppression of ideology. This would be an enormous relief to the regime's subjects. In his *Letter to the Soviet Leaders*, Solzhenitsyn judges that this step would be sufficient to make the regime acceptable, no matter how despotic it remained in other domains.

Such a step would also bring enormous relief to the regime's leaders, who bear the heavier brunt of the obligations of ideology; they would at last be free to rule the USSR in conformity with good sense. Even if the system were to preserve its goals of power and expansion, it could attempt to attain them by rational means instead of by following the detours of absurd organization and meaningless speech.

Although a change of course toward a "National Bolshevism" might be tempting, and much as the natural evolution of the Soviet world seems to point in that direction, it ineluctably runs aground on the question of the legitimacy of power. Once the ideological magic has been destroyed, there would only be one source of magic left—the imperial or colonial legitimacy of the Russian people in a world that today is entirely decolonized. This anachronistic legitimacy would immediately stimulate the resistance of the non-Russian nations, who would call forth their own legitimacies, necessitating military occupation. The Russian people is not sufficiently populous for that task.

Consequently, the only viable political action left for Gorbachev, and very likely for any successor, is to navigate between an impossible return to Stalinism and the dangerous currents of National Bolshevism. The Russian people now reap all the satisfactions of the most chauvinistic Russianism, including the evocation of Dmitry Donskoi and the partial revival of Slavophile and Dostoevskian miscellany. But the party maintains its control over the alliance and its supremacy over the language of ideology. In the name of proletarian internationalism, Soviet patriotism, and the struggle against bourgeois nationalism, the party can conduct periodic purges of the non-Russian nationalities and send their militants to the Gulag. At the same time, the system will continue and may even expand—when unavoidable—its real concessions to the national republics, meanwhile affirming that these concessions are not rights and can be revoked.

In a word, the system's overall policy is to unleash Great Russian nationalism—one measure is the spread of anti-Semitism—while simultaneously allowing some progress for the non-Russian nationalities of the Soviet Union. To keep both sides of this double process well under control, the system uses more and more of the wooden language of Marxism-Leninism. This unstable mixture characterizes the present state of the compromise, but any compromise, seen from the Bolshevik perspective, is temporary and circumstantial.

It should be pointed out that this policy has parallels in the European people's republics, in Cuba, and in Vietnam. For many of these countries, nationalism provided the store of energy that permitted the socialist regimes to take power, and nationalism remains an important supporting force. The government in each of these countries developed a chauvinistic nationalism that recalls the country's glorious historic past, even in some rather suspect cases (Dracula, for instance, in Romania). The call to nationalism aids Soviet policy to the extent that it closes these countries on themselves, hardens their frontiers, impedes regional groupings, and keeps attention from straying to Western Europe and the United States. In Poland, for example, this nationalism helps to clothe the politics of the Communist Party in patriotic garb, even to the point of stimulating the acceptance of essentially communist goals as a lesser evil and a means of struggling against Russian imperialism. In this way Bolshevism puts to use what is contrary to its nature. The Bolshevik art of governing consists of making people accept the Russification that accompanies Sovietization, first in the name of proletarian internationalism and the socialist legitimacy of power, and then as a sacrifice that must be offered to assure the greatness, or the survival, of the nation.

Henri Queuille, who thrice served as prime minister during the Fourth French Republic, once said that there was no problem for which the absence of a solution would not bring a resolution. This observation is true of all things except national problems. In 1913 the government of the tsar thought that it had good possibilities for solving the economic, social, and even the political problems of the empire, but it had no way to solve the national problem. Consequently, it gave up on resolving the other problems, because their solution would have aggravated the national problem and threatened the Russian state.[10] The national problem was what led astray the Russian Revolution and prevented it from evolving as the English and French revolutions had. Bolshevism could restore what looked like the Russian empire; a liberal democracy would have caused it to fly apart. Nationalism had the effect of giving a bonus to Bolshevism. Things are the same today, with the important difference that now neither the economic nor the social and political problems faced by the Soviet regime are susceptible to solution. The system can only try to get by, to make things last for one year, for a thousand years, no one knows how long. Nationalism has become both the principal force holding the USSR together—Russian nationalism—and the principal force tearing it apart—the non-Russian nationalisms. The balanced tension of these two forces, pulling in opposite directions, keeps the Soviet Union in working order.

NOTES

1. Lenin, *Du droit des nations à disposer d'elles-mêmes* (1914), *Oeuvres choisies*, v. 1, p. 597, Moscow, 1975. Translations are by Peter S. Stern.

2. Ibid., p. 588.

3. Stalin, *Le Marxisme et la question nationale*, 1913.

4. M. Agursky, Ideologiia natsional-bol'shevizma (Paris: YMCA Press, 1980). See also the Agursky essay in this volume.

5. Lenin, *Du droit des nations*, p. 597.

6. Stalin, *Sochineniia*, v. 4, p. 87.

7. In the Soviet vocabulary, the word *compromise* has a pejorative sense and is almost always associated with the adjective *rotten* (*gniloi*). The Soviet term that corresponds most closely to my usage is *shag nazad*, meaning a step backwards or a tactical retreat. I nevertheless retain use of the term *compromise* as having a clear meaning for us.

8. Stalin, *Sochineniia*, v. 8, p. 138.

9. A. Bennigsen and C. Lemercier-Qualquejay, *Les Musulmans oubliés* (Paris: Maspero, 1981).

10. In fact, except for Poland and Finland, the national problem in imperial Russia was far from being as severe in 1913 as it has since become.

Russian Nationalism
in Historical Perspective

Hugh Seton-Watson

Any discussion of Russian nationalism as a historical phenomenon must begin with some clarification of the concepts of nationalism and nation. The word *nationalism* ought not to be used, as it all too often is, simply to describe selfish or aggressive behavior by governments of states. It should, I believe, be restricted to two meanings: a doctrine about political organization that puts the perceived interests of the nation above absolutely everything else, and a movement (usually a political party or several parties) whose professed aim is to promote the interests of the nation.

The history of nations is inextricably connected with the history of states, but a nation is not the same thing as a state, although the two are frequently confused in the language of the media and in the rhetoric of world politics. A state is a legal organization, based on a hierarchy of officials. A nation is a community of people who believe themselves to share a cultural heritage. That heritage may include a common language, literature, religion, and folklore; a complex of mutual economic interests; and a body of historical memories and myths—usually a combination of several, or even all, of these. A state may be inhabited by numerous language groups and religious or communal groups that coexist fairly amicably. But a nation is born as soon as a substantial minority from one of these communities (1) becomes convinced that its community is a nation, (2) puts forward claims for political recognition and political institutions of its own, and (3) is at least passively accepted in a leadership the merchant class than among the peasant masses, but even these were not unaffected.

The growth of Russian national consciousness can be seen in the lives of three outstanding men with very different political outlooks.

Pavel Pestel, the Decembrist, was a Jacobin in his views and methods and was also a social revolutionary who planned not only to emancipate the serfs but also to endow them with landed property and make them equal members of the Russian nation. For Pestel, the Russian nation clearly meant those whose language was Russian. He was the first political thinker to insist on the domination of Russians over all other peoples of the empire. These must "completely fuse their nationality with the nationality of the dominant people." The Poles were the only non-Russians of the empire to whom Pestel, in his theoretical work, *Russkaia pravda*, conceded independent national status. He limited the independence of the future Polish state by three important conditions. The Polish-Russian frontier was to be settled according to the convenience of Russia; there was to be a military alliance between the two states; and the Polish political system was to be based on the same principles as the Russian system.

Yuri Samarin, the Slavophile writer, was a landowner who served in the civil administration as a young man and later played a large role in the 1861 emancipation of the serfs and in the land reforms in Poland after suppression of the insurrection of 1863. In his thinking, as in Pestel's, social reform and Russian patriotism were closely connected, and they involved the subordination of the other nations of the empire to the Russians. During his service in the Baltic provinces, Samarin was infuriated by the conviction of the German landowning class that their culture was superior to Russia's and by the Baltic Germans' successful preservation, under the rule of the tsar, of legal, administrative, and educational systems quite distinct from the Russian. Samarin's thinking combined the natural inclination of the bureaucrat to impose a uniform administrative structure on all with passionate pride in Russian culture—based on the Russian language as well as on Russian Orthodox Christianity. He felt an obligation to liberate the Estonian and Latvian peasants from German economic and cultural domination, which, however, was to be replaced not by development of their own cultures but by the blessings of the superior Russian culture.

Count S. S. Uvarov was minister of education under Nicholas I from 1833 to 1849. A highly cultured and intelligent man, Uvarov was a confirmed conservative. He did, however, sympathize with those who insisted on the superiority of Russian culture and the predominance of

Russians over the other peoples of the empire. In his famous report to the tsar in 1832 Uvarov recommended, as the basis for all education, "the truly Russian saving principles of Autocracy, Orthodoxy, and a National Outlook (*narodnost*)." This threefold formula became the slogan of Russian conservatism and, indeed, defined the essence of the legitimacy of the regime for the next three-quarters of a century.

Yet there was a contradiction within the formula. Uvarov had added a third to the two traditional principles of legitimacy. The Russian nation had been placed on the same level as the tsar and the church, entitled to the same allegiance from Russian citizens. The introduction of this third principle had potential democratic implications. As such, it was objectionable to Nicholas I. The emperor was content that his subjects should loyally serve him in whatever roles the social hierarchy assigned them. It was of little importance to him whether or not their mother tongue was Russian. Nicholas disliked and repressed the Poles not because he wanted to make them into Russians but because they had rebelled against him. He resolutely refused to interfere with the institutions of the Baltic Germans and the Finlanders (Finnish or Swedish), or with the Armenian church, because all these peoples had shown themselves to be his devoted and loyal servants. Nicholas personally rebuked Samarin for his anti-German activities in the Baltic provinces. His successor, Alexander II, had the same attitude toward the Baltic Germans and was not persuaded by Samarin to change his view. It was not until the reign of Alexander III (1881–1894) that Russian nationalism received encouragement from the throne and began to be part of official policy.

Several different trends contributed to the new policies that became known as Russification. One was the anxiety of military leaders about frontier areas inhabited by non-Russian peoples, especially the Baltic coast and the Caucasus. A second was the zeal of the Orthodox hierarchy to spread its authority to new areas and, in some cases, to defend itself against the spread of other faiths, especially of Islam in the middle Volga valley. A third was the passion of bureaucrats for uniformity of administration, law, and education in all parts of the empire: they resented especially the existence of long-established advanced European systems in the Baltic provinces and Finland. A fourth trend, less easily identifiable but increasingly powerful, was an ideology of Russian nationalism that insisted on the superiority of Russian culture to all others and on the right and duty of the Russian government to impose it on all subjects of the empire.

The 1890s were the years when European imperialism, both in theory and in action, was at its height. The Russian nationalism that developed the revolutionary outbreaks of 1905–1906. In the brief period of quasi-parliamentary rule, non-Russian nationalist parties grew rapidly, and Russifying policies were modified or altogether abandoned. After the coup d'etat of June 1907, however, the old policies were renewed. The renewed pressure was especially severe in Finland and in the Volga valley. But the gains in national self-confidence, and even in the creation of national cultural institutions, could not be undone. The conflict between Russian official nationalism and non-Russian nationalism was a major feature of the last decade of imperial rule. It is also true that the ideological factor in Russian official nationalism was becoming relatively more important than the earlier military, bureaucratic, and ecclesiastical elements.

The appeal of nationalist demagogy to the Russian masses in this period has been underrated. Because it was the left that triumphed in 1917, and because almost all historians of Russia, whether Russian or foreign, have disliked nationalism, the view that Russian nationalism and Russification were confined to the ruling clique has prevailed. In particular, the Russian working class, "the most revolutionary in history," was presumed immune to this odious infection. But the truth is that in the last decade of imperial Russia strong political parties based on Russian nationalism appeared, favored of course by the post-1907 franchise but still winning their votes from a rather wide range of social forces. The pogroms organized by these people involved large mobs composed of the urban poor. The conventional formula states that participants in pogroms were limited to the *Lumpenproletariat* (the crudest and least educated workers). But this is a category that defies definition. The proposition that only members of the *Lumpenproletariat* indulged in pogroms is really tautological: it means essentially that only workers who enjoy mob violence, enjoy mob violence. That part of the working class that was linked to a socialist party was clearly unaffected by nationalist demagogy and did not join pogroms; but to equate the whole urban labor force with the politically conscious socialist workers is absurd. In reality, glorification of Russia and the Russian nation, combined with hatred of Jews, made a strong demagogical appeal. Anti-Semitism operated rather effectively as "the socialism of the imbecile," concentrating primitive anti-capitalist feeling against Jewish shopkeepers, who in large parts of the empire were the flesh-and-blood capitalists with whom the urban poor most frequently came into contact. Of course, not only Russian nationalism made use of anti-Semitic demagogy: Polish, Ukrainian, Lithuanian, and Bessarabian Romanian nationalists acted likewise.

In 1917 it was the left that triumphed, and it was Lenin who seized the leadership of the left and won a civil war that made him and his party the heirs to the tsars. Of Lenin's utter rejection of Russian nationalism and

Russification there cannot be the slightest doubt. He had long realized that Russian nationalism provided his enemies with a means of diverting the energies of the masses from social revolution to nationalist conflicts and imperialism. Lenin had also recognized the potential revolutionary force underlying the national discontents of the non-Russians. In the civil war his slogan of national self-determination was without doubt more attractive to the non-Russians than the White slogan of "one indivisible Russia." The Bolsheviks benefited from the nationalities' negative preference, and even at times from their positive support. At the end of it all, however, the non-Russians received no opportunity to exercise the right of self-determination. Only where the military balance was against them—in Poland, Romania, the Baltic lands, and, for a short time, Transcaucasia—did the Bolsheviks accept secession. Elsewhere the non-Russians were incorporated, willingly or unwillingly, into a state more centralized even than the empire of the tsars and covering almost all the same territory, although it called itself by a different name and was organized on quite different political and social principles.

In the USSR of the 1920s some of the non-Russian nations improved their lot, at least in some respects. They were allowed, indeed encouraged, to use their own languages in administration, in schools, and in published literature, and the officials of state and party who ruled them consisted largely of members of their own nations. But, in return, no political ideas other than the Bolshevik form of Marxism, and no political organization other than the Communist Party, could exist, and even the content of imaginative literature was confined within very narrow limits. In the 1930s the limits were drawn much tighter. In Lenin's lifetime the conventional wisdom had been that Communists must avoid two deviations, "Great Russian great-power chauvinism" and "local bourgeois nationalism." The former was thought the greater danger and so had to be fought most vigorously, whereas some allowances were to be made for the latter. From the sixteenth CPSU congress in 1934 onward, Stalin specifically reversed these priorities. Denunciations and repression of "bourgeois nationalism" among the nationalities have been a major feature of Soviet public life since then, but very little has been heard of "Great Russian great-power chauvinism."

In practice, nationalities policy (the government's attitude to the non-Russian nations) has varied according to the fluctuations of general central government policy. In periods of comparative stability and prosperity, national antagonisms have not been very obvious. Such were the NEP years of 1921–1928, and, to a lesser extent, the years 1934–1936 and much of the Brezhnev era. In periods of acute crisis, whether economic or political, discontent directed against the government by the non-Russians took the form of hatred not only of the government but of Russians as such. This in turn provoked Russian nationalist hostility to the other nations. Such was the case during the years of collectivization, especially in the Ukraine and in Kazakhstan in 1931–1933, and during the great purge of 1936–1939. During the Second World War the Baltic nations and Ukrainians at first hoped that the German invaders would be their liberators, but they soon found that Hitler's *Gauleiters* were no better than Stalin's *obkom* first secretaries. Stalin deported whole small nations from their homelands: in the case of the Volga Germans, from fear that they might help the advancing Germans, and, in the case of Chechens, Ingush, Balkars, and Crimean Tatars, as collective retribution for the actions of some collaborators. In the first post-war years of great material hardship, when the ruins were being rebuilt, Stalin viewed most non-Russians with deep mistrust. This period was marked not only by repression of the nationalities but also by falsification of their histories and interference with national literatures, in particular of the Caucasian and Central Asian nations. The intent can almost be described as cultural genocide.

Since Stalin's death, non-Russians have been treated more mildly. For a time Khrushchev flattered the national pride of the Ukrainians, and both Georgia and Armenia have been allowed a certain sovereignty over their cultural affairs. In the Baltic republics, too, the pressure of the central government, exercised through Russians, has been somewhat relaxed. Nevertheless, the Moscow authorities have not relaxed their vigilance about "bourgeois nationalism." From time to time denunciations and purges take place, affecting even so eminent a figure as the Ukrainian party boss, Piotr Shelest, who was removed in January 1973. These occasional outbreaks of overt nationalist conflict do not prevent the Soviet leaders from claiming that the USSR is, unlike any other state in the world, a harmonious commonwealth of brotherly socialist nations linked by mutual love. Brezhnev himself, speaking in 1972 at the commemoration of the fiftieth anniversary of the formation of the USSR, concluded that "the national question, as it came down to us from the past, has been settled completely, finally, and for good."

Soviet policies toward individual nations, and the wider economic, ideological, and demographic problems relevant to the issue raised in this essay, form the subject of later chapters. I shall conclude by briefly considering what has happened, during the sixty-eight years of the Soviet regime, to Russian nationalism and Russification.

Leading Communists would fiercely deny that the party has ever promoted Russification, and in this matter there is no cause to doubt their sincerity. They would also deny that Russian nationalism has been a motive of policy, or that the supremacy of Russians over others is its aim. From the beginning of their regime the Bolsheviks did their best to discredit most Russian national traditions. To nationally minded Russians, outside or inside the CPSU, it has seemed that Russia has been ruled by non-Russians. Among the top leaders since 1917 has been a high proportion of Poles, Georgians, Jews, Armenians, and even a few Muslims. Traditional Russian culture, in which Orthodox faith and liturgy and the mythology of paternalist monarchy played so important a part, was contemptuously rejected in November 1917, and there has been no public change of party line in this respect. What has become clear in the Brezhnev years is that the Orthodox church has held, or even regained, ground. In Russia today there is a growing interest in the history, personalities, and monuments of the past. This revival of the cultural dimension of Russian national consciousness has affected persons inside the party as well as dissidents, whose outstanding spokesman in this field is of course Alexander Solzhenitsyn. Those affected by the revival cannot be content with the past or present attitude of the party leadership. This complex and interesting problem is discussed in later chapters.

From the non-Russian point of view, things look rather different. Although individual non-Russians have reached the top of the pyramid of power, the higher and middle levels of the party apparatus have always been dominated by Russians. In most republics many key posts have been in Russian hands: the best-known example is the pattern in Central Asia, where party first secretaries at the republic and *obkom* level are usually Asians but second secretaries are Russians, and similar combinations are found in government ministries and in the administrative hierarchy. Under the Soviet regime, colonization of non-Russian regions by Russian immigrants has far surpassed that of the tsars. The Kazakh, Latvian, and Estonian republics (but not the Lithuanian) are the most striking cases. Riga is well on the way to becoming a Russian city.

Inevitably, the instruments of Soviet power have been predominantly Russian bureaucrats (whether of state or of party), and so there has been some continuity with the tsarist public ethos and political culture. Arrogance toward the public, bowing and scraping to the *nachal'nik*, and ritual denunciation of officials who fall from favor mark the socialist *chinovnik* (and the party *apparatchik*) no less than the tsarist variety. It is inevitable that bureaucrats' disagreeable characteristics should be attributed to the fact that they are Russians. This is not necessarily a fair judgment; there is little reason to imagine that officials of non-Russian nations are or would be a noticeable improvement. Nevertheless, such discontent almost always develops in a society where one nation is, or feels itself to be, dominated by members of another. The situation is not modified by the flood of rhetorical praise for Russian virtues that pours from the Soviet propaganda machine. It is worth noting the constant use of the laudatory phrase "great Russian people" (*velikii russkii narod*) as opposed to the merely descriptive "Great Russian" (*velikorusskii narod*).

Attempts to impose on non-Russians falsified versions of their national histories, in which the Great Russian people always play the role of unselfish friend, have been counterproductive. So, almost certainly, have been the assertions, endlessly repeated for both foreigners—especially in the Third World—and Soviet citizens, that because the Asian peoples of the USSR have made progress in industry and education since 1917—which is certainly true—they therefore love the Great Russian people who brought these blessings with an infinite and disinterested benevolence. Such assertions more often irritate the Asians, who are much more inclined to attribute the obvious progress to their own efforts and to feel (perhaps unjustly) that they would have done better still if they had not had Russians sitting on their necks. This is a matter on which evidence is too thin to permit certainty, but it would be surprising if the Soviet empire alone were exempt from that *zakonomernost'* of modern history, the law of colonial ingratitude, which states that opposition arises not when an imperial power brutally suppresses a conquered people, but when it brings them material improvements and opportunities for education and social mobility.

It is inevitable that so vast a country should require an official language of government and that this language should be Russian, the speech of slightly more than half the population. In the Brezhnev era great efforts were made to ensure that non-Russians knew Russian as well as their own language. Such an enterprise, though defensible on rational grounds, needs to be implemented with great tact. This virtue does not seem to have been in large supply. Mass production of texts in Russian has been accompanied by restriction of publication in other languages, especially Ukrainian, and the tendency has been to make Russian the language of instruction not only in the more advanced and esoteric spheres of the natural sciences, but throughout higher and even secondary education. The official statistics show substantial success in the diffusion of knowledge of Russian, but it is unwise to draw oversimplified conclusions. Even if we accept the fantastically high figures for the increase of knowledge of Russian in the Uzbek republic between the censuses of 1970 and 1979, it would be rash to assume that this shows enthusiasm and love for Russians. To learn the language of the dominant nation is useful for the dominated, but it does not necessarily make for happy, grateful submission. Czechs efficiently learned German in the last decades of Austria-Hungary, and Bohemian Germans efficiently learned Czech in the Czechoslovak Republic, but in neither case did much love result.

My tentative conclusion is that in the Soviet period there has been more Russification than Russian nationalism. The Russification has been less a conscious policy than an unintended consequence of the political and economic centralization of the Soviet empire. The Soviet leadership, from 1917 to the present day, has not been inspired by Russian nationalism. Its rhetoric has flattered the Russian nation although its actions have been designed to dismantle the whole Russian cultural heritage—just as its rhetoric has extolled the proletariat as the leading class in a socialist state while flesh-and-blood workers are exploited by their employer, the Moloch state. Soviet citizens, Russians and non-Russians alike, are expected to be subservient to their masters and arrogantly chauvinist toward all outside the socialist camp who might pose a threat to the Soviet empire or might perhaps be brought under its sway. They are offered in reward the pleasures of pride in a mighty empire, the essence of which is undiluted power, with no cultural content whatsoever. The bullying boastfulness of Soviet imperial demagogues is reinforced by a strong dose of anti-Semitism. The appeal is to the emotions that flared up in the pogroms of the turn of the century. These emotions are deeply rooted and have remained latent but strong in the Russian urban masses for decades past, used sparingly by Stalin and increasingly by his successors. The appeal's attractiveness and power to mobilize mass support should not be underrated; but those who use it or are seduced by it look more like Black Hundreds than socialists.

The legitimacy of the Soviet regime still derives from the truths of scientific Marxism, exclusively revealed to the great Lenin and passed on by pseudoapostolic succession to subsequent members of the Central Committee. (Among whom, admittedly, has been a certain number of agents of imperialism—or victims of the cult of personality, as the case may be—mere "mistakes," which in no way diminish the CPSU's exclusive infallible possession of Marxist-Leninist science.)

It is arguable that the Soviet regime's effective source of legitimacy has evolved, just as the effective basis of tsarist legitimacy evolved in the nineteenth century. There is, indeed, a superficial similarity between the effective principles of the present regime and Uvarov's formula. Of Uvarov's three, the one that is closest to present-day operational doctrine is autocracy—a word that is not held in public esteem today but whose substance has hardly altered. Orthodoxy is replaced by residual Marxism-Leninism, in whose terminology all members of the Soviet political class are fluent. That faith today commands about as much genuine belief as Belinsky, in his letter to Gogol, attributed (wrongly) to the peasant adherents of the Russian Orthodox Church. Uvarov's *narodnost'* is replaced by the imperial chauvinism of the USSR in the 1980s—more ambitious in scope but not very different in quality.

Nationalism is not the right word to describe Soviet official attitudes and policies. Nationalism, whether of Russians or of others, must include defense of national cultures, and this is conspicuously absent from the Soviet official scene. The braggart barbarians who praise and magnify the imperial Moloch have no culture of any sort to defend. The half-century of efforts to destroy the national cultures of Russians and other peoples of the empire has failed. Counterproductive policies have raised a host of problems that have already begun to plague Soviet rulers. It would be nice to think that in a common struggle to defend their national cultures the Russians and the nationalities would respect and help each other; but the historical record does not, alas, suggest that this is likely.

Russian Nationalism and Soviet Politics: Official and Unofficial Perspectives

Frederick C. Barghoorn

INTRODUCTION

Since the mid-1960s, a broad spectrum of Russian nationalist opinion has been expressed in the censored Soviet media as well as in the writings of some Russian dissidents. Russian nationalist sentiments permitted dissemination in Soviet media are obviously regarded by at least some powerful members of the elite as politically expedient and desirable.[1] Soviet authorities have reacted violently, however, to the critical, independent versions of nationalist thought expressed by the novelist and poet, Alexander Solzhenitsyn, and by the editor of the now suppressed "patriotic" journal *Veche*, Vladimir Osipov. This essay will seek to systematically describe, analyze, and, to the extent possible, account for the surfacing in the USSR of attitudes scarcely compatible with the socialist internationalism that, according to innumerable *Pravda* editorials, is the heart of Soviet ideology.

Perhaps the most useful definitions of *patriotism* and *nationalism* have been offered by the distinguished social psychologist, Leonard W. Doob:

> Patriotism: the more or less conscious conviction of a person that his own welfare and that of the significant groups to which he belongs are dependent upon the preservation or expansion (or both) of the power and culture of his society.
>
> Nationalism: the set of more or less uniform demands (1) which people in a society share, (2) which arise from their patriotism (3) for which justifications exist and can be readily expressed (4) which incline

them to make personal sacrifices in behalf of their government's aims, and (5) which may or may not lead to appropriate action.[2]

Doob's emphases on the contribution of political leaders to the creation and nurturing of nationalist attitudes and on the links between external threats and nationalist reactions are useful to students of patriotism and nationalism in all types of political systems. Certain difficulties, of course, arise in applying Doob's categories to multiethnic, multinational entities like the USSR. Matters are complicated by Soviet leaders' claims that, as a socialist community, the USSR is or should be free of nationalist attitudes, which are among the ugliest products of capitalism. Leonid Brezhnev frequently denounced nationalism and chauvinism as tools of imperialist efforts to undermine Soviet society by sowing discord among the various peoples of the USSR. In a statement at the twenty-sixth congress of the Communist Party of the Soviet Union (CPSU) he declared that it was the "sacred duty" of the CPSU to train the Soviet people "in the spirit of Soviet patriotism and socialist internationalism," with pride in belonging to the great "United Soviet Motherland." Non-Russians, however, in statements on Russian–non-Russian relations in the USSR, customarily praise the Russians for their "unselfish help" to the latter.[3] The demand that non-Russians pay symbolic tribute to "the leading nation of the Soviet Union," as Joseph Stalin called the Russians in his toast to the Russian people in May 1945, had been abandoned, or at least attenuated, during the relatively liberal period of Khrushchev's leadership. In contrast, at the twenty-fifth CPSU congress in 1976, the leaders of the non-Russian delegations paid tributes to the Russian people whose fulsomeness was unprecedented in the post-Stalin period.[4]

Renewed pressure on non-Russian leaders to, in effect, publicly pledge allegiance to the Russians reflected a development in the history of Soviet nationalities doctrine that ranks second only to Stalin's authoritative pronouncements on the nature and significance of capitalist and socialist nations. Stalin in 1913 had set forth his four-part definition of the nation as "a historically developed, stable community of people, arising on the basis of community language, territory, economic life and psychological pattern, manifested in a community of culture." But until 1929 Stalin clung to the orthodox Marxist-Leninist view that nations were a product of capitalism. In that year he argued, in an essay entitled "The National Problem and Leninism," that new socialist nations had developed in the USSR. In addition, Stalin argued that the Russian language was the language of socialism and would, in struggle with other languages, emerge victorious. This, combined with his emphasis on the leading role of the Russian people, amounted to an implicit claim that a new Soviet Russian nation, imbued with a new socialist patriotism, was coming into being in the USSR.[5]

Brezhnev continued Stalin's policy of maximum feasible Russification. Brezhnev's approach to nationalities policy, at least in terms of its doctrinal rationalization, was more inimical to ethnic pluralism than was Stalin's. It clearly reflected the views of assimilationist-minded scholars—officials like P. M. Rogachev and M. A. Sverdlin. For decades they have lobbied for deletion of Stalin's psychological-cultural factor from the official Soviet concept of ethnicity. They favor a more purely economic, environmental, and social explanation of ethnicity.[6] They have stressed "internationalization" and "internationalism" in Russian–non-Russian relations—under Soviet conditions, code words for pressure on the non-Russians to submit to Russification and Russianization.

In December 1972, celebrating the fiftieth anniversary of the establishment of the Soviet Union (prior to 1922 only the Russian Soviet Socialist Republic [RSFSR] had existed), Brezhnev proclaimed the existence of the "Soviet people, a new historical community (*obshchnost'*)." Brezhnev called attention to the "special role" of the "most developed and powerful" Russian republic, the bulwark and brotherly helper of all the other republics of the Soviet federation.[7] Comment in an authoritative work by Rogachev and Sverdlin, though not rejecting the traditional claim of the "sovereignty" of the non-Russian republics of the USSR, emphasized that the latter were "organic parts" of the "United International Soviet Union"—a formula reminiscent of the tsarist concept of "Russia one and indivisible." The assimilationist intent of the "Soviet people" concept is also suggested by Rogachev and Sverdlin's assertion that the building of communism would mean achievement of "oneness" (*odnorodnost'*) in the spheres of both social class and national relations.[8]

In tormented language, doubtless reflecting the ticklishness of their subject, Rogachev and Sverdlin assert that the patriotism associated with the community of Soviet people is of a higher order than national patriotism. They allow that the new community is in "many essential respects" similar to a nation: it has a common economy, territory, culture, psychology, consciousness of being Soviet, presence of an all-union language of international communication, and so on. But, they add, the USSR is an "international community," composed of "distinctive," and "relatively separate," "national units." This community is characterized by the fusion (*slitnost'*) of Soviet and national elements.[9]

Rogachev and Sverdlin are authoritative spokesmen for what I call "Soviet Russian nationalism." They disparage any "limited patriotism" that distracts attention from the CPSU's "mission," the salvation of

Russia from "the threat of enslavement by foreign capital," or from the party's leadership role in scientific and industrial development.[10] And in the domains of history and culture they reject approaches that assert continuity between the Soviet and pre-Soviet periods or that, by excessive concern with the cultural heritage of one particular nation, hinder perception of "what unites the peoples into a single whole." Interestingly enough, one of the writers the Rogachev-Sverdlin team named as an opponent of an objectional variety of patriotism was the pseudo-Slavophile publicist, Viktor Chalmaev, whose exuberant Russian nationalist views I shall describe later at some length. Recently, other experts on nationality questions, such as Vadim Pechenev, Chernenko's assistant on nationality problems, have surfaced.

There are good reasons to believe that increasing numbers of both non-Russians and Russians are dissatisfied with official Soviet nationalities policies. Unfortunately, much of the evidence is circumstantial. Recent years have seen a transfer of decisionmaking powers, formerly reserved to the non-Russian constituent republics, to the central government in Moscow. Simultaneously, Russian membership in the central organs has increased at the expense of non-Russians. In the meantime, Russification of certain non-Russian ethnic groups, particularly the Slavic Belorussians and Ukrainians, has proceeded rapidly; among many of the non-Russian peoples, however, only a minority have learned Russian even as a second language. Carrère d'Encausse says that among the "Moslem peoples, we find the knowledge of Russian becoming weaker and weaker."[11]

Better known to the Western public than these persistent, underlying trends are a series of protests by non-Russians, in some cases supported by democratic dissidents, against what they regard as intrusions into their local concerns or even threats to their national identities. Limitations of space do not allow more than reference to the numerous samizdat petitions and letters or the sometimes surprisingly successful demonstrations—for example, the 1978 success of the Georgians, Armenians, and Azerbaijanis in persuading the Moscow authorities to allow them to retain the unique clause in their republic constitutions that establishes the local language as the "state language" of their republics. Suffice it to echo Carrère d'Encausse's view—shared increasingly by Western Sovietologists, particularly those expert on nationalities problems—that "of all the problems facing Moscow, the most urgent and the most stubborn is the one raised by the national minorities."[12]

But what of the Russians? Has not their dominance of the economic, cultural, and political life of the USSR been growing since Stalin established his mastery over the CPSU and the Soviet state? One can hardly answer in the negative.[13] And yet, the strident tone of much Russian nationalist discourse bespeaks frustration rather than self-confidence or contentment.

Generally speaking, Soviet censorship allows access to the official media only to aspects of Russian tradition and sentiments that the authorities believe can infuse life into the ritualized propaganda of Marxism-Leninism. Most useful for this purpose are the authoritarian-xenophobic themes inherited from the tsarist past. Certainly the heritage of Russian orthodox religiosity, central to the Russian spiritual heritage, is totally incompatible with Soviet communism. Even Russian traditional patriotism, however useful it can be to bolster "proletarian internationalism," is also dangerous, for it is offensive to non-Russians at home and to some of the most important foreign audiences of Soviet propaganda.

The versions of Russian nationalism allowed expression in the USSR are not likely to be fully satisfactory either to full-blown Russian chauvinists or to religiously oriented persons like Osipov or Solzhenitsyn. Any Russian whose image of Russia differs substantially from the official one is likely to find himself in conflict with the authorities and sooner or later is subject to repression. Only in the late 1960s was the Russian nationalist grouping that I call the "pseudo-Slavophiles" permitted to articulate more freely a form of Russian nationalism that went beyond the Stalinist amalgam of selected elements of Marxist and Russian ideology.

Finally, Russian democrats like Andrei Sakharov and Vladimir Bukovsky, who believe deeply that they can best serve the interests of the Russian people by disseminating in the USSR universally applicable principles of personal and civil rights, have spoken out as vigorously as Solzhenitsyn and Osipov against what they regard as narrow, chauvinistic images of Russia. Bukovsky, in an open letter to the late Soviet prime minister Kosygin, skillfully described and forcefully repudiated, from the point of view of the Soviet democratic movement, the chauvinism that lurks behind the facade of official Soviet "internationalism." He wrote:

> I am a Russian, but I grieve that in this country high officials openly preach chauvinism and make russification into the highest principle of state policy. I regret that the Russia of today is an even worse prison of peoples than it was sixty years ago. I am a Russian national but I declare that national discrimination exists in the Soviet Union.[14]

SOVIET RUSSIAN NATIONALISM

"Soviet patriotism" or, as I shall refer to it in this essay, Soviet Russian nationalism, has for several decades been described in Soviet sources as one of the main "driving forces" of Soviet public life. In 1948 the German Sovietologist Klaus Mehnert, in his book, *Weltrevolution durch Weltgeschichte*, aptly compared Soviet Russia to an airplane running on two motors, a Marxist-Leninist socialist one and a nationalist one. He predicted that the two motors would soon cease to synchronize, and as a result Soviet ideology would disintegrate. Although premature, Mehnert's prediction called attention to the dilemma of a regime whose legitimation rests on a doctrine composed of not fully compatible elements.

Stalin in the early 1930s injected the adrenalin of Russian nationalism into the Soviet political bloodstream. Until he fully legitimized the public use of terms such as *rodina* (motherland), nationalism and patriotism had been excluded from the Soviet political vocabulary as weapons of the "reactionary bourgeoisie." Yet it should be noted that Lenin himself, in various ways, helped to pave the way for Stalin's full-blown nationalist policies and doctrines. Stalin could perhaps regard "Soviet patriotism" as consistent with Lenin's advocacy of proletarian national pride in his pamphlet, "On the National Pride of the Great Russians." There also is an affinity between Lenin's summons to the fledgling Red Army in 1918, calling on it to defend the "socialist fatherland" against Western "interventionists," and Stalin's patriotic propaganda during the "Great Fatherland War" against Nazi Germany—though the latter slogan not only appealed to class loyalties but also evoked memories of an earlier Russian struggle for national survival against Napoleon's army. Both Lenin and Stalin, particularly the latter, considered that the flourishing, even the survival, of Soviet power depended heavily upon establishing a sense of identity between the regime and the dominant ethnic element of Soviet society, the Russians.[15]

The Stalinist heritage and the mind-numbing impact of decades of terror left an imprint on Soviet life that the brief years of Khrushchev's "liberalization" could not erase. The regime created by Stalin was dedicated to generating what the Soviet leaders proudly refer to as the "military-economic might" of the USSR. The central element of Stalin's now largely unacknowledged legacy was a tightly centralized, bureaucratic, and militarized state. To create and preserve this state Stalin imposed his well-known "revolution from above" in all spheres of life. Repudiating the egalitarian-libertarian aspects of Marxism, Stalin substituted for them materialism, hierarchy, privilege, and a chauvinistic nationalism. In Stalin's foreign policy doctrine, Lenin and Trotsky's denunciation of tsarist colonialism, militarism, and expansionism gave way to glorification of Russian statecraft and feats of arms. Stalin's achievements, above all his flawed but largely successful leadership of Russia during World War II and the USSR's dramatic emergence from prewar pariah status to political equality with the United States, generated considerable pride among Soviet people, especially among Russians of elite status.

Stalin's terror, however, left bitter memories among the peoples of the USSR, Russians and non-Russians alike. Many non-Russians, especially if they were the unlucky members of the seven small "deported peoples"—whose plight was painstakingly investigated by Robert Conquest in his book *The Nation Killers*—had no affection for Stalin. The Jews' remarkable contribution to the Soviet struggle against Hitler's armies went largely unacknowledged, as Grigory Svirski shows in his memoir, *Hostages*, and for them the war against Nazi racism marked a new chapter in the long history of Russian anti-Semitism. The tiny but in some cases deeply committed Soviet minority that favored reformist Marxism or Western-style democratic values abhorred all aspects of Stalinism, not least Stalin's nationalism. These citizens tended to regard any espousal of nationalist goals, even if accompanied by criticism of Stalin, as neo-Stalinist or at least reactionary, and perhaps even "fascist" in its implications.

Neo-Stalinist nationalism has bulked large in Soviet propaganda since the late 1960s, especially in that directed at Soviet youth and the Soviet educational process. For a few years it appeared that the Russian component of propaganda might soon overshadow its Marxist-Leninist element. The Brezhnev leadership, about to embark on "détente" with the West and accelerated pursuit of influence in the Third World, apparently decided that success in achieving its new foreign policy priorities would be hindered by flaunting Russian ethnocentric impulses. At any rate, since 1970 what Mehnert called the two motors of Soviet ideology have operated more or less in synchronization. The Kremlin has proclaimed its devotion to internationalism—often in the form of demands that the non-Russians appreciate the blessings of their association with the Russians—while continuing to tap the wellsprings of Russian nationalism.

After a Politburo meeting in 1970 some of the most flamboyant expressions of Russian nationalism were criticized in the Soviet press and mild penalties were imposed on their authors. This does not, in my opinion, mean that these sentiments ceased to influence Soviet opinion and policy.[16] To be sure, some of the prominent exponents of overt Russian nationalism, including the editor of *Molodaia gvardiia*, who was dismissed in November 1971, suffered somewhat. But, in comparison with the persecution inflicted on democratic dissidents, believers in Russian traditional values, and pseudo-Slavophiles like Viktor Chalmaev and Vladimir Soloukhin, the within-system nationalists suffered only a slap on the wrist.

Of great significance was historian Sergei Semanov's August 1970 article, "On Values, Relative and Eternal."[17] This was a tough, militant tract, that—reminiscent of the novelist Sholokhov's harsh statements about the writers Sinyavsky and Daniel at the twenty-third CPSU congress in 1966—seems to have been a demand for short shrift to intellectuals regarded as blasphemers against sacred Stalinist doctrines. It articulated a truculent, expansionist-messianic, authoritarian-statist outlook and was thoroughly Stalinist in spirit and style. Semanov sharply rejected the proposition that "everything is relative," which, he complained, was common currency not only in everyday speech but even in works pretending to be serious and theoretical.

Semanov defended his fellow *Molodaia gvardiia* contributor, M. Lobanov, against criticism by A. Dementev, a member of the staff of the main "liberal" Soviet journal, *Novyi mir* (New World). Dementev had accused Lobanov of an excessively nationalist, effectually non-Marxist, attitude toward Russian patriotism.[18] In his attack on anti-Stalinist intellectuals, Semanov accused them of resorting to "allusions, hints, and subtexts," and other subterfuges, to conceal their true thoughts. Semanov was apparently hinting that the targets of his attack were close to being engaged in some sort of conspiracy. According to the well-connected nationalist critic, Anatoli Lanshchikov, also a *Molodaia gvardiia* contributor, it was common in the literary polemics of the late 1960s for participants to accuse authors with whom they disagreed of engaging in "political hints," a practice that, Lanshchikov archly implied, smacked of "administrative interference in literary affairs."[19]

Semanov devoted part of his article to expressing satisfaction that, "during the last ten years," Soviet historians clearly had demonstrated that despite harmful foreign influence, which had been an obstacle to Russia's economic and social development, Russia had definitely not been a "semicolony" of the West—an assertion that would have amazed Lenin. This and other findings of Soviet historians, added Semanov, should be incorporated into the intellectual equipment not only of the historical profession, but also of the literary community and the intelligentsia generally. From a political viewpoint, the most startling feature of this superpatriotic tract was a paragraph beginning with this sentence: "It is now clear that in the struggle with the wreckers and nihilists the turning point came in the mid-1930s," and going on to praise, for example, "our Constitution," which, among other merits, bound all "honest toilers" together into a "united and monolithic whole."[20] He added that although the "virus" of "nihilism" was not as potent as it had been in the 1920s and early 1930s, it was tenacious and must still be fought. He concluded his article by urging the Soviet intelligentsia to fulfill its "duty" of preserving the "monolithic unity of society."

Semanov's references to "monolithic unity," his calling the Bolshevik revolution the "Russian" revolution, and other features of his article indicate that his conception of Russian–non-Russian relations was a centralist one, not unlike the tsarist "Russia one and indivisible." At times he did refer to the contributions of non-Russians to Russian and Soviet political and cultural development. Thus, he asserted that the Soviet people were "proud of the artists of ancient Kiev, Erevan, and Samarkand, of our great literature and music, of the glory of Borodino, and of the great feats of the people who mastered the gigantic expanses of Europe, Asia, and America." This was truly a remarkable assertion. But equally remarkable was Semanov's argument that, though it was fitting to preserve the monuments, traditions, and customs of the distant past, it was also necessary to honor "our great Russian revolution," for this revolution was "our priceless national property (*dostoianie*)." Thus, as Raisa Lert pointed out, Semanov was carrying some of Stalin's ideas to their logical conclusion.[21]

The publication of a book of Semanov's articles in 1977 indicated the continued vitality of neo-Stalinist Soviet Russian nationalism. The collection, consisting of items originally published in a wide range of journals, tooks its title, *Serdtse rodiny* (The Heart of the Motherland), from its long opening piece, mainly devoted to extolling statesmen like Ivan the Terrible, who had built the Muscovite state, and Russian commanders and fighting men who had defended the ancient capital against Armenian Tatar raids and attack by Napoleon's Grand Army. Among other things, Semanov here asserted that the ringing of the Kremlin chimes symbolized the beating of "the pulse of the heart and our power," and that Moscow's significance as the center of the Soviet state was a phenomenon unlike anything else in the world.

Semanov's harsh attitude toward "relativism" and "nihilism" and his plea for "monolithic unity" reflected the anger generated among Soviet neo-Stalinists by Khrushchev's partial relaxation of controls over freedom of expression. This had permitted the expression, particularly in Aleksandr Tvardovsky's journal, *Novyi mir*, of sometimes vigorously anti-Stalinist opinions. The post-Khrushchev leadership only gradually tightened controls from 1964 to 1970, permitting opponents and defenders of the growing neo-Stalinist tendencies to engage in a relatively open debate. Parallel to this debate there occurred a more uninhibited underground struggle between advocates of piecemeal, gradual, and limited within-system reform (like Roy Medvedev, whose dissent from many established policies proceeded from "Leninist" premises) and a wide range of far more objectionable dissidents. The Soviet authorities objected not only to "democrats" like Sakharov, Bukovsky, Leonid Plyushch, and many others, but also to some "nationalists" who did not hesitate to openly articulate and disseminate criticisms that the authorities considered subversive.[22]

Khrushchev's collective successors labored to contain public controversy of any kind. That is probably the reason for their embarrassment over publication in the fall of 1969 of Vsevolod Kochetov's ferociously anti-Western spy thriller, *Chego zhe ty khochesh?* (What Do You Really Want?). Kochetov's novel was published in the journal *Oktiabr'* (of which he was editor), regarded as the mouthpiece of the anti-Tvardovsky "dogmatists." The fact that it never appeared in book form in the USSR is evidence of the possible official embarrassment, which in turn may have been related to criticism of the book's allegedly anti-Lenin, pro-Stalin character by highly respected Soviet "establishment" intellectuals. It may also have been thought advisable to indicate displeasure with Kochetov's thinly disguised attack on prominent Western opinion makers. One of his characters was a crude caricature of the Italian "Eurocommunist," Vittorio Spada, and another was a distorted representation of a leading American woman journalist and expert on Russia, cast in the role of an intelligence agent. Such crudity was inexpedient in view of the Soviet leadership's intention, taking shape in 1969, to embark on East-West détente.[23]

Kochetov died, under something of a cloud, in 1970. He was, however, favorably mentioned in a long propaganda tract on "Communist Indoctrination of Youth and Literature," by Vyacheslav Gorbachev, deputy editor of *Moladaia gvardiia*, in its July 1981 issue. It is interesting to note that the career of Semanov, one of the most Stalinist of the Soviet nationalists, has continued to flourish. In keeping with the relative decorum expected of publicists in the 1970s and 1980s, he has so far exercised a certain restraint. The last publication of his known to me was a typically harsh, conventional attack on Leon Trotsky, in the form of a book review, in a journal that over the years has vied with *Molodaia gvardiia* in implementing CPSU Central Committee directives on the patriotic indoctrination of Soviet youth.[24]

PSEUDO-SLAVOPHILISM

There is considerable overlap between the attitudes articulated by people like Semanov and Kochetov and the current of opinion that I call pseudo-Slavophile, but there are also differences sufficient to warrant regarding it as a distinct subcurrent of Russian nationalist thought. Semanov and like-minded people chiefly focus on the virtues and achievements of tsarist and Soviet autocracy. The pseudo-Slavophiles, by contrast, focus more on Russian "spiritual" values, which they more or less openly depict as derived from the pre-Soviet Russian past. There is even, regarding some matters, an affinity between pseudo-Slavophiles like Vladimir Soloukhin, a writer and critic who has not been, to my knowledge, harassed by the Soviet authorities, and the present Soviet rulers' archenemy, Alexander Solzhenitsyn. Soloukhin and Solzhenitsyn share, for example, nostalgia for some aspects of the Russian past and enthusiasm for the beauties of the Russian countryside. Solzhenitsyn, however, has unflinchingly fought the Soviet regime, while the Chalmaevs and Soloukhins have served it as zealous anti-American propagandists. Unlike Solzhenitsyn, the pseudo-Slavophiles have never uttered a word of condemnation of Stalin's purges and slave labor camps, or of the persecution of dissidents in the contemporary Soviet Union.

Chalmaev's two 1968 *Molodaia gvardiia* articles, "Exalted Aspirations" and "Inevitability," especially the latter, it is clear from Soviet press reactions, had a sensational impact.[25] In the first article, devoted mainly to a discussion of the significance of Maksim Gorky's writing, Chalmaev contrasted Russian "spirituality" (*dukhovnost'*) with Western, especially American, "soullessness," "philistinism," and "rationalism." Like other Soviet nationalists of the *Molodaia gvardiia* school, Chalmaev interpreted the Bolshevik revolution as largely the product of a distinctive Russian national character and outlook, which, he indicated, had such vast breadth and power that it could not possibly content itself with such trivia as the "parliamentary boiler" (*kipiatil'nik*) or recipes for social welfare "suitable for tidy (*akkuratnoi*) little Denmark." Gorky, maintained Chalmaev, had shown in his novels that the Russian people needed a revolution that could enable the Russian character to break out of the "moral norms and limits of bourgeois law and order." Citing Dostoevsky in the need for extracting "the beauty from the barbarism in the Russian common people," Chalmaev seemed—confusingly—to be suggesting that the historical service of the Bolshevik revolution consisted in liberating the Russian soul from forces that were preventing it from achieving its moral-emotional potential.

Chalmaev saw inherent goodness in the simple Russian people—in this connection he cited the poet Sergei Esenin on the superiority of Russian village culture to the "mechanical existence" of the West. Nevertheless, he also praised Gorky for rejecting Alexander Blok's image of the Russians as "Scythians" and "God-bearers." According to Chalmaev, Gorky realized that the icon could not save Russia from invasion by the "cheap culture" of the West. And Lenin, Chalmaev indicated, was right in wanting to eliminate the "village muzhik" portrayed by Chekhov and Bunin.

In 1982 Soloukhin was severely criticized in the CPSU Central Committee's main theoretical journal, *Kommunist*. He was also criticized at a meeting of the party organization to which he belongs for having expressed views so alien to official Soviet doctrine that he was charged with "flirting with God." However, in connection with his sixtieth birthday in 1984, he was awarded the Order of the Red Banner of Labor—in sharp contrast to the disfavor into which he had fallen during the leadership of Andropov, who was less tolerant of "nationalist" sentiments than Brezhnev or Chernenko. For his "rehabilitation" Soloukhin paid the price of proclaiming publicly that he was an athiest. Apparently his restoration to grace resulted not only from his expression of contrition but from realization in official circles that, like a number of other important "patriotic" Russian writers, he had often in his writings expressed deeply anti-Western attitudes.[31]

Having examined some typical expression of pseudo-Slavophile opinion, let us now look at some samizdat evidence that sheds light on both the hidden springs of pseudo-Slavophilism and the official concern that led to its diminished access to official Soviet media after 1971.[32] This material is drawn from reports on what was said at a high-level, 1969 official literary "seminar" and at meetings of the Communist Party organization of the Union of Soviet Writers. The source from which I cite this material is Number 1009 of *Arkhiv samizdata* (*The Samizdat Archive*), the Munich-based Radio Liberty samizdat series.[33]

This material makes more understandable the Politburo's eventual decision to stop both the *Novyi mir* "liberals" and the *Molodaia gvardiia* "nationalists" from publishing anything controversial or provocative. That action was followed, in 1970 and 1971, respectively, by the enforced resignations of Aleksandr Tvardovsky, editor of *Novyi mir* and Anatol Nikonov, editor of *Molodaia gvardiia*. Reports on the seminar indicated that its participants turned to the subject of *Molodaia gvardiia* after discussion of reportedly intemperate attacks, in the magazine *Zhurnalist*, on *Novyi mir*. When the discussion turned to *Molodaia gvardiia*, its contributors were subjected to orthodox Marxist-Leninist criticisms. Thus, F. Levin accused "Chalmaev and his supporters" of not seeing "any class struggle in Russian history," of somehow deriving Marxism from the Archpriest Avvakum, and of seeing "the sources of our history in the patriarchal peasantry." Kozhinov, who appeared to qualifiedly support Lanshchikov's qualified defense of Chalmaev, asserted that the discussion had so far ignored "the most important point, the relation between literature and life." He added that, fascism having been defeated, "the danger today stems from left extremism"—he noted the popularity of

Marcuse in the West—and "not from the banks of the Elbe, but from the banks of the Ussuri." He hedged, however, by saying that there were threats to the USSR from both West and East.

Another participant, Feliks Kuznetsov, asserted that if previously there had been, in the Soviet literary world, "two poles," represented respectively by *Novyi mir* and *Oktiabr'*, now a third had taken shape, around *Molodaia gvardiia* and *Nash sovremennik*. He added that this development was not a merely literary matter, but grew out of "life" and had "spiritual roots." He traced two "traditions," namely, the Westernist, revolutionary democrat, narodnik, Marxist one, and the Chaadaev, early Slavophile, Dostoevsky, Vekhi, Berdyaev one. Calling the third, or Chalmaev, position "extraordinarily interesting," Kuznetsov nevertheless indicated that he was troubled by Chalmaev's failure to demonstrate the relationship between his position and Marxism, or the relevance of the "national, popular principle" to "contemporary life." He added that all of the "patriarchal peasants" in contemporary literature were old people, suggesting that they were irrelevant, and concluded by saying that "today there is nowhere to turn to escape from the October revolution." Kogan echoed Kuznetsov's last statement, adding that it was time to understand that "the trouble is not socialism, but an insufficiency of socialism, not Europe, but not enough Europe," and he also deplored what he called a widespread "naively sentimental attitude toward the village." Thus Kogan presented himself as an "enlightened" socialist-Westernizer, rejecting the "village school," nationalism, and the pseudo-Slavophile approach.

The prominent psuedo-Slavophile, Anatoli Lanshchikov, sought at this seminar to explain and justify the *Molodaia gvardiia* point of view. He said,

> We seek a lost ideal. Our youth is not finding an ideal. That worries even the Komsomol Central Committee. More accurately, ideals can't be found once and for all, they change from generation to generation. A literature that stops searching for an ideal stagnates.

Lanshchikov asserted that it was time to stop merely criticizing the "cult of personality" and to seek "positive ideals." Then followed the startling statement that "Our country has a special path. Dostoevski spoke of that." In response to a reply from the floor that he was presenting a "Berdyaev conception," Lanshchikov affirmed that there were positive elements in the thinking of Berdyaev and Leontev. It was, he said, easy to understand how people could be attracted by their ideas. He become a human being."[38] The elements of the Russian cultural heritage most valued by Solzhenitsyn, he indicated in an essay on "Repentance and Self-Limitation in the Life of Nations," belong mainly to the period before "the soulles reforms of [Patriarch] Nikon and Peter the Great began the extirpation and suppression of the Russian National spirit, and our capacity for repentance also began to wither and dry up."[39] In keeping with Solzhenitsyn's preference for the pre-Petrine period of Russian history is a reference in the Lenten Letter of 1972 to a "thousand years" of "ethical Christian atmosphere."

The most systematic treatment of nationalist themes is available in Solzhenitsyn's nonfiction, especially *The Nobel Lecture*, "Repentance and Self-Limitation in the Life of Nations," and the *Letter to the Soviet Leaders*. *The Nobel Lecture* was, of course, not delivered in person by Solzhenitsyn. Solzhenitsyn refused to go to Stockholm in 1970 to receive his Nobel Prize for Literature, because he had good reason to believe that if he did he would not be allowed by the Soviet authorities to return to his country.[40]

The Nobel Lecture begins with a few pages expressing agreement with Dostoevsky's statement that "Beauty will save the world"—provided, Solzhenitsyn insists, that the artist "joyfully works as a common apprentice under God's heaven." A "whole national literature," he says, is "buried without a coffin" in the Gulag Archipelago. Prisoners in the Gulag, he says, dreamed of one day bringing a message to the "world outside," but now that world, in its lack of comprehension, has turned out to be "not at all what we had hoped." Solzhenitsyn strikes a hopeful note, however. He asserts that art and literature alone "can overcome man's unfortunate trait of learning only through his own experience, unaffected by that of others." This transcendent function of art, he makes plain, is coordinate with its function as the "living memory" of individual nations—which are, he insists, "the wealth of humanity." The least among them, he asserts, "has its own special colors, and harbors within itself a special aspect of God's design."

Returning to an internationalist perspective, Solzhenitsyn identifies what he regards as international threats—the "spirit of Munich," generating passivity in the face of aggression, and the "stoppage of information," which, he says, makes international treaties "unreal." He concludes with an expression of hope that WORLD LITERATURE (capitals in original), by exposing the lies on which violence relies for the maintenance of power, can bring the collapse of violence. Along the way, Solzhenitsyn made many remarks hailing the "growing spiritual unity of mankind" and of course rejecting the doctrine of "some ministries of internal affairs" that literature is an "internal affair" of the countries under their jurisdiction. On the contrary, he replies, "no such thing as INTER-

NAL AFFAIRS remains on our crowded earth." And, he adds, "Mankind's salvation lies exclusively in everyone's making everything his business, in the people of the East being anything but indifferent to what is thought in the West, and in the people of the West being anything but indifferent to what happens in the East"—an opinion that in one way or another has, of course, also been expressed by Academician Andrei Sakharov and other Soviet dissidents who disagree with Solzhenitsyn on many matters. Certainly in *The Nobel Lecture* Solzhenitsyn spoke as a man who cherished his Russian roots, but whose aesthetic and spiritual horizons were not only national but international—far more so, obviously, than those of the Soviet elite whose suppression and destruction of art and artists represented, he indicated, a tragedy for Russia and a danger for mankind.

In "Repentance and Self-Limitation" Solzhenitsyn calls upon the Russian people to repent the attitudes and behavior that made possible the crimes of both pre-Soviet and Soviet history. As far as the prerevolutionary period is concerned, he condemns the "monstrous punishment" of the Old Believers, with the approval of the Russian Orthodox Church, and the failure to abolish serfdom in time to avoid a legacy of hatred. Here Solzhenitsyn avoids specifics, but the context indicates that he had in mind the attitudes of the radical intelligentsia, which crystallized in Bolshevism. This is suggested by his statement that "in the twentieth century the blessed dews of repentance could no longer soften the parched Russian soil, baked hard by doctrines of hate." In the broadest terms, Solzhenitsyn calls on the Russian people to repent of what they have done to make Bolshevik rule possible in Russia. In a section of the essay replete with reproaches directed at his people for complicity in the operations of the Gulag, Solzhenitsyn says "This realm of darkness, of falsehood, of brute force . . . this slimy swamp was formed by *us* [italics in original], and no one else." He sees a "glimmer of hope" that his country can, by "shedding the burden of our past," go forward to a "just, clean, honest society." However, unlike Marxist reformers and civil rights activists, he warns that "even the cleverest" economic and social reforms are the wrong building blocks for the change that he desires.

Expressing a view he shares with a number of other "nationalist" dissidents, Solzhenitsyn at several points in this essay states that the Russian, Ukrainians, and Belorussians have suffered more than any of the other people of the USSR. In part, this conviction may explain Solzhenitsyn's angry comments on several samizdat articles that atttributed the content of Bolshevism to Russian traditions. Solzhenitsyn rejects this view, asserting that "the main content of Bolshevism is unbridled militant atheism and class hatred." In connection with his attack on Russians who have grossly misinterpreted the history of Russia, Solzhenitsyn verged on a theme to which he was to devote a great deal of attention after his expulsion from his country—the necessity of establishing a "reliable record" before it is too late.

"Repentance and Self-Limitation" contains many lively pages of criticism of Russian treatment of non-Russian peoples, ranging from "oppressing and destroying" the indigenous people of Siberia to numerous other crimes, both tsarist and Soviet. Solzhenitsyn did not hesitate to mention the forbidden subject of "the destruction of the flower of the Polish people in our camps, Katyn in particular." However, he also criticized the behavior of Poles toward Russians at times when the balance of force was different, and he concluded his discussion of the Russian-Polish relationship with a plea for "mutual repentance and mutual forgiveness." He also took a very negative view of Soviet foreign policy, which, Solzhenitsyn asserted, "might have been deliberately devised as in defiance of the true interest of our people." Soviet policy assumed "a responsibility for the fate of Eastern Europe incommensurable with our present level of spiritual development and our ability to understand European needs and ways," and, Solzhenitsyn continued, it involves meddling on every continent in pursuit of artificial aims. Russia, he asserted, must get away from the "hurly-burly of world rivalries" and turn its attention inward, "healing its soul, educating its children, putting its own house in order."

Solzhenitsyn concluded this essay with a recommendation he was to repeat and develop at greater length in his *Letter to the Soviet Leaders*, composed, like "Repentance and Self-Limitation," in 1973. Russia's national energies, he suggested, should be diverted from external matters to the development of the vast "untamed expanses" of the Northeast, defined by Solzhenitsyn as the northern portion of European Russia plus north central and eastern Siberia. According to Solzhenitsyn, the Northeast "is a reminder that . . . our ocean is the Arctic, not the Indian Ocean, that we are not the Mediterranean nor Africa and that we have no business there!" Anticipating criticism of a program that might be regarded as excessively isolationist and defensive, Solzhenitsyn added that defense forces must be retained but "only on a scale adequate to real and not imaginary threats," and "in the hope that the whole atmosphere of mankind will soon begin to change." His final words are, "And if it does not change, the Club of Rome has done the arithmetic: we have less than a hundred years to live."

The most political of Solzhenitsyn's writings was certainly his well-known *Letter to the Soviet Leaders*. It contained the most comprehensive analysis of the Soviet and international political situation he has offered

and also his most detailed—and in some ways startling—recommendations for curing the ills of the USSR and the world. Moreover, dispatch-
ing this "letter" to the Soviet hierarchy was a dramatic and puzzling act.
In his memoir, *The Oak and the Calf*, Solzhenitsyn shed light on his
motives in taking a step that, one might think, could only have been a
fruitless gesture. In one of numerous references in *Oak and Calf* to the
Letter, Solzhenitsyn remarked that while he was being held in the Lefor-
tovo prison before expulsion from his native land he had felt certain that
he was about to be taken for a conversation with Soviet leaders. The
Letter, he said, was written "as a substitute for such a conversation." He
added that "We cannot give up all hope of converting them: we would be
less than men if we did. Surely they are not bereft of every last trace of
humanity." In the same work he also referred to the *Letter* as "purely
impulsive, quite unpremeditated."[41] Whatever hopes Solzhenitsyn may
have had at the beginning of September 1973 when he sent off his
message to the men in the Kremlin, they were dashed not only by the
unresponsiveness that he doubtless anticipated but also by KGB discovery of a hidden manuscript copy of the *Gulag Archipelago*. As soon as
Solzhenitsyn learned of this calamity, his publishers in the West set in
motion publication of *Gulag*, his most damaging work as far as the Soviet
rulers were concerned. What followed was a firestorm of harassment,
vilification, and even death threats against Solzhenitsyn and his family.

In the *Letter to the Soviet Leaders* Solzhenitsyn struck a "national" note
in the introduction, where he conjectured that his addressees shared his
concern for the fate of all people, especially those "dependent on us" and
especially the Russian and Ukrainian people, whose sufferings have been
incomparably severe.[42] The leaders, he hoped, "are not alien to their
origins, fathers, grandfathers and native haunts," and they are not indifferent to nationality. He then launched into a set of prescriptions for
strengthening the USSR, ending hostile relations with the West, and
avoiding war with the People's Republic of China (or if such a war should
break out, assuring Russian victory). As one way of assuring security
vis-à-vis communist China, Solzhenitsyn urged the replacement of
Marxist indoctrination by Russian patriotism. "Witness," he said to the
leaders, "how mighty America lost to tiny North Vietnam," because
"the United States has a weak and underdeveloped national consciousness."[43] It should be noted that although official Soviet Marxism
was blamed in the *Letter* for a host of evils, including tension with China
and the West, deflection of the USSR's attention from internal development, and even for immorality (which Solzhenitsyn attributed in part to
the substitution of ideology for religion), Solzhenitsyn did not ask for
suppression of Marxist-Leninist doctrine. Rather, he suggested that a

variety of world outlooks, including Marxism and various religions, be allowed to compete for public support.

Perhaps the most interesting statement in the *Letter* was a footnote to the section in which Solzhenitsyn set forth his recommendation that the "center of gravity of national activity" be shifted "from distant continents, even from Europe and even from the Southeast of our country, to its Northeast." The note read as follows. "Of course such a shift must sooner or later lead to our lifting our tutelage over Eastern Europe. Also, there can be no thought of the forcible retention within the borders of our country of any borderland nation."[44]

The third volume of *The Gulag Archipelago* contains statements confirming Solzhenitsyn's position on this question. Solzhenitsyn had warm words for the Estonian and Lithuanian prisoners he had known. Before them, he indicated, he had felt "ashamed," since their people had to suffer "because they lived cheek by jowl with us and stood in our path to the sea." He commented at length on Russian-Ukrainian relations, arguing that "since the two people have not succeeded over the centuries in living harmoniously," it would be the wise and decent course to leave the decision as to the future status of the Ukrainians "to the Ukrainians themselves."[45]

Both *From Under the Rubble* and the *Letter to the Soviet Leaders* discussed the authoritarian principle in Russian history. In "Postscript, 1973" to "As Breathing and Consciousness Return," Solzhenitsyn admitted that the vast majority of Soviet people "whose opinions do not conform to the official stereotype" agreed that Soviet society should strive for *"freedom* [italics in original] and the multiparty parliamentary system." To achieve this, he added, the prerevolutionary Russian intelligentsia had believed that "their cause and that of the nation could only be [the people's] freedom and happiness." The price paid for the intelligentsia's pursuit of material welfare had been "the blood of millions." Some members of the intelligentsia did not care about nonmaterial values, but there was little understanding of "freedom" among the Russian people and little meeting of minds between intellectuals and people.

Having said all that, Solzhenitsyn launched into a dismissive discussion of what he called "external freedom" and of the "dangerous," "perhaps mortal," defects of parliamentary democracy. Those defects, he said, have become "more and more obvious" in a period when "the historical democracies prove impotent, faced with a handful of snivelling terrorists." In an era of crisis for Western democracy, Solzhenitsyn asserted "it ill becomes us to see our country's *only* [italics in original] way out" in that system. Rather tentatively, he weighed the advantages and disadvantages of authoritarian rule. It can, he admitted, lead to arbitrary decisions, even to tyranny. The "autocrats of our own time," he said, "are dangerous precisely because it is difficult to find higher values which would bind them"—unlike those of "religious ages," who "felt themselves responsible before God."

Solzhenitsyn asked, in view of the inability of Russia's 1917 democracy to endure more than eight months, if "the evolution of our country from one form of authoritarianism to another would be . . . the least painful path of development for it to follow." Reverting again to "spiritual" matters, he asserted that the evil of the existing political system lay not in its authoritarianism, but in its demand for "total surrender of our souls," and "continuous participation in the general, conscious *lie*" (italics in original). But to fight the lie, he said, people require "no physical, revolutionary, social organizational measures," but only a "moral step" within the power of each individual.[46] The last and longest of Solzhenitsyn's contributions to *From Under the Rubble* demands that "the smatterers," whom he regards as conformist, careerist, and Western-oriented Soviet intellectuals, start doing their duty to country and people by speaking out against official lies.

In the *Letter* Solzhenitsyn in effect urged the Soviet rulers to take such a moral step by ethically purifying their regime. He assured them—and this assurance was consistent with the nonviolent approach to politics he shared with Sakharov and almost all other Soviet dissidents—that he is no revolutionary. A mere change in political leadership would lead only to a destructive struggle. Moreover, he continued, he is no champion of the kind of democracy that exhausts itself every four years in election campaigns and in which a court finds innocent a man who has stolen and published military documents. Having thus rejected "turbulent" democracy, Solzhenitsyn asserted that freedom was "moral," but only to the extent that it was not unrestrained; order was not immoral if it did not become tyranny. This was followed by a harsh judgment on the forces of constitutional democracy in the Russia of 1917. Russia was unready for democracy in 1917, Solzhenitsyn concluded, but he added that the country was even less ready as he wrote.

One of the most interesting features of the *Letter* was Solzhenitsyn's proposal that the soviets, deprived of real power since June 1918, be revived. Solzhenitsyn again recommended that full freedom of competition among all ideological, moral, and religious doctrines be instituted, and that appointment to government posts no longer depend on membership in the CPSU. He offered a wide range of other humane and, indeed, enlightened and liberal proposals, with special emphasis on mercy to prisoners and freedom for art and literature, as well as uncensored publication of philosophical, ethical, economic, and social studies.

B. Dunlop's study of ASCULP, *The New Russian Revolutionaries*, stated, among other things, that "liberation of the peoples from the Communist yoke" required an "underground liberation army which would overthrow the dictatorship and destroy the oligarchy's security forces."[56] It should be noted that ASCULP never actually attempted any violent action and did not contemplate undertaking any before it had recruited an underground army of 10,000 men—certainly a fantastically utopian goal. Because Ogurtsov and his fellow conspirators never committed any violent acts (their organization remained clandestine from its founding in 1964 until the KGB discovered it three years later), a number of Soviet dissidents wrote indignant protests against the draconian sentences imposed in 1967 on its leaders. Ogurtsov is still in a camp, after having served seven years in the notorious Vladimir prison.

At the time of its destruction by the KGB, ASCULP had almost thirty members and also some thirty probationary members. Its small size, and the fact that its underground character deprived it of the possibility of disseminating its views in samizdat, meant that ASCULP could not have nearly as much impact on Soviet opinion as Solzhenitsyn, Osipov, or their associates. However, the severe repression visited upon the leaders indicates that the authorities took very seriously indeed this expression of Russian religious-nationalist opposition (opposition rather than dissent, for ASCULP actually envisaged a drastic change in the structure, policies, and leadership of the Soviet political, social, and economic system).

ASCULP's program can be briefly characterized as a mixture of Berdyaev and Djilas. It envisaged a society based on Berdyaev's principle of "personalism," or "social-christianity," rejecting both capitalism and socialism and seeing in communism and the "false religion" of Marxism-Leninism the source of the dehumanization, poverty, and danger of world war that threatens the USSR and the world. Pointing to the Hungarian uprising of 1956 and other events, ASCULP proclaimed that communism was doomed. It recommended a new order, inspired by "Christianization" of social life; an economy with elements of worker self-management, profit-sharing, and state control; and a state structure based on "theocratic," "social," and "representative and popular" principles, headed by a popular assembly and a head of state with great executive and administrative powers. This program—or constitution—made no provision for political parties but did call for an independent judiciary, the abolition of capital punishment, and a new legal system conforming to "the spirit and letter of Social-Christianity."

Although ASCULP's program had very little to say about foreign relations, it contained a section promising help to countries in which

Soviet forces had been "temporarily stationed" in the achievement of "self-determination." This plank, and the prescription that the Communist Party be disbanded, were among the many drastic demands in this radical document. It must have been a shock to the Soviet authorities that a group of highly educated Russians could have developed such a program for the radical transformation of Soviet society based on Christian principles.

A miscellany of extremist, perhaps one should say eccentric, expressions of nationalist attitudes appeared in an anonymous, alarming, and somewhat bizarre document often mentioned but probably seldom read in the West. In "Slovo natsii" (A Nation Speaks), which began to circulate in samizdat in December 1970, "Russian patriots" tackled a wide range of topics.[57] One discussed the origin of dictatorships in failed democracies, another predicted that a loss of Anglo-Saxons' national pride would make the industrial potential of America an instrument of world domination by the black race, and another advocated a strong central state in Russia and a privileged elite to lead it. One-fourth of the document dealt with "the national question" and the "religious problem." The "patriots" dismissed the view that the Russians dominated the USSR—the fact was, they insisted, non-Russians, particularly Ukrainians, had more than their share, as was proved by the lack of a Russian party organization (all of the non-Russian republics have their own Communist parties). The authors declared themselves in favor of the old tsarist slogan, "Russia one and indivisible." They asserted that Soviet Jews almost monopolized the arts and sciences in the USSR. Non-Russians, they went on, need not fear being treated as second-class citizens if they behaved properly.

The brief section on religion contained a few sentences declaring that the world was the arena of struggle between the servants of God and Satan. It attacked the Jews for preaching doctrines of egalitarianism and cosmopolitanism, which could only lead to "a universal processing of mixing of blood and degradation." There must, the document insisted, be a revived national state in which the "traditional Russian religion," obviously Russian Orthodoxy, would occupy an appropriate place of honor. In conclusion the "patriots" called for cooperation by Russians, Armenians, and Indians against the "Chinese threat," and they looked forward to the triumph of "Christian civilization" over "chaos."

Similar political views have been expressed by Gennadi Shimanov, an elevator operator, former victim of psychiatric harassment, military officer, one-time acquaintance of Bukovsky, and a prolific writer of nationalist-religious tracts. Shimanov, who describes the USSR as a "mystical organism," has been extensively quoted and described by the former Soviet journalist, Alexander Yanov.[58] Yanov interprets Shimanov's views as a vision of the USSR as "the chosen people's laboratory for conducting experiments for the future 'Russian Orthodoxization' of the world." Shimanov, Yanov argues, seeks to persuade Soviet leaders that his doctrine of totalitarianism with a religious face can bring about a transformation first of Russia, then of the world. Shimanov, incidentally, shares with the "Russian patriots" (and to a degree with Solzhenitsyn) a belief in salvation through suffering. Since the Russian people have suffered as no other people, he argues, they are prepared to lead a movement for the salvation of the world. Unlike Solzhenitsyn, however, Shimanov—as presented by Yanov—is unalterably opposed to secession of the non-Russian borderlands from the USSR. This perhaps explains why Leonid Borodin reported, in an article published after the closing of *Veche* in 1974, that "Shimanov's point of view" was "extremely popular among the nationalistically inclined Russian intelligentsia."[59]

Russian nationalist attitudes, including some virulently anti-Semitic ones, are reported in a considerable number of sources. There were, for example, the "Russian fascists," headed by economist A. Fetisov.[60] And there were the anti-Semitic tracts to which Mikhail Agursky called attention in his 1975 *Novyi zhurnal* article, mentioned earlier. Agursky, in keeping with his support for the Solzhenitsyn orientation, declared in that article that only a "Christian revival" could save the Jews of Russia from the "neo-Nazi danger." A rather different tendency, represented by the international "solidarist"—or corporatist—movement NTS, perhaps still has a few members in the USSR and probably a considerably larger number of sympathizers.[61]

CONCLUDING REMARKS

Explaining Russian Nationalism in the USSR

Probably the most important factor in the growth of nationalist attitudes is the continuing decline in the ability of official Marxism to generate more than passive support for the Soviet system. Even the avowed Leninist, Roy Medvedev, predicted in his 1975 book, *On Soviet Democracy*, that the unattractive nature of official Marxism would cause increasing reliance to be placed on the political indoctrination of Soviet youth with "deepseated nationalist sentiments."[62] Vladimir Bukovsky reported in a perceptive article in *Kontinent* in 1980 that, during his 34 years in the USSR, he had observed that the common people despised rank-and-file Communists and hated those at the *raikom* (county) level, and that he had met only one Soviet citizen who affirmed belief in the idea of communism.[63] Bukovsky is perhaps the keenest, most realistic observer among leading Soviet dissidents. Of course, the Soviet regime is still dependent on Marxism-Leninism for its ideological legitimacy and in part for its ability to exploit "liberation" movements in the less developed countries, and so it thunderously claims to uphold the banners of "socialism" and "anti-imperialism." However, the samizdat material on the 1969 Moscow dispute over the *Molodaia gvardiia* nationalists indicates that "establishment" figures such as Lanshchikov (who, according to one well-informed emigrant, has KGB connections) reject Marxism as an ideology in favor of Russian nationalism. This brings us to a second factor or set of factors—the function of external security concerns. Reliance on nationalism to elicit support for the Soviet regime and its policies has of course always been greatest in the face of external threats, particularly when they were perceived to endanger the very existence of the Soviet state.

A hostile, billion-strong China has long been perceived by both Russian elites and nonelites as the greatest potential threat to the Russian nation. To be sure, anti-Chinese propaganda has not been as shrill in the 1970s and 1980s as it was in the 1960s. After the clash on the Ussuri River in 1969, in which Soviet forces apparently crushed the Chinese, it was believed that for years to come the Chinese threat would be more potential than actual. The Soviet public was reminded of the threat in 1980 by extensively publicized celebrations of the 600th anniversary of the battle of Kulikovo Pole (where Russian forces defeated the Tatar Golden Horde).[64]

There is a third set of factors that fosters among some Russians the belief that they are worse off than other nationalities in the USSR or the peoples of communist countries in Eastern Europe. Perhaps most important among these factors is the unfavorable demographic trend—the well-known fact that the Muslim Turkic people of the USSR are increasing in numbers much more rapidly than are the Russians. There is also a belief, apparently not unfounded, that outside of Moscow—which, although a Russian city, is also the communist capital—Russians live worse than non-Russians. In the face of what some Russians perceive as an unfair situation, they may be experiencing a "defensive" nationalist reaction.

Fourth, the peoples of the USSR have inherited from the tsarist past anticapitalist attitudes and a belief in the virtues of a strong, centralized, authoritarian state and government guidance of the national economy. This heritage renders Soviet people receptive to the appeal of traditionalist and nationalist doctrines, both official and dissident. I agree with name, Vovsi, was incidentally the same as that of one of the leading doctors accused.) The "treacherous Zionist" Mikhoels was also brought into the openly anti-Semitic Slansky trial in November 1952. It was the first overt and avowed anti-Semitic act of policy by the Soviet authorities—although, as I have argued elsewhere, the anti-Jewish aspects of the doctors' plot may have been incidental to Stalin's main purpose, which was to stage an elaborate move against Beria.[7]

The policy of more or less open anti-Semitism was pursued under Khrushchev and survives to this day. Khrushchev indeed was quite frank in his conversations with visiting socialists, as, for example, when he explained how "new" cadres had been created since the early days when Jews were numerous in the party and state leadership (another Soviet party leader present emphasized that by new cadres was meant "our own intelligentsia"). Khrushchev went on to point out that the appointment of too many Jews created anti-Semitism, since a Jew, once appointed, "surrounds himself with Jewish colleagues."[8] There were also periods when Soviet authorities deliberately stimulated nationalist feelings against Jews as an alien and non-Soviet community. This occurred particularly in 1961–1965 when Jews were used as part of a campaign against the universal financial dishonesty that is endemic in Soviet society. The disproportionate number of Jews prosecuted (50 percent of the defendants; 80 percent in the Ukraine) and the accompanying propaganda campaign convinced the International Commission of Jurists that this was a deliberate policy of shifting the odium for economic offenses onto the Jews, so as to disguise the fact that the lawbreaking was prevalent among all sections of the population.[9]

The year 1963 saw the intensification of an aspect of overt Soviet anti-Semitism that has continued virtually unabated ever since. This was a campaign against "Zionism" that by its very nature soon revealed that it was an attack not merely on Israel and its rulers but on the Jewish people as a whole, wherever they might be found, including the Soviet Union. A landmark in the campaign was the publication by the Ukrainian Academy of Sciences of a book entitled *Judaism Without Embellishments* by one T. K. Kichko, illustrated with appropriate cartoons. The book argued that Judaism is a faith that promotes hypocrisy, greed, and usury and is linked in one great conspiracy with Zionism, imperialism, and the Jewish bankers. Kichko's work provoked foreign protest, especially from Communists, and was mildly criticized by the Ideological Commission of the party's Central Committee on the grounds that it "might be interpreted in the spirit of anti-Semitism," but the book was not withdrawn, and its author subsequently received a prize.[10]

The anti-Semitic campaign has since continued in its anti-Zionist guise, and a whole host of experts on the subject has emerged. Anti-Semitism has in fact become a vested interest, which means that, quite apart from party policy, an interest group has emerged that is deeply concerned to keep anti-Semitism alive. One of the experts, Valery Emelianov, even urged the Central Committee to found an anti-Zionist institute (no doubt with himself in mind as director), but nothing came of this idea. The flow of books (published in mass editions), pamphlets, articles, films, lectures, and television shows has continued since 1963, and with special intensity since the six-day Arab-Israeli war of 1967. In the four years from 1975 to 1978, for example, no fewer than fifty full-size books were published on the theme of Zionism and Judaism. The main themes of this propaganda are the following: the Jewish religion is immoral and racist, and Zionism derives its philosophy from that religion. Both Jews and Zionists engage in immoral and criminal activities. They are accused of acquiring enormous financial power through the exploitation of others. They are said to use international finance, as well as subversion and espionage, to dominate the world. In Soviet eyes, Zionism is a racist philosophy akin to Nazism. Zionists are even accused of fomenting anti-Semitism and collaborating with the Nazis in the extermination of fellow Jews. The Zionists are depicted as enemies of the Soviet state and of socialism, and past anti-Semitism is justified in part by the Jews' misdeeds as exploiters of the poor.

The practical forms that anti-Semitism takes in the USSR today may be summarized under three main headings. First, there is widespread discrimination against Jews in many areas—especially in certain coveted employments and in the universities and academic institutions, where a secret *numerus clausus* operates. Analysis of Societ statistics, for example, shows a substantial decline of the Jewish student population between 1970 and 1976, and recent reports suggest that there may have been a further decline.[11] Second, there are the staged trials, in which the cynical indifference to truth is so evident that one can only infer that they are intended to pander to a very low level of political perception. For example, the release of Dr. Shtern, obviously prompted by an imminent tribunal organized abroad to investigate the case, was followed almost immediately by the *Izvestiia* article of March 7, 1977, which attacked Jewish activist Anatoly Shcharansky as a CIA agent. (Dr. Shtern was actually told privately by the trial judge that the charges against him were trumped up—which was indeed evident even from Soviet reports of the case.) And, third, there has been a determined effort to suppress anything that could encourage a Jewish sense of identity or nationalism. This includes the interdiction of virtually all Yiddish, let alone Hebrew, cultural activities; the blotting out of Jewish history by control over the courses taught in schools and universities; censoring of accounts of the fate of the Jews under Nazi occupation; greater religious harassment than that suffered by the other tolerated denominations; and, above all, the denial of the kind of communal organization that is permitted to the churches.

There have been some sops to outside protests. Some minor Yiddish cultural activity is permitted. Hebrew is now taught as an academic subject at Moscow University. And recently *Oktiabr'*, hitherto inclined to be anti-Semitic, carried a novel about the life of Jews under Nazi occupation. The work not only portrayed Nazi oppression but also painted Jewish resistance in a favorable light.

In 1981 and 1982 there were again signs of an increase of repressive measures against Jews. Emigration to Israel (or ostensibly to Israel—the great majority of emigrants now end up elsewhere), once extensively permitted, fell to a trickle. A samizdat journal dealing with Jewish history and culture, which had appeared for some years, was closed down. Many more Jewish activists were arrested and tried between October 1980 and December 1981 than had been the case for many years. Since it has long been evident that foreign protests are one of the most effective influences on Soviet policy toward Jews, the inference is that by the end of 1980 these protests no longer had the same effect. Possibly the explanation lies in the fact that, having assessed the extent of American and West European reaction to such events as the invasion of Afghanistan and the routing of Solidarity in Poland, the Soviet authorities had decided that they need no longer fear. The Western powers had shot their bolt, and it was therefore safe for the Soviet authorities to get rid of the nuisance of dissent without apprehension over foreign reaction. (There has also been an intensification in repression of non-Jewish religious dissent.)

What are the reasons for Soviet anti-Semitism, and how does it relate to nationalism? From the forms that anti-Semitic propaganda has taken it seems clear that one of its functions is to stimulate Soviet nationalism and a consequent rallying behind the Soviet "establishment" against that alien and dangerous element, the international Jew. Folk anti-Semitism is never far below the surface among the Soviet masses—at any rate in the RSFSR and the Ukraine—and can be readily exploited. How successful it has been is difficult to judge. It may well be, for example, that Jewish emigration, and the abuse showered on Jews who emigrate, has produced a response quite different from the one expected, namely: "they got us into this communist mess, and now they are getting out while we have to stay." Anti-Semitism may also be a useful counter to dissidents: it may be exploited as a means of driving a wedge between loyal Russian or Soviet citizens and "these dissidents, who are all Jews." Again, it is impossible to say to what extent this has been successful. (This particular employment of anti-Semitism has also been used in Czechoslovakia against Charter 77 and in Poland, where the communist authorities have long specialized in the political use of anti-Semitism.) Anti-Zionism, of course, has implications as a part of Soviet Arab policy. It serves to mobilize Arab opinion, and indeed African opinion, in the international sphere. The Afro-Asian solidarity movement, which is an important element in the Soviet strategy of mobilizing opinion against "imperialism" by means of a "front," has paid good dividends. In this sense, anti-Semitism is part of the Soviet endeavor to mobilize world opinion behind the PLO, as part of Soviet Middle Eastern strategy—and again this effort has not been unsuccessful.

Whatever benefits the USSR may have derived from encouraging anti-Semitism, there is no doubt that, as a direct result of this policy, it has lost much support in foreign communist and left-wing circles. Although the effects of so-called Eurocommunism should not be exaggerated so far as any serious decline in Soviet power is concerned, it has, at all events, been a considerable nuisance. The facade of lies that the Soviet Union has relied on for years to build its image as a perfect society that others should strive to emulate is gone for good. The immediate effect is that the work of hard-nosed Soviet agents has had to be intensified in order to replace the free services of the starry-eyed innocents. Inside the country, the most significant fact is that anti-Semitism has achieved no respectable intellectual adherents of the kind who played so big a part in the rise of National Socialism in Germany (and who were influential in Russia before 1917). Its exponents now are the riffraff of the ideological establishment or writers with low-level mass appeal. So far as respectable intellectuals are concerned, there is some evidence that they find the anti-Semitic campaign repugnant. Andrei Sakharov has repeatedly protested against manifestations of anti-Semitism and was one of the first to draw attention to the existence of anti-Jewish discrimination. There have been reports of efforts made by some of the institutes of the Academy of Sciences to circumvent the *numerus clausus* laid down for the employment of Jews. A samizdat account of a conference of Zionism held at the Academy's Institute of Oriental Studies in February 1976 shows that scholars do not unanimously accept the official policy and unease exists concerning the anti-Semitic character of anti-Zionist propaganda. Academician Korostovtsev, who is known from other pronouncements as a critic of anti-Semitism, attacked one of the most influential "establishment" anti-Semites, E. Evseev, as a "peddlar of cheap, journalistic anti-Semitism." There were other more or less veiled attacks on Evseev, especially in the form of exclamations from the audience, though some defended him. The meeting ended with a warning by the chairman against the use of violent and insulting language about Jewish history and culture, though the warning did not have much effect in subsequent years.[12]

So far as the most respectable section of the Soviet intelligentsia is concerned—the dissidents—anti-Semitism has won no serious adherents. Among the democrats such prejudice would be unthinkable. They have frequently deplored anti-Semitism, and Sakharov has repeatedly condemned it. Much of our information on official acts of anti-Semitism comes from the dissident *Chronicle of Current Events*. Even among dissenting groups that profess strongly nationalist views, anti-Semitism is far from universal. One must, in fact, be wary of the frequently made assumption that all Russian nationalism is by definition anti-Semitic. If one looks to the past, the strongly nationalist Slavophiles of the mid-nineteenth century had no place for anti-Semitism in their outlook. This element entered Russian nationalist thought when the epigones of Slavophilism took over, who were much more intent on chauvinist expansionism and much less concerned with spiritual matters than their predecessors. There is a parallel situation today, in that anti-Semitism belongs to the extreme politically nationalist groups much more than to those nationalists whose values are religious and spiritual. In the case of Solzhenitsyn, for example, the frequently made charge of anti-Semitism is totally false. There are certainly anti-Semites to be found among some of the nationalist religious groups, but in general this is the exception rather than the rule. Perhaps potential anti-Semites are restrained by the climate of opinion in dissident circles, which is definitely opposed to all nationalist and racial prejudice. Even Ukrainian nationalists condemn anti-Semitism. It is, perhaps, significant that the most violent samizdat anti-Semitism has emanated from nationalist groups that also condemn the church and have been suspected of being inspired by the KGB.

Folk anti-Semitism is not likely to disappear in the Soviet Union. Government-sponsored anti-Semitism will continue as long as the authorities find it expedient to use this well-tried political instrument that dictators wield over their ignorant populations. It is, perhaps, consoling for those who hold the principles of civilized behavior dear that anti-Semitism may be losing the relative respectability that it once enjoyed in some Russian educated circles. At least this applies to those who succeed in raising their voices through the barrier of Soviet censorship.

NOTES

1. V. I. Lenin, *Polnoe sobranie sochinenii*, 5th ed. (Moscow, 1959), 5: 338–39.

2. See my *The Communist Party of the Soviet Union*, 2d ed. (London, 1970), p. 309.

3. Article quoted in S. M. Shvarts, *Antisemitizm v. Sovetskom Soiuze* (New York, 1952), pp. 74–76.

4. Ibid., pp. 118–19.

5. William Corey, *The Soviet Cage: Antisemitism in Russia* (New York, 1973), p. 67.

6. Solomon Schwartz, *The Jews in the Soviet Union* (Syracuse, N.Y., 1951), p. 126.

7. See "The Jewish Anti-Fascist Committee," in Bela Vargo and George L. Mosse, eds., *Jews and Non-Jews in Eastern Europe, 1918–1945* (New York, 1974), pp. 295–97.

8. *Les Réalités*, no. 136, 1957.

9. *Journal of the International Commission of Jurists* 5, no. 1 (1964).

10. *Pravda*, April 4, 1964.

11. Institute of Jewish Affairs (London) Research Report, November 1977.

12. E. L. Solmar, "Protocols of the Anti-Zionist Elders," *Soviet Jewish Affairs* 8, no. 2 (1978).

The Prospects of
National Bolshevism

Mikhail Agursky

WHAT IS NATIONAL BOLSHEVISM?

The prospects of National Bolshevism are linked to the political future of
the USSR in general. Many (practically all) social, economic, and political factors, both internal and external, will influence its fate.

National Bolshevism is now more than an abstract political idea that
has its partisans. It is an ideology that expresses the vital political interests
of a certain segment of the Soviet political system. That is why, to
estimate the prospects of National Bolshevism, it is necessary to define its
social and political base and to understand what chance this group has
in the internal political struggle. We can only do this in a historical
framework. But the history of National Bolshevism has not yet been
written, and one has almost nothing to refer to.[1]

First let me define what I mean by National Bolshevism. *National
Bolshevism is the ideology of a political current that legitimizes the existing
Soviet political system from a Russian national point of view*, contrary to its
exclusive Marxist legitimacy.

National Bolshevism does not reject the existing political and social
system. It does not challenge communist ideology, though it strives to
minimize its importance to the level necessary for political continuity. Its
objectives, however, are different from the objectives of communist
ideology. If a perennial aim of communist ideology is a world communist
system, National Bolshevism can limit itself to the creation of a Russian
superpower or a Russian-dominated international conglomerate able to
coexist with the rest of the world in spite of mutual antagonism. This is

not, of course, to exclude the possibility that such a power might strive for Russian world domination, though not an empire possessed by utopian visions.

National Bolshevism is thus by no means a political antagonist of the Soviet political system. Throughout Soviet history there has been a conflict between Russian nationalism and communist ideology—a conflict solved differently at different times. Meanwhile National Bolshevism has always been an evolutionary, not a revolutionary, force. It is supported mainly by groups that are parts of the system. According to them, the ruling party is a vital political formation that can substantially survive any weakening of communist ideology.

FORMATION OF NATIONAL BOLSHEVISM

National Bolshevism emerged as a political alternative in Soviet Russia soon after the revolution. There were two leading factors that influenced its emergence: Russian demographic dominance in the country and the new geopolitical situation. Revolutionary Russia was in a state of total confrontation with the West and was not supported by other revolutions in Europe. These two factors could not fail to give a national character to the Soviet system, which had not hitherto had national objectives either formally or factually.

Thus the Russian Bolshevik revolution, which was regarded by its leaders only as the first stage of the world revolution, turned out to be a geopolitical confrontation between Russia and the West. Early National Bolshevism was originally formulated outside the Soviet political system in different forms, which turned out to be, however, prototypes for later development. Its right-wing isolationist formulation came from Professor Nikolai Ustrialov, who verbalized it for the first time in 1920. According to Ustrialov, Bolshevism is a form of Russian national revival that grew in the critical conditions that followed the Russian political disaster of 1917. He saw communist ideology as only a temporary instrument of Russian national policy. According to Ustrialov, the objectives of this policy are the restoration of a powerful Russian state and détente with the West. He rejected an escalation of Russian expansion beyond the limits of the former Russian empire. His views provoked feverish intraparty discussion after 1922.

Another model of National Bolshevism that was expansionist and even messianic was proposed by the literary critic, Isaiah Lezhnev (Altshuler). He called his model "Turkestan" socialism, in contrast to the classic Marxist "Basel" socialism.[2] According to Lezhnev, there is no need for a class formulation of socialism. The duty of Russia is to lead the struggle of nations with high fertility against those with low fertility (that is, the West).

Lenin himself had, of course, laid the foundations of a Bolshevik Asian strategy. Asia for Lenin was a vital reserve of the world revolutionary movement, which it was necessary to direct against the capitalist West. According to Lenin, Soviet Russia must not be overly scrupulous about Asian ideologies; on the contrary, it must rely on any anti-Western movement.

Both Ustrialov and Lezhnev's views were rejected and condemned officially, but they nevertheless exercised an important influence on the imperceptible infiltration of Russian nationalism into the Soviet system. Their views were taken up by Stalin in 1924 in his famous slogan, "socialism in one country." The adoption of this slogan was an important tactical move that corresponded to the contemporary geopolitical situation: namely, the stabilization of the West and the isolation of Soviet Russia.

The USSR did much to support anti-Western movements in various Asian areas in the 1920s, though even then the danger had emerged (especially in China) that a revolutionary movement in a large Asian country could go beyond any Soviet control and be transformed into an independent force. This is why Stalin was very restrained vis-à-vis the Asian revolutionary movement; its later successes can be explained rather by the internal dynamics of the world communist movement than by Soviet support.

The quick success of this type of isolationist National Bolshevism was achieved because of several factors: (1) Russian demographic pressures; (2) popular reluctance to be involved in a new revolutionary adventure on a world scale; (3) the necessity of stabilizing the Soviet system, which did not enjoy broad popular support; and (4) Stalin's personal tendency to rely on Russian nationalism against the opposition, which was led mainly by non-Russian (Jewish) leaders.

Thus, from the very emergence of National Bolshevism, the Jewish question was an important structural element. The mobilization of Russian nationalism and its integration happened not only in the process of the confrontation with the West but also in its confrontation with the Jewish political and social presence that had highly increased since the revolution. The Jewish presence was regarded by the majority of the Russian population as a negative consequence of the revolution, as an alien invasion. The early stage of the trend to push Jews away from political life was relatively moderate. The Jewish question had its own dynamics; anti-Jewishness within the system increased after the 1920s.

Russian nationalism, as used by Stalin, had no cultural content. It was for him only a method of political mobilization. Stalin partly changed his policy in 1928–1929 under the impact of the world economic crisis, which demonstrated, on the one hand, the inherent weakness of the West and, on the other, switched on the green light for imports of Western industrial equipment needed for Soviet industrialization.

Yet the relative isolationism expressed by the slogan "socialism in one country" remained. And with political consolidation Stalin could trust in an organic Russian nationalism that relied on Russian confrontation with the West. One of its symptoms was a Russian emigré movement, the "Young Russians" (Mladorossy), who regarded the five-year plan as a victory for nationalism in Russia, affirming the country's international status as a great power.[3] According to the Mladorossy, the USSR was on its way toward a national revolution in its internal development. Up to 1938, they regarded Stalin as a Russian national leader. Without any doubt, Stalin understood that, even during the barbarous collectivization campaign and the crazy industrial crash plans, he could rely on a certain sympathy from Russian nationalism if even a monarchist movement like the Mladorossy could accept such means as the way to a national revolution. Besides, by 1930 Stalin had started an attack against non-Russian nationalism and especially against Ukrainian and Belorussian nationalism. Thus his image as a Russian statesman was crystallized.

Stalin was not alone in his attempts to take political advantage of Russian nationalism. He relied on a group of party officials of Russian origin, especially Sergei Kirov and Valerian Kuibyshev, who supported him during his struggle against the opposition. As a result, the new concept of so-called Soviet patriotism was formulated as early as 1934. On the one hand, this ambivalent concept was a slogan of national integration within the multinational Soviet country. On the other, it was a very convenient formulation of Russian nationalism.[4] The integration of Soviet and Russian nationalism increased during the 1930s, but Marxist ideology did not decline and was still officially dominant. Any attempt to limit this ideology was regarded as a crime.

All this changed sharply after the German invasion in 1941. Indeed, Russian nationalism in an extreme form exercised a decisive role in the hour of mortal danger. Marxist ideology temporarily lost its centrality and was reduced to a very vague revolutionary continuity. The Bolshevik revolution was itself treated as a national liberation movement. The use of Russian nationalism during the war was the result of the USSR's desperate situation. The Red Army consisted mainly of Russian peasants. Besides that, the Western part of the country, which was populated by non-Russians (and in part by non-Slavs), was lost quickly, which increased even more the weight of Russians, especially since Muslims (apart from Tatars, Bashkirs, and, to some degree, Kazakhs) were not regarded as a reliable battle force.

Thus the destiny of the country depended mainly on Russians. Wartime Russian nationalism was a political alternative that was represented mainly by Alexander Shcherbakov, who played an extremely important role at this time. He was Stalin's closest adviser during the first three decisive years of the war. He was probably responsible for several very important political decisions adopted then: (1) the deideologization of literature and art; (2) the compromise with religion and especially with the Russian Orthodox Church; (3) the dissolution of the Comintern; and (4) the adoption of the new Soviet hymn with Russian overtones.

A major aspect of wartime Russian nationalism was Shcherbakov's policy toward the Jews. The Jewish Antifascist Committee was established—the first Jewish all-union formation permitted since the dissolution of the Jewish Section in 1930. A wide-ranging Yiddish publication program was also permitted. It is impossible to claim that all this was done only to mobilize the Western Jewish lobby on behalf of the USSR. Indeed, Shcherbakov's Russian nationalism was extremely hostile to any idea of Jewish political participation on the highest level. But, at the same time, Russian nationalism accepted and even encouraged a certain Jewish cultural autonomy. There is important evidence that wartime National Bolshevism had no anti-Semitic character. Indeed, its main spokesman, paradoxically, was an assimilated Jew, Ilya Ehrenburg, who nevertheless always claimed his Jewish identity. Ehrenburg verbalized the boldest Russian nationalist statements during the war. One can even argue that Ehrenburg was a source of several important political statements made by Shcherbakov during the war. On November 11, 1943, Ehrenburg said that "Russia could have lost its state independence and betrayed its historical mission without the revolution."[5] And Shcherbakov, in his official speech on the Lenin anniversary on January 21, 1944, said that on the eve of the revolution, "the country went on a way which faced it with the imminent loss of state independence. The Bolshevik Party saved our country from such a shame."[6]

Another important feature of this wartime Russian nationalism was its basic isolationsim. The view dominating the Kremlin until the spring of 1944 was that Soviet military actions should be limited to the liberation of Soviet territories within 1941 frontiers. Only Stalin's instruction, given on May 1, 1944, to "finish off the enemy in his den" manifested the rejection of isolationism and the quick retreat from mere Russian nationalism.[7] Shcherbakov's influence began to erode. His liberal literary policy was violently attacked by critics of such leading Soviet writers as Simonov, Platonov, Zoshchenko, and Chukovsky. In April 1945, Ehrenburg himself was criticized for his rabid anti-German assaults, and he was dismissed as the main spokesman of Russian nationalism.[8] Shcherbakov disappeared from the public scene in November 1944. He died on May 10, 1945, at the age of 44. His death may have been unnatural, as was claimed officially in 1953.[9] What brought Shcherbakov down and why was wartime Russian nationalism rejected?

There are several explanations. Naturally, the increasing influence of Shcherbakov provoked a struggle against him, mainly waged by Zhdanov and Malenkov.[10] But his opponents had to do more than discredit him personally. They had to use a political argument against his policy, too. Indeed, Shcherbakov's isolationism was discredited first by Western allies of the USSR, when they first dismissed, on the spot, Soviet proposals to discuss the USSR's frontiers after the war. The USSR was then asking only for recognition of its 1941 frontiers.[11] This rejection helped to arouse Soviet suspicions and to consolidate the resistance of the ideological hard-liners, who had temporarily been pushed aside. Delays in the Western landing in Europe probably played a decisive role in the Russian nationalists' defeat. It seemed that neither England nor the United States wanted to sacrifice lives to prevent a Soviet invasion of Eastern Europe.

Meanwhile the ideological party faction was not passive. The Zhdanovist alternative of a large-scale Soviet expansion, with Communists as its main agents, won. Zhdanov relied on the powerful communist tradition; he could easily argue that Russian nationalism could not integrate new countries within the Soviet orbit. Pan-Slavism was at that time a tentative ideology for such an integration, but it could not work in Romania, Hungary, Albania, East Germany, North Korea, or even Poland. Zhdanovism was the leading Soviet policy until 1948. Russian nationalism, however, was not completely rejected. Many of its elements were integrated into Soviet political life, but they were subordinated to the new policy. Communist expansion in its pure form, however, had an inherent danger. The Yugoslavian conflict with the USSR was the first alarming signal: it demonstrated that a communist expansion not controlled by the imperial center in fact endangers the political stability of the new international system. That discovery was used immediately by Zhdanov's archenemy, Malenkov. Zhdanov was discredited and died very soon after, probably in the same way Shcherbakov died.

As a result of the political failures of both Shcherbakov's Russian isolationism and Zhdanov's communist expansionism, it was necessary to make a synthesis of these two approaches, which separately did not suit the new geopolitical situation. Suslov became its main proponent. He proposed (or was the mouthpiece of) an expansionist and even messianic

Russian nationalism that operated through communist ideology. This new synthesis was close to the early Lezhnevian National Bolshevism. One can say, within certain limits, that Suslov's ideology was a messianic National Bolshevism. Moreover, the concept of the external enemy, which earlier had a purely class interpretation, changed during Zhdanov's time, and this change survived him.

The West, according to the new image, challenges Russia as an existential, perennial enemy that embodies world evil. The West is the source of destructive cosmopolitanism; Russia is the main proponent of national independence. National independence was stressed by Stalin as the highest value in his last public speech in October 1952.[12]

In this way, the ideological foundations of what can be called a Pax Sovietica were laid down. This peace was perceived then as a conglomerate of national states subordinated, however, to a single center. Nationalism was recognized as a foundation of Pax Sovietica; but it must not cross certain limits or endanger the political stability of the new formation. The least clear aspect of the new synthesis was the attitude toward the non-Western (mainly Asian) world. Stalin never relied on Lenin or Lezhnev's idea of Asia as the main revolutionary reserve, because of the potential dangers that proceed from such a realization. Nevertheless, events developed in this very direction regardless of Stalin's wishes. The success of the Chinese Communists in 1949 caused Stalin to recognize communist China for what it was, and he tried to integrate it within the Pax Sovietica. This, however, did not rehabilitate Lenin's old Asian strategy. The emergence of a communist China that was impossible to keep under control for long made Lenin's doctrine dangerous. Indeed, China has since been developing not into a support for Pax Sovietica but into an independent power that could endanger the USSR itself. Stalin was also very suspicious and reserved vis-à-vis the Arab world and did not want to intervene in that area. For example, he did not want to take advantage of the Arab-Israeli conflict. Probably he felt a general fear and distrust of the Muslim world, which was manifested, for example, in his deportation of millions of Muslims from the Crimea and the Caucasus in 1943–1944.

Thus an aggressive and expansionist National Bolshevism dominated the USSR at the end of Stalin's rule. Its Marxist component was reduced to an ideology of national integration within the USSR and within the new Soviet camp. National Bolshevism also became an instrument of further expansion.

Stalin's death strengthened aggressive National Bolshevism. Contrary to various estimations, his death made Soviet foreign policy even more dangerous. Its most radical turn was directed toward what Lezhnev called "Turkestan" socialism. Since 1955, the USSR has been engaging in a very active policy of supporting radical movements in the Third World. It has again made Marxist ideology a dominant element of the Soviet system. The relative importance of the Russian nationalist component in expansionist National Bolshevism has declined (but never disappeared). The policy of world expansion gained momentum when several Soviet interest groups turned out to be interested in it: first, the Soviet military-industrial complex and, second, the ideological section of the party.

The party's ideological branch controls the Soviet mass media, the educational system, and the world communist and procommunist movement. It is also linked to foreign policy and to the powerful KGB international network. The Soviet military-industrial complex has also become a major power center.

The USSR's world expansionist drive reached its culmination in 1966, when, for the first time, the program of a world communist victory was put forward as a real political target for a foreseeable future.[13] This major political change was a result of a new geopolitical situation. The weakness of the West, which started with a general retreat from the Third World, created a political vacuum there. The situation is reminiscent of what happened to Eastern Europe in 1944–1945. The party ideological branch, together with the military-industrial complex, sought to fill this vacuum immediately. Western policy, in fact, encouraged Soviet expansion. Moreover, the West decided to finance this expansion by giving the USSR large credits.

The Russian demographic base was not, however, sufficient to guarantee Soviet world domination. This is why it was decided to start large-scale national integration within the USSR in order to create a new entity—the Soviet people. This Russian-speaking entity must be Russified as much as possible. Yet this might lead not to Russification but to denationalization, even of Russians. Thus an early idea of National Bolsheviks like Lezhnev and Nikolai Rusov, who appealed for the sacrifice of Russia as a national entity for the sake of all humanity, was close to realization.[14]

PAX SOVIETICA CONTESTED

In the very moment of its triumph, however, the policy of transforming national Russia into its imperial extension to achieve world communist victory (even if conceived as the Russian world mission) was contested. One could first see a visible pocket of resistance among Russian intellectuals, who could not accept a program according to which Russia was to be sacrificed to a dangerous political utopia. But resistance to a Pax

Sovietica emerged also within the Soviet political system itself, within the party apparatus. Indeed, the party apparatus, as compared to the ideological branch, was multinational in the first days of the revolution; but only Jews, Letts, Poles, Germans, and sometimes Armenians and Georgians got important political nominations. Even the Ukrainian representation was almost negligible, and Muslims were almost never represented in central party bodies. Party officials from such minorities were committed integrationists. They disappeared (with the exception of Georgians and Armenians), however, after the Great Purge of 1938.

After that, the central party apparatus was monolithically Russian, and the government had more or less the same monolithic character. This demonstrates more than most things the genuine structure of Soviet nationalities policy.

From this point of view it was useless and even harmful to create a separate Russian republican party organization, which would have immediately provoked a request for national representation in the central party apparatus. When Zhdanov's group proposed the creation of such a separate organization, with a view to strengthening its own political position, it was apparently accused of Russian nationalism.[15] After Stalin, and especially after Beria, Russian political dominance even increased, since Georgians and Armenians, too, were purged from central political bodies. The infiltration of such officials as Khrushchev or Brezhnev into the central ruling body brought a powerful political group of former Ukrainian party officials into the party, thus tending to make the apparatus rather more Slavic than Russian.[16] The Russian (or Slav) dominance in the party apparatus is, according to Seweryn Bialer, a condition of Soviet political stability.[17]

Meanwhile, the policy of national integration adopted in 1966 has challenged Russian dominance of the central party apparatus, since it would be irrational to strive for a new entity—the Soviet people—while leaving the national structure of ruling Soviet bodies as is. The same problem emerged in the army, where the high command was almost entirely Slavic and predominantly Russian.

The situation was aggravated by profound demographic changes in the structure of the Soviet population.[18] Indeed, the relative weight of the Russians and the Ukrainians in the Soviet population as a whole has been quickly declining since the 1960s. Their strength has been undermined by wars, terror, and especially by the mass urbanization of the Slavic population. Meanwhile, the strength of non-Slavic nationals, mainly Muslims, has increased quickly. Thus the pressure for the national integration of the central ruling bodies can only increase. And here we should stress that nationalism in the Soviet republics is now manifested not only by centrifugal forces but also by centripetal forces. The republican party elite strives not for separatism but for access to the Kremlin, to central ruling organs.

This is why the Russian-dominated central party apparatus tried to sabotage the policy of national integration. The Russians have enough reasons to regard the program of national integration, and even the master program of world communist domination, as dangerous to their own political position.

Of course, the motivations of high-ranking apparatchiks can be mixed. Besides their personal vested interests and the organic Russian nationalism that is their common denominator, they may also realize that the utopian policy of a worldwide Pax Sovietica could bring their own country to disaster by ruining the political stability based on Russian dominance. The geopolitical situation that seems favorable for expansion could not be a justification of this policy, since the Russians, who would be only a small demographic minority in such a new world order, would not be able to guarantee the stability of such a peace. The Pax Sovietica could easily turn into a Pax Orwellica, with permanent global conflicts between different communist blocs.

THE RUSSIAN OPPOSITION

The apparatus (or at least a part of it) started supporting the isolationist Russian opposition, which was essentially a natural reaction of Russian intellectuals.[19] It was a new stage of National Bolshevism. Naturally, the party apparatus, in spite of the fact that it was in a state of acute confrontation with the ideological-military-industrial bloc, did not want to ruin its own revolutionary legitimacy. Thus the party apparatus sabotages only the following points of the new master program:

1. The extensive industrial growth and program of new investments in the strategic sector of Soviet economics.
2. The program of superindustrialization of the Russian rural sector (a mortal danger for the last Russian demographic rampart).
3. The national integration program.
4. The atheistic campaign, regarded as dangerous to the Russian traditional family and to the morale of the Russian population.
5. The extreme anti-Zionism waged by the ideological branch of the party.

6. The unlimited support of the world revolutionary movement.

7. Any orientation toward Eurocommunism.

8. The dangerous confrontation with China, which could involve the USSR in a hopeless and destructive war.

In addition, very sharp criticism has been extended against the subsidizing of the Soviet strategic budget by the large-scale and expanding sale of alcoholic beverages. The party apparatus also wants to achieve mutual arms control with the United States, since that would limit the dangerous political power and economic demands of the military-industrial complex.

If one analyzes the permitted expression of isolationist Russian nationalism, one can find the verbalization of all these points.[20] First of all, there is violent criticism of the new industrial society that ruins the authentic Russian life (voiced by such writers as Valentin Rasputin and Viktor Astaf'ev).[21] There is a persistent escalation of ecological concern (Rasputin, Astaf'ev, Vladimir Chivilikhin, Oleg Volkov, and many others), which has turned out to be a serious obstacle for many new industrial sites. The Soviet space race was condemned on several occasions as ruinous and useless (for example, by Petr Proskurin and Fedor Abramov). One major demand is to stop the policy of rural industrialization, especially the destruction of small villages. This demand has been the subject of numerous literary and publicist efforts by such authors as Vasily Belov and Fedor Abramov.

Emphasis is also put on the necessity for a multinational structure of the USSR, as it was conceived earlier. The principle of multinationality is set against the principle of national integration. A leading Russian organ, *Nash sovremennik*, now gives a regular place to local republican literature in a section entitled "Unified and Multinational." This is essentially the Russian nationalist approach to the Soviet nationality problem. Valentin Rasputin verbalized this approach more explicitly. He said that the Russians will stay Russians, Tatars will stay Tatars, and so on.[22] (That is, he disbelieves the official policy of national integration.) Thus it is quite evident that it is perfectly legitimate to regard the Russian nationalist trend as a Russian opposition.

There are indications that this opposition is now trying to reformulate its approach to the very sensitive Jewish problem by implicit criticism of official anti-Zionism, which is, in fact, anti-Semitism. A new novel by Yevgeny Yevtushenko was published in 1981 in a literary monthly, *Moskva*, which has always belonged to a moderate wing of the Russian opposition and is published under the auspices of the Moscow party organization. Yevtushenko is not important (he is a political opportunist), but the magazine itelf is. Moreover, the introduction to his novel was written by Valentin Rasputin and emphasizes the political implications of what Yevtushenko says in his novel. Indeed, the novel categorically rejects anti-Semitism and condemns extreme forms of Russian nationalism.[23]

There are several indications that the central party apparatus's approach to the Jewish problem includes the rejection of extreme anti-Semitism. Even before the last Lebanese war, Israel was probably regarded by the Russian opposition as a potential ally of Russia and a counterbalance to the Muslim world. This idea is not something entirely new in contemporary Russian policy—it is merely a repetition of Stalin's support of Israel in 1947–1948. *Partiinaia zhizn'*, the main organ of the central party apparatus, conspicuously gives a very low profile not only to Arab Communist parties, but to Communist parties of the Muslim world in general. This trend started at least as early as 1977. There is an example of this tacit policy in an article by the notorious Valery Emelianov, a spokesman of the ideological branch who is known for his wild anti-Semitism. In his article, published in *Nash sovremennik*, Emelianov had to stress (he did not do this in other publications) that "anti-Zionism" has nothing to do with a rejection of the state of Israel, it is only the rejection of Israeli policy.[24]

It seems that this trend found a reflection in Brezhnev's speech to the twenty-sixth party congress, in which he balanced his condemnation of Zionism with a condemnation of anti-Semitism.[25] For the first time, too, Brezhnev did not say that the Middle East conflict was a global conflict and a danger to world peace. This demonstrated a major change in Soviet Middle Eastern policy. Brezhnev's approach was probably a result of a compromise between different trends in the Soviet leadership.

Criticism of the atheist assault against religion, and especially against Russian Orthodoxy, occupies an important place in the struggle of the Russian opposition against the ideological branch of the party. They claim that official atheism leads to demoralization and the destruction of the traditional Russian family—the Russian demographic stronghold. Moreover, Christianity is regarded as a very important barrier against national integration. And, as we will see below, Christianity is also regarded as a link to the West.

The campaign against alcoholism is also a major operation of Russian nationalists. The essence of it is to cut, as much as possible, the sales of alcohol, a main source of the arms-race-oriented budget. According to a Soviet source, one province alone (Kalinin) sent 400 million rubles each year to the central Soviet budget as a result of the sales of alcoholic beverages! (Yevtushenko, in the previously mentioned novel, also implies, without approval, that alcohol is a main source of the Soviet budget.)[26]

THE STRUGGLE FOR POWER

I have said that Russian nationalism and communist ideology were always in a state of conflict. Nevertheless, Stalin did enjoy almost absolute power to resolve that conflict, either by suppressing one participant of this conflict or by making a cocktail of both of them. The importance of communist ideology has been steadily rising since Stalin's death. Neither Khrushchev nor Brezhnev enjoyed Stalin's power. Moreover, Suslov, as the leader of the party ideological branch, eventually defeated Khrushchev and then overruled Brezhnev, at least in one vital field—the formulation of Soviet long-range objectives.

Thus isolationist Russian nationalism turned out to be in a state of confrontation not only with communist ideology but also with the aggressive, expansionist National Bolshevism that was defended by Suslov after 1948. The two trends of Russian nationalism clashed. This clash certainly had its intellectual foundation, but this foundation was closely linked to the organizational conflict within the Soviet system.

The party ideological branch, together with the Soviet military-industrial complex, was challenged by the party apparatus as such, which realized that the party as a national administration can essentially survive the end of ideology. The model of Shcherbakov, whose nominees achieved a high degree of power, was not forgotten.

Brezhnev turned out to be only a moderator between two competing forces. Since his own power was essentially determined by several republican party organizations (Ukrainian, Moldavian, Azerbaijanian, Georgian, and Uzbek) that sought the national integration of the central party apparatus, Brezhnev had to hesitate constantly.

One can see that the 1966 program has been eroding. The national integration policy was hampered, and its original slogan of full integration was replaced by the slogan of rapprochement. The policy of superindustrialization of the Russian village, with the consequent annihilation of small villages, was eventually discredited, at least in its extreme form. There is a clear indication of a sharp internal struggle on this issue, as was made clear in 1981 by the first secretary of the Moscow provincial committee, Vasily Konotop.[27] The escalation of the ecological movement has created troubles for industry. In 1979, the SALT-II proposals were used for an attack against the Soviet military and strategic budget.[28] As a reaction against this trend, the Afghan invasion was provoked by the ideological-military-industrial bloc in order to escalate international tension. The Russian opposition almost openly demonstrated its political objectives in 1979, as one can judge from *Sovetskaia Rossiia*, which suddenly started publishing Aesopian editorials that explicitly condemned the Western military-industrial complex and implicitly attacked the Soviet military-industrial complex, together with the party ideological branch. The same newspaper, in a listing of Soviet military-technical obligatory holidays, completely ignored one key holiday, the day of the Strategic Rocket Forces on November 19, 1979, since these forces are a main consumer of the giant Soviet military budget. It is interesting to note that the only other newspaper that ignored this holiday was *Radianska Ukraina*, a Ukrainian-language party organ published in Kiev. It probably demonstrates some cooperation between the Russian opposition and the Ukrainian party apparatus, as a kind of united Slavic front.

Relying on the analysis of Soviet leaders' speeches and their participation in public events, one seems to find in the Russian opposition such men as Mikhail Grishin and Ivan Kapitonov, the latter of whom long played a decisive role in party nominations in Russia proper.[29] Both started their party careers under Shcherbakov. Another product of the Moscow party organization, Petr Demichev, might also be numbered with this group, though owing his ideological promotion under Khrushchev to opposition to Suslov.[30] Mikhail Solomentsev seems to have worked with them, but his connections were with Kirilenko, and his cooperation with the "Muscovites" might only be temporary.

An important problem is the late Yuri Andropov. One source called him "the leader of the Russian party."[31] It is impossible to draw any conclusions from his early speeches and actions that would confirm such a claim. His speech on April 22, 1982, however, did imply that he was somehow linked to the Russian opposition.[32] It thus seems that Andropov was a leader of the Russian segment of the central party apparatus. But there is not enough information about Andropov to make any final judgment.

As far as one can judge from their publications in *Sovetskaia Rossiia*, Marshals Viktor Kulikov, Nikolai Ogarkov, and Sergei Sokolov, who constitute the nucleus of the Soviet high command, also support the Russian opposition.

But these are not the only people who count. A considerable number of Russian provincial party committees (though not all of them) support the Russian opposition. The Russian opposition probably controlled another key Central Committee department, the Department for Administrative Organs which controls nominations in the army, the KGB, and police. This department has probably been supervised in general by Kapitonov.[33]

The Russian opposition is also represented in the Presidium of the Supreme Soviet, which is now an important body since it controls, for example, nominations of ministers, marshals, army generals, and ambassadors, and it can veto any proposed candidate.

Soviet ambassadorial nominations form an important field in the struggle for power in the USSR. Ambassadors' nominations for communist countries at least manifest evident links between a Soviet leadership group and the particular countries. For example, the Soviet ambassador in Bulgaria was a former Dnepropetrovsk party provincial secretary, Tolubeev, and, indeed, Bulgaria was a personal stronghold for Brezhnev. Two former senior party officials from the Moscow party organization, Pavlov and Stepakov, were simultaneously appointed in 1971 to the two most "liberal" communist countries: Hungary and Yugoslavia (though Pavlov was moved in February 1982 from Hungary to Japan). Hungary, which has a reputation as a liberal testing ground for the communist bloc, has extremely friendly relations with the Moscow party organization.

This picture is seemingly violated by the nomination of Boris Chaplin from the Moscow party organization as the ambassador to Vietnam, but his appointment might be explained by the wish of the Russian opposition to have control over the dangerous Chinese-Vietnamese conflict, which might involve the USSR in a serious confrontation with China.

One indication of the internal struggle was a growing stress on Shcherbakov—which was, however, somewhat selective. It can be easily explained both by the growing interest in his ideological stance and by the fact that he is a symbol of the ambitions to power of the main nucleus of the Russian opposition—the "Muscovites" whose leaders were Shcherbakov's nominees. *Pravda, Krasnaia Zvezda, Moskovskaia Pravda,* and even *Kommunist* celebrated the eightieth anniversary of Shcherbakov's birth on October 10, 1981: a political victory for the Russian opposition. Meanwhile, the ideological-military-industrial bloc challenges this campaign by celebrating Zhdanov without mentioning Shcherbakov.[34] Neo-Zhdanovism is one of many indications of the persistent struggle waged against the Russian opposition. This struggle has many other forms and its own symbolism. There are several other indicators of attacks against the Russian opposition: for example, criticism of a trend toward patriarchalism, criticism of a nonclass approach to the past or even to the present, criticism of an underestimation of the leading role of the working class, and so on.

There are also direct assaults against Russian nationalism, which is presented as a danger that might destroy the Soviet system and is allegedly inspired by foreign intelligence.[35] But the favorite tactic in this struggle is an imperceptible substitution for isolationist Russian nationalism of its expansionist messianic version. This is probably the main task of monthlies like *Molodaia gvardia* or weeklies like *Ogonek*. It is not a difficult task since there is a common denominator between the two trends. It is very easy, relying on the same assumptions, to come to opposite conclusions. Violent attacks against Zionism are important in this imperceptible substitution, and they have been waged persistently by the party ideological branch since 1968. This branch has delivered to the Soviet and world book market such radically anti-Semitic books as those by Iu. Ivanov, E. Evseev, V. Begun, and Iu. Kolesnikov. These books even resurrect the old Black Hundred mythos of the worldwide Jewish conspiracy, whose main objective is to destroy Russia. This campaign has a very important internal danger. It is designed to discredit the neo-Stalinist "Israeli" option in Soviet orientation by demonstrating that Zionism is a mortal enemy of Russia, and it seeks to discredit all within the Soviet system who would dare to rely on such a neo-Stalinist option. Isolationist Russian nationalists challenge Jewish political participation within Russia and use the term *Zionism* to stress Jewish political infiltration; their opponents use the word for Jewry and Israel as such.

This duality was manifested again during the Israeli intervention in Lebanon, when the Russian opposition for the first time succeeded in avoiding intervention in the Arab-Israeli conflict. The Soviet propaganda machine, however, started a violent campaign against Israel, in open contradiction to actual Soviet policy in the Middle East.

Suslov's death in January 1982 probably considerably weakened the position of the party ideological branch. Only a month later, the Central Committee, in an official document, warned against any acceleration of national integration. Suslov's old enemy, Petr Fedoseev, claimed later that the Russian language is not an ethnic factor of the Soviet people. The expression "multinational mother country" (a slogan of *Nash sovremennik*) was again used in official May Day party slogans after a long period of neglect.[36]

In 1982, after eighteen years of open hostility, Brezhnev publicly proposed a reconciliation with China and acknowledged the socialist character of the Chinese system, which had been decisively denied by Suslov.[37] It is also significant that the May Day slogans considerably reduced the role of the party ideological branch. In October 1981 slogans it had been responsible for education, information, and ideology; its only duty in May 1982 slogans was to pass party decisions to the masses. This was a denial of its independent role.

After a short period of embarrassment, the ideological-military-industrial bloc counterattacked. Mikhail Gorbachev (probably a Suslov protégé) did not repeat Brezhnev's proposal to China, made only a few days earlier, during his visit to Vietnam. A candidate Politburo member and Suslov's former right-hand man, Boris Ponomarev, the head of the International Department, delivered a very aggressive speech on the occasion of the nomination of Yuri Zhukov (a leading Suslov spokesman and *Pravda* columnist) as chairman of the Soviet Peace Committee. It was Zhukov who had been first to accuse West Germany of the attempt to invade Czechoslovakia in 1968. Zhukov has also claimed that Zionism was behind Dubček and Solidarity. In at least two *Pravda* editorials, the Russian opposition was implicitly criticized. One editorial attacked the nonclass approach to the past, a second stressed the need for "personnel stability" and accused anonymous party organizations of taking a wrong approach to the selection of personnel.[38] In fact, this demand is a main political slogan of the *apparat*.[39]

IS RUSSIA EUROPE OR ASIA?

It is possible to single out from all this struggle a truly central political discussion about Russian national strategy. It started in 1980. First of all, Fedor Nesterov made a very important attempt to create an ideological platform that would mobilize all Russian nationalists around the party ideological branch. Nesterov, who is employed by the notorious Lumumba University, a main Soviet center of the international revolutionary movement, wrote a book that delivers an extreme, anti-Western interpretation of Russian history.[40] According to Nesterov, Russia is separated from the West by an abyss. Even the same words have different meanings in the two civilizations. Nesterov claims that the Russians acquired their extraordinary national qualities because they had to fight external enemies throughout history. That is why they worked out the idea of complete submission of personal interests to the state. Nesterov justifies autocracy by saying that the creation of absolute autocracy was a healthy national reaction, given the necessity of the centralization of national efforts for the defense of the mother country. Unfortunately, autocracy was Germanized and became an antinational force after the eighteenth century. Russian expansion, Nesterov says, differed in princi-

ple from European colonization. Europeans regarded colonized people as
inferior races. Only the Russians accepted other people as equals. The
socialist revolution could happen only in Russia, since only Russians
could reject an imperialist war that was artificially imposed on them. All
other nations, according to Nesterov, wanted further expansion.

Naturally the Russian opposition accepts, in principle, any national
interpretation of the revolution. But it could not accept Nesterov's platform in general since it broke all links with the West and was extremely
dangerous in twentieth-century demographic conditions. Another evident obstacle was the anti-Christianity of Nesterov's book. *Nash sovremennik* criticized Nesterov for several mistakes, including a wrong
approach to the role of the church in Russian history. *Ogonek*, however,
welcomed Nesterov's book without any reservations.[41]

In 1980, too, open polemics concerning national strategy broke out.
They were provoked by the 600th anniversary of the Kulikovo battle
(when the Russians for the first time defeated the Tatars). This sensitive
holiday was used for a Russian national mobilization and a reconsidera-
tion of Soviet policy vis-à-vis Europe and Asia. Vladimir Chivilikhin
suddenly violently attacked the so-called Eurasian movement—a religious version of the early National Bolshevism, presented by a group of
Russian emigrants.[42] According to the Eurasians, Russia is an organic part
of Eurasia, together with the Asian peoples. Eurasia is a unique civilization, mortally hostile to the West and waging an uncompromising struggle with it. Chivilikhin claims, on the contrary, that Russia is part of an
admittedly ungrateful Europe, which was saved by Russians from the
invasion of cruel savages who were purely a destructive force. Russia
civilized these savages only by violence.[43]

Another writer, Vasily Lebedev, resorts to the same line, but adds
that the spiritual foundation of Russia and its common denominator with
Europe is Christianity, which the Tatar Khan Mamai wanted to uproot
everywhere in 1380. This view is absolutely contested by Soviet historian
Lev Gumilev, writing in *Ogonek*. According to Gumilev, Kulikovo was a
battle not against Asia, but against an international cosmopolitan horde
that was sent against Russia by an international financial center in Genoa
(with a clear hint that it was a Jewish conspiracy). It was the Tatars who
saved Russians from a true mortal danger in the thirteenth century—the
West.[44]

A more elaborate concept of a Russian-Asian union with the messianic objective of uniting all humanity was proposed in 1981 by an
extreme Russian nationalist, Vadim Kozhinov. According to Kozhinov,
only Russians, for the first time in history, have expressed the idea of
universalism, which allegedly one cannot find either in Judaism or

Christianity. Thus only Russians deserve to accomplish the historical mission of uniting humanity.[45]

Kozhinov's views (though his name was not mentioned) were immediately criticized by Vladimir Shubkin, who claims that Christianity is the foundation of Russian culture and links Russia to the West. Russian universalism, Shubkin says, rejects violence. Nothing can be built on hatred. The political philosophy that rejects confrontation with the West is behind Shubkin's abstract statements. Kozhinov's article was also attacked by a literary critic, Vladimir Kuleshov. A main target of his criticism is Kozhinov's ideas of Russian-Asian union against the West. Kuleshov claims that this idea has nothing in common with the views of Lenin to which Kozhinov refers.[46]

CONCLUSIONS

There is no reason to believe that the struggle between isolationist Russian nationalism and its opponents within the Soviet system will be peaceful. Its result is difficult to predict. There is an enormous expansionist momentum in the Soviet political system that is irrelevant to the positions held by certain leaders or to public or secret agreements with the West they may have signed. There is a segment of Soviet political life where the escalation of extremism will always take place because of the internal struggle for power. No moderate can be a leader in this branch, especially if the cost of expansion is not high. Nevertheless, the Russian opposition has good prospects in the struggle for power. The demographic crisis, the economic crisis, and other crises of Soviet society are so sharp that the lack of an urgent response could lead to disaster. Even now, the Russian opposition exercises an enormous restraining influence. Without it, Soviet policy could very easily lose control and go berserk.

One has to point out an incorrect estimation of Soviet internal political life that circulates among Western experts, an estimation that unfortunately is an integral part of general Western policy toward the USSR. This estimation regards a Russian nationalist victory as an international threat. According to the same view, the USSR is now ruled by moderates. This belief does not distinguish between different trends among Russian nationalists. People who resort to it do not realize that the aggressive Russian nationalism against which they warn is already professed by the existing ideological branch that now shares a considerable part of political power.

It was a radical turnabout when Richard Pipes, for the first time, recognized that the victory of Russian nationalism in the USSR would signify a major improvement of Soviet policy.[47] Nevertheless, Pipes does not see how to encourage this victory. Historical experience, however, demonstrates that the very readiness of the West to recognize Russian nationalism as a peaceful alternative could strongly influence the internal development of the USSR.

Every nationalist explosion frightens American politicians, who regard nationalism as a major evil of the contemporary world. But it is time to get rid of the traditional political philosophy according to which world progress must go in the direction of denationalization.

It is not out of the question that Russia will go through a long period of National Bolshevism and perhaps change its internal structure toward federalization. All this is possible only in conditions of a strong regime. If such a strong regime is not achieved, it is impossible to predict the internal development of the USSR; its internal conflicts may lead to a global conflict, since one faction is always inclined to an escalation of extremism and can decide eventually to enter into any adventure, as Cornelius Castoriadis has so brilliantly demonstrated.[48]

NOTES

1. The first attempt to deal with the early period of National Bolshevism (1917–1927) is my *Ideologiia natsional-bol'shevizma* (Paris: YMCA Press, 1980).

2. Isaiah Lezhnev, "Moi pokazaniia," *Rossiia* (1924), no. 3.

3. Mikhail Agursky, "The Soviet Legitimacy Crisis and Its International Implications," in M. Kaplan, ed., *The Many Faces of Communism* (New York, 1978).

4. E. Oberlander, *Sowjetpatriotismus und Geschichte* (Cologne, 1967).

5. See, for example, the collection of his articles published during the war, *Voina*, 3 vols., 1942–1944. The quote is from vol. 3, p. 392.

6. *Pravda*, January 22, 1944.

7. Ibid., May 1, 1944.

8. Georgi Aleksandrov, "Tovarishch Ehrenburg oshibaetsia," *Pravda*, April 14, 1945.

9. This is suggested, for example, by Edward Crankshaw in his comments in *Khrushchev Remembers* (New York: Bantam, 1971), p. 170.

10. See, for example, Franz Borkenau, "Was Malenkov Behind the Anti-Semitic Plot?" *Commentary*, May 1953.

11. See, for example, Alexander Werth, *Russia at War* (London, 1971).

12. *Pravda*, October 15, 1952.

13. See, for example, my *Sovetskii golem* (London: Overseas Publications, 1982).

14. For example, Isaiah Lezhnev, "Vosstanie kul'tury," *Rossiia* (1925), no. 5, p. 162; and Nikolai Rusov, "Zhivaia smert'," *Vestnik Man'zhurii* (1925), nos. 3–4.

15. Crankshaw, *Khrushchev Remembers*, p. 271.

16. See, for example, Robert Conquest, *Power and Policy in the USSR* (New York: St. Martin's Press, 1961).

17. Seweryn Bialer, *Stalin's Successors* (Cambridge, 1980), p. 208.

18. See, for example, M. Rywkin, *Moscow's Muslim Challenge* (Sharpe, 1982); Hélène Carrère d'Encausse, *L'Empire éclate* (Paris, 1979); and Agursky, *Sovetskii golem.*

19. Agursky, "The New Russian Literature," Soviet and East European Research Centre, Hebrew University of Jerusalem, Research Paper no. 40, 1980.

20. Ibid.

21. Astaf'ev's violent criticism of the destruction of Siberia was awarded a state prize.

22. *Literaturnaia gazeta*, March 26, 1980.

23. Evgeny Evtushenko, "Iagodnye mesta," *Moskva* (1981), no. 10. pp. 120–21, and no. 11, p. 99.

24. *Nash sovremennik* (1978), no. 8, p. 189.

25. *Pravda*, February 24, 1981.

26. P. Dudochkin, "Trezvost'—Norma zhizni," *Nash sovremennik* (1981), no. 8, p. 134, and no. 11, p. 103.

27. I. Vasil'ev, "Zemlia russkaia," *Nash sovremennik* (1981), no. 12, pp. 39–40.

28. The situation is described in detail in four articles I published in *Russkaia mysl'* (September–October 1980). See also my article "The Soviet Golem," *Jerusalem Post Magazine*, July 11, 1980.

29. See, for example, T. Rigby, "The Soviet Regional Leadership: The Brezhnev Generation," *Slavic Review* (1978), no. 1, pp. 11, 23.

30. See Michel Tatu, "Le Pouvoir en URSS" (Grasset, 1967), p. 217.

31. See *Montreal Star*, June 17, 1982.

32. *Pravda*, April 23, 1982.

33. There is such a claim in M. Voslensky, *Nomenklatura* (Paris, 1980).

34. For example, there is an apologia for Zhdanov in A. Chakovsky's "Blokada," *Roman-gazeta* (1967), nos. 1–4.

35. A. Anan'ev, "Gody bez voiny," *Roman-gazeta* (1980), no. 1, pp. 43, 47.

36. *Pravda*, February 21, April 9, and April 11, 1982.

37. *Pravda*, March 25, 1982.

38. *Pravda*, March 27, March 29, April 5, and April 13, 1982.

39. For example, Ivan Kapitonov, "Kadrovaia politika KPSS," *Partiinaia zhizn'* (1980), no. 14, p. 19.

40. Fedor Nesterov, *Sviaz' vremen* (Moscow: Molodaia gvardiia, 1980).

41. V. Kargalov, *Nash sovremennik* (1981), no. 1; and M. Liubomudrov, *Ogonek* (1981), no. 4.

42. On the so-called "Eurasians" see, for example, my "Ideologiia natsional-bol'shevizma."

43. Vladimir Chivilikhin, "Pamiat'," *Nash sovremennik* (1980), nos. 8–12.

44. Vasily Lebedev, "Iskuplenie," *Nash sovremennik* (1980), nos. 8–9; and Lev Gumilev, "Epokha Kulikovskoi bitvy," *Ogonek* (1980), no. 36.

45. Vadim Kozhinov, "I nazovet menia vsiak sushchii v nei iazyk," *Nash sovremennik* (1981), no. 11.

46. V. Shubkin, "Neopalimaia kupina," *Nash sovremennik* (1981), no. 12; and Vladimir Kuleshov, *Pravda*, February 1, 1982.

47. Richard Pipes, *Time*, March 1, 1982.

48. Cornelius Castoriadis, *Devant la guerre* (Paris: Fayard, 1980).

from Russian history and to illustrate the works of the classics of Russian literature, especially those of his favorite author, Dostoevsky.[4]

The party bureaucrats who thought that they had broken Glazunov were bitterly disappointed when, in June 1977, he defied them by canceling his largest-ever personal show, planned for the Central Exhibition Hall (Manège) in Moscow. Glazunov canceled the show because his sponsors refused to display a number of works that he considered indispensable, including his magnum opus, the huge, ten-by-twenty-foot canvas, *The Mystery of the Twentieth Century*.

THE THREE MOST CONTROVERSIAL PICTURES

In *The Mystery*, which he has called "a work of philosophical realism," Glazunov apparently aims at portraying a spiritual dilemma of our age by juxtaposing such major political and cultural figures as Lenin, Trotsky, Winston Churchill, Franklin Roosevelt, John F. Kennedy, Albert Einstein, and Pablo Picasso with the more sinister figures of Hitler, Mussolini, Mao, and Stalin. Stalin seems to dominate this century by occupying center stage. Significantly, Stalin is portrayed as lying in state on a bier floating in a sea of blood. Even more indicative of Glazunov's philosophical thrust is a sympathetic portrayal of Tsar Nicholas II and Alexander Solzhenitsyn. The tsar holds in his arms the murdered crown prince, Aleksei, with a Russian church tumbling in the background. The innocence of the martyred prince is emphasized by a halo. Such was the beginning of the bloody bacchanalia of the twentieth century, the artist seems to be saying. Solzhenitsyn, with a zek number on his chest, is placed at the right flank of the picture, whereas, at the left, Glazunov places his own self-portrait. Thus, an affinity between the two, in their roles as principal witnesses of the age, is suggested. The only bright spot in the picture is the white-clad figure of the Savior that hovers over it all.

In spite of the obvious "anti-Soviet" implications of *The Mystery*, to everyone's surprise, Glazunov not only eluded punishment but was allowed to hold the exhibit a year later.[5] When the exhibit opened on June 3, 1978, *The Mystery* was not there, but Glazunov managed to show two other highly controversial pictures, *The Return* and *To Your Health!*

The theme of *The Return* is the story of the prodigal son. It depicts a young man, clad only in jeans, kneeling before a Christ-like figure with features of a Russian peasant. Behind the "son," in the foreground of the picture, is a macabre scene of rural desolation, misery, sacrilege, debauchery, crime, barbed-wire, and death—symbolized by a table on which a severed head is served on a plate. The scene seems to be presided over by the devilish grin of a half-concealed figure in which one may recognize Lenin. Behind the "father," and receding into the upper left background, are easily recognizable figures of Russia's past, including Sergei of Radonezh (the foremost Russian saint), the saintly prince Alexander Nevsky, Suvorov, Dostoevsky, Pushkin, Lomonosov, Tchaikovsky, Peter the Great, a Russian beauty, and several others. The symbolism of the picture is clear: the salvation of today's "prodigal" Soviet Russia is in the return to her historical, cultural, and spiritual roots. The only other exit from the dead end of Soviet life is suggested at the bottom of the painting, where another young man seems to be escaping from under barbed-wire into a trough over which three huge, fat, obnoxious swine are standing. The swine are shown as if they were coming from a modern metropolis, symbolized by a skyscraper. This may suggest that the "son" has rejected not only the misery of Soviet existence but also the materialist alternative to it, whether at home or abroad. Just as ominous and unappealing is the upper right corner of the picture, where a black sky is pierced by a sort of missile or spacecraft soaring under a conspicuously red sail.

In *To Your Health!* Glazunov portrays a typical Russian muzhik who could be a kolkhoznik or a factory worker. Shabbily dressed in a padded laborer's jacket decorated with a medal that shows that he is a veteran of World War II, he sits in front of a wall covered by Soviet propaganda posters and appears ready to down a glass of vodka. His only *zakuska* is a loaf of bread and a cucumber lying on a newspaper whose headline reads "Today in the World." He has led a hard and far from prosperous life but his indomitable spirit is evinced in his mischievous and ironic smile. The main effect of the picture is produced by the sharp contrast between the reality of the muzhik and the boastfulness of the posters. The figures on the posters include the Marx and Lenin tandem, appealing for unity of the communist movement; an African calling for liberty and equality; a Vietnamese soldier proclaiming communist victory; a triumphant Soviet cosmonaut; two happy Soviet workers congratulating each other because a tractor is now doing their heavy manual work; and the hammer-and-sickle emblem of the USSR, proclaiming pride of Soviet citizenship, with a superimposed Soviet passport refracted in the glass of vodka. The suggested message is crystal-clear: all the achievements Soviet propaganda boasts of have been paid for by the Russian muzhik, the veritable Soviet workhorse in war and peace.[6] It is a Soviet variant of the old Russian saying about serfdom: "While one works with a plough, seven are waiting with a spoon" (*Odin s soshkoi, semero s lozhkoi*). The picture raises the question of whether the Soviet government cares for the laborer's health.

The above three paintings are indicative of the ideological thrust of Glazunov's art. Obviously, his art is not only contrary to the dogmas of socialist realism but has strong, thinly veiled, "anti-Soviet" implications. In any event, it is a far cry from anything the Soviet government has ever tolerated, much less allowed to be shown in public. Why was such an exception made for Glazunov? One plausible explanation is that Glazunov's popularity at home and his reputation abroad are such that the government simply could not afford another scandal caused by forcing an established artist into open dissidence. Another possible explanation is that Glazunov may have enjoyed support and protection from the highest levels of the KGB, army, and party apparatus. The third explanation (which does not exclude the other two) is that the government decided to use his exhibits as a sort of opinion poll in order to gauge the strength of Russian nationalism as a cohesive bond for the regime, in the event the leadership might need to revise the official internationalist ideology.

In any case, the Moscow exhibit cannot be explained away as a mere slip on the part of the ideological watchdogs. For one thing, it was shown for a full month as announced. Moreover, fifteen months later, it was followed by an identical exhibit in Leningrad, which was also shown for a month, from September 28 through October 27, 1979. The latter was held in spite of the efforts of the Cultural Department of the Leningrad party organization, headed by G. Pakhomova, to have it canceled or, at least, shown without the most controversial pictures. Only after Glazunov again threatened to cancel the exhibit was the local party organization overruled by someone higher up, and the exhibit was shown in full.[7]

THE TWO BOOKS OF COMMENTS

In the West, both exhibits created sensations, not only because they were allowed to take place at all, but also because they attracted the largest crowds ever in the history of Soviet art. Whereas the Moscow exhibit had drawn some 600,000 visitors, the Leningrad exhibit was seen by nearly a million people.[8] On both occasions, visitors were allowed to write their opinions in special comment books (*knigi otzyvov*), as is customary in Soviet exhibition halls. Thanks to the Kitezh publication, the contents of these two comment books are now available in the West. Needless to say, in the absence of public opinion polls these books are unique documents that offer Western scholars a rare opportunity to peep into the minds of Soviet people, a terra incognita for most outsiders.

There are about 1,465 entries in the Moscow book and 622 in the Leningrad book. Together, they represent well over two thousand comments, which form perhaps the largest statistical body of opinion on Soviet art available in the West. It should be kept in mind, however, that the source does not easily lend itself to statistical analysis, for which it was not specifically intended. For one thing, the majority of entries are anonymous. By spot-checking, I estimate that about 57 percent of all entries in the Moscow book are anonymous, and the corresponding figure for Leningrad approaches two-thirds. Although the majority of the signed entries are signed by a single person, many entries are signed by a group of people or refer to some unnamed friends and colleagues who are said to share the same opinion. No attempt was made to quantify entries according to sex, age, profession, or the number of signatures per entry. Nonetheless, if we consider each entry as an act of civil expression, the totality of comments is certainly reflective of a general trend in public opinion.

A most striking feature of both books is the spontaneity, directness, and passion of expression. It is as if the volcano of public opinion, dormant for over sixty years of Soviet power, had suddenly erupted, and people who had been mute too long suddenly acquired the gift of speech. Although the overwhelming majority of comments are positive, there is not a trace of that obligatory unanimity that has been a hallmark of Soviet propaganda. Leaving no one indifferent, the exhibits introduced a degree of polarization that is highly uncharacteristic of Soviet society. The comments themselves are widely divergent in size, form, content, and tone. They range from one-word remarks, such as "Great," "Thanks," and "Agree," to lengthy essays and even poems about the virtues or faults of Glazunov and his works. Their language is remarkably free from the usual cant of Soviet propaganda.

I have divided all entries into three categories: positive, negative, and other (see Table 1).[9]

TABLE 1

RESPONSES TO THE GLAZUNOV EXHIBITS

	Moscow		Leningrad		Total	
	Number	*Percentage*	*Number*	*Percentage*	*Number*	*Percentage*
Positive	1,174	80.1	428	68.8	1,602	76.7
Negative	249	17.0	176	28.3	425	20.4
Other	42	2.9	18	2.9	60	2.9
Total	1,465	100.0	622	100.0	2,087	100.0

That the majority of comments were positive is hardly surprising, but the margin of difference is. In Moscow, eight out of every ten visitors liked Glazunov, and in Leningrad more than two-thirds did. In both cities combined, only two out of ten visitors disliked Glazunov's art.

Why Did Some Dislike Glazunov?

As far as the reasons for positive and negative comments, I was able to quantify only the latter category (Table 2).[10]

TABLE 2
CRITERIA FOR NEGATIVE EVALUATIONS

	Moscow		Leningrad		Total	
	Number	*Percentage*	*Number*	*Percentage*	*Number*	*Percentage*
Aesthetic	123	49.4	109	61.9	232	54.6
Ideological	96	38.6	41	23.3	137	32.2
Ethical	30	12.0	26	14.8	56	13.2
Total	249	100.0	176	100.0	425	100.0

The majority of negative comments, 232 (54.6 percent) out of 425, used aesthetic criteria; nearly a third (32.2 percent) were dominated by various ideological considerations, and 56 (13.2 percent) raised objections to Glazunov on ethical grounds.

Let me now illustrate each category of criteria. An example of ideological reasoning can be seen in a lengthy entry signed "Kasatkin, K. B., military." Kasatkin scorns Glazunov for failing to notice that "the teachings of Marx-Lenin have been triumphant in our country for sixty years." Reproaching Glazunov for his preoccupation with the theme of the Russian past and his failure to glorify the Soviet army, he argues that "the Great Patriotic War and many other things are incomparably dearer to us visitors than the old Russia relegated to the past." He also reproaches the artist for his "neutrality" in the "intense battle that goes on in the modern world, the battle of two systems." Paraphrasing Gorky, Kasatkin asks a pointed question: "With whom are you, painter Glazunov?" He ends with a threat reminiscent of the Stalin era: "Not only your future but also the fate of your past work depend on how you answer this question." Another visitor does not object to Glazunov's Russian theme but reproaches him for the "sadness and pessimism" with which he treats "our days"; then the writer indulges in wishful thinking: "if you could imbue your talent with a deep party spirit, the result would be excellent!" An anonymous Muscovite wishes Glazunov "to love our Soviet power. This is very much lacking in his portrayal of today's life. Our days and life are brighter than he depicts." Kislova, a woman from Leningrad who says she is writing "in the name of the Kirov factory workers," is "upset and shaken by Glazunov's attitude to the Soviet system and people." She berates him for seeing "nothing bright and beautiful [in Soviet life]" and for preaching a "return" to the past. She calls it "blasphemy" that he dared to show a Soviet passport refracted in a glass of vodka.[11]

Although the above examples are typical of the 137 (6.6 percent of 2,087) negative comments, which are dominated by ideological criteria close to the official ones, they are just about the only ones that rely on such clichés of Soviet propaganda as "the teachings of Marx-Lenin," "party spirit," and "Soviet system." Apparently, such clichés are considered so trite that even the most dogmatic of Glazunov's detractors avoid using them lest they undermine their own arguments.

As to the negative comments using ethical criteria, I counted 57 of them. None specifically refers to Glazunov's alleged KGB connection, but many vaguely allude to his making some kind of deal with Soviet authorities. An anonymous Muscovite writes, "One cannot be a people's leader and a prophet, if one had eaten well from the master's table." Another anonymous visitor, a student of the Mukhina Institute of Industrial Arts in Leningrad, makes it clear that he is "not against a return to the past and religion" but nonetheless asks, "how could they allow your exhibit to take place? How did you manage it?" Yet another visitor points out the similarity of Glazunov's moral dilemma to that of Yevgeny Yevtushenko.[12] In some instances, visitors condemn Glazunov for his moral compromise but seem ready to forgive him because his art works wonders. As one such visitor put it poetically,

Having betrayed and forgiven yourself,	*Predav, sebia i prostiv*
You touch the Wondrous.	*I vnov' obretaia Chudo*
You are your own Christ,	*Vy sami sebe—Khristos*
As you are your own Judas.	*I sami sebe—Iuda!!!*[13]

The majority of the negative comments, 232 (54.6 percent) out of 425, appear to be aesthetically motivated. Often authored by artists, they are as vituperative as the positive ones are enthusiastic. The most frequent epithets are "charlatan," "banality," "cheap imitation," "mass-culture," "profanation," "self-promotion," "weakness in composition," and "lack of professionalism." Only rarely is Glazunov accused of not following the precepts of "Soviet art" or "socialist realism." An entry signed "Graduate students of Moscow University" enjoins Glazunov to overcome various artistic "deviations" in order to promote "socialist realism." An anonymous visitor accuses Glazunov of pushing "banality" (*poshlost'*) in the guise of "pseudopatriotism." "Nothing more abhorrent has ever happened in Soviet art," says he. Since this visitor is one of the very few who resorts to the phrase "Soviet art," one may suspect that his main objection to Glazunov is ideologically motivated and he simply uses an aesthetic argument to disguise his pro-Soviet bias.[14]

Why Did So Many Love Glazunov?

As stated earlier, the great majority of all comments, 1,602 (76.7 percent) out of 2,087, are positive. Although I was unable to break them down according to preponderant arguments, the overwhelming majority of them are obviously inspired by Glazunov's Russian theme, which can be defined as a longing for a return to Russia's historical, cultural, and religious heritage. These comments are not only most numerous but also most intensely enthusiastic, even ecstatic. Reading them is like being swept away by an avalanche of feeling or a torrent of passion. They come down on one with such a force that one realizes that they must have been pent up for quite a while, only to find an unexpected release. In many entries, enthusiasm turns into rhapsody; in fact, about 28 visitors were so moved that they wrote their comments in poetry. In addition, there are dozens of entries in which quotations from the Russian classics are used to underscore one point or another. Many commentators were moved to use forms of expressions that are more characteristic of old Russia. Thus, to express gratitude, they do not simply say "Thank you" (*Spasibo*) but "We bow low before you" (*Nizko tebe klaniaemsia*). These entries abound with such epithets as "genius," "magician," (*mag*), "sorcerer" (*charodei*), "Russian knight" (*bogatyr'*), Ilya Muromets, and Elijah the Prophet (*Ilya-prorok*). Among other typical comments that echo the Russian theme are: "Bard of the Russian soul," "Russian in everything," "Thank you for restoring our national self-awareness," "For the first time I felt proud to be a Russian," and "In everything one can read the Russian truth (*russkaia pravda*)." But, if I were to choose the one description that best sums up the Russian theme, it must be the lead line of many a Russian fairy-tale, "Here is the Russian spirit, here one senses the true Rus'" (*Zdes' russkii dukh, tut Rus'iu pakhnet*).

Although most comments refer to the exhibit as a whole, quite a few focus on sundry variations of the Russian theme (there are thank you notes for the portrayal of the "Russian woman," "Russian muzhik," and even "Russian eyes") or praise individual works, most notably *The Return* and *To Your Health!* The pivotal role of these two pictures is frequently emphasized, as in this comment by V. Yanushin:

> Ilya Glazunov is a genuine Russian artist, a true patriot of his long-suffering Motherland. One could be proud of his work even if he had created nothing but *To Your Health!* and *The Return*, in which his attitude to both the past and the present of our Motherland and to the Russian people is clearly expressed.

Another visitor writes that, thanks to the two pictures, Glazunov "has earned immortality." "*The Return* is an apotheosis of our life," says yet another. A comment signed "A Russian woman" says that in *To Your Health!* Glazunov "revealed the Russian soul. How mighty is the Russian man who holds on his shoulders almost the whole globe."[15]

The Russian theme is intimately intertwined with the theme of Russian art. In fact, the exhibit is often seen as a "celebration (*prazdnik*) of Russian culture," and Glazunov is compared with such giants of the Russian history genre as Vasnetsov, Surikov, and Repin. Among the more modern painters, he is sometimes compared with Mikhail Vrubel', Mikhail Nesterov, Boris Musatov, Boris Kustodiev, Pavel Kuznetsov, and Nikolai Rerikh. But most frequently Glazunov is compared with the medieval icon painter Andrei Rublev. The implicit meaning of that comparison is that what Rublev did for the liberation of the Russian spirit from the Tatar yoke, Glazunov is doing for the emancipation of Russian culture from the yoke of "foreign" Marxist ideology. Similarly, many visitors compare him with Dostoevsky. One, perhaps on account of Glazunov's use of the Biblical parable in *The Return*, sees him as "a psychologist comparable in stature with Dostoevsky." Another, referring to the cathartic impact of his art, paraphrases Dostoevsky (and, one might add, Solzhenitsyn) by saying that "Art will save the world." There are also some who allude to Glazunov's affinity with Soviet ruralist writers (*derevenshchiki*), most notably the late Vasilii Shukshin, "because in the art of both, there are the same roots."[16]

The majority of utterances about Glazunov's art are chiefly inspired by his themes rather than his technique. One visitor attempts to explain this philosophically: "since in any creative work (art, science, literature) *unexpectedness* is the main thing, the success of this exhibit is understandable and deserved. Whenever there is an *élan vital* (*tvorcheskii moment*), the technique recedes into the background."[17] This visitor is no other than Lev Nikolaevich Gumilev, the son of the acmeist poets, Anna Akhmatova and Nikolai Gumilev. His father was executed in 1921. Although he had been imprisoned under Stalin, Lev Gumilev managed to establish himself as a Soviet anthropologist.

Disagreeing with those critics who denounced Glazunov for turning his back on Soviet reality, a certain Marenich argues that "our roots contain in them a promise of our greening tomorrow."

> Your paintings do not lead to pessimism or a loss of faith, because they tell of the greatness of victory, which has been bought at such a terrible cost; they tell of the enormity of the heroic deeds of our fathers who have preserved for us our Rus'. Your pictures inspire noble feelings, dignity, and moral earnestness, which are becoming a force in our age of disbelief. Who is going to win? The invincible power of evil or we, the people? All depends on us, and each must give his answer. You have already given your answer to us, through your work.
>
> Let everyone answer this question about your place in twentieth-century art. Who are you: the great artist of the past who picked up Rublev's fallen brush, or a prophet of a new age of Renaissance?![18]

Although comments like the above are seemingly apolitical, their unmistakable thrust is against the official ideology based on Karl Marx's teachings about class struggle. If they mention any struggle at all, it is a struggle against evil, not imperialist oppressors or a class enemy.

Not all who admire Glazunov's Russian theme are as optimistic as Marenich. The architect Kliucharev thinks that Glazunov came too late and therefore his art is but "a requiem" to ethnic Russia. Like many other visitors, he points out that Glazunov is "the only Russian artist who has raised the national theme." This melancholic note is echoed by an anonymous visitor: "All this is Russia! Thank you. But we are now almost speechless (*bezgolosye*). And all this is very difficult, for one man!" Such comments, and there are quite a few of them, seem to confirm the opinion of Alexander Solzhenitsyn that ethnic Russians, in spite of their numerical predominance among the Soviet ruling elite, feel that they are just as oppressed and dispossessed culturally as any minority. Their attitude to Glazunov was perhaps best summed up in a pun on the artist's name made by one of the visitors: "*Glazu—nov, a russkomu serdtsu mil*" (New to the eye, and dear to the Russian heart).[19]

The Russian theme is most frequently intertwined with the theme of spiritual and religious revival. Although there are numerous references to Christ and Holy Russia, they usually lack a specifically Orthodox meaning, and there are no traces of interdenominational bickering. One entry symbolically signed by *Vera, Nadezhda,* and *Liubov'* (Faith, Hope, and Charity) says: "People! Love each other! Because God is with us."[20] It is followed by another entry that echoes the same theme. Levin, a medical doctor, says that, seeing the exhibit, "One feels a deep faith in Christ, the Savior of our poor fatherland." He reproaches the sponsors for not showing *The Mystery* and for deliberately limiting access to the comment book, because "otherwise people would have written even more."[21] An entry signed by "A group of like-minded students" says: "Many Christian thanks. *The Return* is a work of genius." In an oblique reference to *The Mystery,* these students regret the absence of "other works" on display. Another entry reads: "In the name of a group of young believers, members of Moscow's Baptist community, I thank the painter for the brilliant depiction of the redeeming essence of Christianity." The author then condemns the "baseness and horror of a world that lacks faith," as depicted in *The Return,* and promises to recommend Glazunov to all believers. Judging by a laconic "Thank you from the Old Believers! You show a great and acute perception of Rus'," Glazunov's art stands above the deepest sectarian division of the Russian church.[22]

One anonymous author reproaches Glazunov for not going far enough in his allegedly messianic Russian theme. He particularly reproaches him for failure to portray, among those "to whom we are to return" (a reference to the group of Russian personalities portrayed behind the father figure in *The Return*), Nikolai Fedorov, a nineteenth-century Russian philosopher who thought that a literal resurrection of the dead should be a common task of all the living. Without Fedorov, the visitor argues, "Russia's mission, her 'idea,' would remain without content, or rather, her orthodoxy would not be really fulfilled."[23] This is just about the only reference to Russian Orthodoxy, and even then it is misapplied insofar as Fedorov is not its representative.

Despite the swell of Russian nationalistic feelings provoked by the exhibits, there are only a few comments that seem to extol Russia above other nations, blame foreigners for Russia's misfortune, or otherwise interpret Glazunov's art in chauvinistic and xenophobic terms. The principal target of accusation appears to be the present "alien" masters of Russia, albeit usually disguised among "other" foreigners. A certain Vladychenko writes:

> Now the Tatars, then Germans, then Frenchmen, and all kinds of other "Swedes" have been subjugating us . . . A talented Russian had to

endure a lot, at times giving his life, in order to make it! Still, we are united with you, Ilya Glazunov, not just by blood and fate, but by Faith; we believe that the Russian people would never succumb to a spiritual slavery under foreigners . . . No one who is not spiritually dead can look at your pictures with indifference.[24]

More frequently, however, the impact of Glazunov's art seems to encourage a respect for other nationalities and humility toward one's own. As one visitor concludes, "It is obvious that one ought to welcome the expression of national dignity and cultural grandeur of [all] peoples populating our Earth. Even more, one should welcome a Rebirth of Russian Culture, because we, the Russians, for too long have been brutally destroying everything that is native to us."[25]

Although it must be presumed that the majority of positive comments were made by ethnic Russians (or Eastern Slavs whose names are often indistinguishable from Russian ones), there were also visitors of other nationalities among Glazunov's admirers. In the Moscow book alone, I counted at least thirty names that appear to be non-Russian. Among them are seven foreigners (two each from Czechoslovakia and Hungary, one Bulgarian, one Spaniard, one who wrote in English), three who appear to be Soviet Armenians, three names suggest a Muslim origin, and the rest seem to belong either to Soviet Jews or Germans. Typical of these comments is the one written by Kabakhan Shtanchaeva, a graduate student at the Institute of Philosophy of the Academy of Science, who apparently is of Muslim origin: "I would call this exhibit a hymn to spirituality and beauty. The spiritual might of his images is tremendous. The ethical intensity of his work is so strong that upon leaving the exhibit, one feels a state near catharsis."[26]

DOES GLAZUNOV'S ART ENCOURAGE ANTI-SEMITISM?

In view of the charges of anti-Semitism made against Glazunov, I paid special attention to those comments that could be interpreted as hostile to the Jews. In the Moscow book, I found two overtly judophobic statements. One is anonymous: "After sixty years of the kike power (*zhidov-skoe zasilie*), finally, one begins to smell Rus'! Long live the Russian state!" It is apparent that, whoever this judophobe is, he equates the Soviets with Jewish power and sees Glazunov's art as the beginning of a revival of ethnic Russia (Rus') at the expense of Soviet Jews. Certainly, when he proclaims "long live," he does not mean the present communist system but an envisioned ethnocentric Russian state. The other anti-

Jewish statement is contained in the collection of poems that a certain Ivan Rukavitsyn attached to the Moscow comment book as a token of his appreciation. One of his poems, "The Secret Train," blames "godless Jews" in general, and Moisha Sverdlov and Lev Bronstein (Trotsky) in particular, for the execution of the last tsar's family. Like the anonymous commentator, he seems to equate the Soviets with Jewish power.[27]

In the Leningrad book, I found just one judophobic statement. It is written in the form of a reply to a preceding comment by "L. Abramova, an editor of the publishing house Khudozhnik RSFSR," who had reproached Glazunov for creating "such a repulsive portrait of the Russian muzhik." Thinking that anyone bearing such a last name must be Jewish, the irate anti-Semite mistakes her for a man and uses the following abusive sentence: "You, damned kike, want to impose on us your shit! Such editors should be chased out of their chairs."[28]

There are, however, about half a dozen entries that express a fear that Glazunov's emphasis on ethnic Russian self-awareness may encourage judophobia or fascism. One anonymous visitor calls Glazunov a *progromshchik*, and then says: "Your ideology is transparent, and it is frightening because of its simplicity." "You are for Russia without, . . ." he goes on, and puts the three dots in lieu of the intended "Jews." A Leningrad painter, Rakhimova, says that the exhibit "reminds me of the official 'art' of Germany during the 1940s." Her statement is apparently intended to suggest that Glazunov's Russian theme may degenerate into the racist and anti-Semitic art of the Nazi era in Germany. "The Family of Ivanovs" sees in Glazunov "a reaction, deep crisis, and deviation from the national democratic tradition. If allowed to develop, it may lead to fascism." The reference to "the national-democratic tradition" suggests a closeness to the official line, which states that Soviet power represents the fulfillment of national aspirations of all "progressive and democratic" Russians. Another anonymous commentator reproaches Glazunov for playing up "base feelings, and that's how fascism begins." There is, finally, an enigmatic remark: "It seems to me that you are a genius, but why did you castrate Sherling?"[29] This is apparently a reference to Yuri Sherling, a Jewish musician, for whom Glazunov designed first sets of a Yiddish-language play performed in Moscow. The remark is possibly intended to suggest that Sherling's Jewishness was diminished after his collaboration with Glazunov.

The few comments expressing fears that Glazunov's art may degenerate into fascism and anti-Semitism are greatly outnumbered by positive, even enthusiastic, comments signed by people whose names suggest a Jewish origin. Thus, M. L. Rabinovich, a student of piano, calls Glazunov "Great artist, great thinker, great humanist, great man, and great citizen." Yuli Naumovich Kantor simply says, "Thank you that you are." Rafael Abramovich Zak, from the city of Omsk, thanks Glazunov "for the joie de vivre (*radost' bytiia*) that you give us" and says that he especially liked the picture *The Russian Venus*. Engineer Tepelbaum says that "a palace should be built to house I. S. Glazunov's exhibit." Engineer L. Vaisman's only regret is that *The Mystery* was not shown. Roza Markovna Shrug calls Glazunov "an artist of genius," thanks him for the "aesthetic pleasure afforded by the exhibit" and volunteers to pose for him. R. Slutsker, a 27-year-old woman engineer from Sverdlovsk, writes: "Today is one of the happiest days of my life, and I feel proud to be your contemporary. You have filled my life with light." Economist Ia. R. Kogan calls Glazunov an "outstanding painter of our time." He is impressed by the "refined brush work and emotional charge" that emanates from his portraits. Engineer V. Vaisberg says: "Finally, I have seen a genuine, original, nonstandard, humane, philosophically thinking, and most talented Russian artist. There is no question that today you are Russia's best painter." Lastly, E. Khaikin calls Glazunov "a nationalist of genius."[30]

This last comment seems to sum up the attitude of those Soviet Jews who feel that ethnic Russian nationalism, as distinct from the "proletarian internationalism" that has plenty of room for official anti-Semitism, is just as legitimate as Jewish Zionism or the exodus movement of Soviet Jews. It may be difficult for unassimilated Soviet Jews to feel the same excitement about Glazunov's Russian theme as ethnic Russians feel, but this does not mean that they do not appreciate it. They do not seem to feel that the revival of Russian nationalism would threaten their existence.

DOES "SOVIET PATRIOTISM" MIX WITH RUSSIAN NATIONALISM?

Among the positive comments are some that seem to conform to the official line—that the Soviet state is but the fulfillment of the national aspiration of ethnic Russians and that, therefore, "Soviet patriotism" is inseparable from ethnic Russians' pride over their past achievements. One such comment dubs Glazunov "a great Soviet-Russian Phenomenon" and "a Leninist and Internationalist, who has proved himself in the paintings of a genius, depicting the long-suffering Vietnam, Chile, and other peoples of the progressive movement." It is signed "Bordiukov, Major-General of the Tank troops, a veteran of the Great Patriotic War." Another visitor underscores that Glazunov is *"our Russian Soviet painter"* and supports that claim by a reference to Glazunov's portrayal of the workers of BAM (the Baikal-Amur railroad, a darling of the Soviet propaganda campaign). This entry is signed: "Sotnikova Engelina [from Friedrich Engels, not an angel], Senior Investigator for Especially Important Cases, the Chief Directorate of Internal Affairs, Lt. Col. of militia."[31]

Engineer-electrician Pilipikov sees in Glazunov's art in general, and in *The Return* and *To Your Health!* in particular, "an example of implementation of the party-spirit (*partiinost'*) in art, in the sense of Lenin's insistence on an honest fulfillment [by an artist] of his duty before the people."[32] These three comments are rather exceptional in that they attempt, rather clumsily, to present Glazunov as "a Soviet Russian phenomenon." Moreover, at least in Pilipikov's case, one may suspect that such comments could have been written tongue-in-cheek and in order to provide an ideological alibi for the suspect artist.

There are, perhaps, half a dozen comments of this kind, but they are greatly outnumbered by those who see Glazunov's art in explicitly non-Soviet and even anti-Soviet terms. A teacher of art, Kuranov from Moscow, courageously signed his name under the statement that Glazunov's exhibit is "an account of the sixty years of Soviet power, during which our demagogues have been shouting slogans from the high platforms, while the low masses (*nizy*) were and remain deprived of all rights." Referring to *The Return*, an anonymous visitor says that "the pigs are *the Fathers of the Capital* who still continue to destroy the architecture of Moscow, the most national city of Russia." He interprets the skyscraper between the pigs as a symbol of modernity, "which denies and defies the right of the Russian people to retain a national school in architecture." Another visitor writes that Glazunov "is the only genuine painter who is not subservient to the ruling elite." Several comments criticize the sponsors of the exhibit for not showing *The Mystery*, and engineer Bakuev expresses a sentiment of many when he accuses the authorities of concealing Glazunov's art from the people "so that he is better known in the West than among us, Soviet citizens." Protesting against the policy of tearing down ancient architectural monuments, medical doctor Zaitseva warns the authorities: "You have no right to kill the soul of the people, to obliterate its history with bulldozers. Who knows what fate may yet befall our country and how the Russian muzhik may serve it. Not for nothing, even Stalin, at the end of the war, raised his first toast to this long-suffering muzhik." Her advice is: "We should do as they have done in Poland: restore our history from ruins!" Others, like engineer Stepanov, warn the authorities that, should they decide to punish Glazunov, "We, the inhabitants of Russia, will not let them hurt you! We shall raise our voice in your defense (and assist you) in every way possible, by words, deeds, letters, etc."[33]

Finally, a female student from Leningrad University writes that Glazunov gave her "a new strength, a new faith. This is a rebirth of Russia, as foretold: 'Russia would rise from her sleep . . .'" She is quoting, of course, from Pushkin's famous poem to Chaadaev, and everyone in the Soviet Union knows how it ends: "and on the ruins of tyranny, our names will be written."[34]

CONCLUSIONS

In an interview with Western reporters during his Moscow exhibit, Glazunov enjoined them to take his exhibit "as a new way of looking at art" in the USSR. Complaining of their preoccupation with well-established dissidents, most of whom dislike him, he used the matroshka-doll metaphor to explain his relative position within the spectrum of public opinion inside the USSR. The Westerners, said Glazunov, only know of "the government on the outside and the dissident physicist, Andrei Sakharov, on the very inside, and they ignore all the other dolls, one inside the other, in-between."[35] A few years later, when it became apparent that the dissident movement had virtually come to an end in consequence of emigration, persecution, and Sakharov's exile, Glazunov repeated the charge that the West ignores "all the other dolls." "Diplomats and foreigners who come here think dissidents are mostly Jewish and that they want to leave," said Glazunov, and then he defined the position of his supporters and himself: "Another kind of dissident wants to stay."[36]

The main significance of the two comment books is precisely that, in addition to whatever they say about the state of Soviet art, they shed a great deal of light on the political attitudes of all the other dolls, that is, on the wide spectrum of public opinion that is suspended in-between the government and those dissidents who want to leave. In the light of this homemade Soviet opinion source, one can clearly see that the "in-between dolls" are far from satisfied with the current official approach to Russia's national heritage. Craving a restoration of national self-awareness, they harbor the kind of dissidence that has the best chance to win broad popular support and thus to succeed.

It is apparent that a substantial majority of ethnic Russians, although perhaps not as many as the over 75 percent who favor Glazunov's art, feel that they are dispossessed of their national heritage and deprived of their ethnic identity. Such a feeling must be especially bitter since they are often accused by outsiders of being the master race of the Soviet empire. In fact, they are but the silenced majority. But since they penetrate all layers of Soviet society and have their closeted adherents at all levels of power, they constitute the greatest potential force for a peaceful transformation of Soviet society—perhaps along the lines suggested by Solzhenitsyn in his *Letter to Soviet Leaders*.

The two comment books contain substantial evidence that the prevailing nationalist sentiments among ethnic Russians are strictly defensive in character and respectful of other nationalities. Their overwhelming concern, no matter how viscerally expressed, is with survival, not expansion or Russification of others. An element of chauvinism, though present, does not seem to be stronger than in any other nation with a long history of competition with superpowers. Unlike other nationalisms, it seems to be motivated not by a belief in racial or religious superiority but by a feeling of exclusivity based on a record of long suffering. Although an element of anti-Semitism is also regrettably present in a few comments, it is not as prominent as one would expect in a country known for its history of both official and popular judophobia. Unlike the official Soviet anti-Semitism that chiefly focuses on the Jewish religion, Zionism, and the state of Israel, the comment books give vent only to the popular variety of judophobia, which seems to be chiefly concerned with the role of Jews in the October Revolution and the establishment of the "internationalist" Soviet state. These judophobes seem to be oblivious of the fact that the state has been hostile not only to Russian nationalism but to Jewish and any other nationalism. Although some Soviet Jews apparently feel that the rise of ethnic Russian nationalism à la Glazunov may threaten their well-being in the USSR, many more realize that his art undermines the official ideology that shackles all peoples of the USSR, including the Jews.

Therefore, if Soviet leaders did indeed commission their trusted party scholars to analyze the two comment books in lieu of an open poll, they must have been greatly alarmed by the results. The fact that the official attitude to Glazunov—to tolerate but not to favor him—has not since changed suggests that they simply do not know how to cope with the swell of ethnic Russian self-awareness. They may just hope that time is on their side and the problem will go away.

In his lead article, "Russian Nationalism," in the collection *The Domestic Context of Soviet Foreign Policy*, Adam Ulam concedes that Solzhenitsyn, whose views "it has become fashionable in certain Western circles to deride . . . has one very perceptive insight: the hold of Soviet Communism can be loosened *only* if it is shown to be incompatible with

Russian nationalism" (emphasis added).[37] This is exactly what the two comment books show. In any case, my analysis of this unique Soviet source supports those Western scholars who, like Donald Treadgold, have held the opinion that "In Russia, the whole heritage of Orthodox Christianity, the liberal aspirations of the nineteenth and early twentieth century, the entire precommunist corpus of village tradition, ceremony, and the arts, and other elements have been subjected to prohibition of scholarly study, direct attack, or grotesque and deliberate distortion by state fiat."[38] It also lends support to the argument that ethnic Russian nationalism does not have to be antagonistic to other nationalities of the USSR and should be viewed as an ally of the free world. That the Soviet government has been able to create and maintain a semblance of symbiosis between communism and Russian nationalism is due, to no small degree, to the unwillingness of the West to admit the legitimacy of Russian nationalism because of unfounded fears that it may develop into an alternative worse than communism.

NOTES

1. *Khudozhnik i Rossiia* (Artist and Russia), published by "Grad Kitezh," Gesellschaft für Förderung russischer Kunst, D-4000 Düsseldorf, West Germany, 1980. On Russian nationalism, see, for instance, Edward Allworth, ed., *Ethnic Russia in the USSR: The Dilemma of Dominance* (New York: Pergamon, 1980); John B. Dunlop, *The New Russian Revolutionaries* (Boston: Nordland, 1976), and *The Faces of Contemporary Russian Nationalism* (Princeton University Press, 1983); and Alexander Yanov, *The Russian New Right* (Berkeley, Calif.: Institute of International Studies, 1978). Allworth's *Ethnic Russia* has only one passing reference to Glazunov. John E. Bowlt dismissed him as "A Reliable Soviet Citizen" (the title of his article) in *Art News*, October 1977, pp. 109–10; and S. Frederick Starr responded to the cancellation of Glazunov's 1977 show with an article, "Soviet Painter Poses a Question" (*Smithsonian* 8, December 1977, pp. 101–4), in which he declared Glazunov a neo-Stalinist but allowed that he is also "as much mystery as his painting." As early as 1972, however, Abraham Rothberg recognized Glazunov as an "exceptional" phenomenon in Soviet art and put his name next to Solzhenitsyn, Pasternak, and sculptor Ernst Neizvestny in his book *The Heirs of Stalin: Dissidence and the Soviet Regime, 1953–1970* (Ithaca, N.Y.: Cornell University Press, 1972), p. 366. For the accusations against Glazunov, see, for instance, John Barron, *KGB: The Secret Work of Soviet Secret Agents* (New York: Bantam, 1974), p. 145; and Frederick C. Barghoorn, "Four Faces of Soviet Russian Ethnocentrism," in Allworth, *Ethnic Russia*, p. 61.

2. Ibid., p. 6.

3. I met Glazunov on the premises of a Moscow University dormitory on the Lenin Hills around 1958. Accompanied by his wife, Nina, and Yevgeny Yev-

tushenko, he was desperately trying to show some of his pictures in students' private rooms. Together with a number of other dissidents, I helped him move pictures from one floor to another. Although all of us felt the excitement of conspiring against the authorities with the "forbidden" artist, the acquaintance remained, on my part, a chance encounter.

4. See Glazunov, *Pisatel' i khudozhnik: Proizvedeniia russkoi klassicheskoi literatury v illiustratsiiakh Il'i Glazunova* (Writer and artist: The works of classical Russian literature illustrated by Glazunov) (Moscow: Izobrazitel'noe Iskusstvo, 1979). Introduced by Vladimir Soloukhin, this is the last book on Glazunov that was published in the USSR after the Moscow exhibit. Previous publications, all in small editions, include I. Iazykova, *Ilia Glazunov* (Moscow: Izobrazitel'noe Iskusstvo, 1973); and Vasilii Zakharchenko, *Ilia Glazunov: Fotoal'bom* (Moscow: Planeta, 1978).

5. The term "anti-Soviet" is used in this article not in a strictly juridical sense but as a label that Soviet propaganda often uses in order to censure certain ideological, ethical, and aesthetic attitudes even when these do not necessarily challenge the Soviet political system or violate Soviet laws.

6. Since one of the posters proclaims "I am a citizen of the Soviet Union," the Russian muzhik may be understood as an everyman, that is, the exploited working person of any nationality of the USSR.

7. *Khudozhnik*, p. 153.

8. Ibid., p. 15. These figures are especially significant because, according to the Kitezh publishers, the exhibit commemorating the sixtieth anniversary of the Soviet Union attracted only 50,000 people in three months.

9. Since some entries include both positive and negative remarks, the main criterion for their classification was the prevalent tone. Admittedly, this is a rather subjective criterion, but the unusual degree of polarization of opinion reduced the number of undecided entries to a minimum. As to the "Other" category, it consists mostly of entries in which the focus of concern is on organizational matters. Most frequently, the authorities are criticized for the failure to advertise the exhibit and otherwise popularize Glazunov's art.

10. In unclear cases, the prevalent argument determined my grouping.

11. *Khudozhnik*, pp. 79–80, 133, 138, 191.

12. Ibid., pp. 88, 166, 82.

13. Ibid., p. 157.

14. Ibid., pp. 98, 174. It is noteworthy that whereas in Moscow only 49.4 percent of all negative comments are aesthetically motivated, their share in Leningrad is 61.9 percent. The respective figures for ideologically motivated comments are 38.6 percent and 23.3 percent. This marked increase of the share of aesthetic comments at the expense of ideological ones may suggest a greater artistic inclination of people from Leningrad. It may also suggest that Glazunov's detractors, for whatever reason, after being routed in Moscow, were better organized to mount an attack on him in Leningrad and chose aesthetic arguments as the most effective ones.

15. Ibid., pp. 53–54, 26, 39, 51.

16. Ibid., pp. 26, 62, 105.

17. Ibid., p. 75.

18. Ibid., p. 79.

19. Ibid., pp. 52, 59, 24.

20. Ibid., p. 53. I have found only two entries (ibid., pp. 73 and 120) in which the respondents welcome a return to Russian "roots" but do not accept the idea of restoration of religion.

21. Ibid., p. 78. This suggests that some people felt inhibited from expressing their pro-Christian and proreligious sentiments, and thus are probably underrepresented in the comment books.

22. Ibid., pp. 38, 110, 77.

23. Ibid., p. 91.

24. Ibid., p. 45.

25. Ibid., p. 185.

26. Ibid., p. 43.

27. Ibid., pp. 41, 71.

28. Ibid., p. 162. In addition to the three openly judophobic comments, one may suspect that some other judophobes could have concealed their true feelings under the mask of russophilism. Their number, however, cannot be significant if we keep in mind that the two comment books are distinguished by an unprecedented degree of spontaneity and that several people were not afraid to express anti-Soviet sentiments.

29. Ibid., pp. 33, 172, 82, 177, 38.

30. Ibid., pp. 63, 134, 120, 57, 90, 126, 195, 185, 191. Other positive comments were signed with such names as M. G. Krol'; Neimark; Galina Gennadievna Rubinshtein; Tatiana Toints; I. A. Miller; and Vladimir Semenovich Vol'man. These may belong to people with a Jewish connection.

31. Ibid., pp. 44, 66.

32. Ibid., pp. 67–68.

33. Ibid., pp. 122, 110, 89, 123, 129, 56.

34. Ibid., p. 185.

35. Craig Whitney, "Unbridled Artist Proving Popular at Soviet Show," *New York Times*, June 18, 1978, p. 121.

36. David K. Willis, "Currents of Nationalism: Dissent Beneath Crust of Communist Conformity," reprinted as "Soviet Memorandum" by the *Christian Science Monitor*, March 1981. It is important to remember that, in spite of being an exception among Soviet painters, Glazunov represents a very broad current of discontent that has ranged from the underground activities of Igor Ogurtsov's All-Russian Social-Christian Union for the Liberation of People (see Dunlop, *The New Russian Revolutionaries*) to Vladimir Osipov's samizdat magazine *Veche*, the ruralist writers, and the All-Russian Society for the Preservation of Historical and Cultural Monuments (VOOPIK), of which Glazunov is a founder. Best known abroad through the

writings of Solzhenitsyn, this current of dissent can be described as the "Russian National and Religious Rebirth Movement."

37. Adam Ulam, "Russian Nationalism," in Seweryn Bialer, ed., *The Domestic Context of Soviet Foreign Policy* (Boulder, Colo.: Westview Press, 1981), pp. 13–14.

38. Donald W. Treadgold, "Alternative Western Views of the Sino-Soviet Conflict," in Herbert Ellison, ed., *The Sino-Soviet Conflict: A Global Perspective* (Seattle: University of Washington Press, 1982), p. 352.

Soviet Minority Nationalism in Historical Perspective

Alexandre Bennigsen

There are many definitions of nationalism, all more or less related to the concept of the nation, a historical phenomenon of the late eighteenth to early twentieth centuries. These definitions—with a few exceptions—could hardly apply to the minorities of tsarist Russia. For the purpose of this chapter, *nationalism* will be used with a broader double meaning:

1. first, to designate the awareness of belonging to a specific community based on and corresponding to various criteria, including a specific religion or national church, allegiance to a state or a dynasty, attachment to a national language and literature or to a certain way of life;

2. second, to represent the will to protect a national community against cultural, linguistic, or biological assimilation by the dominant aliens—in this case, the Russians. In this sense, nationalism is understood as a reaction, a response to a challenge.

The last Soviet census (1979) listed 104 nationalities in the USSR, but only a few among them present a "national problem." Twenty-two of these nationalities are foreign minorities (border groups or immigrant colonies). This is the case for the Germans, the Poles, the Greeks, the Koreans, and the Hungarians, whose languages have no legal status in the USSR. Thirty-four are small ethnic groups with vernacular languages, and sixteen form larger groups belonging to the Christian Orthodox tradition (Chuvash, Gagauz, Yakuts, Mordvinians, and others) and therefore lacking a distinct cultural background. These three categories are doomed to a more or less rapid assimilation by the Russians.

Certain other nationalities, however, can be considered as authentic historical nations. Each possesses a specific culture, a religion of its own or an autonomous church, and, in some cases, an old tradition of statesmanship. This is the case for the Ukrainians, the Georgians, the Armenians, the Jews, the Lithuanians, and the Muslims—these last belong to a group of twenty-four nations that speak and write different languages but share the same religious cultural, and historical traditions. Together these national groups (in prerevolutionary Russia there were two more, the Poles and the Finns) form 41 percent of the total population of the Soviet Union. They are the only nationalities of the USSR that present a "national problem."

It can be stated without exaggeration that the survival of the Soviet empire depends largely on the positive solution of the nationality problem, which can be summarized as the problem of relations between the dominant community, the Great Russian "elder brother," and the junior "lesser brothers." For the last fifty years, Soviet theorists have been repeating ad nauseam that the problem has already been solved, but there is ample evidence that this is just wishful thinking on their part.

In this chapter I will endeavor to trace and analyze the historical roots of nationalism, with an emphasis on Muslim nationalism. Although less known, Muslim nationalism is probably more dangerous for the final stability of the USSR than the better known Ukrainian, Georgian, and Baltic nationalist movements.

RUSSIAN PRESSURE

The nationalism of ethnic minorities is a response to the pressure exerted on them by a dominant community. In Russia's case this pressure has been conditioned by several factors:

1. The specific, practically unique, character of the relations between the Russians and the conquered minorities.
2. The constantly changing character of the political regime in Moscow and St. Petersburg during the period of the conquest of the borderlands, that is, between the sixteenth century and 1917.

3. The more or less serious resistance encountered by the conquerors.

The Soviet Union is the last of the great European and Asian empires but has characteristics distinct from those of its predecessors. Indeed, in the USSR some of the dominated junior brothers, long before their Russian elder brother, had created their own national states—in some cases great empires—and had acquired deeply rooted national consciousnesses. This has given a unique character to the relationship between the Russians and the minorities. Not only do the latter have no inferiority complex with regard to the Russians, but they often have a feeling of superiority vis-à-vis their would-be masters. In the case of the Muslims, this characteristic is reinforced by the never-forgotten legacy of the "Tatar yoke," which lasted for three hundred years. Almost all Russian (and Soviet) historians who have commented on the impact of the Tatars on Russia ascribe Russian cultural backwardness, the despotism of Russian rulers, and the abject servility of their subjects to the Mongol-Tatar example. It is outside the scope of this essay to analyze this theory and to decide whether it is correct. Nevertheless, it must be pointed out that the same unfortunate legacy did not befall other countries—Armenia, Georgia, Iran, China, and Turkestan—that were conquered by the Mongols and placed under their direct rule, whereas in Russia the "Tatar yoke" was only an indirect one. One thing is, however, certain: the Tatar rule inspired in the Russians a deep respect for the military and political superiority of their Tatar conquerors and, as a corollary, gave the Russians a lasting sense of inferiority toward their former masters. This gives Russian-Muslim relations their specific character, so different from the classic colonial type. Today Soviet Muslims, though forced to yield to the overwhelmingly superior strength of their Russian elder brother, do not feel inferior in a cultural and political sense. Their attitude is best summed up by a Tatar prerevolutionary politician, Ayaz Iskhaki: "How did it happen that we became slaves of our former slaves?"

The expansion of the Russian empire lasted 360 years, from the conquest of Kazan in 1552 until about 1900. During this period, the character of the Russian state and its political ideology underwent numerous variations, and its treatment of the minorities varied accordingly. Ivan the Terrible, following the Mongol tradition of religious liberalism, was tolerant in religious and national matters and welcomed Muslims as his subjects, especially those belonging to the Chingissid aristocracy, such as the descendants of the Silverian, Crimean, Kazan, and Astrakhan khans. Ivan's second wife, Maria Temrükovna, was born a Muslim and her father, the Kabardian prince Temrük—the tsar's father-in-law—remained Muslim, as did several brothers of the tsarina who took service with the tsar.

This period of religious liberalism came to an end with the death of Ivan the Terrible. Under his son and successor, Fedor, a long era of religious intolerance began that was to last until the end of the eighteenth century. Muslims of the Middle Volga were treated as "citizens" of the empire and had to submit to the same obligations (military service, for instance) as the Russians, although they were denied the privileges enjoyed by the Christians (education, cultural freedom, and so on). For two centuries, an intense effort was made to assimilate the Muslim subjects of the empire through conversion to Orthodoxy. The anti-Islamic campaign reached its peak during the reign of Tsarina Anna, between 1738 and 1755, when 418 out of the 536 existing mosques in the Kazan *guberniia* were destroyed. A direct consequence of this attempt to solve the Muslim national problem was the active participation of the Tatars and Bashkirs in the great popular uprisings of Stefan Razin and Emilian Pugachev.

Catherine II reversed the national strategy spectacularly. She understood that a multinational empire, in which the proportion of non-Russians was steadily increasing, could only survive if all the subjects—whatever their religious and cultural backgrounds—were treated as equals. The anti-Muslim campaign was halted, Tatars were allowed to build mosques, and Tatar merchants were granted important economic privileges. This tolerant policy was a great success. For almost a century the Tatar merchant class acted as loyal partner of the Russian state, and Muslim merchants served as scouts and middlemen between the Russian government and Central Asia and China.

This era of cooperation, beneficial for both partners, lasted until the reign of Alexander II, when a new attempt was made to solve the nationality problem. This time, however, cultural Russification was rejected as counterproductive. It was replaced by a new endeavor to assimilate the various nationalities—whether Muslims, Buddhists, animists in the East, or Protestants in the West—by converting them to Orthodoxy while preserving their national languages and traditional cultures. However, in the two Muslim areas, the North Caucasus and Central Asia, the Russians applied a totally different policy. The Caucasian mountaineers, subjugated after a century of bloody war, were not granted the status of citizens of the empire. They remained "natives" (*inorodtsy*) and did not perform military service. In Dagestan and in Chechnia Russian rural colonization was discouraged, and Russian authorities refrained from interference in the internal affairs of the country.

No assimilation policy was pursued there and Orthodox proselytism was strictly forbidden. The rich plains of the northwestern Caucasus (the Cherkess country) were, on the contrary, open to Russian rural colonization, and the natives—Cherkess and Abkhazian Muslims—were encouraged to emigrate to the Ottoman empire. By 1865, almost a million Muslims had left the newly conquered territory.

In Central Asia, a country of overpopulated oases, Russian rural colonization was impossible and, until the revolution, the number of Russians there remained insignificant. The general lines of the national policy elaborated by the first governor-general of the territory, General Konstantin Kaufmann, were somewhat similar to the apartheid policy in South Africa. The natives were not drafted into military service and the territory was cut off from any outside source of influence, whether Tatar, Turkish, or Russian. Orthodox proselytism was forbidden and the local Russian authorities tried to preserve the most archaic form of Islamic culture. The aim of this simple strategy was to maintain Turkestan in a state of medieval backwardness and social and intellectual stagnation, in the hope that the local population, thus cut off from external influence, would wither away and finally die out. Jews within the Pale of Settlement were condemned to the same fate.

Although there was discrimination against the Jews, the Muslims, and the Catholic Poles, Protestants, on the contrary, were viewed with favor and treated as equals. Thus the attitude of the tsarist government appears constantly changing and illogical, in strong contrast to the uniform policy of the Soviet government. Behind this seeming incoherence, however, certain permanent lines are discernible that add up to what could be called the "imperial Russian strategy" toward the minorities.

The most notable features of this imperial strategy were the monolithic character of Russian administration and the distrust of indirect rule displayed by Muscovy as early as the sixteenth century. That distrust grew steadily throughout the ensuing 350 years. All attempts to decentralize the empire or to preserve the autonomy of the local rulers were eventually abandoned and, on the eve of the revolution, the Russian empire appeared an almost perfect monolith.[1] The same model of bureaucracy was compulsory for all provinces of the empire with two minor exceptions—the emirate of Bukhara and the khanate of Khiva. Paradoxically, at the end of the nineteenth century, the Russian empire, in which Russians accounted for no more than half the total population, was administered as though it were a Great Russian national state.

By the late nineteenth century, Orthodoxy was truly the state religion. A Russian could only be a Christian Orthodox (or an atheist). Only one Orthodox church—the all-Russian Orthodox Church—could exist on the territory of the empire. The Georgian Orthodox Church, founded in the fourth century and autocephalous since the sixth century, was abolished in 1811 and became a mere exarchate of the church of Moscow.[2] The Orthodox Church of the Ukraine, separated from Moscow in the fifteenth century, became a subordinate of the church of Moscow in 1657. Moreover, all attempts to decentralize the Orthodox church, by creating non-Russian Orthodox communities with their own liturgical languages, were promptly discouraged by the state church.[3] At the Missionary Congress of Kazan in 1913, it was declared that the term "Orthodox" was synonymous with "Russian."[4]

Non-Orthodox and non-Christian religions were tolerated and received more or less favorable treatment according to criteria not easy to determine. Those whose religious centers were on the territory of the empire were viewed with favor. Such was the case with the Armeno-Gregorian church. Religious freedom was granted to the highly decentralized Lutheran churches, the Buddhists (Kalmyks, Buryats, Altays), the Nestorians (Assyrians), and even to the so-called devil worshippers (Yezidis), who were persecuted in the Ottoman empire and Iran but protected in the Russian Caucasus. Whenever the spiritual center of a religion was situated abroad, it was viewed with strong suspicion and its members were often discriminated against.[5] Thus Catholics and Muslims, Russia's "hereditary enemies," were suspected of being more loyal to the pope or the Ottoman sultan-caliph than to the Russian state. The Jews, accused of having sold Jesus Christ (*Khristoprodavtsy*), had very limited rights, and members of certain sects of Orthodox origin (Khlysty, Skoptsy, Molokans, and Dukhobors) were practically considered criminal elements.

THE RESPONSE OF THE MINORITIES

We have seen that Russian pressure on the minorities was changeable and unequal. As a result, the reactions of the minorities varied according to regions and periods and their nationalist movements presented a wide spectrum of trends. Western public opinion has endorsed the Bolsheviks' depiction of tsarist Russia as a "prison of peoples." The reality was more complicated. Although some nationalities posed a more or less strenuous resistance to conquering Russians and, when subjugated, endeavored to rid themselves of their conquerors, others—including several culturally important minorities—accepted and even welcomed, for various reasons, the Russian annexation of their lands. Their national awareness did not assume a xenophobic, anti-Russian character and, in many cases, these minorities never developed a conscious structured nationalism. In some instances their national movements were viewed with favor and were even sponsored by the Russian authorities, since they were directed against a foreign enemy, not against the Russians.

Minorities That Accepted
Or Did Not Oppose Russian Domination

The voluntary acceptance of Russian supremacy or the absence of resistance may be explained by several historical factors. The minorities that welcomed Russian rule fall into five categories.

The first group included minorities with a high cultural, social, and political development (sometimes higher than that of the Russians themselves) whom the Russians protected against a greater external danger. Such was the case of the Armenians, whose national existence was threatened by the neighboring Muslim states, the Ottoman empire, and the Iran of the Qadjars. The Armenians had a strong, deeply rooted national awareness and an old and brilliant culture, and they had had an independent national church since the Council of Chalcedon. Their national movement, well structured and aggressive, was focused on liberation from the rule of the Ottoman Turks and never assumed an anti-Russian aspect. Armenians never felt threatened by the Russian presence; even when their national political parties (Hintchak and Dashnaktsütün) opposed the tsarist regime, they never adopted an anti-Russian position. This pro-Russian attitude survived the October Revolution. At present, Armenians are probably the most Russophilic of all Soviet minorities, even when firmly anticommunist. Their main enemy is still, as in the past, the Turk.

Similarly, the Russians protected the Mongols from the Chinese and, from the sixteenth through the eighteenth centuries, defended the Kazakh hordes against the more powerful Buddhist Jungans who threatened their existence. The Mongol national movement is now, as in the past, anti-Chinese and pro-Russian.[6] As for the Kazakhs, their first national leaders, Chokan Valikhanov, Ibray Altysaryn, and Abay Kunanbaev, were the most pro-Russian of all Muslim *Kulturträger* of the nineteenth century. Chokan Valikhanov used to proclaim that "Without Russian help, we, the Kazakhs, would be wild Asiatics." It was only after 1895, when the Kazakh steppes were submerged by waves of Russian and Ukrainian settlers, that the Kazakh national movement began to acquire a xenophobic, anti-Russian face.

In the case of the Belorussians, the Lithuanians, the Estonians, and the

Latvians, Russian conquest was not a national disaster but only a "lesser evil," or, at least, "one of the many possible evils." At the time of their incorporation into the Russian empire, they were downtrodden rural communities, oppressed by their Polish or German lords. Russian rule did not save them from oppression, but at least these new citizens of the empire could make a choice between several oppressors. The Russians did not enjoy a monopoly in this respect and did not have the privilege of being the *only* enemy.

A second group of nationalities that did not resist Russian rule included minorities that, at the time of their annexation to the Russian empire, had not succeeded in forming national states or had already lost them. Armenia also fell into this category, since it had been conquered by the Muslim Seljuks in the eleventh century. Supreme authority in Armenia was represented by the head of the Armenian church, the catholicos of Echmiadzin. Similarly, Azerbaijan was in a state of feudal anarchy when the Russians moved in, bringing with them a peace and order that Transcaucasia had not known for centuries.

Third, minorities whose cultural level was markedly lower than Russia's posed no serious opposition at the time of their incorporation into the Russian empire. Such was the situation of the pagan tribes of eastern Russia: the Finns (Mariis, Mordvinians, Udmurts, Komis) or the non-Muslim Turkic peoples (Chuvashes, Yakuts, Altays). For them, conversion to Orthodox Christianity and assimilation by the Russians represented a social and cultural promotion. With few exceptions, these "nonhistorical" minorities, generally without national cultures of their own, did not mount serious resistance to Russian rule. They were converted to Christianity and their upper classes welcomed linguistic Russification.[7] The national awareness of these minorities remained vague and their nationalism was embryonic.

A fourth group encompassed immigrant colonies who had suffered from discrimination or persecution in their original homelands and had sought refuge in the tsarist empire. Examples include the Uygurs and Dungans from China (after the defeat of the revolt of Yaqub Beg in the Sinkiang in 1865) and the Assyrians, Muslim or Yezidi Kurds, and Greeks from the Ottoman empire and Iran. All of these small minorities had an acute national consciousness, and the Uygurs and the Kurds had embryonic national movements. Their nationalism, however, never took an anti-Russian bias; on the contrary, they considered the Russian state their traditional protector. It is significant that at present these minorities are still among the most pro-Russian and pro-Soviet of all the Soviet nationalities, and most of them enjoy an authentic extraterritorial cultural autonomy.[8]

Finally, a fifth category of nonresistant minorities included nationalities from which the tsarist government selectively co-opted members of the nobility, clergy, or merchant bourgeoisie. These elites received ranks and privileges in accordance with the corresponding social classes of the empire. This policy was applied in the seventeenth and early eighteenth centuries to the Swedish nobility in Finland, the German aristocracy in the Baltic states, the Ukrainian higher clergy, and the Volga Tatar merchant bourgeoisie. These elements had a well-developed national consciousness and often a strong sense of superiority vis-à-vis the Russians. As a rule, they kept their religion (Lutheran in the case of the Swedes and the Germans) and their national culture and way of life. They did not readily mix with the Slavs. Though the vast majority were loyal subjects of the tsar, they refused to consider themselves Russians or to accept an allegiance to the Russian state, much less to the Russian nation.[9] Because of their privileged position, however, there was no solidarity between them and their fellow countrymen and, with rare exceptions, they did not take part in the national movements of their communities.

Minorities That Opposed Russian Domination

The minorities that resisted Russian rule and developed strong national movements generally were "historical nations" or remnants of historical nations. Each was endowed with a strong national consciousness and most considered themselves superior to the Russians. Their nationalism, generally of a strongly anti–Russian nature, focused on the defense or restoration of various national institutions like the state, church, religion, culture, or language.

"Historical nations" whose national states were liquidated by the Russians or whose ruling dynasty was replaced by a purely Russian administration made up one such group. The memory of lost independence was one of the most powerful incitements to nationalism, all the more so as, with the passage of time, the pre-Russian era acquired a glorious and heroic character. To this category belonged the Georgians, Ukrainians, Poles, Crimean Tatars, North Caucasians, Kazakhs, and the Turkestani peoples. The recovery of their independence constituted the central point of the Polish and Georgian national movements. The restoration of the Crimean Tatar and Ukrainian states was one of the main aspirations of Tatar and Ukrainian nationalism. In 1918, the re-establishment of Shamil's theocracy was the avowed goal of the North Caucasian mountaineers' movement led by the conservative elements.[10] The fountain of Bakhchisarai and the tower of Süyümbike were the symbols of Muslim nationalism.[11] The slogan "tsarist Russia—prison of peoples" was eagerly accepted on the eve of the revolution by these minorities.

A second determinant of resistance was an old Christian Orthodox tradition, such as that of Georgia or the Ukraine.[12] In these regions the earliest stage of nationalism centered on the defense and re-establishment of the autocephaly of the national church.

In other cases, anti-Russian sentiment was provoked by a threat to the national culture. In these regions, the creation or defense of the written national language and national schools, together with the struggle for freedom of the national press and literature, represented the initial phase of resistance to the assimilation policy of the Russian state. The most typical case is probably that of the Volga Tatars. Their national revival began in the early nineteenth century. Its first phase was a religious reform, a reaction against the severe, Muslim conservative scholasticism that had dominated the Tatars' spiritual life since the Russian conquest in the sixteenth century. It was followed in the mid-nineteenth century by what was called, without exaggeration, the Tatar Renaissance. That interesting historical phenomenon had numerous facets: modernization of the literary languages, creation of a new educational system, and the emergence of a modern, politically engaged literature. Without these efforts, which lasted a whole century, the sophisticated political movement of the Russian Muslims in the early twentieth century would have been impossible. Cultural *jadidism* (modernism) was a precondition for political revival. Significantly, it was Ismail bey Gasprinski—the Crimean Tatar reformer, the "Father of Russian Jadidism," the promoter of the modernization of the Tatar literary language, and the creator of the first reformed *madrasah*—who chaired the first (clandestine) Congress of Russian Muslims in Nizhni Novgorod in 1904.[13] This congress was the first manifestation of political life among Russian Muslims.

Nationalism also flared with particular strength among the minorities whose existence was threatened by Russian rural or urban colonization: Muslims from Dagestan and Chechnia who were expelled from the rich lowlands of the North Caucasus and forced into the mountains when their lands were taken over by Russian settlers; Kazakh nomads whose pastures were reduced after 1895 by waves of Russian and Ukrainian colonists. Their resistance culminated in the great uprising of the nomadic tribes in 1916. In these instances, the national movement started as a deeply rooted, popular, elemental tide. The intellectual elite, formerly pro-Russian, was obliged to follow and to adopt an anti-Russian attitude.[14]

Nationalism was especially strong in the case of minorities split between the Russian empire and other countries, because such nationalities could and in fact often did receive their nationalist impulses from abroad. Thus, the Ukrainian language was officially recognized as one of the administrative and educational languages of the Austro-Hungarian empire although it had no legal status in Russia. The Ukrainian cultural center in Lvov represented a model for the Ukrainians of the Russian empire. The attraction of Istanbul and Tabriz was an even greater stimulus for the development of nationalism among the Azerbaijani Turks.

Where religious discrimination existed, resistance to the missionary activity of the Russian Orthodox church was at the very heart of the national movement. In this instance, a more or less complete symbiosis existed between the national and the religious consciousness. A Lithuanian could only be a Catholic. An Orthodox Lithuanian became ipso facto a Russian. The same was even truer of the Muslims, because Islam was more than a religious belief—it was a way of life, a culture, and, above all, the basis of the national consciousness. Only a Muslim could be an Uzbek, a Dagestani, or a Turkmen. Inversely, an Uzbek or a Dagestani was necessarily a Muslim. On the eve of the 1917 revolution, Muslims of the Russian empire still defined themselves primarily as Muslims. A Christian Uzbek (or Turkmen, or Dagestani) was a contradiction in terms: he was considered a Russian. Only the Volga Tatars represented an exception. The two Christian Tatar communities—the Starokriashens who converted to Orthodoxy in the sixteenth century and the Novokriashens who converted in the eighteenth century—spoke and wrote Tatar (in cyrillic script), were distinct from both the Russians and the Tatars, and formed a separate minority that maintained its specific identity long after the October Revolution. (They were listed as a separate nationality in the Soviet census of 1926.)[15]

The situation did not change after the revolution, and at present Catholicism and Islam represent, as they did a century ago, the main elements of Lithuanian and Muslim self-identification. An Uzbek may be a believer or an atheist (the expression "nonbelieving Muslim," often used in Central Asia, corresponds to a certain reality), but he cannot be a Christian.[16] Paradoxically, conversion to Christianity (the Orthodox creed or any other) is still, as it was before the revolution, the only way for a Muslim to cut his ties with his *millet*—his national community.

It is noteworthy that the Armenians represent a different case. Their national identity cannot be reduced to the Armeno-Gregorian (Monophysite) creed. There is in the Caucasus a certain proportion (impossible to evaluate) of Catholic, Protestant, and even a few Orthodox Armenians, who are first and foremost Armenians. Even the small Muslim Armenian group (some one to two thousand "Hemshins" who were converted to Sunni Islam in the seventeenth century by the Ottoman

Turks) is not entirely excluded from the Armenian community. In spite of being devout Muslims, they still speak and write Armenian.[17]

THE HERITAGE OF PRESENT-DAY NATIONALISM

The best approach to the understanding of nationalism among the minorities is the analysis of present-day references to the past. My analysis will focus on Soviet Islam because Muslims represent the least Russified community of the USSR. They have managed better than other minorities to resist cultural and biological symbiosis with the Russians.

During and immediately after World War II, intellectuals in Central Asia started to rediscover the national past with which they had somewhat lost contact because of two changes in alphabets (from Arabic to Latin in 1928–1929 and from Latin to Cyrillic in 1939–1940). This rediscovery was a spectacular process, a struggle for the rehabilitation of the national inheritance, known by the specific term *mirasism* (derived from the Arabic word *miras* [patrimony]). The resulting struggle opposed Muslim intellectuals—who considered the greatest part of their cultural and political inheritance as "progressive" and therefore deserving preservation in the new Soviet society—to the Russian central authorities who were trying to confine the local patrimony only to elements that could contribute to friendship between the Soviet peoples (*druzhba narodov*). All other elements, especially those springing from Islam, were rejected and condemned as "clerical" and "bourgeois nationalist."

The conflict reached its climax in 1951–1952, when Russians and Muslims violently opposed each other over the question of the status of the Muslim national epic songs (*dastan*).[18] The Muslims rightly considered them an essential part of their national culture, but the Russian authorities wanted to suppress them as "clerical" and "feudal." This dispute was one of the most dramatic episodes in the history of *mirasism*. It resulted unexpectedly in a Muslim victory, the first one won by the native intelligentsia over the central Russian authority. After Stalin's death, the polemics became less intense and more academic, but the *miras* process still continues. Every year, practically every month, new literary and political figures of the past are being rediscovered and rehabilitated as admirable and inspiring models of national tradition for the younger generation of native intellectuals.

Four aspects of *mirasism* are especially significant: the imperial tradition, the resistance to the Russian conquest, the perceived superiority of the classical Muslim culture to the more recent Russian culture, and the progressive character of the Muslim Renaissance of the nineteenth century.

The Imperial Tradition

One heroic figure dominates the *miras* process in the history of Central Asia: Timur (Tamerlane).[19] There are many aspects of the cautious rehabilitation of the great Turkic conqueror; Timur is both a symbol of past glory and a promise of future revival. Timur is a symbol of Turkism (*Türklük*). He ruled over the greatest Turkic world empire in history and all of Central Asia was united under his sway. Thus, the rehabilitation of Timur acquires a pan-Turkic significance. It recalls the glorious period when all Turkestanis formed one Muslim nation (*millet*). Significantly, Timur has now been monopolized by the Uzbeks, the largest Central Asian nationality, who increasingly play the part of the local "elder brother" in Central Asia. Timur thus has become the symbol of the unity of Central Asia if not of the whole of Soviet Islam.[20]

Timur, a pious and orthodox Muslim who protected the Sufi brotherhood and built numerous mosques and *madrasahs*, is also the flag-bearer of the pan-Islamic revivalist movement that can be observed at present in the Muslim republics of the USSR.[21]

Resistance to the Russian Conquest

Several leaders who fought the tsarist armies are today considered symbols of nationalism. All had been banned from official Soviet historiography in Stalin's time, when the tsarist conquest was deemed a "positive historical fact" and the leaders of the resistance were branded as traitors and agents of foreign imperialism. Some have been rehabilitated since Stalin's death, but the majority remain officially *personae non gratae*.

Among these heroes, the most important figure is the *imam* Shamil, leader of the Caucasian mountaineers between 1828 and 1859. Denounced as a Turkish and British agent under Stalin but since partly rehabilitated, Shamil is the pre-eminent hero not only of the Caucasians but of all Russian (and Soviet) Muslims.[22] He was at once a successful military commander, an Orthodox Muslim (an adept of the Naqshbandiya Sufi brotherhood), and a model of heroism. For over twenty years he fought, with a handful of followers, against the immense might of the Russian empire and the best generals of the tsar—who had recently defeated Napoleon. It is no exaggeration to speak of a cult of Shamil. The word is not too strong to describe the attitude of Muslim intellectuals (members of the Communist Party included) toward the Dagestani hero. This is easy to understand: Shamil's resistance proved that Russian armies can be defeated. If this was possible in the past, the same might happen again, especially now that the Afghan *mujahidin* are helping to demonstrate that the Soviet army is not invincible.

Other resistance leaders also serve as symbols of nationalism. Such are Khan Kenesary Kasymov of the Middle Kazakh Horde, who fought against Russian rule in the central Kazakh steppes (1837–1847), and Salavat Yulaev, Pugachev's Bashkir lieutenant, who died in the Schlüsselburg prison in 1797. In the 1950s Kazakh historians tried in vain to rehabilitate Kenesary Kasymov by presenting him as a "national patriotic figure." More recently, in the late 1970s, Central Asian intellectuals have displayed a new interest in the great guerrilla uprising of the rural masses of Central Asia against Soviet rule, the Basmachi movement of 1920–1928.[23]

In the Caucasus, where resistance to the Russian conquest was led by the mystical Sufi brotherhoods, religious "dramatis personae," especially those who died fighting the Russians, have acquired the profile of national leaders. Their posthumous reputations as flag-bearers of Caucasian nationalism can be measured by the prestige of their mausoleums. According to recent Soviet surveys, some of the most popular holy places of the Caucasus are the following mausoleums:[24]

1. The tomb of Uzun Haji in the village of Dyshne-Vedeno in the Chechen-Ingush Autonomous Soviet Socialist Republic (ASSR). Uzun Haji, a sheikh of the Naqshbandiya brotherhood, was, together with the *iman* Najmuddin of Hatso (Gotsinsky), the principal leader of the conservative religious elements of the North Caucasus. He fought the Russians on principle, whether they were the Whites of Denikin or the Bolshevik Reds. In 1919–1920, he founded in the mountains of Chechnia the *Imamat*, modeled on the theocratic state of Shamil. Uzun Haji died in the spring of 1920 at the age of 90. After his death, Najmuddin Gotsinsky took charge and led the great uprising of the Dagestani and Chechen mountaineers that started in the summer of 1920 and was quelled only in 1923.

The Soviet authorities closed this holy place in 1961. A few years later, however, there were still mass pilgrimages to this tomb from all the districts of the Chechen republic, as well as from other republics, the autonomous regions of the North Caucasus, and even from Georgia. Pilgrims came on foot, by train, and in cars.[25]

2. The tomb of Sheikh Abdurrahman of Sogratl, a Naqshbandi sheikh, near the *aul* of Kazanishchi in the Dagestan ASSR. This is the second most venerated holy place of the North Caucasus. The sheikh Abdurrahman, one of the Dagestani leaders of the 1877–1878 revolts, was hanged by the Russians.

3. The tomb of Sheikh Mohammed of Balakhany, near the village of Gergebil in Dagestan. Mohammed of Balakany, another Naqshbandi sheikh, commanded a rebel unit that in the valley of Arakan in November 1920 destroyed to the last man an important Red Army unit, the "First Rifle Regiment of Model Revolutionary Discipline" of Moscow.

4. The tomb of the Sheikh Tasho Haji in the village of Sayasan in the Chechen-Ingush ASSR. This is the third most popular place of pilgrimage. Tasho Haji, a companion of Shamil, introduced the Naqshbandi brotherhood into the Chechen country.[26]

5. The tomb of the mother of Kunta Haji Kishiev in the village of Haji Otar, in the district of Vedeno of the Chechen-Ingush ASSR. Kunta Haji, the first Qadyri sheikh in the North Caucasus, was arrested by the Russian authorities in 1864 and died in a Russian prison. The veneration of his followers has been transferred to the tomb of his mother.

6. The tomb of the Sheikh Ali Mitaev in the village of Shali in the Chechen-Ingush ASSR. Ali Mitaev, a Qadyri sheikh, was the chief of the brotherhood of Bammat Giray Hoja, one of the four Qadyri branches formed after the death of Kunta Haji. He was executed by the Soviets in 1925 in Rostov-on-Don for "counter-revolutionary activity."

Superiority of the Traditional Muslim Culture

Since Stalin's death Muslim intellectuals have been engaged in a battle against their Russian "comrades" for the rediscovery and rehabilitation of their national culture. This battle is not spectacular, but the stakes are of tremendous importance. It is no exaggeration to claim that the future of the USSR depends largely on its final outcome.

After World War II the Russians themselves managed to rehabilitate practically all of their cultural patrimony (including personalities and aspects unlikely to favor the emergence of a "Soviet culture," such as Fedor Dostoevsky, Andrei Rublev, Novgorod ikons, and N. S. Leskov). Similarly, Muslim intellectuals of Central Asia are rediscovering, rehabilitating, and translating into modern Tadzhik and Uzbek (or transliterating into Cyrillic script) the entire Irano-Turkic literature from the tenth to the twentieth centuries. This literature, thoroughly penetrated by the spirit of Islam, includes such rich Sufi writings as the mystical poems of Jelaleddin Rumi, Feriduddin Atar, and Amir-i Khosrow-i Dehlevi.

The younger generation of Muslim intellectuals thus considers its cultural patrimony an important element in the arsenal of minority nationalism. Cultural rehabilitation has acquired two aspects:

    1. The prestigious classical literary patrimony—from Rudaki, the Persian poet of Bukhara who lived in the ninth century, to Mir Ali Shir Nava'i in the fifteenth century, the bilingual (Persian and Chagatai Turkic) poet of Herāt—is not limited to one nation but belongs to the whole of Central Asia. This is an argument in favor of the pan-Turkic and pan-Islamic theories condemned by the Soviets, according to which Turkestan is great when it is united into one nation and one state.

    2. There is another and simpler aspect to this literary revivalist movement, which expresses itself thus: "We do not have to imitate the Russians. Our culture is older and greater than theirs . . . Rudaki was composing his *ruba'i* at the court of the Samanid rulers of Bukhara when the ancestors of our 'elder brother' were still hiding in forests."

The Progressive Character of the
Nineteenth-century Muslim Reformist Movement

During the last five to six years, Muslim intellectuals have opened a new front in their struggle for the rehabilitation of their patrimony. It concerns the *jadid* (modernist) movement, a cultural and political phenomenon promoted in the late nineteenth and early twentieth centuries by the liberal Tatar and Caucasian bourgeoisies. Their bold objective was to radically modernize Muslim society to enable it to survive in the hard technical world of the twentieth century and to compete with outsiders without in the process losing its religious basis. It was a brilliant endeavor covering every field of activity: religion, female education, language, literature, and, finally, politics. The October Revolution disrupted the *jadidad* Renaissance. Some of the leaders joined the counterrevolutionary camp; others sided with the Bolsheviks and later became the leaders of "national communism." They tried in vain to conciliate Islam and Marxism and were physically liquidated by Stalin in the 1930s. Since then Soviet historiography has described the *jadids* as archenemies of Marxism-Leninism and *jadidism* as an obnoxious bourgeois-nationalist phenomenon. The current effort to rehabilitate at least the main protagonists, if not the movement as a whole, has a clear implication for the Muslims and an absolutely unacceptable one for the Soviet authorities. It reminds all that in the recent past Islam inspired a great progressive, liberal, intellectual, and social movement, which successfully tackled the numerous aspects of Muslim backwardness and removed obstacles on the way to progress. Consequently, some conclude, social change may be obtained through a democratic evolution under the banner of Islam. Marxism-Leninism is not therefore the only way to progress.

CONCLUSION

Even a superficial analysis of the evolution of nationalism among the minorities reveals that, contrary to the oft-believed assertion, Russia has never been a melting pot of nations. Attention has focused too much on individuals who came to Russia to serve the prince—not the people— and sometimes adopted the prince's religion. Their descendants became Russified. We tend to forget the national minorities, including small and downtrodden groups that have successfully resisted for over four hundred years a more or less systematic assimilation policy: Muslim Tatars and Bashkirs, but also the smaller heathen Finnish tribes that have survived until today (Mariis, Udmurts, Mordvinians, Komis, and others).

Before the revolution, the only way to assimilate individuals or entire communities was through conversion to Orthodoxy. The Russian church was well equipped for missionary work, but its activity was curtailed and results over the last four centuries have generally been modest.

In our time, it is still religion, not Marxism, that remains the best instrument of fusion. An Uzbek or a Lithuanian Communist remains Uzbek or Lithuanian, but if converted to Orthodoxy, they become Russians. Nowadays the Russian church is not allowed to exercise missionary activity, and it is Marxism-Leninism alone that is supposed to play the unifying role that was reserved for Orthodoxy before 1917. Sixty-eight years of the Soviet regime have demonstrated beyond any possible doubt that communism is no longer what it was for a short while half a century ago—a philosophical doctrine and pseudo-religion capable of mobilizing the masses. Today it is but a way to make a career in the Soviet bureaucracy. A "Soviet man" (*sovetskii chelovek*) endowed with supranational loyalties has not emerged, and there is plenty of evidence that he will dwell forever in the dreamland of Soviet theorists.

NOTES

1. For a short while, in the late seventeenth century, the Ukrainians partly preserved their autonomy under the rule of their hetmans. The Georgian monarchy disappeared in 1801 shortly after the extension of the Russian protectorate to Trans-caucasia. The administrative autonomy of the khans of the three Kazakh hordes was abolished between 1822 and 1842; Finland lost its own administration, which was replaced by the Russian one. The only tolerated exception of a lasting autonomy was the Muslim Tatar kingdom of Kasimov, whose rulers, the "tsars of Kasimov," were vassals of the tsar of Moscow. The tsardom, founded in 1445 under the reign of the Grand Prince Vassily II, survived until the reign of Peter the Great in 1715.

2. The Georgian Orthodox patriarchate was established in Mtskheta by King Vakhtang Gurgasal (446–495), but the first Christian sovereign, Mirian, was baptized around 295.

3. Three spectacular attempts were made: in the fourteenth century by St. Stefan, bishop of Perm, who evangelized the Zyrians (in our days, Komis); by St. Gurii, the first Archbishop of Kazan in the sixteenth century, who converted some Volga Tatars and granted them the right to have a liturgy in Tatar; and in the late nineteenth century by Nicolas Il'minsky, who translated the Orthodox liturgy and the Bible into Tatar, Kazakh, Cheremiss, Votiak, and Mordvinian.

4. Cf. *Missionerskii S'ezd v gorode Kazani, 13–26 iunia, 1910 goda* (Kazan: Tsentral'naia Tipografiia, 1910).

5. Catholics were excluded from certain governmental careers (for instance, from the General Staff); Muslims obtained the full freedom of religious education only in 1905.

6. All references to a possible "Mongolization" of Afghanistan are therefore absurd. Mongolia was never conquered by the Soviet army and the Mongols consider Russians their natural protectors against their stronger neighbors and enemies, the Chinese.

7. The Cheremiss (now called Mariis), who had a strong and warlike tribal organization and in the fifteenth and the sixteenth centuries provided the khanate of Kazan with its main fighting force, were the only Volga nationality seriously to oppose Russian rule. It is significant that at present the Mariis are the least Russified of all mid-Volga nationalities. According to the last Soviet census (1979) the proportion of linguistically Russified individuals is 18.3 percent among the Chuvash, 27.5 percent among the Mordvinians, 23.7 percent among the Udmurts, and only 13.4 percent among the Mariis. Before the 1917 revolution there was a revival of paganism among the Mariis.

8. This is the case of the Uygurs, the Kurds, the Assyrians, and the Dungans. Each has a national press (in 1978, five Uygur newspapers in Alma Ata, Panfilov, Chundzha, and Chilik; a Kurdish newspaper in Erevan; and a Dungan newspaper in Frunze) and a network of schools teaching in the national language.

9. Their Russification depended upon their conversion to Orthodoxy, which

was often the consequence of mixed marriage. According to Russian law, the children of mixed marriages (between Orthodox and non-Orthodox) had to be Orthodox.

10. The great Dagestani revolt of 1920–1921 against the Soviet regime, headed by the Sufi Naqshbandi leaders, sheikhs Najmuddin of Hatsa (Gotsinsky) and Uzun Haji of Salty, aimed to re-establish a theocratic state on Shamil's model.

11. The fountain of Bakhchisarai is in the old palace of the khans of Crimea; the tower of Süyumbike in Kazan was supposedly built by the last Tatar queen of Kazan (in reality it is a seventeenth-century Russian monument). It is also significant that it was in Kokand, the old capital of the khanate, that the nationalist leaders in January 1918 convened the Assembly of Muslims of Central Asia and proclaimed the autonomy of Turkestan.

12. The Orthodox church of the Ukraine remained separate from Moscow and was under the control of the Holy See of Constantinople until the middle of the seventeenth century. The last metropolitan of Kiev, Sylvestr Kossov, was elected on February 25, 1647, by the Ukrainian clergy, and was confirmed by the king of Poland and the patriarch of Constantinople, who made him his exarch. When Muscovy occupied part of the Ukraine, several Ukrainian bishoprics were placed under the control of the patriarch of Moscow. At the time of Sylvestr's death (April 13, 1657) the Ukrainian church was, according to Makarii (*Istoriia russkoi tserkvi* [St. Petersburg, 1883], 12:111), de facto if not de jure annexed by the Russian church, but the patriarch of Moscow was already called "Patriarch of the Great, Little, and White Russias."

13. Ismail bey Gasprinski (Gaspraly), 1831–1914, a Crimean Tatar reformer, publicist, and philosopher, was elected in 1877 mayor of Bakhchisarai. In 1882, he founded his first reformed (*jadid*) *madrasah* and launched his famous newspaper, *Terjüman* (The Interpreter), which became one of the greatest Muslim newspapers. Gaspraly was the first exponent of pan-Turkism among Russian Muslims, but he rejected its most violent anti-Western manifestations.

14. Such was the case of the first Kazakh political party, the Alash Orda (the Horde of Alash—a mythical ancestor of the Kazakhs). It began as a liberal, moderate national group, whose leaders, Ahmet Baytursun, Ali Bukeykhanov, and Mir Yaqub Dulatov, followed the tradition of the early Kazakh *prosvetiteli* and were the most pro-Russian of all Muslim political leaders. After 1916, however, in order to maintain their leadership, they were forced to adopt a much more anti-Russian attitude.

15. Today the number of Christian Tatars is still estimated at between 100,000 and 150,000. They form a rural community and, as a rule, do not mix either with their Muslim brethren or with the Russians.

16. There are no absolute atheists in Muslim lands, however. The word *atheist* (*bîdîn* in Iranian, or *dinsiz* in the Turkic languages) is still synonymous with "marooned" or "idiot," and *imansiz* (without faith) designates a "faithless scoundrel." Even militant atheists perform all the essential rites in the life of a believer: circumcision, religious marriage, and religious burial in a special Muslim cemetery.

17. The entire Hemshin community was deported to Central Asia in 1944 together with the Meskhetian Turks. It is probable that in their place of exile they are rapidly losing their Armenian identity and are being assimilated by the Meskhetian Turks.

18. The 1951–1952 conflict concerned the following epic songs: *Dede Korkut* (Azeri), *Korkut Ata* (Turkmen), *Alpamysh* (Uzbek), *Koblandy Batyr* (Kazakh), *Er Sain* (Nogay), *Shora Batyr* (Crimean Tatar), and *Manas* (Kirgiz). On this subject, see my article, "The Crisis of the Turkic National Epics, 1951–1952: Local Nationalism or Internationalism?" *Canadian Slavonic Papers* 8 nos. 2, 3 (1975): 463–74.

19. He remains a bloodthirsty tyrant in official Soviet historiography.

20. Other rulers played a similar role: in Central Asia, for example, Khan Abdul-Khair (1412–1468), who managed for a short time to unify all Turkic nomadic hordes; in Lithuania, Grand Prince Vitautas (Vitold, Vitoft), the last great ruler of Lithuania (?–1430).

21. See the collective work published in 1953 in Tbilisi by the Department of the Archives of the Ministry of the Interior (MVD), Sh. V. Tsagareishirli, ed. 2, *Shamil— Stavlennik sultanskoi Turtsii i angliskikh kolonizatorov* ("Shamil: Agent of the Sultan's Turkey and of the English Colonizers").

22. The interest of Central Asian intellectuals in their grandparents who fought the Red Army in the 1920s is indirectly demonstrated by the growing number of Soviet publications that denounce the Basmachis as "tools of English and American imperialism." The most recent anti-Basmachi book was published in 1981 by A. I. Zuvelev, Iu. A. Poliakov, and A. I. Chugunov (*Basmatchestvo: Vozniknovenie, sushchnost', krakh* [Moscow: Nauka, 1981]). The authors draw a clear parallel between the Basmachis and the Afghan *mujahidin* and declare—contrary to the historical evidence—that, as in the case of the Afghans, the main factor for the vitality of the movement was "the extensive support from outside" ("Anglo-American imperialism was the true organizer and inspirer of the Basmachi movement"). See B. Tulepbaev's review of the book in *Pravda*, January 19, 1982. See also *Radio Liberty Research*, 44/82, January 26, 1982.

23. The best sources on the subject are V. N. Basilov, *Kul't sviatykh v Islame* (Moscow: Mysl, 1970); A. A. Salamov, "Pravda o sviatykh mestakh v Checheno-Ingushetii," *Trudy Checheno-Ingushskogo Nauchno-Issledovatel'skogo Instituta* 9 (Groznyi, 1964), pp. 155–69; S. M. Gadzhiev, *Puti preodoleniia ideologii Islama* (Makhach-Qala, 1963); and V. Makatov, "Kul't sviatykh v Islame," *Voprosy Nauchnogo ateizma* 3 (Moscow, 1967), pp. 164–85.

24. V. Makatov, "Kul't sviatykh v Islame," p. 180.

25. A. A. Salamov, "Pravda o sviatykh mestakh v Checheno-Ingushetii," p. 167.

26. As of the spring of 1982, the following leading figures of Tatar *jadidism* had been wholly rehabilitated: Abu Nasr Kursavi (1783–1814), Shihabeddin Marjani (1818–1899), and Abdul Qayyum Nasyr (1824–1904). Others will certainly follow. The mechanism of rehabilitation generally follows the same pattern: the first article appears as a rule in the quarterly journal published by the Muslim spiritual Board of Central Asia (Tashkent), *The Muslims of the Soviet East* (in Arabic, Uzbek in Arabic script, Persian, English, and French). Then a second article appears under the signature of a native historian in the Tatar literary journal *Kazan Utlary* (The Fires of Kazan). Only then is official rehabilitation crowned by articles or books in Russian.

The Ukraine and Russia

Roman Szporluk

The view that the Soviet Union is an empire is commonly held today. The imperial character of the Soviet state, many authors hold, is reflected in the relations of the Russians with the non-Russian nationalities of the USSR as well as in the Soviet Union's relations with Eastern Europe.[1] How does the Ukraine fit into this overall picture? What is the specific nature of its own dependency in the Soviet framework?

The dependence of one people or territory on another may take many forms: political, military, economic, or cultural. The situation of the Ukraine in these regards is roughly analogous to that of the other republics that form the USSR under the leadership of the Russian Soviet Federated Socialist Republic (RSFSR). At the same time, however, the Ukraine is special because of its population, location, and certain economic and strategic factors. Its importance can be summed up in the simple proposition that without the Ukraine the Soviet Union would not be a superpower. The Ukrainians are the largest non-Russian nationality in the USSR (42.3 million, of whom 36.5 million live in the Ukrainian republic), and the Ukraine is the most populous of the fourteen non-Russian republics (50 million). The Ukraine's capital, Kiev, is the third-largest city in the USSR and the primate city of the Ukrainian republic, which includes such other major urban centers as Kharkov, Dnepropetrovsk, Odessa, and Donetsk. The industrial and agricultural potential of the Ukraine is well known. The Ukrainian party organization is the largest if not the most powerful regional machine in the CPSU, and its head customarily holds a seat on the Moscow Politburo. Among the Soviet republics, only the Ukraine and Belorussia enjoy a measure of international recognition as members of the United Nations and its affiliated bodies. However illusory their actual role on the world scene may be, this fact appears to have a genuine significance for some Ukrainians. There is no doubt whatsoever that the Ukraine is strategically located insofar as the Soviet Union's relations with Eastern Europe are concerned. It is small wonder, then, that a substantial literature in English exists on its politics, economy, demography, culture, and religion.[2]

According to British sociologists Jaroslav Krejčí and Vitězslav Velímský, the USSR is a "Federation as a Holding Company." Successful empire builders, Krejčí and Velímský point out, long ago discovered that indirect rule serves their purposes better than direct rule. They have, accordingly, put to good use "the holding company principle," under which "the holding of 51 per cent of the shares in a parent company which holds, in its turn, 51 per cent of the shares in a number of daughter companies can eventually give the empire-builder a degree of effective control much greater than is warranted by his actual financial strength."[3]

Krejčí and Velímský argue that the Russians have implemented this principle in the USSR: they hold a very comfortable majority in the "parent company," the Russian Soviet Federated Socialist Republic (RSFSR), and that republic in turn controls the USSR. The USSR, furthermore, is the dominant influence in the "socialist camp," which contains a narrower group of countries, such as those in the Warsaw Pact plus Mongolia and Afghanistan, but also includes the more loosely attached Cuba and Vietnam. Krejčí and Velímský calculate that in 1970 the Russians held a majority of 82.3 percent in the RSFSR, a majority of 53.4 percent in the USSR, and a minority of 36.7 percent in the more narrowly defined Soviet bloc. That minority further declined to a minority of 28.8 percent in the wider version of the bloc. All this has not prevented the Russians from being the dominant element: "in spite of the fact that the non-Russians represent 71.2 percent of the population of the 'Camp' and 46.6 percent of the population of the USSR, there is no doubt about who effectively runs the show."[4]

The more recent assessment by a political scientist and a scholar of international relations fully matches the judgment of the two sociologists. Zbigniew Brzezinski, in an article characteristically titled "The Tragic Dilemmas of Soviet World Power: The Limits of a New-Type Empire," writes:

> The Soviet Union is the political expression of Russian nationalism. The
> Great Russians dominate the multinational Soviet Union, populated by

some 270 million people; and through the power and resources of that Union, they dominate in turn a cluster of geographically contiguous states numbering approximately an additional 115 millions of people. In effect, about 135 million Great Russians exercise political control over a political framework that cumulatively encompasses some 385 millions spread over much of the Eurasian continent.[5]

Considering that the Russians represent just a bare majority of the Soviet population (52 percent, according to the 1979 census), the Ukrainians and, to a smaller extent, the Belorussians are critically important if the Russians are to remain in numerical control of the USSR. (This control, in turn, affects their capacity for retaining a controlling position in the Soviet bloc as a whole.) Accordingly, the special place of the Ukrainian and Belorussian element in Soviet internal politics has been recognized by both Soviet and Western scholars for a long time. For example, the prominent Soviet political geographer, V. V. Pokshishevsky, has characterized the role of these two East Slav nations as that of "fellow-travelers" or "companions" of the Russians (*sputniki russkikh*) outside their own republics, for example, in Central Asia or the Baltic states. The American scholar, John A. Armstrong, has described them as the Russians' "younger brothers."[6] Taking this into account, Armstrong predicted in the 1960s that "the major thrust of Soviet nationality policy . . . will be toward drawing the younger brothers (especially the Ukrainians) into indissoluble junior partnership with the Russians as the dominant ethnic group."[7]

Armstrong's prediction, made some twenty years ago, has since been fully confirmed by the Russifying turn in Soviet policy toward the Ukraine, which took place after the fall of Shelest (1972). The importance for Moscow of the "Ukrainian connection" has been reaffirmed by the demographic explosion of the Soviet Muslims, on the one hand, and the political and social upheavals in Poland, on the other.

Although linguistic assimilation seems to be a major goal of the Soviet regime with regard to the Ukraine, Moscow understands that a separate Ukrainian identity as a political factor is not exclusively, perhaps not even basically, rooted in the difference between the Russian and Ukrainian languages. Without admitting it publicly, Moscow probably agrees with the Western scholar of nationalism, Walker Connor, who has argued that for Ukrainian nationalists language has chiefly a symbolic value.[8]

But if this is so, what is it that makes the Ukrainian problem a political problem? It would seem that memory, history, is that necessary factor that any group like the Ukrainians must have if it is ever to be capable of acting as an autonomous agent. According to Karl W. Deutsch, who has formulated in the language of modern social science what generations of men have understood instinctively, "Autonomy in the long run depends on memory." A self-steering society must receive a "full flow of information" about the outside world, itself, and its parts as well as information from the past, "with a wide range of recall and recombination." If any of these kinds of information is cut off, "the society becomes an automaton . . . It loses control over its own behavior."[9]

Milan Kundera, a Czech writer living in the West, draws the logical conclusion. A character in his novel, *The Book of Laughter and Forgetting*, says: "The first step in liquidating a people is to erase its memory. Destroy its books, its culture, its history. Then have somebody write new books, manufacture a new culture, invent a new history. Before long the nation will begin to forget what it is and what it was. The world around it will forget even faster." The struggle for survival, says another character in the novel, is "the struggle of memory against forgetting."[10]

It is a well-known fact that the Soviet regime has used its power to formulate the historical ideas of the peoples under its control. Accordingly, the main theme of this essay is Ukrainian history as a political problem in the USSR or, to put it differently, my concern here is to explore the status of the Ukraine in the Soviet imperial system from a special but by no means insignificant angle—official control over history. One of the peculiarities of the Soviet system is precisely that, among empires of the modern age, it has been so concerned to control historical ideas. Other imperial rulers were usually satisfied to control the present and the future of their subjects but not their past; their bodies and their material resources but not their souls and memories.

The preoccupation of successive Russian governments (this applies also to tsarist predecessors of the Soviet state) with the problem of Ukrainian history has had broader concerns than the aim of simply controlling the Ukrainians. As I shall show, the history of the Ukraine (and also that of Belorussia, to which unfortunately I shall be unable to give attention in this brief essay) is also related to a central problem of Russian history, indeed, to the broader question of *Russian* national identity. These considerations justify our concentration on what might appear to be a marginal or narrowly academic topic.

In light of the quotations from Deutsch and Kundera we can easily understand what the Soviets are doing when they try to shape the historical consciousness of the Ukrainians—or, for that matter, of other nations under their control. The Soviet goal is to regulate the flow of information "from the past," to narrow the "range of recall and recombination" that is at the Ukrainians' disposal. The ultimate goal is to deprive the Ukrainians of a capacity to steer themselves. Having deprived captive peoples of control over their own politics, economy, and culture, Moscow is trying to take away their past, which it rightly views as the last surviving element of their spiritual independence. Once they adopt the official history as the framework in which to view themselves, they will cease to be distinct nations and thus will lose the capacity to act on their own. To deprive a people of its past may thus be a colonialism more destructive and more vicious than the one that expropriates a nation's mineral resources, imposes discriminatory terms of trade, disbands its army and civil service, or puts foreigners in all official positions.

The battle over the past of the Ukraine is especially intense and bitter for two reasons: first, because the concept of a Russian history and a Russian nationhood is closely related to, and vitally affected by, the history of the Ukraine, and, second, because the great-power status of the USSR requires that the Ukraine be dependent on Moscow. Without the Ukraine, Russia would no longer be a world power of the first rank. In this respect, the Ukraine is fundamentally different from any other nationality of the Soviet Union, just as it was fundamentally different from any other people under the Romanovs before 1917. A prominent Russian nationalist made it quite clear, in 1911, when he explained that "the Polish, Armenian, Finnish, and other problems are peripheral, i.e., secondary problems." The "Mazepist" (that is, Ukrainian) problem, however, "injures Russia at the origin of its existence as a great power." Unlike the Ukraine, "Poland, Finland, and other borderlands did not give Russia her greatness."[11]

Hostility to the very idea of a separate Ukrainian nationality was not the monopoly of reactionary Russian nationalists. Peter Struve, a dedicated Westernizer and liberal, fully agreed on this count with the "Black Hundredist" Savenko. The Ukrainian idea, Struve argued, was an attempt to carry out "a gigantic and unprecedented schism of the Russian nation, which, such is my deepest conviction, will result in veritable disaster for the state and for the people. Borderline problems will pale into mere bagatelles," he warned, "compared to such a prospect of bifurcation and—should the 'Belorussians' follow the 'Ukrainians'— 'trifurcation' of Russian culture."[12]

It might seem that Lenin would have taken a stand opposing Struve, let alone Savenko. Lenin, after all, had recognized the right of all nations of Russia, the Ukrainians emphatically included, to self-determination, including the right of secession. Long before 1917 (when the Bolsheviks in practice repudiated this "right"), however, Lenin's concession was negated by his insistence that workers of all nationalities of the empire, especially the Ukrainian workers, must have one, ostensibly supranational, social democratic party—which, of course, was Lenin's party.

This Leninist position happened to contradict the stand that Engels had taken when the problem of the Irish and Polish socialists had arisen. Engels believed that, if the socialists of Poland were to join the socialist parties of the powers that then ruled the partitioned nation (Germany, Austria, and Russia), they would thereby acquiesce in, and accept, the denial of Poland's right to be a free nation. Similarly, Engels did not think that the socialists of Ireland should be part of a broader British socialist organization. Engels's statement on this subject had a more general significance:

> What would be said if this Council called upon Polish sections to acknowledge the supremacy of a Russian Federal Council in Petersburg, or upon Prussian, Polish, North Schleswig, and Alsatian sections to submit to a Federal Council in Berlin? Yet what was asked to do with regard to Irish sections was substantially the same thing. If members of a conquering nation called upon the nation they had conquered and continued to hold down to forget their specific nationality and position, to "sink national differences" and so forth, that was not Internationalism, it was nothing else but preaching to them submission to the yoke, and attempting to justify and to perpetuate the dominion of the conqueror under the cloak of Internationalism.[13]

Understandably, the Ukrainian Marxists, without Engels telling them this, grasped very well the implications of Lenin's "internationalism." One of those Ukrainians, Lev Iurkevych, writing as "L. Rybalka," challenged Lenin on this score. In retrospect, I have to agree with Charles Halary that the Leninist principles of party organization replicated exactly the principles on which the tsarist imperial state— which the Bolsheviks sought to destroy—was based.[14] But of course the Leninist position was not based on any abstract considerations of ideology: Kazimierz Kelles-Krauz, the leading Polish socialist theorist of the nationality problem, reported in 1901 from London to his Polish comrades that the Russian socialists from the Iskra group (with whom he was in contact) absolutely opposed the existence of a separate Ukrainian socialist party—even though they were prepared to tolerate a Polish or Finnish or even a Lithuanian party. To allow the Ukrainians a party of their own "would be political suicide."[15] (As we have just seen, this was also the view of Struve and Savenko.)

The uncompromisingly negative position of so many Russians toward the idea of a distinct political identity of the Ukraine was not solely caused by geopolitical considerations, that is, fear that without the

Ukraine Russia would be a much weaker state. The hostile (one is almost tempted to say hysterical) response to the refusal of nationally conscious Ukrainians to be Russian (for this is how Russian opinion perceived the Ukrainian phenomenon) was related to the fact that the Russians themselves had not solved their own problem of identity in modern times. In this connection it is helpful to recall the point made by Richard Pipes, who writes that to understand the nature of the nationality problem in the USSR it is necessary to bear in mind the peculiarities in the formation of the Russian national identity during the late medieval and early modern eras. Pipes has taken as a point of departure a comparison between the nation-building processes in the West and in Russia, and he points out that the empires of the West were founded after the rise of national states in Europe. For reasons of geography, "European imperial expansion directed itself across the seas and into other continents; hence there was never any doubt about the spatial separation between colony and metropolis. In sum, Western empire-building—that is, the acquisition of masses of other ethnic groups—was always chronologically and territorially distinct from the process involved in building the national state."[16]

These processes took a different course in Russia, which expanded along its territorial frontiers. Gradually, it conquered and absorbed foreign ethnic groups, beginning with Finnic and Turkic nationalities and finally including Asian and some European peoples. "The chronological and geographic contiguity of the processes leading to the building of both the nation-state and empire has had the effect of blurring the two phenomena, tending to make Russians remarkably insensitive to ethnic problems." Pipes notes that even liberal and social democratic groups ignored ethnic problems and treated "the demands of nationalities for a greater role in self-government as reactionary and enemy-inspired."[17]

I conclude then, in agreement with Pipes, that it is a special feature of Russian historical development, as compared with the rise of West European nations, that Russia became a multinational empire—in other words, a colonial power—before a modern Russian nation had been formed.

As a result of this reversal of stages—the formation of an empire before the completion of nation-building—the Russians themselves have never been quite sure what is "Russia" and what is not Russia even if it is under Russian rule. By contrast, even the most chauvinistic Frenchmen sensed clearly that Indochina or Madagascar were not French in the same sense that Champagne and Burgundy were, just as the English knew that Calcutta was not British in the same way that Manchester was. (In fairness to the Russians, one might recall that not so long ago some French people fought for a "French Algeria.")

In Russia the confusion was compounded by another major factor impeding the rise of a Russian nation distinct from the Russian empire: the political system and ideology of the state itself. Of necessity simplifying a complex issue, we might say that in the West, in the course of developments extending over several centuries, there emerged societies as entities independent of the monarch. That development, in turn, had been made possible by the emergence of a fundamental distinction in the public sphere between the status of the monarch as a political ruler and his status as an owner. Although the tendency to view the kingdom as the personal patrimony of the prince had arisen in the West, too, "it never struck root in the west, where theorists steadfastly adhered to the fundamental distinction between ownership and authority, between *dominium* and *imperium* or *iurisdictio*."[18] As a medieval jurist put it, the emperor "was lord in the political sense, but not in the sense of an owner."[19] (In other words, he had *imperium* or *iurisdictio*, but not *dominium*, over his subjects.)

In Muscovy, sovereignty acquired "the attributes of patrimonial or dominial power, i.e., full ownership of the land and its inhabitants." The external side of this process of the rise of Moscow expressed itself in the claim of its ruler to sovereignty over all of historic Rus'. Thus, the diplomats of Ivan III claimed Kiev and Smolensk, then held by Lithuania, as the tsar's inheritance (*votchina*), and, when, later, Ivan IV invaded Livonia (which had never formed part of the Kievan state), he also called it his *votchina*.[20] Since the concept of state was lacking in Russia "its corollary, society, was also unknown." (Pipes thinks that even after it had emerged in the middle of the seventeenth century, it "remained imperfectly assimilated.")[21]

This political system denied any independent legal identity to the subject of the tsar and thus did much to slow down the process of the rise of a modern Russian nation: the latter did not begin to form until after the reforms of Catherine II. It is proper to view the great intellectual and political controversies of the first half of the nineteenth century—the Westernizer-Slavophile controversy—as a debate over the definition of the Russian nation. It was then, in the nineteenth century, that even tsarism felt forced to acknowledge the new era of nationalism: accordingly, its spokesmen counteracted with the formula of "Official Nationality," with its triad of Orthodoxy, autocracy, and nationality.

Much confusion about the nature of Russian nationalism has been caused by the oversimplified idea that in the nineteenth century, and by extension even in our times, the Russian debate over the real nature of Russian nationality has been waged in terms of the controversy between the Slavophiles and the Westernizers. In fact, any discussion of the problem of Russian national identity, and along with it, of the nationality problem in Russia, especially with reference to the Ukrainian question, has to take into account the fact that there has always existed a third party in those debates, to wit, the view that considered the state—autocratic and imperial—the essential marker of Russian nationality. Much of Russian political and intellectual history up to the revolution of 1917 will remain misunderstood if one fails to acknowledge the powerful presence of that statist or imperial-statist concept of the Russian nation, with its official religious ideology of Orthodoxy.[22]

The official ideology legitimized the partitions of Poland—which resulted in the transfer to Russia of all of Belorussia and the Ukraine west of the Dnieper (but not Galicia, taken by Austria in 1772)—in terms of the tsars "recovering" their dynastic patrimony. The ideologues simultaneously considered the Ukrainians and Belorussians to be Orthodox Russians for the same reason, their descent from Kievan Rus'.

Thus, as can be easily seen, the theory and practice of official nationality had nothing to offer the Ukrainians (or Belorussians). On the contrary, it denied them any separate identity precisely on the principle of dynastic identity: they had been recovered by the tsar, the heir of Kiev. The fact that some Ukrainians and most Belorussians had become Catholic in the course of the several centuries during which they were associated with the West (Poland) did not deter the tsarist regime: St. Petersburg ordered their reconversion to Orthodoxy so that they might fit the image of what they were supposed to be. The same applied to the political tradition and institutions the Ukrainians had developed during the centuries of their association with Poland-Lithuania, the period of their supposedly forced separation from the tsar. That element too was to be extinguished, and this is what the tsarist regime did when it gradually destroyed the autonomy of the Hetmanate and the Sich (that is, those parts of the Ukraine Muscovy had ruled as autonomous entities, since the seventeenth century). The official ideology was not prepared to recognize any Ukrainian claims (let alone Belorussian, which at that time were infrequently raised) to the status of equality with Russia. The celebrated agreement of Pereiaslav (1654), which was contracted by the Ukrainians with the representatives of the tsar, was interpreted in conformity with official ideology.[23]

As I noted, in official tsarist ideology, which gradually permeated also the emerging Russian national consciousness, the partitions of Poland in 1772, 1793, and 1795 were a process of recovery by the tsars of their patrimony. As ethnic nationalism began to replace dynastic autocratic ideology as the principle of political legitimation, however, the Russians increasingly invoked the principle of alleged ethnic unity of the people of Kievan Rus' in justification of their territorial claims and of their denial of a separate national identity to the Belorussians and Ukrainians. In the nineteenth century, the Russian public began to view those lands as belonging to Russia for ethnic reasons. After all, they were not Polish, were they?[24]

The difference between the Ukrainian and Belorussian languages on the one hand and Russian on the other was frequently attributed to alleged contamination of the former by Polish influences. Thus, the same type of argument was invoked that had earlier been used to justify the suppression of a separate religious and political identity of the Ukraine and Belorussia. In sum, both the official tsarist and the emergent ethnic-nationalist concept of Russia held that, whatever history the Ukrainians and Belorussians may have had that kept them apart from the rest of the Russians, it really was a nonhistory or antihistory, a "time-out" that deserved to be blotted from their memory.

It would carry us too far from our main theme to explore the full implications of the fact that the Poles continued to think of the lands of the Ukraine, Belorussia, and Lithuania as Polish long after an independent Polish state ceased to exist in 1795. Unlike Russia, which was a state or, better still, an empire without a nation, Poland after 1795 was a nation without a state. Russo-Polish relations in the nineteenth century—perhaps also a considerable portion of the twentieth century—was the history of the struggle for control over those territories. The Polish claim to those lands, however, unlike the Russian one, was based on a political concept of the Polish nation, that is, a community created by common rights and institutions, not any alleged ethnic or linguistic closeness or identity.[25] Thus, we have to mention the Polish connection because the formation of a Ukrainian national identity took place amid this controversy between the Russians, who had a state but were not yet a nation, and the Poles, who were a nation but had lost a state.

During their national revival of the nineteenth century, the Ukrainians created their own conception of national history as a process that followed its own inner dynamic; they did not view their history as a variation of, or departure from, the mainstream of Russian (or "all-Russian") history. The concept of a Ukrainian historical process—the "national myth"—was elaborated by several generations of scholars and received its most consistent and detailed formulation in the work of Mykhailo Hrushevsky (1866–1934) in this century.[26]

At the grave risk of a gross oversimplification, I would venture to say that the modern Ukrainian national identity, insofar as it is based on historical ideas, incorporates the following key concepts that set it apart, and against, the Russian conception of history. (Comparable points can be made about the Belorussians.) First, Ukrainian historical ideology does not accept the view according to which Kievan Rus' had been an ethnically uniform, homogeneous entity. Second, it refuses to recognize the Muscovite state as the main, let alone the only, successor of Kiev, and of course it rejects entirely the conception of Russian unity implied in the concept of the patrimonial state. On the contrary, it insists on making distinctions between the history of the Russians treated as a people, the history of Kievan Rus' as a whole, and the histories of the Belorussian and the Ukrainian peoples.

It is clear that the Ukrainians have a different conception of the role of the state in their national development, and, it goes without saying, they can find no beneficial effect of the actions of the tsarist state in their nation. Whereas Peter the Great, Catherine II, Nicholas I, and Alexander II are associated in Russian history with important and often beneficial undertakings, for those Ukrainians who are nationally aware, Peter and Catherine stand for the destruction of Ukrainian liberties (any reader of an unexpurgated Shevchenko knows this) and Nicholas I is remembered for his decision to forbid the Ukrainian national poet Taras Shevchenko "to paint or to draw" while in prison and exile. The "tsar liberator," Alexander II, in Ukrainian historical memory is associated with the decrees that banned the use of Ukrainian in print, in school, and on the stage (1863 and 1876).

Just as even communist Russians have found it possible to approve of tsarist Russia's foreign policies, wars, and conquests, so have many anticommunist Russians been able to recognize the Soviet regime as a national force at least in some of its aspects and actions. Even some of the staunchest opponents of communism think of the Soviet army, for example, as a *Russian* national force. It is hardly possible for nationally conscious Ukrainians (or Belorussians) to sympathize with the Soviet cults of Suvorov, Kutuzov, Nakhimov, and other tsarist figures, or to view the Soviet state or army as Ukrainian national institutions.

The Ukrainians view themselves as history's victims, as underdogs. When they compare their fate with that of other nations, they look to the Slovaks, Czechs, Slovenes, or Bulgarians. The common Russian perception of Russia's past and present status is quite the opposite: the Russians are aware that they have been and now are a great power, and, by and large, they are proud of the fact even when they disapprove of their country's regime or specific policies at any particular time. The Ukrainian view of the world of nations is also unlike the Russian view, because their experience of living with foreigners has been so different. For the Russians, foreign rule in their own country ended about five hundred years ago, when the "Tatar-Mongol yoke" was overthrown. The Tatar rule is remembered in Russian collective consciousness as an unmitigated disaster. Even official Soviet propaganda, so expert in finding good aspects of Russian rule over non-Russians, seems unable to discover any benefits to be drawn from Tatar domination over Russians. Later, the Russians themselves expanded their state and their country to become a multinational empire. The Russians were unfailingly the dominant element in the empire and accepted the ever-expanding state as their homeland. It seems quite important for the formation of Russian attitudes toward the outside world that no significant numbers of Russians have ever lived for long under a *western* neighbor of Russia, for example, Poland-Lithuania or Sweden. They have known the West only in war, as a temporary invader, never as a regular civilian authority. "The West" was known only when one traveled abroad. This factor seems to have contributed to the emergence of that celebrated dichotomy in Russian political thought between Russia and Europe (or Russia and the West).

The Ukrainians have lived for centuries within states in which they were just one of several ethnic groups, and they were never the master nation in those states, even though, as in Poland-Lithuania, they were not really an oppressed nationality in the modern sense. Poland and Austria, under which many Ukrainians lived, were European powers, but the Ukrainians did not blame Europe for their problems: they wanted to enjoy those rights that others had.

Russian social and political thought contains a theme that poses Russia in opposition to the West. One of the differences supposedly separating the two worlds was the alleged creative role of the state as a force standing above society in Russia, as contrasted to the state's subordination to society in Europe. This is one of the ways in which both Russians and non-Russians have tried to explain the phenomenon of autocracy in Russian history. Whatever the merit of those interpretations (and, as the works cited earlier indicate, there is some validity to them), such problems do not exist in Ukrainian history: there is no "Ivan the Terrible Complex" (to cite the title of Alexander Yanov's study) in Ukrainian history. On the contrary, Ukrainian national mythology idealized the epoch of the Cossacks as a period of freedom and a time of the supremacy of society over the state.

Finally, in Russia religion and nationality were united under the state in a common identity, and to be Russian meant to be Orthodox. (Catholics, Jews, and Muslims were among the tsar's subjects, to be sure, but they were not Russians.) Even the Old Believers, who were ethnic Russians, were not only excluded from the official church but were for this reason also persecuted by the state. Many sectarians were forced to leave Russia altogether. The Ukraine had lost its ecclesiastic unity in the sixteenth century, when a significant portion of the Ukrainians and Belorussians recognized the authority of the pope. (At that time those Ukrainians and Belorussians in the Polish-Lithuanian Commonwealth who remained Orthodox had a strong sense of religious and cultural unity, but it was different from Muscovite Orthodoxy.) The affiliation with Rome did not sink into the popular consciousness until the eighteenth century, however. By that time, in the areas under Russian control, where Orthodoxy had survived, the Russian Orthodox Church had subordinated the Kievan Orthodox metropoly to itself (before 1685 Kiev had been under the patriarch of Constantinople) and helped the state in its empire-building by suppressing Ukrainian autonomy in religious matters.[27] After the partitions of Poland, the Russian government forcibly "reconverted" the Ukrainian and Belorussian Catholics to Orthodoxy. Catholicism survived, however, among the Ukrainians of Galicia and the Transcarpathian Ukraine (Ruthenia) until after World War II. Thus, religious dualism and the lack of state support for one official religion has been a fact of Ukrainian history for the past several centuries.

One might push this contrast further and argue that the Ukrainian nation as such has functioned, as an organized entity, through a network of diverse social, economic, cultural, and political organizations within those states that allowed such activities, but it has tended to virtually disappear where the state did not tolerate any voluntary associations, whether cultural, political, or religious. Millions of Ukrainian migrants to Siberia, the Far East, and other parts of Russia thus lost their language and identity and became assimilated, whereas those Ukrainians who had emigrated to America managed to preserve and even develop many of their old traditions thanks to the political pluralism prevailing in Canada and the United States. Even under Austria and Poland, which were much less liberal societies than either the United States or Canada, the Ukrainians established a complex structure of social, religious, economic (cooperative societies of consumers and producers), and political organizations. Just as they functioned where there was freedom of association, the Ukrainians found the Russian state openly inimical to their very existence as a nation.

This simple distillation of some basic features of Ukrainian historical consciousness makes it easy to understand why such diverse figures as the socialist and populist Mykhailo Drahomanov (1841–1895) and the conservative and monarchist Viacheslav Lypynsky (1882–1931) interpreted Ukrainian national identity in historical terms and emphasized the Ukraine's relations with the West as a formative factor. Thus, according to Drahomanov, "Most of the national differences between Ukraine and

Muscovy can be explained by the fact that until the eighteenth century, i.e., until the establishment of Russian rule—Ukraine was linked to Western Europe. In spite of the handicaps caused by the Tatar invasions the Ukraine participated in Europe's social and cultural progress." Lypynsky arrived at essentially the same conclusion: "The basic difference between Ukraine and Moscow does not consist in the language, race or religion, . . . but in a different, age-long political structure, a different method of the organization of the *elite*, in a different relationship between the upper and the lower social classes, between the state and society."[28]

This view that the basis of Ukrainian-Russian differentiation is historico-political rather than ethno-linguistic has had a famous formulation in an essay on "The Two Russian Nationalities" by Mykola Kostomarov (1817–1885), published in the Ukrainian journal *Osnova* in 1861. That essay, says Doroshenko, was for a long time regarded as "the gospel of Ukrainian nationalism." Here is what Kostomarov wrote:

> The Ukrainians are characterized by individualism, the Great Russians by collectivism . . . In the political sphere, the Ukrainians were able to create among themselves free forms of society which were controlled no more than was required for their very existence, and yet they were strong in themselves without infringing on personal liberties. The Great Russians attempted to build on a firm foundation a collective structure permeated by one spirit. The striving of the Ukrainians was towards federation, that of the Great Russians towards autocracy and a firm monarchy.[29]

Kostomarov contrasted Russian and Ukrainian folk belief systems, attitudes toward nature, relations between the individual and the group, and attitudes toward property:

> In their social beliefs the Great Russians are different from Ukrainians as a result of their different historic heritage. The urge to unite individual parts into a whole, the denial of personal interests in the name of social good, the highest respect for social judgment—all these features manifest themselves in the large family life of the Great Russians and in their sacrifices for the community (mir). A Great Russian family is one unit, with property in common . . .
>
> The Ukrainians, on the other hand, hate this system . . . A common duty, not voluntarily undertaken but inevitable, they regard as a great burden, while among the Great Russians these duties substitute their strivings for personal liberty.
>
> Compulsory common use of the land and responsibility of all for one appear to a Ukrainian to be the worst and most unjust kind of servitude.

His history has not taught him to suppress his feelings for private property or to regard himself as a servant of some abstract commune and be responsible for other members of it.[30]

It is interesting that Kostomarov purported to see certain similarities in the national character of the Ukrainians and the Poles though admitting that linguistically the Ukrainians were closer to the Russians. As a nation of peasants, the Ukrainians were allegedly democratic whereas the Poles were aristocratic, but then the Polish aristocracy was "very democratic" and the Ukrainian democracy was "very aristocratic."[31]

Up to 1917, the Ukrainians in the Russian and Austrian empires developed under quite different conditions. In tsarist Russia they suffered from the general restrictions on political activity, which, in the Ukrainian case, were compounded by administrative prohibitions on the use of the Ukrainian language (in effect until the revolution of 1905). Even after 1905, organized Ukrainian life in Russia operated under an extremely unfavorable regime. All of this was reflected in Ukrainian politics during the post–March 1917 era. However, scholars generally agree that the establishment of an autonomous Ukraine with the consent of the Provisional Government, the success of the Ukrainian parties in the elections to the All-Russian Constituent Assembly, and, finally, the struggle of the Ukrainian nationalists for an independent state during the upheavals of 1918–1921 demonstrated the capacity of Ukrainian nationalism to present a political program and to reach the masses.[32] The conditions under the Habsburgs were quite different: from the late 1860s, Austria was a constitutional state and the Ukrainians of Galicia and Bukovina availed themselves of the opportunities this provided. Their failure to maintain an independent West Ukrainian People's Republic (1918–1919) was due to a combination of circumstances, primarily the determination of the Poles to hold all of Galicia, but also errors on the part of the republic's leaders.[33]

It is instructive to see what Thomas G. Masaryk, the great scholar and practitioner of nationalism, had to say about the Ukrainian problem. In a political memorandum prepared for Allied leaders during the final stages of the First World War, he commented:

In the Ukrainian problem we must carefully distinguish the question of language and nationality from the political question. The point lies in this: Are the Ukrainians a separate nation or a Russian tribe? Is the Ukrainian language a separate language or a Russian dialect? Even the philologists (Slavic) are divided on this question. Following the analogy of other nations, however, we may say that the Ukrainians, even granting that their tongue is merely a dialect of the Russian—and that is my opinion—may separate themselves from the Russians on other grounds as well—on grounds economic, social, and political.[34]

Masaryk's comment on the Ukrainian question deserves to be compared with his judgment on the Russians as a nation, to be found in the same work: "the Russians themselves have not developed to the point of national consciousness; the masses of the people have their religious viewpoint, and the *intelligentsia*, as far as it is Socialistic, does not feel nationally." The reason why the Russians themselves had remained so politically underdeveloped was the continuing political impact of tsarism, which survived the fall of the tsar (this was written in early 1918): "The tsarism of the Romanoffs was without culture and brutal, and for that very reason less noxious [than "the tsarism of Vienna and Berlin, a more dangerous species of tsarism because it uses science and developed capitalism"]. The tsarism of the Russian masses and revolutionaries is worse; they rid themselves of the Tsar, but they have not yet ridden themselves of tsarism."[35]

The history of the post-1917 period is too well known to require more than a most elementary summary. Initially, the Bolsheviks viewed their revolution as simply the first act of a broader international revolution that would establish a proletarian federation based on principles completely opposed to those of nationalism. Lenin viewed the formation of the Union of Soviet Socialist Republics in 1922–1924 into an association of formally equal republics (one of which was Russia, now styled as the RSFSR) as a transitional step dictated by expediency. It was his idea that Russia should formally recognize itself an equal of the Ukraine (Ukrainian Soviet Socialist Republic) and other Soviet republics in a new federation "of Europe and Asia." Stalin, however, favored the inclusion of the Ukraine, Belorussia, Armenia, and so on in the *Russian* Socialist Federated Soviet Republic, as the latter's "autonomous" subdivisions. Lenin's concept preserved at least formally the original supranational dream of the revolution; Stalin's quite openly amounted to the restoration of a Russian state embracing all those parts of the former tsarist empire that the Bolsheviks had managed to retain under their control.[36]

Looking back at those issues from the contemporary perspective we see that what Stalin proposed—only to be overruled by Lenin—was what Communists of various nations actually did after winning power after 1945. As Benedict Anderson has recently pointed out, "since World War II every successful revolution has defined itself in *national* terms." Anderson has cited the cases of the People's Republic of China and the Socialist Republic of Vietnam, noting that each has grounded itself firmly in a territorial and social space inherited from the prerevolutionary past. Conversely, the fact that the Soviet Union shares with the United Kingdom of Great Britain and Northern Ireland the rare distinction of refusing nationality in its naming suggests that it is as much the legatee of the prenational dynastic states of the nineteenth century as the precursor of a twenty-first century internationalist order.[37]

How did the Soviets in the decade of the 1980s, nearly seventy years after the inauguration of what had plausibly appeared a new "internationalist order" in the making, find themselves with a polity that can persuasively be compared to the prenational dynastic states? For the opinion of Anderson is by no means uniquely his: an identical view underlies the work of Krejčí and Velímský, whom I quoted in the opening section of this essay. These two authors note that of the empires in existence before 1914—Britain, France, Germany, Portugal, Belgium, the Ottoman Porte, the Netherlands, Austria-Hungary, and Russia— only Russia remains today. It is natural, they say, that questions arise regarding the causes of the Russians' success. One of these questions is "how do the Russians manage to run an imperial structure in a period when other empires have run aground?" The second, "where does the 'charisma' come from?" is concerned with the principle of legitimacy. Krejčí and Velímský answer their first question simply: the Russians manage to hold their possessions because "the others do not." (They cite the example of Hitler's "total mismanagement of the Ukraine" during World War II to illustrate how the others have failed.) As for the charisma, they argue, the Russians have not one but two charismas: one for "consumption abroad," the other "for internal consumption."

> The charisma "for consumption abroad" does not mention the specificity of the Russian ethnie [*sic*] but stresses the invaluable experience of the Communist Party of the Soviet Union in two areas—that of overthrowing capitalism and that of constructing "real" socialism. Accordingly, the path of other countries to socialism, if it is to be a successful one, cannot differ from this universally applicable paradigm, except in minor points of detail related to different historical circumstances.[38]

According to Krejčí and Velímský, the other charisma, "charisma for internal consumption," is less visible in the media but is "accepted as self-evident truth" in "the three institutions that successively form the mind of a Russian": the family, the school, and the army. It is also accepted in parts of the bureaucracy. This internal charisma is Great

Russian nationalism, which they note is "shared to some extent by both the establishment and the dissidents."[39]

This statement requires modification, for, though it is undoubtedly true that a Russian nationalism is one of the "charismas" of the Soviet regime, that Russian nationalism is presented to the non-Russian half of the Soviet population in a special hybrid form—by means of the concept of the "Soviet people."[40] The "Soviet people," according to the official doctrine, is a new historical community embracing the Russians and the non-Russians in an entity that is not ethnic per se, though it has certain ethnic features, for example, the Russian language as a medium of "inter-nationality communication."

The domestic nationalist charisma aimed at the Russians (which glorifies the old Russian state) and the version for the non-Russian half of the Soviet population have an important common denominator: both assume that the nation/people exists through the state, and that it has a common ideology—Marxism-Leninism. Thus, current Soviet doctrine may be seen as a secularized and updated edition of tsarist "Official Nationality" or a variant of statist or imperialist Russian nationalism, to be distinguished from, and contrasted with, the culturalist versions of Russian nationalism represented most prominently by Alexander Solzhenitsyn.[41]

The rehabilitation of the Russian tsarist state and its incorporation into official Soviet ideology was a gradual process. It began in the 1920s and was accelerated in the 1930s, when Stalin openly condemned the previously orthodox communist line represented by Mikhail Pokrovsky. Pokrovsky's view, which had also been Lenin's, was highly critical of the role of the tsarist state in history, both internally as an oppressor of the working people and externally as the oppressor and conqueror of foreign peoples.[42]

In the Ukraine, an independent Marxist Ukrainian historiography was represented by Matvii Yavorsky, "the Ukrainian Pokrovsky." Other historical schools were also tolerated: the founder of modern Ukrainian historiography and the leader of a Ukrainian anti-Bolshevik government during the revolution, Hrushevsky, was allowed to write and publish as well.

The 1920s were the only period in the history of Ukrainian-Russian relations when Ukrainian history was treated as an autonomous process, developing alongside Russian history, rather than as a provincial or regional variant of the latter. In this regard, the treatment of history corresponded to the formally equal status of the Ukraine and Russia in the Soviet federation as it was understood at that time.[43]

In the early 1930s, the school of Pokrovsky was condemned in

Russia. Even before this, an attack had been launched against the alleg- edly nationalist tendencies of Ukrainian Marxist historians. These developments in ideology were part of a larger transformation of the USSR that is associated with the concept of Stalinism. A new, clearly Russocentrist conception of history was advanced on the direct orders of Stalin, and even though a neutral term, "history of the peoples of the USSR," was used, it became clear that the Russian state and the Russian nation had been restored to pre-eminence. Under this new line, the tsarist state was viewed as a force that protected the non-Russian peoples of the USSR from foreign enemies. Thus, by some strange logic, the Russian conquerors of those non-Russian peoples somehow were no longer "for- eign" masters of the Ukrainians, Tatars, Uzbeks, Estonians, and others.[44]

After the death of Stalin in 1953 there was a toning down of the more extreme expressions of Russian patriotic fervor, but at no time was the basic premise of Stalinist historiography challenged: it was still held that association with Russia, tsarist and communist, has at all times been for the "peoples of the USSR" an absolutely positive experience. Within this broader formula, however, it became possible to revive a genuine study, albeit limited in scope, of Ukrainian history (during the so-called Shelest period).[45]

The political formula of the Shelest regime, it would appear from what is now a historical perspective, was an attempt to legitimate the Soviet regime in the eyes of patriotic Ukrainians by providing them, in return for political loyalty to the Soviet state as a whole (without even questioning the Russian dominance in that state), with genuine conces- sions to Ukrainian cultural individuality, both in the present and in the study of the past. Using concepts suggested by Farmer, I might say that the nationality policies of the Shelest era corresponded to the stand of the "cultural pluralists," who advocated "a demotic, rather than an organic, basis of cohesion: a genuinely multinational and multicultural federation based on *class* unity." Their position was distinct from those of the "assimilationists"—who favor the linguistic and cultural Russification of all non-Russians—or the "nationalists," for whom a separate cultural identity was the justification and also the basis of political independence from the Russians. The relatively liberal policy of the Shelest era (as compared with Stalinism or what came after the fall of Shelest) did not, however, signify a return to the ideas of the 1920s: it continued to endorse the positive role in Ukrainian history of the Russian tsarist state. For this reason it was the subject of denunciations by several prominent Ukrai- nian historians and other intellectuals. Those critics included Ivan Dziuba and Mykhailo Braichevsky in the 1960s and, more recently and most incisively, Yuri Badzio. Their critique of the current status of the Ukraine included a very prominent challenge to the official, statist interpretation of history, which these critics rightly see as incompatible with Marxism and even with Leninism.[46]

The efforts of these critics have been, of course, wholly unsuccessful. On the contrary, with the dismissal of Shelest (May 1972) and his replacement as first secretary of the Communist Party of the Ukraine by V. V. Shcherbitsky, there came a broad purge of the cultural apparatus in the Ukrainian republic. A comprehensive policy of Russification, especially in the educational system and in the media, was launched.[47] Making use of Farmer's terms again, I might say that a major victory was won by the assimilationists, whose goal is the creation of a single, culturally homogeneous—not only politically integrated—Soviet nation. These assimilationists clearly believe that cultural pluralism is in principle dangerous to the political unity of the USSR as a successor of the former tsarist empire.[48]

The concept of the Soviet people as now elucidated has all the marks of a synthetic, artificial device and is treated with the utmost suspicion by the non-Russians. They suspect, with good reason, that behind the talk of a Soviet people as a new international community lies a much less noble design—the desire to transform the peoples of the USSR into a Russian political nation, in other words, to realize a goal that eluded earlier Russian nationalists. This much has been almost literally admitted by the man who is the chief of the Soviet "brain trust" in charge of designing nationality policies—Academician Yuli V. Bromlei. In a recent authoritative statement, Bromlei declared that the "Soviet people" typologically belongs to the class of "historical communities" that includes such entities as the "Indian people" or the "people of Indonesia." Also typologically analogous to the Soviet case, Bromlei thinks, are the communities now being formed in Czechoslovakia and Yugoslavia.[49]

This might seem nothing but the program of Peter Struve—minus the latter's political liberalism. Because of this political factor, however, the Bromlei concept of a Soviet people appears to have been literally stolen from N. V. Ustrialov, the post-1917 National Bolshevik, who as early as the 1920s and 1930s spoke of a "Soviet nation" (sovetskaia natsiia) emerging in the USSR. Ustrialov felt that the rise of such a nation, united in a common state by the Russians and ideologically cemented by Marxism, might be thwarted by the victory of communism in other countries, which, he implied, would weaken the role of the Russians in an expanded communist world.[50]

The idea of a Soviet people reflects the realization on the part of the Soviet ruling elite that Marxism, not only in the USSR but also in all other lands where Marxists have come to power, has failed to transcend the traditional state forms and national identities. What has emerged thus refutes not only the expectations of the Russian Communists in 1917 and immediately thereafter, but also the assumptions of generations of Communists since "The Communist Manifesto" proclaimed the imminent abolition of national conflicts and, indeed, even of national differences.

Clearly, Moscow does not relish the suggestion that the USSR is an updated version of a nineteenth-century empire. The Marxist dream of internationalism having failed, and Moscow having prevented the peoples of the old Romanov empire from establishing their own national states after 1917, the Soviets now face a choice: either they will belatedly grant their non-Russian peoples equality with the Russians (which might lead to secession) or, to resolve the existing tension, they will have to deprive those peoples of their nationhood and thus solve the problem by abolishing its source.

If there is a sense of urgency in current Soviet treatment of the nationalities it may be because what Ustrialov had thought a remote possibility has in the meantime become a reality. The victory of communism in other countries of the world, especially in Eastern Europe and China, has in all cases resulted in the affirmation of old national identities, opening anew the question of why, for the non-Russian peoples of the USSR, communism must be synonymous with their submergence in a Russian political nation. If the Poles can have a country of their own, why not the Lithuanians or Ukrainians? There is evidence that the Soviets seriously fear the spillover effects of East European developments in their own domestic life.[51]

For reasons that by now should be clear, the Ukrainians may be especially susceptible (along with the Lithuanians and Belorussians) to the "Polish infection." Because of this, and because of the linguistic closeness of the Ukrainians and Belorussians to the Russians, these two East Slavic peoples have been selected, it appears, to serve as guinea pigs in the process of accelerated Russification. The tendencies in the reinterpretation of Ukrainian history (as well as those in Belorussian history) are likewise even more extremist than anything said under Stalin. Projecting their goals into the past, official party spokesmen today claim to discover in the early recorded history of the Eastern Slavs and non-Slavic peoples of the USSR the first indications of their alleged unity. Particular care is taken to associate the Ukrainians and Belorussians with the Russians, and some evidence cited in support of these ideas has clear racial undertones.[52]

After a careful review of recent statements of Soviet political and academic figures, Roman Solchanyk has concluded that the current interpretation of Ukrainian history makes one point: "that Ukraine and the Ukrainians emerged on the face of the earth for the sole reason of 'reuniting' with Russia and the Russians. The Ukrainians, as a result, are deprived of a separate and distinct identity either in the past, present, or future." The same scholar sees the Soviets' "quest for unity" as the source of this treatment of the past, and he implies that the Soviets may be trying to prevent in this way any potential impact of Poland on her Ukrainian and Belorussian neighbors.[53]

How likely is Moscow to succeed in its goal of eliminating the Ukrainians (and others) as politically and, in the longer run, culturally meaningful entities? This will depend on several factors. One, perhaps the most important, concerns the character of the Ukrainian response to Moscow's policies. Will the Ukrainians define themselves as a basically linguistic and cultural entity, and will they accordingly fight for their language and thus accept the spread of the Russian language in the Ukraine as tantamount to the liquidation of the Ukraine as such? Or will they treat the language as important, but one of several ingredients of a Ukrainian identity, ingredients that include a political message—striving for freedom—rooted in history?

Second, very much will depend on how the Russians, including those who for one or another reason are termed "nationalists," will react to the imposition from above of a statist form of Russian nationhood. Some Russian liberals and democrats on the one hand, and religious and cultural patriots of Russia on the other, have dissociated themselves from the myth propagated by the regime, which holds that the empire is a vital necessity for the Russian people.[54] Will those anti-imperial Russian patriots manage to win enough support among their fellow Russians to help force the regime to abandon its present policies?

In this connection it may or may not be significant that the prominent Russian philosopher, Alexander Zinoviev, should have expressed himself in a recent interview in favor of the "destruction" of the Soviet empire as a precondition of the liberation of the Russian nation:

> My sole concern is the future of the Russian people . . . I want the Russian people to be educated, cultured, and self-confident so that they can share the treasures of world culture and contribute to them. I want to lift the Russians out of centuries-old backwardness and subjection. It is impossible to attain any of these things within the Soviet empire.[55]

One feels certain that Masaryk would have understood what Zinoviev is trying to say. (So would Tocqueville, according to whom "nothing is more inimical to human prosperity and freedom than great empires.") Zinoviev's interview, however, contains a number of quite bizarre statements as well, and, even more ominously, Zinoviev offers in it a justification of the murderous collectivization of the 1930s with the argument that "Without it our country would have disintegrated."[56] What is this but that ancient idea that a people exists for the state?

Finally, there are the questions of resistance to Soviet endeavors in Central Asia, where a battle over the past has also been waged, and of the possible role of Eastern Europe, especially Poland.[57] Will Poland be able to encourage the resistance in the USSR and perhaps help the forces of reform to design less oppressive policies? At this particular moment of history this is obviously a utopian hope, but a number of important intellectuals in Eastern Europe have in recent years shown that they understand that their own nations may in the longer run be subjected to the same kind of treatment that is the lot of the Ukrainians and Lithuanians today.[58]

NOTES

1. See, for example, Edward Allworth, ed., *Ethnic Russia in the USSR: The Dilemma of Dominance* (New York: Pergamon Press, 1980); Jeremy Azrael, ed., *Soviet Nationality Policies and Practices* (New York: Praeger, 1978); Zev Katz, Rosemarie Rogers, and Frederic Harned, eds., *Handbook of Major Soviet Nationalities* (New York: Free Press; London: Collier-Macmillan, 1975), especially the chapter on "Russia and the Russians," by Dina Rome Spechler; Hélène Carrère d'Encausse, *Decline of an Empire* (New York: Newsweek Books, 1979); and Peter Zwick, *National Communism* (Boulder, Colo.: Westview Press, 1983). Among older works, Frederick C. Barghoorn (*Soviet Russian Nationalism* [New York: Oxford University Press, 1956]) and Elliot R. Goodman (*The Soviet Design for a World State* [New York: Columbia University Press, 1960]) remain especially useful, as do the books of Walter Kolarz (*Russia and Her Colonies* [New York: Praeger, 1952], and *Communism and Colonialism* [New York: St. Martin's Press, 1964]). Kolarz argued that the colonial label was fully applicable to the non-Russian peoples of the USSR.

2. Among these works, the most recent and especially valuable are Roman Solchanyk, "Politics and the National Question in the Post-Shelest Period," Bohdan Nahaylo, "Ukrainian Dissent and Opposition," Myroslav Shkandrij, "Literary Politics," Gennady Ozornoy, "The Ukrainian Economy in the 1970s," and Bohdan Krawchenko, "Ethno-Demographic Trends," in Bohdan Krawchenko, ed., *Ukraine After Shelest* (Edmonton, Alberta: Canadian Institute of Ukrainian Studies, 1983). For the religious situation, see Bohdan R. Bociurkiw, "The Catacomb Church: Ukrainian Greek Catholics in the USSR," *Religion in Communist Lands* 5, no. 1 (1977); Ivan Hvat', "The Ukrainian Catholic Church, the Vatican, and the Soviet Union During the Pontificate of Pope John Paul II," ibid. 11, no. 3 (1983); and Frank E. Sysyn, "The Ukrainian Orthodox Question in the USSR," ibid. 11, no. 3. Works that retain topical importance are Peter J. Potichnyj, ed., *Ukraine in the Seventies* (Oakville, Ontario: Mosaic Press, 1977); and I. S. Koropeckyj, ed., *The Ukraine Within the*

USSR: An Economic Balance Sheet (New York and London: Praeger, 1977). Roman Szporluk ("The Ukraine and the Ukrainians," in Katz et al., *Handbook of Major Soviet Nationalities*, pp. 21–48) presents the social, economic, and cultural data for the early 1970s. The special place of the Ukraine (and Belorussia) in Soviet politics was already noted in the 1960s by John A. Armstrong, "The Ethnic Scene," in Erich Goldhagen, ed., *Ethnic Minorities in the Soviet Union* (New York: Praeger, 1968), pp. 3–49. The same question in the 1980s is discussed by Roman Solchanyk, "Molding 'the Soviet people': The role of Ukraine and Belorussia," *Journal of Ukrainian Studies* 8, no. 1 (Summer 1983): 3–18.

3. Jaroslav Krejčí and Vitězslav Velímský, *Ethnic and Political Nations in Europe* (New York: St. Martin's Press, 1981), pp. 112–13.

4. Krejčí and Velímský, *Ethnic and Political Nations*, p. 114.

5. Zbigniew Brzezinski, "Tragic Dilemmas of Soviet World Power: The Limits of a New-Type Empire," *Encounter* 61, no. 4 (December 1983): 10. Brzezinski's argument concerning the prospects of Soviet-American relations and Soviet attitudes toward the problem of stability in international relations is based on the premise that the USSR is a Russian-dominated colonial-type empire. The same premise is used by Colin S. Gray, "The Most Dangerous Decade: Historic Mission, Legitimacy, and Dynamics of the Soviet Empire in the 1980s," *Orbis* (Spring 1981): 13–28; and Rebecca V. Strode and Colin S. Gray, "The Imperial Dimension of Soviet Military Power," *Problems of Communism* 30, no. 6 (November–December 1981): 1–15.

6. I have discussed this problem, with reference to the Pokshishevsky and Armstrong theses, in my "Russians in Ukraine and Problems of Ukrainian Identity in the USSR," in Potichnyj, *Ukraine in the Seventies*, pp. 195–217, and in "West Ukraine and West Belorussia: Historical Tradition, Social Communication, and Linguistic Assimilation," *Soviet Studies* 31, no. 1 (January 1979): 76–98.

7. John A. Armstrong, "The Ethnic Scene in the Soviet Union," in Goldhagen, *Ethnic Minorities*, p. 32. See also Szporluk, "West Ukraine and West Belorussia," p. 94. Although the Belorussians are in many ways very much like the Ukrainians, their case is sufficiently important to merit a separate discussion, which cannot be offered here. A brief note on the literature will have to do as a substitute: Jan Zaprudnik, "Belorussia and the Belorussians," in Katz et al., *Handbook of Major Soviet Nationalities*, pp. 49–71; Ivan S. Lubachko, *Belorussia Under Soviet Rule, 1917–1957* (Lexington: University of Kentucky Press, 1972); Steven L. Guthier, "The Belorussians: National Identification and Assimilation, 1897–1970," *Soviet Studies* 29, no. 1 (January 1977): 37–61, no. 2 (April 1977): 270–83; Nicholas P. Vakar, "The Belorussian People Between Nationhood and Extinction," in Goldhagen, *Ethnic Minorities*, pp. 218–28; Stephan M. Horak, "Belorussia: Modernization, Human Rights, Nationalism," in Ihor Kamenetsky, ed., *Nationalism and Human Rights: Processes of Modernization in the USSR* (Littleton, Colo.: Libraries Unlimited, 1977), pp. 139–54; and the contributions by Vitaut Kipel and Jan Zaprudnik in George W. Simmonds, ed., *Nationalism in the USSR in the Era of Brezhnev and Kosygin* (Detroit, Mich.: University of Detroit Press, 1977), pp. 96–104 and 105–14.

8. See Walker Connor, "Nation-Building or Nation-Destroying," *World Politics* 24, no. 3 (April 1972): 338.

9. Karl W. Deutsch, *The Nerves of Government* (New York: Free Press; London: Collier-Macmillan, 1966), pp. 206–7. Alexander Solzhenitsyn expressed the same idea in the language of art when he characterized literature as "the living memory of a nation." The suppression of a nation's literature, said Solzhenitsyn, signifies "the sealing up of a nation's heart, the excision of its memory. A nation can no longer remember itself, it loses its spiritual unity, and despite their seemingly common language, countrymen cease to understand one another" (Alexander Solzhenitsyn, *The Nobel Lecture,* trans. Alexis Klimoff [New York: Ad Hoc Committee for Intellectual Freedom, 1973], pp. 14–15).

10. Milan Kundera, *The Book of Laughter and Forgetting* (New York: Knopf, 1981), pp. 159, 3.

11. A. I. Savenko, *Kievlianin,* November 17, 1911, as quoted in Jurij Borys, *The Sovietization of Ukraine, 1917–1923,* 2nd ed. (Edmonton, Alberta: Canadian Institute of Ukrainian Studies, 1980), p. 383.

12. Peter Struve, "Obshcherusskaia kultura i ukrainskii partikularizm: Otvet Ukraintsu," *Russkaia mysl',* no. 1, pt. 2 (1912), p. 85, quoted in Richard Pipes, *Struve: Liberal on the Left, 1870–1905* (Cambridge, Mass.: Harvard University Press, 1970), pp. 211–12. See also Pipes, *Struve: Liberal on the Right, 1905–1944* (Cambridge, Mass.: Harvard University Press, 1980).

13. Karl Marx and Friedrich Engels, *Ireland and the Irish Question* (New York: International Publishers, 1972), p. 303, as quoted in Andrzej Walicki, *Philosophy and Romantic Nationalism: The Case of Poland* (Oxford: Oxford University Press, 1982), p. 375.

14. See Myroslav Yurkevich, "A Forerunner of National Communism: Lev Iurkevych (1885–1918)," *Journal of Ukrainian Studies* 7, no. 1 (1982): 50–56; Lev Iurkevych [L. Rybalka], "The Russian Social Democrats and the National Question," ibid., pp. 57–78; and Charles Halary, "Lutte nationale et cadre étatique," in Jacques Dofny and Akinsola Akiwowo, eds., *National and Ethnic Movements* (Los Angeles: Sage, 1980), p. 72.

15. Kazimierz Kelles-Krauz to Foreign Committee of the Polish Socialist Party, London, March 14, 1901, as quoted by Jerzy Targalski in his review of Walentyna Najdus's *SDKP i L a SDPRR, 1893–1907* in *Przegląd Historyczny* 65, no. 3 (1974): 574.

16. Richard Pipes, "Introduction: The Nationality Problem," in Katz et al., *Handbook of Major Soviet Nationalities,* p. 1.

17. Ibid., p. 2. The leading Marxist historian of Russia, M. N. Pokrovskii (1868–1932), observed that Russia had been a multinational state for much longer than is commonly thought: some Finnic tribes, for example, the Karelians of Tver, had been conquered in pre-Muscovite times. See M. N. Pokrovskii, "The Prison of Nations," in Roman Szporluk, ed., *Russia in World History* (Ann Arbor: University of Michigan Press, 1970), p. 109. For a broader view of Russian imperial treatment of nationalities, see Marc Raeff, "Patterns of Imperial Policy Toward the Nationalities," in Edward Allworth, ed., *Soviet Nationality Problems* (New York: Columbia University Press, 1971), pp. 22–42; and Andreas Kappeler, "Historische Voraussetzungen des Nationalitätenproblems im russischen Vielvölkerreich," *Geschichte und*

Gesellschaft 8, no. 2 (1982): 159–83. Also see Michael Cherniavsky, "Russia," in Orest Ranum, ed. *National Consciousness, History, and Political Culture in Early-Modern Europe* (Baltimore, Md. and London: Johns Hopkins University Press, 1975), pp. 118–43; and Walter M. Pintner, "Russia," in Raymond Grew, ed., *Crises of Political Development in Europe and the United States* (Princeton, N. J.: Princeton University Press, 1978), pp. 347–82.

18. Richard Pipes, *Russia Under the Old Regime* (New York: Scribners, 1974), p. 65.

19. Paul Vinogradoff, *Roman Law in Medieval Europe* (Oxford, 1929), p. 62, as quoted in ibid., p. 65.

20. Pipes, *Russia Under the Old Regime,* pp. 64–65.

21. Ibid., p. 70. Cf. Marc Raeff, *Understanding Imperial Russia: State and Society in the Old Regime,* trans. Arthur Goldhammer (New York: Columbia University Press, 1984).

22. Nicholas V. Riasanovsky, *Nicholas I and Official Nationality in Russia, 1825– 1855* (Berkeley and Los Angeles: University of California Press, 1967), is essential reading for anyone who wants to rise above the simplistic "Westernizer-Slavophile" concept of modern Russia.

23. For an account of Russian-Ukrainian debates with reference to language and literature as well as history, see George S. N. Luckyj, *Between Gogol and Shevchenko: Polarity in the Literary Ukraine, 1798–1847* (Munich: Fink, 1972). Much important material is to be found in Ladis K. D. Kristof, "The Russian Image of Russia: An Applied Study in Geopolitical Methodology," in C. A. Fisher, ed., *Essays in Political Geography* (London: Methuen, 1968), pp. 345–87. On Pereiaslav, see John Basarab, *Pereiaslav 1654: A Historiographical Study* (Edmonton, Alberta: Canadian Institute of Ukrainian Studies, 1982), a review of successive interpretations of that momentous event in the history of Eastern Europe.

24. There is no systematic study of Russian perceptions of the Polish problem after the partitions, but interesting material on aspects of the Russian-Polish conflict may be found in Julia Brun-Zejmis, "'The Russian Idea' and 'The Polish Question': Some Russian Views on the Polish Insurrection of 1830," *East European Quarterly* 14, no. 3 (Fall 1980): 315–26; J. L. Black, "Nicholas Karamzin's 'Opinion' on Poland: 1819," *International History Review* 3, no. 1 (January 1981): 1–19; David B. Saunders, "Historians and Concepts of Nationality in Early Nineteenth Century Russia," *Slavonic and East European Review* 60, no. 1 (January 1982): 44–62; Frank Mocha, "The Karamzin-Lelewel Controversy," *Slavic Review* 31, no. 3 (September 1972): 592–610; and Dietrich Geyer, "Funktionen der russischen Nationalismus, 1860– 1885," in Heinrich August Winkler, ed., *Nationalismus* (Königstein: Verlagsgruppe Athenäum, Hain, Scriptor, Hanstein, 1978), 173–186.

25. For Polish reflections and debates about the meaning of Polish nationhood after the loss of a state, see the magisterial work of Andrzej Walicki, *Philosophy and Romantic Nationalism.* Walicki cites the case of Piotr Semenenko, "a polonized Ruthenian" (i.e., a Ukrainian or Belorussian), who proposed, in an article published in 1834, to make "Ruthenian" the official language of the future independent Poland in

view of the fact that the majority of the common people spoke that language. Walicki thinks this was rather an exceptional stand but he stresses that in Poland "almost nobody advocated a programmatic linguistic assimilation of the Ukrainian, Belorussian, Lithuanian, Latvian, and German inhabitants of the former Commonwealth" (Walicki, *Philosophy and Romantic Nationalism*, p. 70).

26. Dmytro Doroshenko, "A Survey of Ukrainian Historiography," special issue of *The Annals of the Ukrainian Academy of Arts and Sciences in the U.S.* 5–6 (1957): 9–304. See also Mykhailo Hrushevsky, "The Traditional Scheme of 'Russian' History and the Problem of a Rational Organization of the History of Eastern Slavs," ibid., 2, no. 4 (1952): 335–64 (reprinted in Andrew Gregorovich, ed., *Michael Hrushevsky* [Winnipeg, Manitoba: Ukrainian Free Academy of Sciences, 1965]); Lubomyr R. Wynar, "Ukrainian-Russian Confrontation in Historiography: Michael Hrushevsky versus the Traditional Scheme of 'Russian' History," *Ukrainian Quarterly* 30, no. 1 (Spring 1974): 13–25; and Stephan M. Horak, "Periodization and Terminology of the History of Eastern Slavs: Observations and Analyses," *Slavic Review* 31, no. 4 (December 1972): 853–62. For an outline of main themes of Ukrainian history as interpreted by Ukrainian historians today, see Omeljan Pritsak and John S. Reshetar, "The Ukraine and the Dialectics of Nation-Building," in Donald W. Treadgold, ed., *The Development of the USSR: An Exchange of Views* (Seattle and London: University of Washington Press, 1964), pp. 236–37.

27. For a concise outline of the history of the Orthodox and Catholic religions in the Ukraine up to 1917, see Volodymyr Kubijovyc, ed., *Ukraine: A Concise Encyclopaedia* (Toronto: University of Toronto Press, 1971), 2: 132–67. I am grateful to Professor Bohdan R. Bociurkiw for his comments on the religious question in the sixteenth–eighteenth century Ukraine in an earlier version of this essay. In a letter of July 13, 1984, he also wrote: "The Russian Church's continuing fanatical hostility to both the Uniate [Catholic] Church and, in modern times, the Ukrainian Autocephalous [Orthodox] Church attests to its concern about religious and political unity of the 'Russian' people (i.e., the Great, Little, and White Russians, whichever terminology one uses). This kind of 'historical community' (excluding the 'Western' Balts and the 'Asiatics') is really the model for the 'one Soviet people' and the institutional 'proof' of a continuous 'Russian' common identity." It appears that the Soviet regime shares official Orthodoxy's hostility toward Catholicism. As a Polish historian recently noted, the latest edition of an old Russian Marxist classic on the history of the church in Russia omits those parts of the previous (1931) edition that depict the coerced conversion of Uniate Catholics to Russian Orthodoxy under the tsars. See K. S. [Kazimierz Stembrowicz], review of N. M. Nikolskii, *Istoriia russkoi tserkvi* (Moscow: Politizdat, 1983), in *Przegląd Historyczny* [Warsaw] 75, no. 2 (1984): 355.

28. Mykhailo Drahomanov, *Vybrani tvory* (Prague, 1937) 1: 70; and Viacheslav Lypynskyi, *Lysty do brativ-khliborobiv* (Vienna, 1926), p. xxv, as quoted by Ivan L. Rudnytsky, "The Role of the Ukraine in Modern History," in Treadgold, *The Development of the USSR*, p. 219.

29. Mykola Kostomarov, "Dve russkiie narodnosti," *Osnova*, no. 3 (1861), quoted in Dmytro Doroshenko, "A Survey of Ukrainian Historiography," p. 137. Doroshenko's reference to "the gospel" is on p. 139.

30. Doroshenko, "A Survey of Ukrainian Historiography," pp. 138–39.

31. Ibid., p. 139.

32. See John S. Reshetar, Jr., *The Ukrainian Revolution, 1917–1920: A Study in Nationalism* (Princeton, N.J.: Princeton University Press, 1952); Taras Hunczak, ed., *Ukraine 1917–1920: A Study in Revolution* (Cambridge, Mass.: Harvard Ukrainian Research Institute, 1977); Ivan L. Rudnytsky, "The Role of the Ukraine in Modern History," in Donald W. Treadgold, ed., *The Development of the USSR*, pp. 211–28; Stephen L. Guthier, "The Popular Base of Ukrainian Nationalism in 1917," *Slavic Review* 30, no. 1 (March 1979): 30–47; and Geoff Eley, "Remapping the Nation: War, Revolutionary Upheaval, and State Formation in Eastern Europe, 1914–1923" (Paper presented at the MacMaster Conference on Jewish-Ukrainian Relations in Historical Perspective, Hamilton, Ontario, October 1983), in a volume edited by Howard Aster and Peter J. Potichnyj (Edmonton, Alberta and Toronto: Canadian Institute of Ukrainian Studies, forthcoming).

33. Ivan L. Rudnytsky, "Polish-Ukrainian Relations: The Burden of History," in Peter J. Potichnyj, ed., *Poland and Ukraine: Past and Present* (Edmonton, Alberta and Toronto: Canadian Institute of Ukrainian Studies, 1980), p. 25. The dean of contemporary Polish historians, Stefan Kieniewicz, describes the Polish-Ukrainian conflict in Galicia as "the most tragic, in its long-term consequences." See Stefan Kieniewicz, *Historyk a świadomość narodowa* (Warsaw: Czytelnik, 1982), p. 279. Andrei S. Markovits and Frank E. Sysyn, eds., *Nationbuilding and the Politics of Nationalism: Essays on Austrian Galicia* (Cambridge, Mass.: Ukrainian Research Institute; distributed by Harvard University Press, 1982), contains essays on the Ukrainians along with those on the Poles and the Jews of Galicia before 1918. See also Paul Robert Magocsi, *Galicia: A Historical Survey and Bibliographic Guide* (Toronto: Toronto University Press, 1983); John-Paul Himka, *Socialism in Galicia: The Emergence of Polish Social Democracy and Ukrainian Radicalism (1860–1890)* (Cambridge, Mass.: Ukrainian Research Institute; distributed by Harvard University Press, 1983), and "Young Radicals and Independent Statehood: The Idea of a Ukrainian Nation-State, 1890–1895," *Slavic Review* 41, no. 2 (Summer 1982): 219–35; and Wolfdieter Bihl, "Die Ruthenen," in Adam Wandruszka and Peter Urbanitsch, eds., *Die Habsburgermonarchie, 1848–1918* (Vienna: Österreichische Akademie der Wissenschaften, 1980), 3: 555–84. All these works remind us that the modern history of the Ukrainian people cannot be fully subsumed under the heading of "the peoples of Russia/USSR": the Ukrainians, or their western branch, to be precise, were also one of the "peoples of the Habsburg monarchy," and, later, they lived for another twenty years in interwar East Central Europe.

34. Thomas G. Masaryk, *The New Europe: The Slav Standpoint*, ed. W. Preston-Warren and William B. Weist (Lewisburg, Pa.: Bucknell University Press, 1972), pp. 119–20. Masaryk further developed this thought: "Political independence does not depend on language alone, as the independent German States best prove. What applies to the West can be applied to the East. Of course, Western history shows that the individuality of dialect became subordinate to the cultural advantages derived from the union with the larger and more cultured nations; in France, for instance, Provencal differs from literary French more than the Ukrainian differs from the Russian. Even

the German Plattdeutsch and other dialects show a greater difference from the literary language than there exists between the Ukrainian and Russian. It is true, of course, that the French and German literature and culture are richer than the Russian, and France and Germany have not proceeded against their dialectic individualities so foolishly as the Russian Tsarism" (ibid., p. 120). Masaryk thus appears to have believed that under Russian conditions, unlike in the West, *cultural* differences—such as the Ukrainian "dialect"—could become politicized precisely because of the *political* oppressiveness of the tsarist system.

35. Ibid., pp. 118, 123. (The words in square brackets are taken from the preceding sentence in the same paragraph.) One might see confirmation of the Masaryk diagnosis in the weakness of the liberal, Westernizer version of Russian nationalism in the civil war. See William G. Rosenberg, *Liberals in the Russian Revolution: The Constitutional Democratic Party, 1917–1921* (Princeton, N.J.: Princeton University Press, 1974); and Richard Pipes, *Struve: Liberal on the Right, 1905–1944*. When the victor in the civil war, the Bolsheviks, eventually adopted a Russian nationalist stand, it was close to the "Official Nationality" version of Russian nationalism, not to that of Struve or Miliukov. Galia Golan ("Elements of Russian Traditions in Soviet Socialism," in S. N. Eisenstadt and Yael Azmon, eds., *Socialism and Tradition* [Atlantic Highlands, N.J.: Humanities Press, 1975], p. 21) comments: "Having chosen the 'etatist' political interpretation of socialism, the Bolsheviks eventually introduced an entire system of institutions connected with autocratic rule and many elements of the Russian state which they were in effect perpetuating. The actual institutions of rule in the Soviet state greatly resemble those of Czarist Russia."

36. See Richard Pipes, *The Formation of the Soviet Union*, rev. ed. (New York: Atheneum, 1968), pp. 270–74. Pipes provides a summary of the Lenin-Stalin exchange of views (which was not made public until 1956).

37. Benedict Anderson, *Imagined Communities: Reflections on the Origin and Spread of Nationalism* (London: Verso Editions and NLB, 1983), p. 12. Anderson quotes approvingly the comment of the British Marxist historian, Eric Hobsbawm, who wrote: "Marxist movements and states have tended to become national not only in form but in substance, i.e., nationalist. There is nothing to suggest that this trend will not continue" (Eric Hobsbawm, "Some Reflections on 'The Break-up of Britain,'" *New Left Review*, no. 105 [September–October 1977], p. 13).

38. Krejčí and Velímský, *Ethnic and Political Nations*, pp. 114–15.

39. Ibid., p. 115.

40. A number of scholars find it very difficult to accept that the ideology of the Soviet regime merits designation as "Russian nationalist." For example, Kenneth C. Farmer (*Ukrainian Nationalism in the Post-Stalin Era: Myth, Symbols, and Ideology in Soviet Nationalities Policy* [The Hague: Martinus Nijhoff, 1980], p. 45) writes: "We should clarify that the myth of Russian primacy is distinct from Russian *nationalism*—both the neo-Slavophilism of Solzhenitsyn and the integral nationalism of *Veche* and *Slovo natsii*. It is clear that a myth of national identity based on blood is incongruous with the merger of nations through intermarriage, migration and assimilation, which is the goal of Soviet nationalities policy, and an integral part of the myth of proletarian

internationalism." Farmer believes that the principal Soviet political myth is the myth of proletarian internationalism, of which the "myth of Russian supremacy" is a *subcategory*: "the myth of Russian patrimony of the former Tsarist empire,—the myth that because Russians have taken responsibility for the Soviet Union, Russians have the first prerogative of rule, and that the international culture that will emerge with the building of communism will in fact be Russian culture" (ibid., p. 30).

41. For an attempt to develop the distinction between culturalist and statist versions of Russian nationalism today, see Roman Szporluk, "History and Russian Nationalism," *Survey* 24, no.3 (1979): 1–17. That article contains numerous references to relevant literature.

42. For a sampling of Pokrovsky's views on these matters see his *Russia in World History*.

43. The most recent and comprehensive account of post-1917 intellectual developments and their political importance in the Ukraine, containing a full bibliography of relevant earlier studies, is in James E. Mace, *Communism and the Dilemmas of National Liberation: National Communism in Soviet Ukraine, 1918–1933* (Cambridge, Mass.: Harvard Ukrainian Research Institute and the Ukrainian Academy of Arts and Sciences in the U.S.; distributed by Harvard University Press, 1983).

44. The standard work on this subject is Lowell Tillett, *The Great Friendship: Soviet Historians on the Non-Russian Nationalities* (Chapel Hill: University of North Carolina Press, 1969). For the historiography of the Stalin era, also see Olexander Ohloblyn, "Ukrainian Historiography, 1917–1957," *Annals of the Ukrainian Academy of Arts and Sciences in the U.S.* 5–6 (1957): 307–456.

45. Jaroslaw Pelenski, "Shelest and His Period in Soviet Ukraine: A Revival of Controlled Ukrainian Autonomism," in Potichnyj, *Ukraine in the Seventies*, pp. 283–305.

46. Farmer, *Ukrainian Nationalism*, p. 77. Farmer discusses representative statements of Ukrainian dissent in matters of historiography, some of which are also available in English translation. See Ivan Dzyuba, *Internationalism or Russification?* (London: Weidenfeld and Nicolson, 1968); Mykhailo I. Braichevskyi, *Annexation or Russification* (Munich: Ukrainisches Institut für Bildungspolitik, 1974); issue 6 of *The Ukrainian Herald: Dissent in Ukraine*, introd. Yaroslav Bilinsky (Baltimore, Md.: Smoloskyp, 1977); and issues 7–8 of *Ethnocide of Ukrainians in the USSR*, introd. Robert Conquest (Baltimore, Md.: Smoloskyp, 1976). The more recent work of Iurii Badzio, "An Open Letter to the Presidium of the Supreme Soviet of the USSR and the Central Committee of the CPSU," was published in English in *Journal of Ukrainian Studies* 9, no. 1 (Summer 1984): 74–94. Badzio argues that the present treatment of the history of the Ukrainian and Belorussian nations is identical with that of the most extreme tsarist ideologues of the prerevolutionary period. Badzio also criticizes Lenin from a position close to that of Engels. (See n. 13 above.)

47. For an analysis of the political situation after 1972, see Roman Solchanyk, "Politics in Ukraine in the Post-Shelest Period," in Krawchenko, *Ukraine After Shelest*. See also Kay Oliver, "Ukrainian Nationalism in the 1970s" (Ph.D. diss., Indiana University, 1981). Since the mid-1970s, the Soviet government appears to

have been pursuing a policy of restricting the circulation of newspapers and magazines in the non-Russian languages of the USSR and simultaneously strongly promoting the expansion of Russian-language media. See Roman Szporluk, "Recent Trends in Soviet Policy Toward Printed Media in the non-Russian Languages," *Radio Liberty Research Bulletin*, Supplement 2/84, November 7, 1984.

48. Farmer, *Ukrainian Nationalism*, pp. 76–77.

49. Iu. V. Bromlei, "XXVI s'ezd KPSS i zadachi izucheniia sovremennykh natsional'nykh protsessov," in *Razvitie natsional'nykh otnoshenii v SSSR v svete reshenii XXVI s'ezda KPSS* (Moscow: Nauka, 1982), p. 25; and Yaroslav Bilinsky, "The Concept of the Soviet People and Its Implications for Soviet Nationality Policy," *The Annals of the Ukrainian Academy of Arts and Sciences in the United States* 14 (1978–1980): 87–133. Bilinsky gives a broad survey of Soviet literature dealing with the problem and provides quotations from representative Soviet statements.

50. The classical statement of this idea is in Ustrialov's article, "O sovetskoi natsii," *Nashe vremiia* (Shanghai, 1934), pp. 38–39. For Ustrialov, see Mikhail Agursky, *The Ideology of National Bolshevism* (Boulder, Colo.: Westview Press, forthcoming); (Russian edition, 1980).

51. See Roman Solchanyk, "Poland and the Soviet West," in S. Enders Wimbush, ed., *Soviet Nationalities in Strategic Perspective* (London: Croom Helm, 1985), pp. 47–69.

52. R. A. Starovoitova, *Etnicheskaia genogeografiia Ukrainskoi SSR* (Kiev, 1979), as cited in Solchanyk, "Molding 'The Soviet People,'" p. 16. See also Roman Solchanyk, "Merger of Nations: Back in Style" and "Literature, History, and Nationalities Policy in the Ukraine," Radio Liberty Research, nos. 84/83 and 318/82; and Yaroslav Bilinsky, "Shcherbytskyi, Ukraine, and Kremlin Politics," *Problems of Communism* 32, no. 4 (July–August 1983): 1–20.

53. Solchanyk, "Molding 'The Soviet People,'" pp. 13, 6–10, 3–4.

54. John B. Dunlop (*The Faces of Contemporary Russian Nationalism* [Princeton, N.J.: Princeton University Press, 1983]) deals with the diverse "non-statist" currents of Russian opinion.

55. George Urban, "Portrait of a Dissenter as a Soviet Man: A Conversation with Alexander Zinoviev," *Encounter* 62, no. 4 (April 1984): p. 23.

56. Ibid., p. 20.

57. Daniel C. Matuszewski, "The Turkic Past in the Soviet Future," *Problems of Communism* 31, no. 4 (July–August 1982): 76–82.

58. For references to certain Polish and Czech statements along these lines, see Roman Szporluk, "Defining 'Central Europe': Power, Politics, and Culture," *Cross Currents: A Yearbook of Central European Culture, 1982* (Ann Arbor: University of Michigan Department of Slavic Languages and Literatures, 1982), pp. 30–38. Russian-Polish relations and the question of continuity between tsarist and Soviet attitudes toward Poland is a subject to which recent Polish writers devote considerable attention. See, for example, Kazimierz Brandys, *A Warsaw Diary, 1978–1981*, trans. Richard Lourie (New York: Random House, 1983), esp. pp. 173–80; and Tadeusz

Konwicki, *Wschody i zachody księżyca* (London: Index on Censorship, 1982), *passim.* (The Konwicki book appeared originally as no. 21 of the Warsaw underground journal, *Zapis.*) Earlier comments of Czesław Miłosz on the same subject may be found in his *Native Realm: A Search for Self-Definition*, trans. Catherine S. Leach (Garden City, N.Y.: Doubleday, 1968). The Czech writer most preoccupied with the same question is Milan Kundera, "The Tragedy of Central Europe," *The New York Review of Books*, April 26, 1984, pp. 33–38.

The Baltic States

Alexander Shtromas

RESISTANCE AND SUPPORT, 1940–1941 AND 1944–1952

The influence and popularity of communism in the independent Baltic states was always minimal by any standards. Indeed, it was rather difficult for communist doctrine to take any deeper root in the still predominantly agricultural and patriarchal Baltic societies. It was even more difficult for the Baltic Communist parties, which openly advocated their countries' Sovietization and eventual incorporation into the USSR, to gain any large following in nations that had only recently, through battle and sacrifice, freed themselves from the Russian colonial yoke. Estonia, Latvia, and Lithuania were immensely proud of their newly acquired national statehood.

This was especially true for the pre-1933 period, when the Communist parties of the Baltic states were purely sectarian bodies consisting of a few dozen committed "professional revolutionaries" linked solely to the Comintern in Moscow. Only Hitler's rise to power in Germany in 1933, amplified by the establishment of right-wing authoritarian-nationalist regimes in the Baltic states themselves, turned some marginal elements of

Some of the basic research for this chapter was done when the author held visiting appointments in the Russian and East-European Center of the University of Illinois at Urbana-Champaign (1982) and at the Hoover Institution (1983–84). For the generous support of both these distinguished centers of learning the author wishes to express his profound gratitude.

the Baltic societies to cooperation with the Communist parties—thus providing them with a certain, though very narrow, base in the indigenous Baltic populations.[1]

After 1933 a few of the so-called progressive intellectuals, faced with the rising Nazi threat, began to consider the possibility of the incorporation of their countries into the "socialist and internationalist" Soviet Union as a preferable, even desirable, alternative to absorption by Hitler's Third Reich; hence, they started to forge links with the Communists and to give the Communist parties their support. A few such intellectuals, because of their now sharpened commitment to the defense of "progress and justice" against the fascist threat, even joined the party. Mečys Gedvilas, a prominent Lithuanian public figure with impeccable liberal credentials who secretly joined the clandestine Lithuanian Communist Party (LCP) in 1933 and later, in August 1940, became the first chairman of the Lithuanian Soviet government, is one such case in point. Some justified their support for the party on purely nationalistic grounds. For example, another very prominent Lithuanian liberal intellectual, Professor Petras Leonas, when asked by a friend (in 1938) why he supported the Communists, answered: "Lithuania is on a crossroad between falling under a long-term German or Russian occupation. The Germans with their characteristic pedantry will liquidate our nation in about 25 years. Russia is a chaotic, anarchic and badly organized country; being occupied by her we have a better chance to survive longer. That is why from these two evils I prefer to choose the Russians."[2]

The policy of the united front against fascism, which the Communists actively embraced after the Seventh Congress of the Comintern in 1935, was congenial to such attitudes and found a favorable response not only among individual (the so-called nonparty-type) intellectuals but also among certain segments of the traditional liberal and socialist parties of the Baltic states. Some of the members of these parties, frustrated by the reluctance of their leaders to accept a united front with the Communists as official party policy, even tried to break away and join the Communist Party directly; in most cases, however, they were advised to stay on and to work for the communist cause from within their own parties. Justas Paleckis, one of the leading figures of the liberal Populist Party (Liaudininkai), who in 1940 became the acting president of "people's" Lithuania and later served for many years as the chairman of the Presidium of the Supreme Soviet of the Lithuanian SSR, recollected in his memoirs how he joined the Communist Party in August 1940: "A few years before 1940 I raised the issue of joining the party. But Meškauskienė [one of the leading Communists of independent Lithuania] . . . replied . . . that I am more useful to the party remaining outside its ranks."[3] There were quite a few communist sympathizers and crypto-Communists like Paleckis among Baltic liberal intellectuals and politicians, which explains how it was possible to form communist governments in the Baltic states without many (and in the case of Estonia, any) members of the Communist party participating in them.

This trend was not limited to liberals and socialists alone. A few right-wing politicians, having been driven from active participation in public life by the autocratic regimes of the Baltic states during 1934–1936, tried to retaliate and to regain a share of power by closing ranks with the Communists and wholeheartedly supporting their subversive activities against the state. In this category were such people as the prominent Lithuanian nationalist poet, Liudas Gira, who was the founding organizer of the Lithuanian countercommunist secret police and, until his removal in 1935, a leading figure of the official establishment. Another was the Lithuanian lawyer and historian, Povilas Pakarklis, one of the most ardent members of the openly fascist and pro-Nazi faction within the ruling Nationalist Party led by the former prime minister of Lithuania, Augustinas Voldemaras.[4]

Of course, there were also direct Soviet agents, both active ones and "sleepers," in all sectors of the Baltic political establishment, even the most right-wing ones. (The Soviet intelligence services even in the 1920s, especially after the failure of the revolution in Germany that they planned in 1923, had acquired the habit of infiltrating these establishments, as the cases of Kim Philby, Richard Sorge, and many others show. The Baltic states were, of course, no exception to this rule.) These Soviet agents played a role in the process of enhancing communist influence in the Baltic societies during this period.

Members of some Baltic minorities, especially the Jews and, to a lesser extent, the Russians, always formed a substantial part of the Baltic Communist parties.[5] Of course, only tiny minorities of these minorities—hundreds rather than thousands—were associated with the Communists, but within the minuscule Baltic communist movements their participation was at any rate disproportionately high.[6] In the mid-1930s, the rising threat of Hitler's Germany and the stronger emphasis placed on ethnic nationalism by the authoritarian-nationalist regimes of the Baltic states naturally drove some members of these national minorities (especially the Jews) to lend support to the Communist parties and, to some extent, contributed to the swelling of the communist ranks.

The fact that during the mid- and late-1930s the Communists managed to acquire at least some social backing in the Baltic countries did not change their influence in any dramatic terms. Suffice it to say that, according to official Soviet data, by the time of the Soviet occupation in

June 1940 the strength of the Baltic Communist parties was: in Lithuania, 1,500 members; in Latvia, less than 1,000 members; and in Estonia, only 130 members.[7] There were at that time not very many active communist supporters and associates outside the ranks of the parties' membership— a few more hundreds or thousands at the most.[8]

The Soviets knew only too well how insignificant and marginal their support in the Baltic countries was and how strongly the nations of these countries were committed to resisting any potential occupying force. Therefore they planned well in advance a series of repressive measures aimed at breaking any actual or potential resistance to Soviet rule in the area. To this effect Order No. 001223 of the NKVD (the People's Commissariat of Internal Affairs) of the USSR, "On the Operative Accounting of the Anti-Soviet and Socially Alien Elements," was issued as early as October 11, 1939, that is, the day after the conclusion of the Pact of Mutual Assistance between the USSR and Lithuania (the last such pact in the series of three) and more than eight months before the Baltic states were in any real terms taken over by the Soviet Union.[9] The only purpose such an order could have had was preparation for purging the Baltic states from all those who had the potential for organizing and carrying out resistance to Soviet rule.

This indeed proved to be the case. Deportations from the Baltic states were ordered by the USSR's People's Commissar of State Security, Merkulov, on May 19, 1941,[10] and the notorious, strictly secret, and extremely detailed "Instructions Regarding the Manner of Conducting the Deportation of the Anti-Soviet Elements from Lithuania, Latvia, and Estonia" were issued by Merkulov's deputy, Serov, sometime between February and June 7, 1941.[11] The ordered deportations started in all three republics simultaneously, on the night of June 13–14, 1941. During the one week that was left before the outbreak of the war (June 22, 1941), 34,260 persons were deported from Lithuania, 15,081 from Latvia, and 10,205 from Estonia.[12] This massive purge marked the peak of the constant wave of repression that, albeit on a much smaller scale, had taken place in the Baltic states throughout the entire period of Soviet rule in 1940–1941. These repressions were directed against political, public, and religious figures of the independence period and, more selectively, against people suspected of resistance or oppositional activities, making anti-Soviet pronouncements, or simply refusing to cooperate with the Soviet regime. It is estimated that Soviet repression and evacuations to the USSR in 1940–1941 cost Lithuania 39,000, Latvia 35,000, and Estonia (where Soviet forces stayed the longest and some conscription into the Red Army was effected) 61,000 citizens.[13] (These numbers do not include many thousands of people imprisoned by the Soviet authorities but neither killed nor deported before the Soviets retreated from the territories of the Baltic states.)

It is interesting, though, to note that these ferocious repressions totally failed to achieve their goal. If anything, they were counterproductive. These measures demonstrated the brutality and deviousness of the Soviet regime to many unsuspecting and, in the beginning phase of Soviet rule, entirely neutral people. In so doing, the repression contributed to the growth of resistance in terms of both the numbers of resisters and the determination to resist. The very massive and indiscriminate character of Soviet repression caused it to harm many innocent people, but it failed, in fact, to destroy the bulk of the organized resistance forces, whose preparations for an armed insurrection continued unabated. Indeed, the day after the German attack on the USSR an armed insurrection of the Baltic peoples against Soviet rule broke out, and it was so well coordinated and organized, so massive and determined to win, that the retreating Soviet troops were unable to quench it.

Of course, the spirit of Baltic resistance to Soviet rule was greatly increased by the precarious international situation and the almost unanimous conviction of the Baltic peoples that the imminent war between Germany and the USSR would spell a rapid end to Soviet rule in the area. This conviction was strengthened and substantiated by the fact that Baltic political emigrés in Germany successfully took on the task of organizing and coordinating the activities of resistance groups within their respective countries. Without explicit German approval and direct support, they certainly would not have been able even to start such activity. The Germans were indeed extremely helpful to these emigrés, providing them with everything they needed to achieve success (including arms supplies, logistics, and the means to transport supplies to the Soviet-controlled Baltic territories). The Germans were keen to ensure that, on the day of the attack against the Soviet Union, insurrection behind Soviet lines would flare as widely and powerfully as possible.

The full story of the organization of resistance and the insurrection against Soviet rule at the outbreak of the German-Soviet war in June 1941 is best documented in the Lithuanian case. The Lithuanian ambassador to Germany, Colonel Kazys Škirpa, who organized and led the resistance from Berlin, published a book of memoirs in which he included all the relevant documents about the organization of that resistance and insurrection. It clearly transpires from these documents that as early as July 1940 Škirpa was busy forming in Berlin the Lithuanian Activist Front (LAF), an anti-Soviet resistance organization uniting all noncommunist segments of the Lithuanian political spectrum. These activities of Škirpa and his associates were supervised and, in a way, guided by the German

Foreign Office via its liaison man with the Lithuanians, Dr. P. Kleist. The LAF was formally inaugurated on November 17, 1940, and, when ready to start combat activities behind Soviet lines, was transferred to the supervision and guidance of the Abwehr Amt (Intelligence Office) of the OKW (High Command of the Armed Forces). The OKW's liaison man with the Lithuanians, Colonel-Lieutenant Dr. Graebe, replaced Dr. Kleist. Very soon four special Lithuanian posts were established within the Abwehr system on the German-Lithuanian (now Soviet) border for constant maintenance of links and supply lines between the LAF center in Berlin and its branches in the country. As Škirpa emphasized, these posts played a crucial role in assuring the success of resistance organization in general and of the insurrection of June 23, 1941, in particular.[14]

What was true for Lithuania must have been true also for Latvia and Estonia, although corroborating documents are less readily available. Undoubtedly German support played a significant role in the successful organization of resistance and insurrection in all three Baltic countries, although one should not overestimate this factor. For without the genuine determination of the masses of indigenous peoples to join the resistance forces, without the faithfulness to the cause of liberation that assured the survival of the widespread organizational network of the resistance movements despite some "successful" arrests and disclosures made by the Soviets, the whole enterprise, with or without German support, could not have gotten off the ground and, even if it had, the result would have been nothing but a great flop.

Only part of the organized resistance forces were directly connected to the coordinating and supply centers in Berlin. Some such forces sprang up and operated independently without ever establishing any links with these centers or, perhaps, without even suspecting their existence. For example, the Berlin-based LAF's local Lithuanian network in 1941 numbered about 36,000 members organized in combat units and ready to strike, whereas the total force of organized combatants who participated in the Lithuanian insurrection of June 1941 was about 100,000, that is, "about three times the size of the members of underground organizations under the leadership of LAF."[15] Hence, without denying the significance of German support in making the resistance movements in the Baltic organizationally and logistically viable, one has to conclude that the German role was secondary and supplementary in nature, unable to determine or even to affect significantly the emergence and scope of these movements.

Popular uprisings on a massive scale took place in all three Baltic republics in June 1941. The Lithuanian insurrection started on June 23, 1941, the day after the German invasion, and it took the insurgents the next three days to free the whole of Lithuania from Soviet rule. Some places in Lithuania were freed more than a week before the advancing German armies marched in. The Lithuanian Provisional Government installed in power by the insurrectionists on June 23 immediately declared the restoration of Lithuania's sovereignty and effectively took charge of the country's affairs. Indeed, when German troops occupied Lithuania they found a country that, to their surprise and to the displeasure of the Reich's leadership, was effectively ruled by a legitimate national government. It took the Nazi authorities six weeks to dismantle this government (it was dissolved on August 5, 1941) and to put Lithuania under the control of their own occupational administration. The Provisional Government (except for three of its members) refused to be a part of the Nazi-installed local administration.

The Latvian insurrection, in which about 60,000 resistance fighters took part, followed almost immediately. On June 26, 1941, an official Soviet broadcast from Riga was forced to admit the fact that "Latvia was in open revolt."[16] On June 28, the insurgents expelled the Red Army from Riga and announced the formation of a Latvian government. Soviet forces, however, regained control of Riga the next day, and they crushed the Latvian government. Nevertheless, the Latvian armed struggle against the Soviets continued until the Germans took Riga on July 1, 1941.[17]

A similar uprising took place in Estonia, with about 50,000 participants. Here it was a more protracted and a less spectacular affair; most of the time the insurgents were involved in guerrilla-style warfare rather than in a direct frontline confrontation with the superior forces of the Red Army. The Estonian guerrillas, however, fared quite well in this warfare: in its course they killed 4,800 Red Army men and took 14,000 prisoners.[18] They themselves lost only 541 fighters on the battlefield.[19] On July 7, 1941, when the Germans crossed the Estonian border, they "found on their arrival the national flags flying everywhere"—an indication of how effective the Estonian guerrillas were.[20] Indeed, in major parts of southern Estonia, the guerrillas had replaced Soviet local administrations with Estonian ones days and even weeks before the arrival of the Germans. "Tartu was under full or partial Estonian control from 10 to 28 July." The Estonian capital of Tallinn, as well as the whole northern part of the country, was under much firmer Soviet military and administrative control, which partly explains why there was no attempt to create an Estonian government.[21] An Estonian National Council for coordination of the activities of resistance forces, however, with the last preoccupation prime minister, Jüri Uluots, at its head, was formed at the very start of hostilities.

These national insurrections made absolutely obvious the illegitimate, antipopular nature of Soviet rule over the Baltic states. Soviet claims that the establishment of their regime was in accordance with the "unanimous popular will," and the masquerades of elections and other gimmicks that were supposed to substantiate these claims, were blatantly exposed as fakes within hours. In other words, the mass insurrections of June 1941 indicated an explicit and total rejection of the Soviet regime by the overwhelming majority of the Baltic populations. The genuine collective will of these nations—to restore their non-Soviet, pre-1940 sovereign statehoods—had thus been actively expressed. In 1941 this will, however, was brushed aside and trampled upon by the new masters, the Nazis, as brutally and unequivocally as by the Soviets in 1940 (and, where they managed, in 1941).

During the German-Soviet war the Baltic nations found themselves in the most peculiar and unenviable situation of being unable to pursue their national aspirations by siding with either of the warring parties; as R. Silde-Karklins succinctly pointed out, "they had to resist equally the imperialist plans of both, the Germans and Soviets, thereby running the risk of being ground between the two."[22] The task of resisting both was indeed formidable. On the one hand, the Baltic peoples were reluctant to be used by the Germans as cannon fodder and tried to sabotage all efforts to this end; but, on the other hand, they were tempted to exploit for their own national ends the acute need of Hitler's embattled Reich to recruit them to military service. The idea was to establish under German auspices (but, if necessary, even by defying the Germans) an independent military force that, after an eventual German retreat, could engage in a struggle against the advancing Soviets. By enlisting Western support for this struggle, it was hoped that such forces would prevent the USSR from re-establishing its rule over the Baltic states and that these states would thus be put back on the map.

The attempts to implement this plan can be illustrated by the example of events in Lithuania. After the dissolution of the Lithuanian Provisional Government, German attempts to mobilize the Lithuanians for either German military service or industrial work in the Reich were so effectively sabotaged that, as E. J. Harrison pointed out, by the end of 1943 the Lithuanians had successfully wrecked almost all plans directed at using them for serving German needs.[23] Indeed, the initial plan to recruit people for work in Germany was fulfilled only by 5 percent, and the later (March 1943) attempt at creating a Lithuanian national SS legion (which was supposed to be not less than 150,000 men strong) was a complete failure, which the ensuing severe German repressions against the Lithuanians were unable to correct.[24]

Faced with such massive passive resistance, the Germans decided to change gear and get what they wanted by applying "cooperative" tactics. They allowed the Lithuanians to form an independent Territorial Defense Force and promised that this force would be used only within the Baltic area (along the Narva-Vilnius line). The Germans also agreed to accept the appointment as commander of this force of the highly popular nationalist general, Povilas Plechavičius. The response to the appeal calling on Lithuanian youth to join this force, which General Plechavičius issued on February 16, 1944 (the day of Lithuanian independence), surpassed all expectations. In a few days, more than 30,000 volunteers signed up, and an even greater number had to be turned down. As soon as the force was formed and acquired a militarily viable shape, however, the Germans broke all their promises. They ordered the incorporation of this force into the SS and thus put it under direct German command.

This turn of events outraged Plechavičius, who bluntly refused to bow to these orders and issued his own disbanding the force altogether. As a result, the Gestapo arrested the general together with the members of his staff, imprisoned them all in a concentration camp, and indiscriminately executed 100 soldiers from among the few the Germans had managed to capture before the force disbanded. (The rest of the captured troops, 3,500 of them, were integrated into the German Luftwaffe and sent to service airports in western Germany.) The main contingent of the force, more than thirty thousand men in full uniform and with all their weapons, successfully went into hiding, thus forming the bulk of the Lithuanian guerrilla army later known as the LLA (Lithuanian Freedom Army), which was to fight against the Soviets for more than eight years.

Similar developments took place in Estonia where, in February 1944, Uluots, the last pre-Soviet prime minister of the country, issued an appeal along the same lines as that of Plechavičius and got the same tremendous response. Even those Estonians who had previously fled to Finland to avoid German conscription voluntarily returned home (after a German pardon for their desertion was granted) to join the newly formed Estonian Territorial Defense Force, assigned to defend Estonia against the Soviet advance. In Latvia, events took a somewhat different turn (because of Germany's extended hold over Courland), but the results were approximately the same.

This is how all three Baltic nations acquired, during 1944–1945, a token military force that, however ill-equipped and weak by any other standards, was sufficient for mounting a protracted guerilla war. It was hoped that by engaging in such a war the Baltic nations would be able to attract Western support for the cause of Baltic independence from the USSR and thus ultimately succeed in achieving independence.

It has been estimated that the initial (1945) strength of these guerilla armies was 30,000 fighters in Lithuania, 15,000 in Latvia, and between 10,000 and 15,000 in Estonia.[25] The number of active supporters, liaison men, and other "part-time" guerillas in each case was several times as large. From 1945 onward, the number of guerilla fighters was steadily rising. The original nuclei of the guerilla armies were joined by forces that had been clandestinely organized to fight the Germans and, after the Germans' retreat, continued to fight against the Soviets.[26] Later, great numbers started to flee to the forests to join the guerrilla forces. These individuals consisted of several categories, which Misiunas and Taagepera have divided as follows:

1. "willing and unwilling German collaborators and draftees";
2. "men avoiding Soviet draft and Red Army deserters";
3. the victims of "Soviet land distribution and other social restructuring measures";
4. actual and/or potential victims of "Soviet screening and deportation campaigns";
5. peasants fleeing from or threatened by the farm collectivization process (and the deportations connected with this process), which was activated in 1949;
6. other individuals "when they could no longer take the insecurity of civilian life."[27]

The absolute number of active guerilla fighters never grew much over the initial numbers. As Misiunas and Taagepera convincingly explained, this was because "the average life span of a forest brotherhood career has been estimated to be two years due to casualties, disease, and return to civilian life." Hence, "over the 8 years of intensive guerrilla activity (1945–52), about 100,000 people may have been involved in Lithuania . . . The Latvian and Estonian forest brotherhood may have involved a total of about 40,000 and 30,000 respectively, at one time or another."[28] This assessment is indirectly substantiated by a statement made by the director of the LCP Central Committee's Institute of the History of the Party, Romas Šarmaitis. In an interview with American journalist George Weller, Šarmaitis stated that, during the eight years of guerilla war in Lithuania, 20,000 guerillas and a similar number of Soviet troops perished on the battlefield.[29]

The last great influx of civilians (peasants fleeing from collectivization and deportation) into the guerilla forces occurred in 1949. That year the guerrilla movements reached their peak, but they started declining sharply soon afterward. In 1950 they were practically over as nationwide movements in both Estonia and Latvia.[30] By 1951–1952 only about 5,000 guerillas operated in Lithuania, and, by the end of 1952, the Unified Command of the Lithuanian Freedom Army (LLA) issued the order to end the armed struggle and proclaimed self-demobilization of the army.[31] In this order, however, the LLA issued a call to all its members and to all Lithuanians to continue the struggle for freedom by peaceful means.

After eight years of incessant and desperate fighting, the guerrilla war in the Baltic thus came to an end; the Baltic nations entered a period of peaceful coexistence with their Soviet rulers.

There is no doubt that in the beginning the guerrillas had commanded almost total popular support. The overwhelming majorities of the Baltic nations were involved in guerrilla activities, carrying out certain duties on behalf of the guerrillas, assisting in hiding and feeding them, and helping them in various ways. Thus, for most of the time during the guerrilla war, the Soviets in the Baltic area controlled firmly only the larger towns and roads, whereas the countryside belonged to the guerrillas almost entirely.

In their struggle against the guerrillas the Soviets used a variety of means, of which straightforward armed combat was the least prominent and successful. From time to time the Soviets "combed" the forests, but their main repressive emphasis was placed on the destruction of the civilian environment that was conducive to guerrilla activities. To this end, annual mass deportations of native Baltic people to Siberia were carried out between 1945 and 1951. Relatives of the guerrillas and families friendly to them, as well as members of the "dispossessed bourgeoisie of towns and villages," were the first affected.[32] The biggest mass deportation took place in 1949, when all the "kulaks" and other peasants "barring the way to the collectivization of agriculture" were affected.[33] Overall, during 1945–1951, not less than 600,000 natives (or about 9 percent of the total native population) were deported from the Baltic area to Siberia and similar inhospitable (or even uninhabitable) places of the USSR; about half the deportees came from Lithuania.[34]

For any contact with the guerrillas a civilian was liable to face the charge of treason and sentencing to twenty-five years in the labor camps. Aiding guerrillas under duress or the threat of death was no excuse; a Soviet citizen was supposed to die rather than help the enemy. In September 1944 instructions were issued to the NKVD troups to shoot any suspect on the spot and to burn down any house, farm, or village suspected of harboring "bandits."[35] These instructions were carried out throughout the following years. These unprecedentedly harsh, indeed genocidal, measures, which initially boosted the guerrilla forces, resulted in the long run in their demise.

Parallel to the mass repressions, the Soviets made every effort to enlarge the base of their indigenous popular support. They managed to retain as champions of their cause the tiny groups that had supported them initially—among them a certain segment of the national intelligentsia that had been antiestablishment during the years of independence. It would perhaps be wrong to suggest, as many people do, that such prominent national figures as Petras Cvirka or Antanas Venclova (Lithuania), Vilis Lacis or August Kirchenšteins (Latvia), and Johannes Vares-Barbarus, Johannes Semper, and Artur and Eugen Kapps (Estonia), chose to support the Soviet regime so unequivocally merely out of opportunism or careerist motivations. At the beginning, their motives were most likely sincere and, indeed, idealistic. And later? Then it was in any case too late: perhaps temptingly comfortable to stay in, too frightening to quit, or both. Having been incorrigible romantics during the years of independence, these progressive intellectuals learned only too well how to be even more incorrigible pragmatists under the incomparably harsher conditions of Soviet reality.

The ability to rely on these people and to use them for the consolidation and representation of the Soviet regime, though an important asset, was far from sufficient to make the Soviet authorities secure in their running of the Baltic countries. Therefore, in order to secure a firmer grip on power in the area, the Soviets urgently needed to sway to their side much larger, truly grass-roots segments of the Baltic population. Their interpretation of events in terms of class rather than national struggle was quite effective for this purpose. Indeed, some natives, especially among those whose position in traditional Baltic societies was at the lower end of the scale and whose prospects for upward mobility were extremely limited, let themselves be convinced by Soviet official propaganda that the ongoing struggle in their countries had nothing to do with national liberty, which was only being used as a cover by the former ruling classes, who sought the restoration of their lost privileges.

Of course, under the "second Russians" (the regime established after the Soviets returned to the Baltic at the end of the war) the ranks of Soviet supporters were joined, in the first place, by great numbers of conformists and careerists, people who would have supported any ruling power either out of respect for its sheer might or, as the Lithuanian poet, Vincas Kudirka, once wrote, "for a nugget of gold, for a spoonful of better food." But there were also quite a few people who went over to the Soviet side because they were genuinely converted to its "truth." The fact that the Soviet regime generously offered to young and ambitious people of humble origins ample opportunities for promotion and thus for leading positions within their respective societies—something that most had not even dreamed of under pre-Soviet conditions—was perceived by some as nothing less than the embodiment of social justice. Hence, by taking such opportunities, individuals were under the impression that they had taken up a great cause—the cause of the construction of communism, of a truly just and affluent society. They were genuinely unable to discern that, in fact, they had fallen for an old trick that newly established dictatorial regimes have used throughout history to compensate for their lack of legitimacy—the trick of recruiting a fraction of the lowest classes in the population to form a new establishment, an uprooted "praetorian guard." Such a group is easily manipulated because of its complete dependence on the regime not only for positions of power and privilege but for sheer physical survival.

Many different methods for the recruitment of that praetorian guard (or, as the official propaganda put it, the winning of the "children of Baltic workers and working peasants for the service to their own working people's state") were employed in the Baltic area as soon as the Soviet regime was re-established there during 1944–1945 by the advancing Red Army. Newly set up educational facilities figured most prominently among them. So-called *rabfaks* (accelerated full-time high school graduation courses that paid their students quite generous stipends) were established in major cities for the most zealous adherents. A wide network of evening high schools for working youths (where one could graduate from high school without interrupting work) was evolved for those who were ambitious enough to attend. The graduates of these educational establishments were given a great deal of preference in getting places in the universities and other institutions of higher learning, whose first task now was to breed "in-house specialists" regardless of their academic qualifications.

For deserving activists—those who joined the Soviet militia forces, agreed to serve in the "extermination battalions" (semimilitary units of native people specially formed to fight against the guerrillas, later renamed "people's defenders' squads"), or otherwise expressed their unswerving willingness to serve the Soviet system—special "educational shortcuts" were arranged. These took the form of either different "academies" preparing barely literate people in a few months to serve as judges, procurators, security and militia officers, economic managers, and so on, or party schools for people specially selected to enter the key apparatuses of party and governmental administration.

Through such means the Soviet regime within a few years managed to build up its Baltic cohorts of faithful and dedicated native cadres. This process was more prominent in Lithuania and Latvia than in Estonia, where the "native cadres" were primarily "Yestonians," that is, people of Estonian origin living in Russia, where they had been assimilated. These "Yestonians" were imported into Estonia in 1940–1941 and 1944–1946 to occupy leading positions and to assure the country's smooth Sovietization. Such people were also imported into Latvia and Lithuania, but there, especially in Lithuania, they were more equally mixed with genuine natives.

The relative success of this policy of promoting indigenous people who decided to rise via Soviet offices "from filth to wealth," apart from assuring the regime the necessary numbers of native workers for its cause, also produced a genuine ideological split within the Baltic societies. What was formerly a straightforward confrontation between occupied Baltic nations and the occupying foreign power thus was extended into a genuine confrontation between a tangible minority (several thousand) of the Baltic population, who for idealistic or opportunistic reasons embraced communist ideology and goals, and the great majority of the people, who refused to accept the Soviet regime and remained faithful to the ideology and goals of national independence.

In this sense, one could say that the guerrilla war acquired the dimensions of a genuine civil war. Indeed, as long as the open battle between the regime and the guerrilla (or partisan) armies went on, it provided a connecting link and a rallying point for the active expression of genuinely popular views and goals. The whole spectrum of the contradictory political orientation of the Baltic nations was manifested in this battle. There was little doubt that only a small minority converted to the new masters; the overwhelming majority was still committed to resist them.[36]

The mood of resistance, so overwhelming in the beginning, started to flounder as years went by. With no support, let alone help, from the West (which preferred to turn a blind eye to the Baltic struggle for freedom), more and more Baltic people started to perceive their lonely struggle against the huge Soviet state machine as not only futile but nationally suicidal. They became keen to end it by any means. Among such people were several leading figures of the resistance movement, for example, the Lithuanians Jonas Deksnys, Juozas Markulis, and Kostas Kubilinskas. Knowing that they would not be able to persuade their colleagues in the resistance leadership to stop the armed struggle, they went so far as to become secret agents of the KGB, actively helping it (mainly by providing vital intelligence) to destroy the resistance movement from within. As a result of their collaboration, many thousands of their former friends and colleagues, together with their families, were killed or imprisoned for long years in Soviet labor camps. But they remained unrepentant, saying that if that was the price for assuring the nation's physical survival, it was worth paying.[37]

Thus, after eight years of desperate armed struggle, the period of open resistance started to come to an end. It did not finally stop because of a decisive Soviet military victory against the resisters. After all, the Baltic guerrillas had been defeated many times before and many times new volunteers had come to restore their ranks. In the 1950s, however, largely for the reasons explained above, no more recruits were available to continue this hopeless struggle. The fact that at a certain point fresh forces for further open resistance did not emerge and that the whole open resistance movement was slowly dying out does not at all mean that the Baltic nations had internally surrendered to the Soviet regime or had decided to accept it wholeheartedly. Rather, they had realized that direct opposition to the occupation, under the continuing circumstances of East-West peaceful coexistence, was not simply doomed to fail but was fraught with consequences that could be literally fatal. Hence, the Baltic peoples ceased their war against the Soviet occupier not out of acquiescence but because of their newly and very painfully acquired realistic perception of their political situation in the world. It was neither the Soviets nor the Baltic nations but political realism that triumphed in this war. And therefore the war is far from over: cease-fire, even if its condition is quiescence, does not necessarily mean peace. The Baltic nations simply have delayed the final act of their struggle with the occupier until better times, knowing quite well that these better times cannot be brought about by their efforts alone. The name of the game today is patience, and the place of the game is Moscow, where the regime is crumbling under the pressure of all oppressed nations, not excluding the Russians themselves.

COMPLIANCE AND PROTEST, 1952–1982

When armed resistance broke down and compliance became the order of the day, the voice for the ideals of national independence vanished together with the identifiable organizational framework of opposition to Soviet rule. These ideals, removed from the visible social surface to take refuge in an atomized shape within the inner consciousness of individual Balts, yielded the social scene to the monopolistic dominance of Soviet official ideology and values. As a result, the latter, though never "interiorized" by the vast majority of people, assumed the position of the only moral and ideological bond holding the Baltic societies together. Needless to say, this situation caused the profound alienation of most individual Balts from the official societies in which they had to live. The hope that in time this alienation would soften and finally be replaced by genuine integration proved futile. In fact, as time went by, this alienation only deepened. Moreover, and this was the most striking development, over time this alienation acquired an absolute and universal dimension that it had never had before.

Indeed, the limited ideological support the Soviet regime had initially achieved in the Baltic countries and had maintained (even increased) during the time of terror was gradually but irretrievably lost after 1952, during the time of the peaceful coexistence of the people and the regime. It is paradoxical but nevertheless true: the apparently total victory of Soviet communism over Baltic societies has gradually brought an equally total rejection of it within the moral and political consciousness of the Baltic peoples.

The ideals and expectations that Baltic people with communist convictions (or, at least, aspirations) had attached to the new regime completely failed to materalize. There was now less freedom and more injustice; poverty, instead of disappearing, sharply increased and, because of the collectivization of agriculture, became clearly irredeemable for all except a handful of top communist bureaucrats. The rivers of blood that had flowed so amply accomplished only one task: the seating of the new elite, the old-time communist apparatchiks and their newly recruited "praetorian guards," in positions of power and privilege. The continuing denial of national and individual rights could no longer be justified by either war or class struggle. In this respect, the new circumstances had a particularly strong, sobering effect on erstwhile communist idealists, who saw in them the betrayal of everything they had believed in and hoped for. It was a shocking discovery that appeared with such blatant clarity that communist sympathizers found it impossible to ignore.

Despite this realization by the new elite (or the "new class," as Milovan Djilas put it), almost all of its members decided to soldier on. The majority continued out of purely selfish and careerist motivations such as fear and greed; a few had mixed motives, including the determination to use their newly acquired positions of influence for the benefit of their countries and people. Some, probably the most naive and idealistic, failed to adjust to reality as it was and, by entering into conflict with its rigorous demands, were crushed or dropped by the system.[38]

The "realistically minded" native apparatchiks who learned how to avoid risks and continued to serve the regime obediently were perhaps more bitter about the situation in which they found themselves than anyone else. After all, it was they who, in their day-to-day activities, constantly experienced the stifling power of Moscow's directing hand

and the humiliation of being deprived of any independent will and reduced to the status of robots blindly implementing whatever arbitrary and repressive decisions were handed down. Whatever their motivations for continuing in the positions of the new elite, their ambitions were deeply frustrated and their inner discontent and disappointment were rather overwhelming. This is how the Soviet regime lost among the indigenous Balts its last genuine, ideologically motivated, support. By the mid-1950s, it had gone completely, and sheer opportunism took its place.

The "breakdown of ideology" inevitably produced certain clashes that at least partially came into the open. The first such manifestations took place in Estonia. They started in 1946 with the suicide of Johannes Vares-Barbarus, the chairman of the Estonian Soviet government (and, before that the head of the "people's" government). There is strong evidence suggesting that the cause of Vares's suicide was the blatant contrast between his expectations for Estonia's future, which motivated him to become one of the main architects of her Sovietization, and the reality of the Soviet Estonia over which he presided.[39] Many, if not all, indigenous Estonian Communists had similar feelings. They tried to preserve Estonia's nationhood by whatever modest means in their power. Alerted to these attitudes by Vares's suicide, the Kremlin closely watched the Estonian Communist Party and in 1950 decided to launch a purge of its indigenous leadership and membership. A great number of leading Estonian Communists, including the first secretary of the Central Committee of the Estonian Communist Party, Nikolai Karotamm; the chairman of Estonia's Council of Ministers, Arnold Veimer; and the chairman of the Presidium of the Estonian Supreme Soviet, Eduard Päll-all, were accused of bourgeois nationalism, narrow localism, ostentatious isolationism from the rest of the USSR, and immersion in narrowly conceived and essentially nonsocialist national traditionalism.[40] As a result, the leadership of the Estonian party as well as the whole apparatus of Estonian administration were "Yestonianized" and Russified more than ever before. The first secretaryship was handed over to Johannes Käbin, another "Yestonian" who hardly even understood the Estonian language; his duty was to assure that no more "deviations" would occur in the future, and he did his best to fulfill that duty.

A similar crackdown took place in 1958–1959 in Latvia. The main culprit there was Eduards Berklavs, the vice-chairman of the Latvian Council of Ministers and former first secretary of Riga's party committee. Together with him, the chairman of the Latvian Trade Union Council, A. Pinskis; the first secretary of the Latvian Communist Youth League, A. Ruskulis; and scores of other leading Latvian Communists were purged—charged with having a "Latvian bourgeois-nationalist deviation."[41] The chairman of the Presidium of the Latvian Supreme Soviet, K. Ozolins, also lost his job in the purge. He was replaced by Janis Kalnberzins, who had been removed from the post of first secretary of the CC of the Latvian Communist Party, which he had held from 1940 until the purge in 1959 (as the man with overall responsibility for the party he was found guilty by association). A Russian Communist of Latvian origin, Arvids Pelše, became the first secretary of the CC of the Latvian Communist Party and vigorously pursued into the early 1960s the task of removing every indigenous Latvian from a position of higher responsibility. (Even Vilis Lacis, the veteran chairman of the Council of Ministers, who publicly dissociated himself from the "deviationists" and was active in denouncing them, was dismissed from his post.) Nevertheless, a 1971 letter from seventeen Latvian old Communists (who preferred to remain anonymous), addressed to several of the world's Communist parties, not only openly defended Berklavs's line but went much further by vigorously denouncing Soviet policies in Latvia. The letter demanded that the "fraternal parties" take up with the CPSU the gross breaches of "Leninist national policy" perpetrated in Latvia. This letter manifested with all clarity that, although suppressed, the national ideals of the native Latvian communist establishment were as much alive as ever.[42]

Matters in Lithuania were different in appearance but not in essence. There were no party purges in Lithuania and no accusations of dissent or deviation against any party members. This was largely due to the fact that, unlike his counterparts in Latvia and Estonia, the first secretary of the CC of the Lithuanian Communist Party, A. Snieckus, was an outstandingly strong, inveterate, and autocratic leader who, without interruption from the end of 1926, had practically been in sole charge of the Lithuanian Communist Party and in full control of everybody in it. There was no question of anyone in the Lithuanian party speaking out or doing anything at all without Snieckus's prior consent. He had total authority over his companions and also managed to carry this authority in his relations with Stalin and the whole Kremlin leadership. Snieckus's ruthlessness and implacability were legendary. During the time of deportations and repressions he would not spare even his closest relatives, let alone anyone else. Stalin personally was extremely impressed with Snieckus's performance and even used to say that the two of them were then the only real Communists left in the whole of the Soviet Union.[43] Mikhail Suslov, who in 1944 was dispatched from Moscow to Vilnius as chairman of the Lithuanian Bureau of the CC of the All-Union Communist Party and whose job was to supervise Lithuanian communists in their fight against the "class enemy" and to "help" them to build a socialist society, was not only full of admiration for Sniečkus, but fell heavily under his influence. Sniečkus carried this influence until his death in 1974, which explains how he was able to get away with so many things that would have spelled the end of a party career for anyone else.

In the end, however, the disappointment with Soviet reality affected the fanatical Sniečkus as much as it did other indigenous Baltic Communists. But he was too experienced a politician to openly deviate from Moscow's line; he knew how to succeed and survive where Karotamm or Berklavs had failed.

A Lithuanian samizdat author writing under the pseudonym of T. Ženklys, who had known Sniečkus quite intimately for a number of years, testified in his obituary for Sniečkus that during his last twenty or so years in power (from the late 1940s or early 1950s) Sniečkus changed beyond recognition. "At the beginning, Moscow could not even dream of a more assiduous servant of its will in Lithuania," wrote Ženklys. But "increasingly from year to year, one could perceive in Sniečkus's activity a national orientation, a defence of the specific interests of Lithuania, an effort first of all to see to the country's proper development, to the rise of its prosperity."[44] So we see that a spiritual evolution, leading to disillusionment with the Soviet order and an understanding that false gods had been served, affected even the most dedicated and Stalinist Baltic Communists, to say nothing of the others. True, some have remained convinced Communists and Marxists, but they have stopped identifying their beliefs with the "real socialism" of the Soviet regime.

By the first half of the 1950s there were no more indigenous Baltic people who continued to support the Soviet regime out of idealism or conviction. Nor did any of the indigenous Balts still believe in communism as represented and implemented by this regime. Hence, the enforced situation of total outward compliance had been complemented by an equally total inward dissent. It goes without saying that inward dissent tends to find some forms of expression in social action and thus partially reduces the totality of compliance. This, however, does not change the peculiar combination of basic compliance with total dissent that has, until the present day, been the characteristic feature of the relationship between the Baltic peoples and the sociopolitical system in which they live. To understand how this combination practically works, it is necessary to distinguish between the *teleological* and *practical-pragmatic* political orientations of the Baltic peoples.

The teleological political consciousness coincides with the people's positive vision of the desirable political future for themselves, their nations, and the world around them. It therefore also implies a certain plan for political change, without which these future-oriented goals would remain unachievable. As I have argued elsewhere, the teleological political consciousness of the Baltic peoples is cohesive, lends itself to a proper definition, and is universal in the sense that it is shared today by every native Balt, including even the most active collaborators with the regime.[45] It could be defined by the following five-trait cluster:

1. Re-establishment within its ethnic boundaries, for each Baltic nation, of a free and truly independent nation-state;

2. Transformation of the present political, social, and economic order into one that would be: (a) consistent with national traditions; (b) committed to put national interests first; and (c) able to provide sufficient room for individuals and their freely formed groups to exercise independent initiative, defend their legitimate interests, and otherwise realize their potential in all spheres of life, first of all in economics;

3. Establishment of direct, tight, and durable political, economic, cultural, and person-to-person links with the Western world, accompanied by the removal of all restrictions on people's foreign travel and aimed in the end at the integration of the Baltic states into the community of Western nations;

4. Restoration on the territory of each Baltic state of an ethnically, linguistically, and culturally compact—if not entirely homogeneous—national society (this aim is considered to be of the highest priority in all three Baltic republics but is more acute in Latvia and Estonia, where the Russians and other aliens are about to rise to the level of 50 percent of the population; in Lithuania the non-Lithuanians are only about 20 percent;

5. Promotion within the framework of a nationally compact society of complete religious and cultural freedom.

How is this teleological orientation translated into the pragmatic attitudes toward social reality that determine everyday political behavior (which is still characterized by basic compliance with Soviet rule)? Compliance requires all Baltic people to accept a certain degree of conformism, which varies from one person to another. One can draw a certain continuum between total conformism and total nonconformism, within which one can place the practical-pragmatic political orientation of the great majority of the Balts. Indeed, very few are total conformists who have built their whole lives and careers on unquestioning subservience to the regime and thus have completely sold out their natural teleological orientation for the sake of security, power, and comfort. The majority of Balts who have invested their lives in rendering political service to the regime manage to combine conformism with what one could call the conservationist orientation, or simply *conservationism*. This orientation expresses itself in the use of official position to do whatever is deemed possible for the preservation of the nation's identity, integrity, and its natural and spiritual resources—as well as for the enhancement of its relative welfare. The degree to which this conservationist attitude expresses itself delineates the limits of one's compliance with the regime. In certain cases, conservationists trespass the limits of official toleration and find themselves in a position of activist dissent.

Outbursts of extrastructural activist dissent (opposing certain policies of the regime or demanding change) started in the Baltic as early as 1956 (four years after the end of armed resistance) and have since continued unabated.[46] It is in these outbursts that the genuine teleological political orientation of the Baltic nations has clearly manifested itself. But, even more important, ever-increasing coincidence between the people's practical-pragmatic and teleological political orientations has been marked. In other words, during the years 1956–1982, a diminution of compliance with official ideological and political demands and a growing assertion of the people's national selves (through protests, demands, samizdat publications, and various other forms of independent activity) have slowly but steadily developed in all the Baltic republics.

Overt dissident activities in the Baltic states during the last decades, especially since the late 1960s, are sufficiently well documented in various publications.[47] What should be said, however, is that, spontaneous mass manifestations apart,[48] systematic protest activities that at first were sporadic and focused on specific issues (religious rights, creative freedom, and freedom of information)[49] gradually began to center on more general issues of national and individual rights. Dissent acquired a more regular organizational pattern in the form of various groups and committees, as well as periodical samizdat publications.

In Lithuania, two such committees were formed in open defiance of the regime: the so-called Lithuanian Helsinki Group (1976), which was one of several such groups formed in the Soviet Union in that year, and the Committee for the Defense of the Rights of Catholics (1980). The Helsinki Group, in spite of having lost through governmental repression (or death) most of its active members, is still trying to recruit new ones and to keep itself alive; from the beginning of 1983, the Committee for the Defense of the Rights of Catholics has been submitted to a repressive onslaught by the authorities, which culminated in the trials of its leaders, Father Alfonsas Svarinskas, in May 1983 (sentenced to seven years of internment and three years of internal exile for anti-Soviet propaganda) and Father Sigitas Tamkevičius, in December 1983 (sentenced, under the same indictment, to six years of internment and four years of internal exile). Nevertheless, the committee has survived and still persists in its activities. A significant boost for the continuation of these activities was the protest letter in defense of Svarinskas and Tamkevičius signed by the unprecedented number of 46,905 people from 71 parishes in May–June 1983. There are a few other organized dissident bodies in Lithuania that do not operate publicly and are known only because of their samizdat output. The latter not only do not diminish but continue to proliferate.

In Latvia, three such groups came into existence in 1975: the Latvian Independence Movement, Latvia's Democratic Youth Committee, and Latvia's Christian Democratic Organization. By 1976 they started to coordinate their activities and issued joint statements addressed to the government of the Latvian SSR, the Australian prime minister (Malcolm Fraser), and others. Another, more activist body, the Organization for Latvia's Independence, has been organizing throughout the 1970s and the 1980s various protest actions, petitions, and demands.

In Estonia, two such groups acquired prominence by 1972: the Estonian Democratic Movement and the Estonian National Front. In 1974 another group, Estonian Patriots, came into existence, and the Association of Concerned Estonians was formed in 1976 after the government crushed earlier oppositional bodies. In 1978 two new groups, the White Key Brotherhood and Maarjamaa, mostly concerned with problems of cultural freedom, were formed in addition to the ones mentioned above.

Lithuania is richest for samizdat periodicals not only in the whole of the USSR but also in Eastern Europe. Apart from the *Chronicle of the Catholic Church*, which in 1982 celebrated the tenth anniversary of its uninterrupted appearance, at least twelve other unofficial periodicals are circulating in this republic. *Aušra* [The Dawn], the secular samizdat periodical, has appeared regularly since 1975. Between 1976 and 1979 a wide variety of different religious and secular samizdat magazines sprang up. Among the religious ones, *Dievas ir Tėvynė* [God and Fatherland] and *Rūpintojėlis* [Sorrowing Christ] are worth mentioning; among the secular, *Varpas* [The Bell], which has appeared since 1977, upholds the Lithuanian liberal tradition; *Alma Mater* (1979) tackles the problems of higher education; *Pastogė* [The Shelter] and *Perspektyvos* [Perspectives] discuss literature, philosophy, and the arts; a few others, such as *Tiesos Kelias* [The Way of Truth] and *Laisvės Šauklys* [The Clarion of Freedom], both appearing since 1976, have no special profile but represent the nationalist orientation of the Lithuanians by dealing with a variety of different subjects. Several of these periodicals were stopped by the authorities, who discovered and severely punished their editors. However, *Perspektyvos* and *Dievas ir Tėvynė* reappeared after a short interval in 1981, and in the same year *Tautos Kelias* [The Nation's Way], an entirely new samizdat periodical publication, was started.

In Estonia the periodical *Eesti Democraat* [Estonian Democrat] has been published since 1971, and *Eesti Rahvuslik Hääl* [The Voice of the Estonian Nation] appeared soon afterward. What is interesting and specific about Estonia's samizdat periodicals is the fact that some of them are published in Russian; thus the *Estonian Democrat* is published in Russian translation and there is also a special Russian-language samizdat periodical, *Luch Svobody* [The Beam of Freedom]. Another Estonian samizdat periodical, *Poolpäevaleht* [The Semi-Daily], was started in 1978, but it was crushed by the authorities a year later (only six issues were published and circulated).

In spite of the ferocious repressions that the authorities have applied (and relentlessly continue to apply) to break down organized Baltic dissent, it not only persists but also develops new forms of organized activities. It is significant that in the last few years dissident groups in all three Baltic republics have started to coordinate their activities and have launched joint ventures. For example, on August 23, 1979 (the fortieth anniversary of the infamous Molotov-Ribbentrop Pact), a joint petition bearing 45 signatures of representatives of all three Baltic republics was issued in Moscow. The petition demanded that the USSR and the two German states declare null and void the Molotov-Ribbentrop Pact, which assigned the Baltic states to the Soviet Union. This document must be singled out not only because it was one of the first exercises in Baltic unity of action but also because it marked a totally new departure in Baltic dissident politics. For the first time since armed resistance to Soviet rule stopped, the demand for full restoration of the national independence of the three Baltic states was forcefully made in clear and unequivocal terms by people prepared to risk the full consequences of such an act.[50] In fact the contemporary Baltic dissidents had taken up, in a unified manner, the banner of their predecessors, the guerrilla fighters, and had committed themselves to carry it on, this time exclusively by peaceful struggle. Thus the resistance movement of the Baltic states, in terms of publicly proclaimed goals, in 1979 returned to its 1940 starting point, in spite of the fact that in 1952 it had seemingly been smashed irreversibly.

The growing cooperation of activist Baltic dissenters with the dissident movement in Russia is extremely significant, too. A unity of purpose has been established, whereby the Balts have joined the struggle of the Russians for the democratization of the Soviet Union, and democratically minded Russians have made the cause of Baltic independence a part of their own program for democratic change in the USSR as a whole. The most symbolic expression of this unity is the fact that the petition of

August 23, 1979, signed by 45 representatives of the Baltic republics and demanding the restoration of the sovereignty of the Baltic states, was amended by a petition of support for it signed by five representatives of Russian democratic dissent: Mal'va Landa, Viktor Nekipelov, Tatjana Velikanova, Andrei Sakharov, and Arina Ginzburg.

The history of the cooperation between Baltic and Russian dissenters goes, however, much farther back. In July 1968, a document written and signed on behalf of "Numerous Members of the Estonian Technical Intelligentsia," titled "To Hope or to Act" gave a sympathetic but critical assessment of Sakharov's *Thoughts on Progress, Co-existence, and Intellectual Freedom* and formulated a program for democratic change in the USSR as a whole, which was conceived by the authors of this document as the prerequisite for the attainment of the freedom of both Russia and Estonia.[51] A similar document, "Program of the Democrats of Russia, the Ukraine, and the Baltic Lands," was circulated by samizdat channels approximately at the same time.[52]

In Latvia in 1968, Ivan Yakhimovichs protested against the Moscow trial of Aleksander Ginzburg and Yuri Galanskov, as well as against other convictions and persecutions of Russian dissidents.[53] Together with Petro Grigorenko and others, Yakhimovichs was active in protest activities concerning the Soviet invasion of Czechoslovakia and other issues. In a statement on the eve of his arrest (March 25, 1969), Yakhimovichs made an appeal addressed to Bertrand Russell, Alexander Solzhenitsyn, Andrei Sakharov, Petro Grigorenko, Alexander Dubček, and others, expressing his commitment to the struggle for freedom and human rights not only in Latvia but in Russia, the Ukraine, Czechoslovakia, Poland, and elsewhere.[54]

In their turn, Sakharov and other Russian dissidents from the late 1960s onward campaigned for the release of Baltic political prisoners and regularly expressed their solidarity with the cause of Baltic freedom. The publicity that the Baltic appeals and samizdat publications received in Western media was possible only because Moscow dissidents transmitted them to Western correspondents accredited in Moscow. (One should note that the August 23, 1979, petition was launched in Moscow and the Lithuanian Helsinki Group was formed there in 1976.) Baltic emigré literature also found its way into the Baltic republics via "transmission points" in Moscow. Moscow's *Chronicle of Current Events* was regularly reporting on events in the Baltic and published extracts from Baltic samizdat documents giving special prominence to the reports from the *Chronicle of the Lithuanian Catholic Church*. The trial of the leading Muscovite dissident, Sergey Kovalev, took place in December 1975 in Vilnius (Lithuania), and one of the charges against him was the dissemination of the *Chronicle of the Lithuanian Catholic Church* via the *Chronicle of Current Events* and other means.[55] Accusations of assisting to propagate the *Chronicle of the Lithuanian Catholic Church* were also raised by the KGB against another prominent Russian dissident, Andrei Tverdokhlebov.[56] The Lithuanian Helsinki Group established in 1976 worked in close cooperation with the analogous group in Moscow. Even closer links between Baltic and other Soviet dissidents were forged in the labor camps where they served their sentences together.[57]

Through all these channels Baltic dissent firmly established itself as a constituent part of the wider USSR's democratic movement and also convinced this movement to embrace the cause of Baltic independence and freedom. As the *Chronicle of the Lithuanian Catholic Church* stated, the work of Russian dissenters for Lithuania "compelled the Lithuanian Catholics to take another look at the Russian nation. Their sacrifice is necessary for all persecuted Soviet people, it is also necessary for the Lithuanian Catholics."[58]

These developments point to the fact that the Baltic peoples have today learned only too well that their goals cannot be realized by local action alone. Only in cooperation with neighboring nations, including the Russians, can they hope to restore their freedom, for nothing will better their lot so long as the regime in Moscow remains unchanged. The Balts now know that if they are to entertain any hopes for realization of their political goals, they have to be united not only among themselves but also with all other Soviet-ruled peoples in opposition to the common enemy, the totalitarian communist Soviet regime.

Activist dissent, based on this awareness, is consolidating, entrenching itself, and acquiring an ever-growing significance in the life of the Baltic republics. So, to a much larger extent, is conservationism, the mass intrastructural dissent that has taken on an increasingly drastic and challenging stance, especially in literature and the arts. As long as the system in Moscow remains stable, however, the correlation between outward compliance and inner dissent in the Baltic republics is bound to stay basically unchanged, with conservationism the dominant practical-pragmatic political orientation of the great majority of the Baltic peoples, and activist dissent remaining relatively marginal. This situation is likely to last until major events outside the Baltic area make it redundant; the political realism of the Baltic nations, borne out by their extremely difficult and long experience of life under oppressive foreign rule, will hardly justify any different course of behavior or action. But the same political realism keeps Balts of every practical-pragmatic political orientation, conservationists and activist dissidents alike, ready to assume an independent existence as soon as opportunity allows them to conceive that as an attainable goal. This common readiness for independence and freedom is the result of the last thirty years, during which the Baltic nations have recovered from the military defeat and physical decimation at the hands of the Soviet regime and have managed, despite all odds, to regenerate themselves into self-reliant, buoyant, and consolidated entities whose identity has become so solidly indestructible that nothing short of a truly genocidal exercise could undermine it.

NOTES

1. Such authoritarian-nationalist regimes were established in Latvia and Estonia in 1934, whereas in Lithuania a regime of that type had existed since December 1926; however, it was only during the years 1935–1936 that a semifascist ban on all oppositional activities was imposed in all three Baltic states.

2. T. Venclova, "Lietuva šiandien ir rytoj" [Lithuania Today and Tomorrow], in A. Štromas, *Politinė sąmonė Lietuvoje* [Political Consciousness in Lithuania] (London: Nida Press, 1980), p. 81.

3. J. Paleckis, *V dvukh mirakh* [In Two Worlds] (Moscow: Politizdat, 1974), p. 349.

4. In this context it is interesting to note that the charismatic leader of the Lithuanian fascists, A. Voldemaras, tried to regain power with Soviet help. In 1940 he was languishing in exile in Germany but, as soon as the Soviets occupied Lithuania and ousted his implacable enemy, Smetona, from power, he packed his bags and returned from Berlin to Kaunas, only to be arrested there and immediately deported to Moscow. By that time the Soviets had already acquired in Lithuania (as elsewhere in the Baltic states) enough stooges with less controversial reputations, and they did not need Voldemaras's services any more. One of such "surprise" Soviet stooges in Lithuania was, for instance, General Vincas Vitkauskas, who at the time of the Soviet invasion was the minister of defense in Smetona's government and chief commander of the army.

5. For a brief explanation of this phenomenon, see A. Shtromas, "The Soviet Ideology and the Lithuanians," *Russia*, no. 3 (1981): 25.

6. In 1941 (after more than half a year of Soviet rule) ethnic Lithuanians, Latvians, and Estonians formed only about half of the membership of the Communist parties of their respective Soviet republics. For example, according to official Soviet data, on January 1, 1941, 53 percent of the members of the Lithuanian Communist Party (LCP) were ethnic Lithuanians. See "Lietuvos Komunistų Partija" [The Lithuanian Communist Party], in *Mažoji Lietuviškoji Tarybinė Enciklopedija* [The Short Lithuanian Soviet Encyclopedia], vol. 2 (Vilnius: "Mintis," 1968), p. 383.

7. For these figures see A. Sniečkus, *Ataskaitinis pranešimas V-me LKP(b) suvažiavime apie LKP(b) CK darbą, 1941m. vasario 5d.* [Report on the Work of the Central Committee of the LCP(b) to the Fifth Congress of the LCP(b) on February 5, 1941]

(Kaunas: State Publishing House of the Lithuanian SSR, 1941), p. 57 (on Lithuania); *Istoriia Kommunisticheskoi Partii Sovetskogo Soiuza* [The History of the Communist Party of the Soviet Union], vol. 5, book 1, *1938–1945* (Moscow: Politizdat, 1971), p. 93 (on Latvia); and A. K. Pankseev, *Na osnove leninskykh organizatsionnykh printsipov* [On the Basis of Leninist Organizational Principles] (Tallinn: Eesti Raamat, 1967), p. 81 (on Estonia).

8. The official (and, no doubt, overblown) Soviet estimate for Lithuania of June 1940 is about 6,000 of such communist supporters and associates outside the ranks of the Communist Party itself; of these 1,000 were members of the League of Communist Youth. (See *Mažoji Lietuviškoji Tarybinė Enciklopedija*, pp. 383, 390.)

9. The text of Order No. 001223, issued by the NKVD of the USSR on October 11, 1939, is not available. Our knowledge of this order springs from explicit references made to it (invoking both the number and the date) in the "follow-up" orders of the people's commissariats of internal affairs and state security of the Baltic republics. Full texts of these orders are available and were published in English translation in the *Third Interim Report of the Select Committee on Communist Aggression* [House of Representatives, Eighty-Third Congress, Second Session, under authority of *H.R.* 346 and *H.R.* 438] (Washington, D.C.: Government Printing Office, 1954) [hereafter referred to as *Third Interim Report*]. Among such orders the following ones should be mentioned: No. 0054 of November 28, 1940, "On the Negligence in Accounting of Anti-Soviet and Socially Alien Elements," issued by the Lithuanian SSR's People's Commissar of Internal Affairs, Guzevičius (pp. 470–72); and No. 0023 of April 25, 1941, "On the Organization of the Operative Accounting in the County (*uezd*) Branches of the People's Commissariat of State Security" (pp. 495–97). The second of these refers twice to NKVD Order No. 001223. See also No. 0037 of May 23, 1941, "On Preparation for the Operation Ordered by the Directive No. 77 of May 19, 1941, of the People's Commissar of State Security of the USSR" (pp. 515–20). Both No. 0023 and No. 0037 were issued by the Lithuanian SSR's People's Commissar of State Security, Gladkov.

10. The "Merkulov Directive," No. 77 of May 19, 1941, is referred to in Order No. 0037 of May 23, 1941, issued by Gladkov as the basis for "the direction, preparation and execution of the operation of purging the Lithuanian SSR from the hostile anti-Soviet and criminal and socially-dangerous element" (*Third Interim Report*, p. 515). The text of this directive is not available.

11. The text of the notorious "Serov Instructions," which does not bear either a number or a date of issue, is published in the *Third Interim Report* under a misleading heading: "1. Moscow Instructions on Deportations, Order No. 001223." In fact, the "Serov Instructions" and the NKVD's Order No. 001223 are two entirely separate documents. Not only are their subjects different (accounting of the people to be purged in Order No. 001223, and the execution of deportation in the "Serov Instructions"), but so are their issuing organs. (Order No. 001223 is consistently referred to as a document issued by the People's Commissariat of Internal Affairs, the NKVD, whereas Serov signed his instructions in his capacity as deputy people's commissar of state security [of the NKGB].) The attribution of a date "between February and June 7, 1941" to the "Serov Instructions" is based on the fact that: (1) the NKGB was only

created, by its separation from the NKVD, in February 1941 (hence, it could not have issued any documents earlier than that); and, (2) the original text of the document was stamped as received in the NKGB office of the city of Šiauliai on June 7, 1941. (For a detailed elaboration on the subject of the dating of the "Serov Instructions," see Dr. Constantine R. Jurgela, "Review of Bronis J. Kaslas, ed., *The USSR-German Aggression Against Lithuania,*" *The Ukranian Quarterly* 29, no. 4 [Winter 1973]: 407–11, esp. pp. 409–11.)

12. For these figures see "Pirmoji sovietinė okupacija (1940–1941)" [The First Soviet Occupation, 1940–1941], in *Lietuvių Enciklopedija* [Lithuanian Encyclopedia], vol. 15 (Boston, Mass.: Lithuanian Encyclopedia Press, 1968), p. 369 (on Lithuania); *Latvju Enciklopedija* [Latvian Encyclopedia] (Stockholm: Latvian Encyclopedia Press, 1950), p. 477 (on Latvia); and E. Uustalu, "Events After 1940," in A. Rei, ed, *The Drama of the Baltic Peoples* (Stockholm: Vaba Eesti Kirjastus, 1970), p. 320 (on Estonia).

13. This estimate is convincingly elaborated in R. Misiunas and R. Taagepera, *The Baltic States: The Years of Dependence (1940–1980)* (London: C. Hurst, 1982), p. 41.

14. See K. Škirpa, *Sukilimas Lietuvos suverenumui atstatyti: Dokumentinė apžvalga* [Uprising for the Restoration of Lithuania's Sovereignty: A Documentary Survey] (Washington, D.C.: The Author, 1973), pp. 26–33, 37–38, 115–16. For an extensive study of these events in English, see A. M. Budreckis, *The Lithuanian National Revolt of 1941* (Boston, Mass.: Lithuanian Encyclopedia Press, 1968). An account of the LAF's inauguration, together with the texts of the minutes of its inaugural meeting and the Inaugural Act itself, is given in Škirpa, *Sukilimas,* pp. 90–100.

15. Z. Ivinskis, "Lithuania During the War: Resistance Against the Soviet and the Nazi Occupants," in V. S. Vardys, ed., *Lithuania Under the Soviets: Portrait of a Nation, 1940–1965* (New York: F. Praeger, 1965), pp. 65, 67. The 100,000 is a conservative estimate; in most other sources the figure given is "at least 125,000 men" (see J. A. Swettenham, *The Tragedy of the Baltic States: A Report Compiled from Official Documents and Eyewitnesses' Stories* [London: Hollis and Carter, 1952], p. 143).

16. Swettenham, *Tragedy of the Baltic States,* p. 143.

17. See Misiunas and Taagepera, *The Baltic States: The Years of Dependence, p. 47.*

18. Swettenham, *Tragedy of the Baltic States,* p. 143.

19. See Misiunas and Taagepera, *The Baltic States: The Years of Dependence,* p. 47.

20. *The Baltic States, 1940–1972: Documentary Background and Survey of Developments* (Stockholm: The Baltic Committee in Scandinavia, 1972), p. 55.

21. Misiunas and Taagepera, *The Baltic States: The Years of Dependence,* p. 47. According to them, only 5,000 fighters were active in northern Estonia, mainly in forests and in the countryside.

22. R. Silde-Karklins, "Formen des Widerstands im Baltikum, 1940–1968," in T. Ebert, ed., *Ziviler Widerstand: Fallstudien aus der Innenpolitischen Friedens- und Konfliktforschung* (Düsseldorf: Bertelsman Universitätsverlag, 1970), p. 215.

23. E. J. Harrison, *Lithuania's Fight for Freedom* (New York: The Lithuanian

American Information Center, 1945), p. 46. For a detailed and well-documented treatment of the German failure to use the Lithuanians for their ends, see A. Dallin, *German Rule in Russia, 1941–1945: A Study of Occupation Policies*, 2nd rev. ed. (London and New York: Macmillan, 1981), pp. 182–98.

24. Z. Ivinskis, "Lithuania During the War," pp. 75, 78–81.

25. The Lithuanian estimate, first given by V. S. Vardys ("The Partisan Movement in Postwar Lithuania," in Vardys, *Lithuania Under the Soviets*, p. 85) on the basis of a thorough analysis of a number of documents, is shared by all other authors who write about this subject. On Latvia, see R. Silde-Karklins, "Formen des Widerstands," p. 216. The Estonian figure follows from the analysis given in Misiunas and Taagepera, *The Baltic States: The Years of Dependence*, p. 81.

26. For example, in Lithuania it was the Legion of Samogitia, which "was formed in 1942 for anti-German purposes" (T. Remeikis, *Opposition to Soviet Rule in Lithuania, 1945–1980* [Chicago: Institute of Lithuanian Studies Press, 1980], p. 60); in Latvia it was the army of General Kurelis, which from December 1944 operated in Courland against the Germans. For more details on Kurelis, see sources as different as the publication of the Baltic Committee in Stockholm, *The Baltic States, 1940–1972*, p. 68; and, from the Academy of Sciences of the Latvian SSR, *Istoriia Latviiskoi SSR* [History of the Latvian SSR], vol. 3, *1917–1950*, ed. K. J. Strazdin (Riga, 1958), p. 581.

27. Misiunas and Taagepera, *The Baltic States: The Years of Dependence*, p. 82.

28. Ibid., pp. 83–84. The facts on life span are referred to Vardys, "The Partisan Movement," in Vardys, *Lithuania Under the Soviets*.

29. *Chicago Daily News*, August 17, 1961. This is a conservative estimate for the guerrillas' death toll. The more generally accepted one, given by the guerrilla sources themselves, is 30,000 (Vardys, "The Partisan Movement," p. 86; and J. Pajaujis, *The Soviet Genocide in Lithuania* [New York: Maryland Books, 1980], p. 108). Some outside estimates deem even this figure too conservative. Since the exact battlefield death toll cannot be established, Misiunas and Taagepera (*The Baltic States: The Years of Dependence*, p. 84) reasonably suggest a compromise solution between 20,000 and 50,000. As for the Soviet casualties, there is overall agreement that they must have been much heavier than those of the guerrillas. The guerrilla sources claim that they killed not 20,000 but 80,000 Soviet troops on the battlefield (see Pajaujis, *Soviet Genocide*, p. 108).

30. On Estonia, see J. Pennar, "Soviet Nationality Policy and the Estonian Communist Elite," in T. Parming and E. Järvesoo, eds., *A Case Study of a Soviet Republic: The Estonian SSR* (Boulder, Colo.: Westview Press, 1978), p. 116. Nevertheless, fighting in Estonia continued well into 1953 when, according to the chairman of the Estonian KGB, Ado Pork, it was largely crushed (A. Pork, "Na strazhe zavoevaniy Oktiabria," *Kommunist Estonii*, no. 12 [1967]:11). Separate guerrillas continued to operate in Estonia even in the 1970s, as A. Küng reports, referring to information about the execution in 1976 of a guerrilla fighter, Kalev Arro, published in the Soviet Estonian press (A. Küng, *A Dream of Freedom* [Cardiff: Boreas Publishing House, 1981], p. 202). On the decline of guerrilla resistance in Latvia, see

J. Rutkis, ed., *Latvia: Country and People* (Stockholm: Latvian National Foundation, 1967), p. 260. The last known major battle between the guerrillas and Soviet forces in Latvia took place in February 1950 (ibid., p. 275).

31. Misiunas and Taagepera, *The Baltic States: The Year of Dependence*, p. 90; and K. V. Tauras, *Guerrilla Warfare on the Amber Coast* (New York: Voyager Press, 1962), p. 95. The actual warfare in Lithuania did not stop even after 1952, since several large guerrilla units disregarded the order and continued to operate well into 1954. Thus one of the guerrilla leaders, A. Jonušas, when interrogated by the KGB, declared: "In December 1952 I was appointed commander of the 'Darius' region. Three units— *Pilis* (Castle), *Jūra* (Sea), and *Geležinis Vilkas* (Iron Wolf)—belonged to this region and were subordinated to me. I continued in this post until June 21, 1954, i.e. until the day of my arrest" (Lithuanian Academy of Sciences, *Archyviniai Dokumentai: IX Rinkinys* [Archival Documents: Ninth Collection], ed. Z. Vasiliauskas [Vilnius: "Mintis," 1968], p. 116). It is also indicative that the "extermination battalions," formed to fight the guerrillas "on the spot" in 1944, were finally disbanded only in 1954. Separate Lithuanian guerrillas remained active in the 1960s and 1970s. In 1965, *Tiesa* [Truth], the LCP daily newspaper, solemnly announced that the last Lithuanian guerrilla, Antanas Kraujelis, had been discovered by security forces and was shot in the battle that ensued, but five years later, in 1971, another such "last guerrilla," Henrikas Kajotas, was found.

32. Each administrative-territorial unit was given a quota for the number of people to be deported from its territory. Then a special commission consisting of the leading party, KGB, and Soviet officials of this unit would prepare a list of people to be deported. Since the deportations were usually performed in one or, at the most, two consecutive days, people on the list could avoid deportation if on these days they happened to be absent from home. However, the quota had to be met regardless of circumstances, and it always was—by deporting an equal number of the neighbors of the absentees, people who originally were not on the list at all.

33. Conservative estimates suggest that in 1949 alone about 200,000 Baltic natives were deported to Siberia and Kazakhstan. Of the 200,000, 60,000 were from Estonia. This is carefully calculated in R. Taagepera, "Soviet Collectivization of Estonian Agriculture: The Deportation Phase," *Soviet Studies* 32, no. 3 (July 1980): 379–97, esp. p. 393. In my view, Taagepera's data allow us to put the estimated number much higher, up to 70,000–75,000. T. Parming, in "Population Changes and Processes" (Parming and Järvesoo, *A Case Study of a Soviet Republic*, p. 27), actually puts it to "at least 80,000." Conservative estimates cite 50,000 from Latvia (calculated in G. King, *Economic Policies in Occupied Latvia* [Tacoma, Wash.: Pacific Lutheran University Press, 1965], p. 83). Again, a conclusion that a higher number, at least 60,000–65,000, was involved, seems to me more justified by the data used. Misiunas and Taagepera arrived at the conclusion that at least 80,000 were deported from Lithuania in 1949 (*The Baltic States: The Years of Dependence*, p. 96). Other, less conservative, estimates arrive at a joint figure more than twice as high, namely 456,000 Baltic deportees (see Silde-Karklins, "Formen des Widerstands," p. 222). The truth must be, as it usually is, somewhere in the middle.

34. According to Remeikis (*Opposition to Soviet Rule*, p. 42), not less than 300,000

were deported from Lithuania during these six years. The estimates for Estonia and Latvia are 145,000 (Parming, "Population Changes and Processes," p. 27) and 144,000 (*The Baltic States, 1940–1972*, p. 82), respectively.

35. In testimony before the U.S. Congress, a former Soviet border guard, Lt. Col. Grigori Stepanovich Burlitski, stated (*Fourth Interim Report of the Select Committee on Communist Aggression*, House of Representatives, Eighty-Third Congress, Second Session [Washington, D.C.: Government Printing Office, 1954], pp. 1368–74), "against these people firearms are to be used and they are to be killed without any further ado. No court is necessary for them. If these people happen to take refuge or run into a house or into a farm or into a village, then this particular house or farm or village is to be considered a bandit farm, a bandit house or a bandit village and those houses or farms or villages are to be destroyed by fire." The facts about guerrilla warfare in Afghanistan show that Soviet instructions on how to fight guerrillas have remained more or less unchanged since 1944.

36. The growth of party membership was slow but steady. Although in Estonia only 56 new party members enrolled in 1944, hundreds followed suit in 1945, so that by January 1946, 1,900 members—or 27 percent of the total membership—were already home-grown Estonians (see Pennar, "Soviet Nationality Policy," p. 118; and Misiunas and Taagepera, *The Baltic States: The Years of Dependence*, p. 77). In Latvia, by January 1, 1946, about one-half of the 10,987 members of the party were ethnic Latvians, of whom about 3,000 or 4,000 were home-grown ones (see King, *Economic Policies*, p. 183). In Lithuania, by June 1946, there were 11,354 party members, of whom about a third were home-grown Lithuanians. Not less than 1,500 were admitted after the war (calculated on the basis of data provided in the *Mažoji Lietuviškoji Tarybinė Enciklopedija*, vol. 2, pp. 384–86). However, one can assume that the growth of the Communist Youth League was much more spectacular, since most of those who genuinely went over to the Soviet side were young people. Unfortunately, no precise statistical data are available on this, except that in Lithuania, in 1945, the Communist Youth League counted 3,800 members, of whom 1,600 belonged to the "extermination battalions" or "people's defenders" squads (their total number at the time is estimated at about 7,000, a figure that is indicative of genuine Soviet support in Lithuania, since membership of these squads was voluntary). It is also known that in 1946 6,000 members of this organization actively participated in the USSR's Supreme Soviet election campaign, and that by 1950 it counted about 34,000 members, of whom not less than 20,000 are supposed to have been indigenous Lithuanians (see "Lietuvos Lenino Komunistinė Jaunimo Sąjunga" [Lithuanian Leninist Young Communist League], in *Mažoji Lietuviškoji Tarybinė Enciklopedija*, vol. 2, p. 391). The steady growth in the number of Soviet supporters is also demonstrated by the fact that the number of people executed by the guerrillas for collaboration increased throughout 1945–1949; according to Soviet sources, 13,000 people were thus executed in Lithuania alone (see Misiunas and Taagepera, *The Baltic States: The Years of Dependence*, p. 86, n24). One should note that only natives were liable to stand trial by the guerrilla tribunals for collaboration. Newcomers— Russians et al.—were not touched. These figures are more or less precise in showing the real extent of genuine Soviet support in the Baltic. As stated before, this support

can be measured in thousands of people, whereas the remaining millions either opposed the regime or supported those who opposed it.

37. J. Deksnys, who, after braving the Iron Curtain three times lost all hope of Western support or help, described his experience and feelings in a series of articles published in the Soviet Lithuanian tabloid, *Švyturys* [Lighthouse] ("Iliuzijų suduži-mas" [The Collapse of Illusions], *Švyturys*, no. 9 [May 1962]: 10–11, no. 10 [May 1962]: 10–12, no. 11 [June 1962]: 16–17, and no. 12 [June 1962]: 10–11). Although there is no doubt that the series was heavily doctored by Soviet editors, an attentive reader can discern in the articles some useful and persuasive pieces of genuine information. On the activities of J. Markulis, see Pajaujis, *Soviet Genocide*, pp. 106–7. Remeikis (*Opposition to Soviet Rule*, p. 56n and p. 269n) is doubtful about the extent to which Markulis's treachery affected the partisan movement and assumes that in his role as one of its leaders Markulis was representative of genuine resistance thinking and action. This is ardently but not very convincingly denied by K.K. Girnius in his review article on Remeikis's book ("The Opposition Movement in Postwar Lithuania," *The Journal of Baltic Studies* 12, no. 1 [Spring 1982]: 66–73, esp. pp. 67–68). There are also eyewitness accounts of Markulis's pronouncements, in which he boasted about his treachery and presented it as an act of patriotic heroism. It seems that K. Kubilinskas, a talented poet, had the hardest lot in trying to reconcile himself with what he had done. He became an alcoholic and died in 1962, before his 39th birthday.

38. Cases of dissent among the native members of the apparat and the party were the earliest ones. Even later "extrastructural" and overtly dissident pronouncements and acts came first from those Balts who held genuinely communist views and criticized the policies of the regime from the standpoint of anti-Stalinist Marxism and communism. It was natural for the naive and idealistic (i.e., those who considered the Soviet regime their own and wanted to adjust it to their idealistic vision rather than to adjust themselves to its oppressive practices) to voice their genuine opinions and protests publicly and in the most simple-minded and straightforward manner. Some of them, like Ivan Yakhimovichs in Latvia or Viktoras Sevrukas in Lithuania, directly founded their petitions and protests on the principles of communist ideology and morality. But it should be noted also that many of those dissidents who did not invoke Marxist-Leninist or communist principles explicitly started their lives as convinced believers in communism and genuine partisans of the Soviet regime and were actually driven into dissent upon finding their convictions inconsistent with the Soviet social and political reality. Such prominent Baltic dissenters as Jüri Kukk (an Estonian scientist and party member who perished in the Gulag in 1981), Lidija Doronina-Lasmanis and Maija Silmale (both Latvian cultural figures), Tomas Venclova and Jonas Jurašas (both Lithuanian cultural figures), and many others belong to this category.

These facts corroborate the thesis that the first and most outspoken Baltic dissidents were former communist idealists. People of the traditional nationalist orientation were much more cautious and realistic in their fearfulness of the Soviet regime and thoroughly avoided any open confrontations or disputes with it. Only much later (in the mid-1970s) did some of them—such as Viktoras Petkus and Balys

Gajauskas (Lithuanians) and others—start to join the overt dissident ventures already well on the move.

39. See A. Küng, *A Dream of Freedom*, p. 167.

40. Although N. Karotamm came from Leningrad, it would be wrong to consider him a "Yestonian" since he left Estonia in the 1930s as a political refugee and, like many other refugees from different countries, resided in the USSR for several years as an emigré. The same, to a certain degree, applies to E. Päll-all, who lived in Russia for many years but whose roots were nevertheless in Estonia.

41. For more details on the so-called Berklavs Affair and the purge in general, see A. Berzins, *The Unpunished Crime* (New York: Robert Speller, 1963), pp. 182–84, 255–62.

42. For the English text of that very revealing letter, see *Congressional Record*, February 21, 1972, pp. E1426–30.

43. This story was told to me by a person who witnessed a few conversations between Stalin and Snieckus.

44. T. Ženklys, "Pasibaigusi Lietuvos gyvenimo epocha" [The End of an Epoch in Lithuania's Life], *Akiraciai* [The Horizons], no. 3 (57), 1974, p. 7. A shortened version of this extremely interesting article is available in Russian; see A. Shtromas, "Dve stat'i T. Zhenklisa" [Two Articles by T. Ženklys], *Kontinent*, no. 14 (1977): 229–41.

45. See A. Shtromas, "Baltic Problem and Peace Studies," *Journal of Baltic Studies* 9, no. 1 (Spring 1978): 3–4. The thesis about the universality of the teleological political consciousness of the Baltic people is elaborated in some detail and corroborated by existing evidence in Štromas, *Politinė sąmonė*, pp. 50–53.

46. In November 1956, on All Saints Day, spontaneous mass demonstrations and meetings broke out in Kaunas and Vilnius (Lithuania). The demands were for "Freedom for Lithuania," "Solidarity with the heroic peoples of Hungary and Israel," "Russians out of Lithuania," and so on.

47. Major dissident activities in and documents from the Baltic were regularly reported in the *Chronicle of Current Events*, clandestinely published in Moscow since 1968 and available in English translation from the publications of Amnesty International. The United Baltic Appeal regularly publishes *UBA Information Services*, a news-release series in which such information is given wide coverage with full texts of major documents made available. The same applies to the ELTA (Lithuanian News Agency in the USA) monthly *Bulletin*, the *Latvian Information Bulletin* (published by the Latvian Legation in Washington), *Estonian/Baltic Events* (published by R. Taagepera), and *Lituanus*. Good collections of Baltic dissident documents are included in P. Reddaway, ed., *Uncensored Russia: The Human Rights Movement in the Soviet Union* (London: Jonathan Cape, 1972); *Documents from Estonia on the Violation of Human Rights* (Stockholm: Estonian Information Centre, 1977); V. S. Vardys, *The Catholic Church, Dissent, and Nationality in Soviet Lithuania* (New York: Columbia University Press, 1978); and Remeikis, *Opposition to Soviet Rule. The Chronicle of the Lithuanian Catholic Church* is regularly published in English by the Lithuanian Roman Catholic Priests' League of America in New York.

48. Mass demonstrations, spontaneous protest meetings, and other similar events have been regular in the Baltic republics since November 1956 when, on All Saints Day, mass manifestations took place in the two Lithuanian cities, Kaunas and Vilnius. Another mass manifestation that developed into a full-scale riot took place in Kaunas in 1960, during the festivities devoted to the twentieth anniversary of Lithuania's Sovietization. On that occasion militia forces started shooting on the demonstrators, killing and wounding several people, which outraged the crowds to such an extent that they attacked and smashed the forces of law and order present in the city. Two more such mass demonstrations that developed into riots took place in Lithuania. One, in May 1972, was the result of the self-immolation in the central square of the city of Kaunas "for the freedom of Lithuania" of a young student, Romas Kalanta; it was his funeral on May 18, 1972, that turned into a demonstration that literally took over the city and held it for almost two days, until the troops were sent in to disperse it. More than five hundred arrests were made. The other, in October 1977, developed from a soccer match played in Vilnius between the local team and a team from the Russian town of Smolensk. On all occasions the overriding slogans were "Freedom for Lithuania" and "Russians out of our country."

In Estonia a mass protest took place on April 20, 1972, in the capital city of Tallinn. It started as a result of the televised hockey world championship. When the Czech team defeated the Soviet team, hundreds of people, mainly students, burst onto the streets shouting "we won." Mass youth manifestations took place in Tartu (Estonia) in 1976 and in Liepaja (Latvia) in 1977 over pop music events. The most significant Estonian youth demonstrations took place in Tallinn, Tartu, and some other places in October 1980 over the issue of increased time allocation to Russian lessons in Estonian schools. Subsequently, a letter from 40 prominent Estonian intellectuals expressed their full solidarity with and support for the demonstrators, who were extremely brutally dealt with by the militia and army troops.

49. In Lithuania, protests against violations of the religious rights of the people and of the Catholic church itself, accompanied by appropriate demands, were systematically launched from 1968 onward. They culminated in a petition signed by 17,054 Lithuanian Roman Catholics and calling for a stop to violations by Soviet authorities of the right of the people to exercise their freedom of conscience, guaranteed by the Soviet constitution. The petition demanded an end to the practice of gross civil discrimination against religious believers. In December 1971 it was sent to the U.N. and, via its offices, to Soviet leaders in Moscow. (For the English text of this petition, see Vardys, *The Catholic Church*, pp. 144–49.) In 1972 the publication of *The Chronicle of the Lithuanian Catholic Church* had started; it reflected the course of the systematic, massive, and regular struggle of Lithuanian Catholics for their rights. In Latvia, similar mass developments took place, mainly insofar as the rights of the Baptists were concerned, but Latvian Catholics were actively involved in protest activities, too.

In Estonia, recorded protests about the lack of free access to information and of freedom for culture-creating activity go back to 1958 and are connected with the activities of the leading Estonian dissident, Mart Niklus. In Latvia, similar acts could be traced to the early 1960s, in connection with the 1961 trial of the prominent Latvian poet, Knuts Skujenieks (later, other cultural figures were also tried). In Lithuania, such cases were recorded only in the early 1970s, as, for example, the 1972 memorandum of Jonas Jurašas, the Chief Director of the State Theater in Kaunas, who refused to comply with the dictates of the authorities and pledged to work only in accordance with his own conscience. Similarly, the poet and architect Mindaugas Tamonis refused to inspect and restore crumbling monuments to the Red Army on nationally and religiously significant Lithuanian sites.

50. For the full English text of this petition, see *UBA Information Service*, news release no. 330/331, November 11, 1979 (supplement). Most of the 45 signatories were arrested, tried, and received heavy penalties, which they continue to serve in the Soviet Gulag. There are unconfirmed reports that 35,000 signatures in support of this petition were gathered in Lithuania alone.

51. For its text in Russian, see Radio Liberty, *Arkhiv samizdata*, no. 70.

52. The Herzen Foundation in Amsterdam published it in Russian in 1970 as a separate pamphlet, "*Programma demokraticheskogo dvizheniia Sovetskogo Soyuza.*"

53. See his letter, "The Duty of a Communist," addressed to M. Suslov, in A. Brumberg, ed., *In Quest of Justice: Protest and Dissent in the Soviet Union Today* (London: Pall Mall Press, 1970), pp. 129–32.

54. Ibid., pp. 359–60.

55. For details, see *Delo Kovaleva*, a documentary report published as a separate pamphlet in New York in 1976 by "Khronika-Press."

56. For the records of his interrogation by the KGB, see *INDEX on Censorship*, no. 3 (Autumn 1975): 56–61; more details on his case are available in *Delo Tverdokhlebova*, a documentary report published as a separate pamphlet in New York in 1976 by "Khronika-Press."

57. For a more detailed review of the links between Lithuanian and Russian dissenters, see Vardys, *The Catholic Church*, pp. 151–55. The various ties between Estonian and Russian dissenters are explored and perceptively assessed by Sergey Soldatov, himself an Estonian and a Russian dissident at one and the same time. See his "Estonskii uzel" [Estonian Knot], *Kontinent*, no. 32 (1982): 223–38.

58. No. 15, 1975; quoted from *Lietuvos Katalikų Bažnyčios Kronika* [The Chronicle of the Lithuanian Catholic Church], vol. 2 (Chicago: LKRŠR Publications, 1975), p. 357.

The Soviet
Muslim Borderlands

S. Enders Wimbush

INTRODUCTION

Since the Great Game began to wind down and the Russians unequivocally established their hegemony in Central Asia and the Caucasus, little
systematic attention has been paid by scholars (with some notable exceptions), still less by policymakers and statesmen, to the Muslim regions
and strategic periphery of the USSR. In part, this lack of attention
followed naturally on the demise of that intrepid class of British soldier-
explorer-scholars who kept the world informed of events in Central Asia
and the Caucasus for more than a century; in part, it resulted from Soviet
efforts to keep prying eyes out, made easier by the explicit and implicit
decisions of most Western governments to avoid close scrutiny. Only
today is a new generation of specialists, who can command the languages,
history, and culture of the region, coming into its own. The rise of this
new generation is due largely to the persistent efforts of a few concerned
and knowledgeable scholars, like Alexandre Bennigsen, to keep these
vital matters in the public eye.

This long hiatus in our understanding of Soviet Muslim affairs
comes at significant cost to our ability to discriminate, inclining various
observers to both overstatement and understatement, when what is called
for is competent research and cool judgment. Currently, the Soviet
Muslim borderlands are neither the fuse that will presage the explosion
of *l'empire éclaté* (to borrow Hélène Carrère d'Encausse's colorful but
misleading phrase) nor are they perfect illustrations of successfully employed social-science theory. Some would like to believe that Soviet

Muslims have undergone social and political mobilization Soviet style, elites have been integrated vertically and horizontally, and most have developed such a stake in the current political and economic system—that is, they have been co-opted—that serious anti-Soviet dissent can be ruled out a priori.

Soviet Muslims are dynamic peoples. They are heirs to one of the most brilliant Islamic civilizations and can rightfully claim to have been at one time the intellectual center of the Islamic world; their populations are in the throes of rapid growth and transition; and they are affected by a backwash of tumultuous political, religious, and military events along their borders. All these forces and others combine to shape the Soviet Muslim's identity and political outlook. On the one hand, he has a national identity as an Uzbek, Kazakh, Tadzhik, Turkmen, Kirgiz, Azerbaijani, or a member of one of the smaller Muslim peoples. This political identity is the result of Soviet efforts in the 1920s and 1930s to create largely artificial allegiances among Soviet Muslims that would undermine pre-Soviet attachments to pan-Turkic and pan-Islamic ideals, which Bolshevik leaders viewed as dangerous to the stability of the new Soviet state. National or tribal distinctions always existed, of course, and Soviet authorities had and continue to have little difficulty convincing people that they are what the leadership says they are. It is ironic, however, to hear Soviet leaders these days inveighing against "nationalism" in the Soviet Muslim borderlands, for which they themselves must accept a disproportionate share of the blame.

On the other hand, Soviet Muslims remain part of the world of Islam, a fact that is not contradicted by the more recent emergence of modern national distinctions. One can easily be an Uzbek and a Muslim, just as one can be a Saudi and a Muslim; but can one be both a Muslim and a New Soviet Man? Again, the answer probably is yes in most cases, but not insofar as being a New Soviet Man means becoming Russified. It is here that Islam's broader scope is felt. More than a religion, Islam is a way of life and a set of historical and social traditions. Even among avowed atheists, Islam today forms the cultural substructure of much social activity. In a very real sense, Islamic tradition has become the fundamental cultural bulwark against assimilation by an aggressive Russian culture, much to the displeasure of Soviet social engineers who seek to assimilate the Muslim peoples but acknowledge the difficulty of attaining this goal. Because of this bulwark, men who have never been to a mosque maintain, wittingly or unwittingly, a substantial psychological distance from Russians. Unlike many other Soviet peoples, the Soviet Muslims' search is not for a national identity that somehow amalgamates aspects of the New Soviet Man in such a way as to assuage the ideological demands of the ruling Russians. Theirs is not an identity crisis, for they cannot cease to be Muslims.

The importance of Islam in the psychological makeup and identity of Soviet Muslim peoples, unfortunately, is frequently discounted and its political implications are ignored. In part, this is because most Western specialists approach any examination of the Muslims of the Soviet Union via Russia and Russian culture and organizations. Few start with a thorough background in Islamic history, culture, and civilization, a preparation that logically would encourage more discriminating instincts. In part, Soviet propagandists have been successful in suggesting that Islam in the USSR is now the province of old men and fanatics, often despite quite compelling evidence to the contrary.[1] Still, common sense suggests that fourteen centuries of brilliant Irano-Turkic-Islamic culture cannot be quickly swept away by sixty-eight years of Russian-dominated Marxist-Leninist pseudoculture, among whose highest offerings—by the Soviets' own admission—figure the complete works of Leonid I. Brezhnev. Has the Soviet experiment really been so effective, an experiment that addresses other cultures almost without exception through negative example? Few specialists would deny the vehemence or importance of Baltic peoples' attachment to their historic identities, which are formed from less well-embedded roots than those of the Muslims of Central Asia and the Caucasus. Why is it that some are prepared to deny or ignore the importance of Islam to the latter?

In the next two decades, Soviet Muslims will be affected by momentous changes inside the Soviet empire and in the non-Soviet borderlands. Only the most optimistic Soviet planner could look at the potential for unwanted change and still believe that Soviet Muslims will enter the twenty-first century much as they are today. The forces that will stimulate change are varied and complex, to be sure; there is no inevitability about them, only uncertainty, which might give Soviet leaders hope, if little comfort.

DEMOGRAPHIC IMPERATIVES

Perhaps more than any other internal Soviet development, the rapid increase in Muslim numbers underlines the potential for new pressures on Soviet domestic and foreign policies.[2] The USSR is now the world's fifth largest Muslim state.

Until World War II, the net demographic gain of the Muslims in the USSR was slower than that of the domestic Slavic populations. Between 1926 and 1959 (years in which censuses were taken), Soviet Muslims registered a modest population increase (41 percent) compared to the overall population growth of the USSR (42 percent) and of the Great Russian population (47 percent). The absence of a census between 1945 and 1959 probably masked a significant population explosion among Soviet Muslims, an explosion that only became evident when the 1970 census appeared. From 1959 to 1970, the Muslim population of the USSR increased by 45 percent, compared to an average Soviet increase of only 16 percent and a Great Russian increase of a mere 13 percent. Although full details of the most recent Soviet census of 1979 have not yet been released, enough is now available publicly to indicate that between 1970 and 1979 the Soviet population as a whole increased by 8.4 percent, the Great Russians by only 6.5 percent, and Soviet Muslims, continuing their high birthrate trend, by 23.2 percent. If one projects these trends to 1995, it is clear that the Muslims of the USSR are the only group that will gain in its share of the overall population during this period. Soviet demographers have estimated that the number of Muslims in the USSR in the year 2000 will be roughly 100 million, or approximately one-third of the entire Soviet population. This may be an excessive estimate; a more logical figure, offered by several Western analysts, is between 65 and 80 million. Even at this more modest rate of increase, by the turn of the century one in every four, or one in every five, Soviet citizens will be from a nominally Muslim people.

Demographic gains by themselves do not necessarily presage major shifts in the internal Soviet balance of power between different national groups or different regions of the state; nor do they foretell the immediate breakdown of Russian control or the inevitable dissolution of the Soviet Russian empire. Soviet leaders, however, can find little comfort in the history of empires that have faced these demographic developments. As Paul Johnson has noted in his history of modern times, "One of the lessons of the twentieth century is that high birth-rates in the subject peoples are a mortal enemy of colonialism."[3] At the very least, demographic gains of this magnitude and speed among Soviet Muslims, however, do introduce new criteria on which critical statewide and regional decisions must be based. The long-term outcome of such changes could indeed alter the political relationship of the Russian center to its Muslim borderlands. As the effects of Muslim demographic gains become more immediate, any hope of muddling through and avoiding important policy changes will recede.

Demographic trends that favor Soviet Muslims underlie a number of increasingly urgent problems with which state, regional, and military planners are grappling. For example, Soviet European regions, which house the vast majority of the USSR's heavy industry and technological development, are chronically short of labor; they are destined to become even more so until the late 1990s, when the problem will begin to ease somewhat. Soviet Muslim regions, Central Asia in particular, have large and growing labor surpluses. If traditional patterns of social behavior had prevailed, large numbers of surplus Central Asians and others would have migrated from their own regions in search of employment in the job-rich western sections of the USSR; but this has not happened. A variety of Soviet and Western demographers have pointed to the unwill-ingness of Soviet Central Asians to migrate, a fact that the Soviet regime finds deeply depressing. Short of using coercive methods to push Soviet Asians westward, the regime really has few palatable options at its disposal. This lack of options almost certainly accounts for the import into the Soviet labor force of Finns, Bulgarians, Koreans, and, most recently, North Vietnamese.

Soviet planners, thus, are faced with some difficult choices. Are they to relocate and give preferential treatment to the development of new industry in Central Asia, or are they to continue attempts to bring Central Asian labor to existing industry? Neither alternative is without costs of some magnitude.[4] Forcing Central Asian labor out must be seen as counterproductive in both the long and the short term. Furthermore, it is directly contrary to all the lip service Soviet leaders have paid over the last sixty-eight years to the equal development of all peoples of the USSR and to the elimination of imperialist exploitation of minorities. Relocating some existing industry and initiating new industrial projects in Central Asia and elsewhere along the Soviet Muslim periphery would be an enormously expensive undertaking that Soviet planners can embark on only with great anxiety. The labor force of Central Asia is largely un-skilled and would require costly and time-consuming education and technical preparation. Even within Central Asia there is little migration from the countryside to the cities; hence, Soviet planners would face the additional handicap of having to locate some industry in the Muslim countryside, far from supplies of raw materials and convenient modes of transportation.

Nor do the problems end here. Soviet planners are facing yet another inherent limitation to the development of the Central Asian periphery: a shortage of water for both industry and agriculture.[5] For nearly two decades, debate has raged in high places about the feasibility of rerouting several central Siberian rivers to Central Asia to provide badly needed water supplies. Yet, to date, no rerouting has been undertaken. Central Asian development thus remains limited from the outset. Native leaders from these regions have become unusually outspoken about this prob-lem, and recently in public forums many have called for the expenditure of the huge sums required to undertake the rerouting schemes.[6] Their pleas have assumed a thinly disguised nationalistic tone. Not surprisingly, Russians have been reluctant to accede to the demands. According to official Soviet estimates made several years ago, the entire project could cost upward of 100 billion rubles, a sum that has certainly become inflated over time. Many Russians, particularly those with strong nationalist leanings, might wish to see this money spent on social welfare and other projects closer to home. Moreover, Russian anxiety is unlikely to be quieted by the certain knowledge that expensive capital investments, regardless of other risks, will be easily within range of Chinese strategic weapons in the event of conflict with the People's Republic of China.

Without new water, Central Asia's largest industry, cotton farming, cannot expand much, if at all, beyond its current boundaries. Assuming that labor surpluses in the Central Asian countryside will continue to grow, any failure to create new agricultural enterprises will leave workers with little to grow into. Of course rural underemployment and redundancies tend to be somewhat easier to absorb than those in urban environments, where the concentration of humans is higher and the opportunities for concerted protest seemingly better.

If Soviet labor sociologists are concerned about the changing demographic balance and its implications for the nonmilitary labor pool, Soviet military planners, especially those assigned to procure the human resources necessary to fuel the Soviet military machine, must be most unsettled by the developing trends. High birthrates among Soviet Muslims and stagnant birthrates among Soviet Slavs are rapidly changing the face of the draft-eligible labor pool.[7] Soviet Muslim populations are now considerably younger than those of Soviet Slavs, and, until at least the 1990s, a larger and larger percentage of the draft-eligible cohort will be represented by Muslim eighteen- and nineteen-year-olds. By the end of the 1980s, approximately one in every three draft-eligible young men will come from a Muslim people.

Historically, with few exceptions among Muslims (the most notable are the Volga Tatars), the Russians have sought to flesh out their armed forces with Slavic recruits, a practice that has become particularly salient in the Soviet period. Soviet Muslims, for the most part, are excluded from positions of technological responsibility and political sensitivity — for a number of reasons.[8] First is the question of ultimate loyalty. Several hundred thousand Soviet Muslims distinguished themselves during World War II by collaborating with the Germans; many in fact joined Hitler's "East Legions" to take an active role in the fight against the

Soviet Union.[9] I can identify nothing to suggest that Soviet leaders have forgotten this lesson; indeed, current Soviet military manning and stationing practices suggest that they remember very well. Second, Soviet Muslims are probably the least proficient of all Soviet peoples in Russian, the language of command. Many arrive for military service with no knowledge of the language and little desire to learn it. Third, with the possible exceptions of the Volga Tatars and some Azerbaijanis, Soviet Muslims, for the most part, have a comparatively low level of technological education. This renders them unlikely candidates for positions requiring technological sophistication.

To these factors, one should add one more of major significance: the psychological dimension. Soviet Muslims simply do not wish to serve in the armed forces because they are clearly the targets of both official and unofficial discrimination on national and racial grounds. Few, beyond the token number that Soviet authorities roll out for parades, become officers; almost none choose to attend military academies despite affirmative action programs that would seem to favor them. Almost none re-enlist after their obligatory service term (usually two years). Most Soviet Muslim troops—there are some exceptions—are segregated into construction battalions, where they often receive no combat or weapons training to speak of and are commanded by their own sergeants, who speak native languages rather than Russian. Conflict between Muslims and Slavs in these battalions is frequent and violent.

Soviet propaganda speaks both to the outside world and to the Muslim soldiers themselves about the successes of the military system as a great social and national equalizer. The armed forces are depicted as a place where many nationalities meet head on, only to depart with their individual and national prejudices tamed and their sense of brotherhood, of "Soviet friendship," strengthened. What really happens is probably closer to the opposite: Soviet Muslim soldiers, like most other minority soldiers, probably leave military service with an enhanced sense of their own nationality and an increased awareness of how their own individual and corporate goals depart from those of Russian society. One must wonder how it could be otherwise, when Soviet Muslims in the armed forces are bombarded daily with evidence of their inferior status and constant reminders that they remain a colonial people in the service of an imperial power.[10]

Assuming that Soviet leaders intend to hold the size of their armed forces at roughly the current level—probably in the vicinity of 4.5 million men, according to many estimates, although some have it as high as 6.0 million—and that manning and stationing practices with respect to

Soviet Muslims will remain largely unchanged, one might seriously inquire whether the supply of incoming Slavic recruits for the next fifteen years can satisfy the demand. Soviets of all kinds, military and nonmilitary alike, live with the nagging fear that, indeed, a significant shortfall of Slavs for the military is likely to occur in the mid-1980s. If these fears are warranted, and I believe they are, the Soviets will be faced with some difficult and unpleasant policy choices. These could include drafting more Soviet Muslims into positions of political and technological responsibility with the attendant cost of diminishing Russian control in these areas; extending the enlistment term, which, though certainly meeting the objective of providing the military with enough Slavs, will require the extended absence of working youth from the already labor-short nonmilitary economy; reducing the size of the armed forces altogether and striving to make up this deficit by the introduction of modern labor-saving technology; or involving Muslim military construction battalions more fully in the nonmilitary labor sector, thereby freeing more Slavs for military service. Other solutions may be envisaged, or even combinations of these. But, most important, no solution is without immediate and substantial costs; all would appear to test the abilities and priorities of the Soviet system. Moreover, any apparent solution to this problem will require Soviet authorities to conduct a strategic reassessment of their military institution and its relationship to the growing Soviet Muslim population.

Any reformulation of the role of Soviet Muslims in the Soviet military, whether to correct for ethnic imbalances in the conscript pool or to plot new operational opportunities, will have to consider the military performance of Soviet Muslims during the invasion of Afghanistan in December 1979. By nearly all accounts, Soviet Muslims were in fact part of the initial Soviet invasion force—a distinct break with past Soviet policy, which strove to eliminate from cross-border operations any soldiers who might have ethnic or religious connections with the populations being invaded. Although information is sketchy, there is sufficient reason to believe that this precedent was broken for practical reasons: a relatively fast mobilization for the Afghan invasion necessarily required that those military units closest to the Afghan border be brought up to complement by local reservists—in this case, poorly trained Central Asians. Of course, Soviet leaders may have seen a political windfall in this as well, namely, that the Uzbeks, Tadzhiks, Kirgiz, and other Soviet Muslims who eventually ended up in the first wave of invaders would blunt the violence of the attack by their ability to communicate with their coethnics, who constitute a large part of the Afghan population north of the Hindu Kush.[11] Yet, when one considers the extraordinary measures Soviet authorities have taken to prevent the Islamic revolution in Iran and elsewhere from infecting Muslims along the USSR's southern border, it is difficult to imagine these same authorities opting to ensure that large numbers of Soviet Muslims would meet face to face some of the world's most devout Islamic fundamentalists, the Afghans.

Regardless of their rationale for sending Soviet Muslims into Afghanistan in the first place, Soviet leaders pulled the great majority out only a few months later, in February 1980. Various media, emigré, and, increasingly, Afghan *mujahidin* reports argue strongly that this move was taken because Soviet Muslims proved unreliable against their Muslim brethren. Reports speak of widespread fraternization between the Soviet Muslims and the Afghans, a heavy traffic in Korans intended for Soviet Muslim regions, desertions and refusals to report for duty among Soviet Muslim reservists, and unwilling combat performance against the Afghan guerrillas. (Several reports, which cannot be verified, claim that Soviet officers and squads of riflemen followed early invasion units into battle with the sole intention of shooting retreaters, a policy that was often used during World War II.)[12]

Whether it was military or political inadequacies that ultimately mandated the withdrawal of Soviet Muslims is of little note, inasmuch as neither is easily correctable without fundamental changes in the Soviet military system. Thus it is that Soviet political *and* military leaders face not only the possibility that more and more Muslims will have to be added to the ranks to satisfy existing and planned manpower commitments but also the real worry that their operational choice may to some extent be determined by this condition. If Soviet Muslims failed to perform to expectations in Afghanistan and, what is more, demonstrated a certain political unreliability as well, then how can Soviet leaders plan military operations in the Muslim-dominated Persian Gulf without leaving perilously undermanned other theaters that require heavy concentrations of Slavic troops, such as the Sino-Soviet border or Poland?

THE BORDERLAND EMPIRE

Along virtually the entirety of its land borders, the USSR shares ethnic groups with adjoining states.[13] Nowhere is this more evident than along the Soviet Union's southern and southeastern rim, from the Caucasus to the Altai Mountains. This border meanders its way through many distinct ethnic groups, most of whom are Turkish-Muslim peoples. So it is that Uzbeks, Uygurs, Tadzhiks, Kirgiz, Azeri Turks, Kazakhs, Turk-men, and others can be found in sizable concentrations not only in the USSR but also directly across Soviet borders in China, Afghanistan, and Iran. Although these borders are well guarded by the KGB border forces and mined where possible, they cannot be made impenetrable—especially to radio broadcasts and foreign visitors—and thereby cannot stem the flow of alien ideas from foreign lands. Most of the ideas that find their way into the USSR from abroad probably are anathema to loyal Marxist-Leninists and Komsomol members, but these same ideas prob-ably find a real or potential resonance in Soviet Muslim society.

Both the Islamic turmoil in Iran and the largely Islamic-inspired resistance to the Soviet invasion in Afghanistan have offered opportuni-ties for Islamic ideas to spill over into the USSR. There is no evidence of a wholesale spillover, but Soviet behavior suggests strongly that some ideological by-products from Iran and Afghanistan have trickled in.[14] Since the Iranian revolution began, but especially after the Soviet invasion of Afghanistan, Soviet media in the Muslim regions of the country have been warning the natives of the dangers inherent in the spread of Islamic ideas. Islam, for the first time, has been characterized as antisocial and antisocialist and is criticized as an irrational belief and reactionary basis for human organization. Gone for the most part are the earlier, more serious attempts by Soviet antireligious scholars to show the logical inconsisten-cies in Islamic doctrine. Soviet presses have increased their output of anti-Islamic propaganda over the same time period.[15]

Another telling measure of Soviet concern for the Islamic turmoil on its borders is a new official emphasis on counteracting "parallel Islam." Parallel Islam is, essentially, underground Islam. Because Islam—at least in its Sunni variant—requires no institutionalized clerical structure to direct religious practice, such as is required in Catholicism and Ortho-doxy, almost anyone with some knowledge of Islamic tradition can conduct the prescribed rituals (birth, burial, circumcision, and so on). Parallel Islam, which is condemned by Soviet authorities and by the official Soviet Muslim establishment in Tashkent, provides these services to the millions of practicing and nonpracticing Muslims in the USSR who find it impossible to have their spiritual and cultural requirements sat-isfied at one of the few officially sanctioned mosques or by clerics licensed by the Soviet state. For millions, a parallel network of itinerant clerics, who often have a very limited knowledge of Islamic doctrine, replaces these servants of the state-approved Muslim organization; these clerics often operate from the thousands of underground mosques that dot the countryside of Soviet Muslim regions.

Parallel Islam has grown dramatically in the last fifty years, all the more so because of the Soviet authorities' heavy-handed treatment of the Muslim clergy (most were liquidated). It continues to proliferate despite sanctions against practitioners and official campaigns to educate the Muslim masses against it.

Parallel Islam began long before Ayatollah Khomeini's revolution, but the latter unquestionably has added new energy to it, as Soviet official media make clear. (One report from the Turkmen press laments the fact that Muslim clerics—taking advantage of advances in electronics— record Khomeini's speeches on tape cassettes so as to make them easier to distribute among the faithful.)[16] Paradoxically, since Islamic fervor has intensified, Soviet leaders have authorized the opening of a number of new mosques in Central Asia and the Caucasus—a transparent attempt to draw believers away from the clandestine mosques where their activities cannot be observed and controlled.

Official condemnation has also centered on another meaningful target: the Sufi brotherhoods.[17] Like nearly all Muslim countries of the world, the USSR is host to several traditional clandestine Islamic orders, or brotherhoods (*tariqa*), which defy government attempts to eliminate them. In the Soviet media, Sufis are usually referred to as "fanatics" and occasionally as "religious terrorists," suggesting that their activities may on occasion be assuming violent dimensions. But the Sufi brotherhoods do not represent an alternative political system to the Soviet state, nor do the Sufis pretend as much. Sufism in the Soviet Union is meaningful primarily within the wider context of Islam. The goal of the secret organizations is to maintain the true faith through organization and discipline. Sufis maintain hundreds of holy places throughout the Muslim borderlands, which are visible proof to believers of Islam's survival under hostile conditions.[18] In the past Sufis played central roles in anti-Russian and anti-Soviet resistance movements in both the northern Caucasus and Central Asia, and the same brotherhoods currently enjoy a prominent involvement in the Afghan *mujahidin* resistance against Soviet forces.[19] Thus, though it would be inaccurate to suggest, except in isolated cases, that the Sufi brotherhoods in the USSR represent active anti-Soviet terrorist organizations, they could become a catalyst for Muslim opposition to Soviet rule in time of crisis.[20] Short of this, the brotherhoods are politically important for their successful efforts to operate clandestinely, apparently with considerable popular support and in defiance of Soviet campaigns to eliminate them. They provide a structure for the rigid discipline of Sufi adepts, who themselves offer to the Muslim masses, through their preaching and maintenance of holy places, evidence of Islam's staying power.

THE CHINA FACTOR

Many visitors to Tashkent and the other major cities of Central Asia return having heard some reference to the neighboring Chinese and how they eventually will send the Russians scurrying from Central Asia. "Just wait until the Chinese come. They'll show you what's what!" is one variation on this theme. Yet, for anyone with a sense of Central Asian history for the last one hundred years or so, this must sound like a hollow threat. The Chinese, after all, have hardly distinguished themselves by their benevolent treatment of the Muslims of Sinkiang province, formerly called Eastern Turkestan. In fact, Chinese rule in that region has been corrupt and brutal at best, all the more so in the last twenty-five years. Moreover, as all Soviet Central Asians know perfectly well, nearly all flights from unacceptable despotism have been from the PRC to the USSR (although there is little doubt that the Soviets encouraged these intermittent migrations in many ways).[21] Taunting the Russians with the Chinese threat can be explained as pure anti-Russianism on the part of some Central Asians—a pointed way of saying that they prefer the devil they don't know to the one they do.

All this may be about to change. The Chinese, who until the fall of the Gang of Four accepted the Soviet model of nationality relations—the forceful assimilation of minorities to the majority—appear to have embarked on a substantial policy change. If fully implemented—and nearly all Chinese officials admit that implementation is the difficult part—Chinese nationality policy, with special reference to Sinkiang, will offer Soviet Central Asians some attractive political alternatives.

Aware at last that their national existence is not threatened by the minority peoples who constitute between 6 and 10 percent of the Chinese empire, Chinese authorities have moved to reverse policies and practices that have alienated minorities, especially Sinkiang Muslims, for decades. Compulsory training in the Chinese language has been rolled back; freedom of religion has been declared, and mosques are being repaired or built at a frantic pace; well-known native political and cultural figures are being rehabilitated; and control of local affairs is increasingly being turned over to native managers. One particularly appealing part of the new policy calls for the removal of at least 50 percent of the Chinese cadres who were relocated to Sinkiang despite the vociferous and violent protests of the local inhabitants. Of all the changes, this one should find considerable sympathy in Soviet Central Asia, whether it can be put into effect or not. Most Soviet Muslims would no doubt welcome a similar commitment by the Russian government: such an action would be a bold statement that Russians and other colonizers in Central Asia and the Caucasus have no inherent right to be there.

For several decades a propaganda war has been fought at various intensities along the Sino-Soviet border. At stake is the allegiance of the border peoples, who are potential fifth columns in the opponent's camp. Even without full implementation of their new policies, the Chinese have provided themselves with some potent psychological weapons for this battle. Moreover, they show every intention of capturing the Islamic issue as their own. Many signs point to a new Chinese Islamic offensive, with the Soviets as the obvious target. (China's head mufti has had the unprecedented privilege of traveling extensively throughout the Muslim world in the last few years, especially since the Soviet invasion of Afghanistan. His message is pro-Islamic and anti-Soviet.) Since the invasion of Afghanistan and the failure of the Tashkent Islamic conference in September 1980, Soviet stock in the Muslim world has apparently been ebbing. The Chinese already have begun to capitalize on Soviet setbacks, and they are likely to make direct appeals to Soviet Muslims—appeals that can be underlined by practice—in the near future. Added to other Soviet concerns for the Muslim regions, then, is this: for the first time in Soviet history, a hostile communist state sharing several thousand miles of common borderland and many nationalities has articulated and moved to implement an aggressive, competing nationalities policy with special provisions for Muslims. It should not take Soviet leaders long to assess this danger and to draw its obvious implications.[22]

CONCLUSIONS

The Soviet Union is a multinational empire that is susceptible to all of the divisive internal and external pressures that have destroyed other multinational empires. The Soviet Muslim borderlands are the classic soft underbelly of the empire. In no other region of the state is the variety of pressures for change greater or the tempo of events faster. This variety of pressures, some of which have been discussed here, and the speed with which they are likely to become real forces, will make unavoidable gradual, perhaps even precipitate, changes in the rules of the game.

Of course there are those who will argue that Soviet Muslims have committed themselves to the Soviet system, that they are now part of that system and are its beneficiaries. In this view, benefits pre-empt dissatisfaction. There can be little doubt that Soviet power has helped Central Asians to develop economically, but this development has come at considerable social, political, and human cost to the Muslim peoples.[23]

Moreover, it is impossible to say whether Soviet Muslims might have developed faster and better under a different political system, for under the Soviets they have never had the luxury of political choice. Because of the costs to Central Asians and other Soviet Muslims of Soviet-style development and the impossibility of making other developmental choices that the dominant Russians might disapprove, one would be very foolish indeed to conclude that Soviet Muslims have "bought" the system.

It may be the case that Soviet Muslims have become very good at playing by the rules of the game and living within a limited set of options established by Moscow. And why shouldn't they? Although the game is not of their making, it is what they have to live with at the moment. Under the circumstances, they wisely advance in different ways by using the instruments at hand. One should not mistake their use of the system for "assimilation" or "integration" without overwhelming proof to that effect. In fact, Soviet Muslim advancement within the political system that embraces them can be interpreted in precisely the opposite way: Soviet Muslims are quietly but steadily reclaiming small parts of the power and authority that the Russians stripped from them in the 1920s. For example, recent research on cadre recruitment and movement in Uzbekistan indicates a strong trend toward "nativization," that is, toward the acquisition by native Central Asians of positions of authority in many spheres that formerly were held only by reliable Russians and other Slavs. Russians, however, have retained ultimate power by evolving new regional positions in which their authority is unchallengeable. Still, according to one expert, Russians are no longer bosses but watchdogs, and he concludes that "further changes favoring the Uzbek Party elite are inevitable, reducing the future political role of Russian cadres to a level more compatible with Uzbek advancement."[24] We should be alert to this trend and to the political implications of Soviet Central Asians in general using the established system to wrest control over many aspects of their lives from the dominant Russians. Our evaluation of their progress should be tempered with the knowledge that history is replete with examples of "committed" colonial peoples turning on their masters when the moment is opportune, regardless of the cost.

The Soviet Muslim borderlands can no longer be isolated from a strategic understanding of the wider Central Asian region, which stretches from western China to western Anatolia. This region, which is bound together by history, culture, language, and religion, is undergoing profound change in every sphere, from political reform in Muslim China to religious reform in Iran to economic reform in Turkey. These are all destabilizing influences on the societies of the Soviet southern flank. The

Russian response to these trends is beyond dispute: everywhere they have tried to disrupt change in the countries bordering their Muslim population, directly engaging in or sponsoring such varied tactics as propaganda and subversion in Sinkiang and Iran, terrorism in Turkey, and military intervention in Afghanistan. Seeing the Soviets committed to changing the prevailing social, political, and economic trends along this entire front should alert us to their anxieties about the region they seek to isolate and protect: Soviet Central Asia.

The time has passed when it was explicable to refer to the USSR as a unified Russian state. An examination of the strategic opportunities that could result from a more discriminating Western policy toward Soviet nationalities, and toward Soviet Muslims in particular, is long overdue. The Soviet periphery with its long stretch of soft underbelly already is subject to all the pressures described above and more; Soviet Central Asia could be the catalyst for substantial political change in the last empire. It will be to our advantage to study the possible dimensions of that change and to plan for the possibilities.

NOTES

1. Soviet scholars and high-ranking authorities of the security organs have recently begun to complain publicly that Islam in the USSR is now finding devotees among the younger generation and the intelligentsia. See, for example, Major General Zia Yusuf Zade, "Protecting the Country and the People," *Bakinskii rabochii,* December 19, 1980; and T. Khydyrov and K. Bagdasarov, "Islam in the Plans of Anti-Communism," *Turkmenskaia iskra,* September 11, 1982.

2. Demographic changes among Soviet Muslims and their policy implications are admirably discussed in Michael Rywkin, *Moscow's Muslim Challenge* (Armonk, N.Y.: M. E. Sharpe, 1982), esp. chap. 5; and in Alexandre Bennigsen and Marie Broxup, *The Islamic Threat to the Soviet State* (London and Canberra: Croom Helm, 1983), pp. 124–35. Good statistical data is found in Murray Feshbach, "Trends in the Soviet Muslim Population: Demographic Aspects," in Yaacov Ro'i, ed., *The USSR and the Muslim World* (London: George Allen and Unwin, 1984), pp. 63–94.

3. Paul Johnson, *A History of the Modern World: From 1917 to the 1980s* (London: Weidenfeld and Nicolson, 1983), p. 711. The American edition of this work is entitled *Modern Times.*

4. For a discussion and bibliography of the outmigration versus regional development question, see S. Enders Wimbush and Dmitry Ponomareff, *Alternatives for Mobilizing Soviet Central Asian Labor: Outmigration and Regional Development,* Rand Corporation, R-2476-AF, November 1979.

5. Discussed in ibid. See also Philip P. Micklin, "Soviet Water Diversion Plans: Implications for Kazakhstan and Central Asia," *Central Asian Survey* 1, no. 4 (1983):

9–43; and Gary Thatcher, "Diverting Soviet Rivers," *Christian Science Monitor,* January 16, 1985, pp. 14–15.

6. Micklin, "Soviet Water Diversion Plans," pp. 34–36.

7. The best discussion of the Soviet military manpower issue is Edmund Brunner, Jr., *Soviet Demographic Trends and the Ethnic Composition of Draft Age Males, 1980–1995,* Rand Corporation, N-1654/1, February 1981.

8. See Susan L. Curran and Dmitry Ponomareff, *Managing the Ethnic Factor in the Russian and Soviet Armed Forces: An Historical Overview,* Rand Corporation, R-2640/1, July 1982. For a discussion of the difficulties Soviet military authorities are facing in their attempts to integrate Soviet Muslims into the Soviet armed forces, see S. Enders Wimbush and Alex Alexiev, *The Ethnic Factor in the Soviet Armed Forces,* Rand Corporation, R-2787/1, March 1982.

9. See Alex Alexiev, "Soviet Nationalities in World War II," in S. Enders Wimbush, ed., *Soviet Nationalities in Strategic Perspective* (London: Croom Helm, 1985).

10. For a comparative view of practices aimed at minorities in military service, see S. Enders Wimbush, "Nationalities in the Soviet Armed Forces," in ibid.

11. See S. Enders Wimbush and Alex Alexiev, *Soviet Central Asian Soldiers in Afghanistan,* Rand Corporation, N-1634/1, January 1981.

12. In late 1985, a serious mutiny in the Soviet military in Afghanistan was reported. The mutiny was based on ethnic divisions and pitted Soviet Uzbek and Tadzhik soldiers against Soviet Slavic soldiers. Fighting between these troops is said to have raged for many hours, with casualties running as high as 450. See *The Daily Telegraph* (London), November 8, 1985; and *Afghan Information Centre Monthly Bulletin* (Peshawar), no. 56, November 1985. See also Taras Kuzio, "Ethnic Problems in the Soviet Army," *Soviet Analyst* vol. 14, no. 24 (4 December 1985), pp. 2–3.

13. For a discussion of the USSR as a borderland empire, see Daniel C. Matuszewski, "Nationalities, Empires, Borders," in Wimbush, *Soviet Nationalities in Strategic Perspective.*

14. For a well-documented discussion of the "trickle-in" phenomenon, see Alexandre Bennigsen, "Mullahs, Mujahidin, and Soviet Muslims," *Problems of Communism* (November–December 1984): 28–44.

15. For an excellent discussion of Soviet concern about the implications of militant Islam along its borders, see Yaacov Ro'i, "The Impact of the Islamic Fundamentalist Revival of the Late 1970s on the Soviet View of Islam," in Ro'i, *The USSR and the Muslim World,* pp. 149–77. See also Bennigsen, "Mullahs, Mujahidin, and Soviet Muslims," pp. 29–32, 38–42, and "Soviet Islam Since the Invasion of Afghanistan," *Central Asian Survey* 1, no. 1 (July 1982): 65–78. For an examination of the impact of the situations in Iran and Afghanistan on Soviet "Islamic diplomacy," see Chantal Lemercier-Quelquejay, "The USSR and the Middle East," in ibid., pp. 43–51.

16. For a discussion of the use of cassette tapes by Soviet Muslims, see "Central Asian Focus," *Arabia,* March 1985.

17. For a comprehensive treatment and bibliography of the Sufi issue in the USSR, see the special issue of *Central Asian Survey* (vol. 2, no. 4 [1983]) that is devoted

entirely to this subject. See also Alexandre Bennigsen and S. Enders Wimbush, *Mystics and Commissars: Sufism in the Soviet Union* (London and Los Angeles: Croom Helm and the University of California Press, 1985).

18. For an interesting discussion of one Westerner's discovery of an important holy place in Uzbekistan, see Pierre Julien, "In Quest of the Holiest Place in Central Asia," *Central Asian Survey* 4, no. 1 (1985). A list, descriptions, and maps of Muslim holy places in the USSR are in Bennigsen and Wimbush, *Mystics and Commissars*, pp. 115–156.

19. Olivier Roy, "Sufism and the Afghan Resistance," *Central Asian Survey* 2, no. 4 (1983), pp. 61–79.

20. During a trip to Kashgar and Ili in the Sinkiang province of the People's Republic of China in late 1983, I was told by leading Islamic figures that Sufi activity enjoyed a remarkable surge during the Cultural Revolution, that is, during a period when Islam in China was under strong attack. Indeed, this is an observable pattern throughout the Islamic world: when "open" Islam is under pressure, Sufi orders thrive.

21. For an examination and analysis of the ethnic politics of the Sino-Soviet border region, see Hans Braker, "Nationalities in the Sino-Soviet Dispute," in Wimbush, *Soviet Nationalities in Strategic Perspective.*

22. New Chinese polices in Sinkiang are discussed in "The Battle for the Hearts and Minds in the Heart of Central Asia," *Arabia*, December 1984, pp. 36–37; and in Hans Braker, *Die islamischen Türkvölker Zentralasiens und die sowjetisch-chinesischen Beziehungen*, Berichte des Bundesinstituts für ostwissenschaftliche und internationale Studien, no. 37, 1984. An analysis of the implications of these important changes in Chinese policy for the Central Asian region may be found in Alexandre Bennigsen, Marie Broxup, Paul B. Henze, and S. Enders Wimbush, *Central Asia in the 1980s: Strategic Dynamics in the Decade Ahead*, FAR-NA-100, (Kansasville, Wis.: Foreign Area Research, June 1984).

23. Two recent studies argue persuasively that the Soviet Central Asians' economic situation is deteriorating badly and that Central Asian dissent, based on economic grievances, is likely in the near future. See Boris Rumer, "Current Economic Problems of Central Asia," paper presented at the conference "Central Asia: The Decades Ahead," Munich, 19–20 August 1985; and Alastair McAuley, "Economic Trends in Central Asia," paper presented at the Second International Conference on Central Asia, Madison, Wisconsin, 10–12 October 1985.

24. Michael Rywkin, "Power and Ethnicity: Regional and District Party Staffing in Uzbekistan (1983/84)," *Central Asian Survey* 4, no. 1 (1985): 46.

Minority Nationalism Today: An Overview

Teresa Rakowska-Harmstone

INTRODUCTION

Minority nationalism in the Soviet Union is an outgrowth of historical conditions as much as a reaction to the establishment and policies of the Soviet system. Thus, to borrow a phrase from Marxism-Leninism, it is a product of both objective conditions and subjective forces.

The objective conditions are the legacy of the Russian empire. Russia's five hundred years of relentless eastward, westward, and southward expansion netted the minority half of the Soviet state's population. The non-Russians are of diverse cultural and historical background and constitute national groups of widely varying sizes and levels of socioeconomic development. The multiethnic society that has emerged in the USSR is of a type characterized by sociologists as a society with a dominant plurality core (the Russians are, in fact, a bare majority) and an aggregate of peripheral groups. The core group views itself as historically entitled to hegemony. This perception has resulted in the Russians' further penetration of the periphery, which has assured for them positions of political and economic authority. This in turn has resulted in the dissemination of Russian cultural patterns and values and their adoption as universal Soviet social norms.

The subjective forces that have shaped national relations in the Soviet period are comprised of (1) Marxist-Leninist ideological assumptions as they have been translated into policies for the construction of a new society and (2) reactions to those policies. Marxism-Leninism assumes that the ownership of productive forces and the resulting class struggle determine social relations and that nationalism—which is the product of national and social oppression under capitalism—is bound to disappear under socialism. Lenin saw two parallel trends in the period of capitalism, the momentum of which was to carry over into the socialist period. The first was a trend toward national self-assertion that emerged in the early capitalist period in reaction to the dual national-social oppression. The second was a trend toward internationalization in social relations that started in the late capitalist period under the impact of monopoly capitalism. In dialectical terms, the internationalist trend was in the ascendant and, once socialism was established, would lead to an eventual replacement of national by class loyalties. Lenin recognized the importance of nationalism, supported the right to national self-determination against the interests of imperial Russia (as his successors have supported self-determination in the Third World), and made concessions to nationalism in the interest of consolidating Soviet power. But he was confident that the policies aimed at the establishment of a socialist society would inevitably result in the disappearance of particular nationalisms (including Russian nationalism) and the emergence of class-based proletarian unity.

The very imposition by the Communist Party of the dictatorship of the proletariat was seen as an act that ipso facto liberated the masses from their erstwhile oppressors, social and national. Thus, theoretically at least, the basis was created for a conflictless society. National conflicts that stubbornly remained were therefore condemned as survivals of the past, and minority nationalism was officially perceived as the vestigial remains of a bourgeois nationalist mentality that had to be combated and suppressed.

In the period of the consolidation of Soviet power, strong centrifugal nationalist forces in the borderlands necessitated the assertion that the right to proletarian unity is historically "more progressive" than the right to national self-determination—an assertion that served to justify the reconquest of the rebellious borderlands by the Red Army.[1] The strength of minority nationalisms was recognized in the adoption of a federal state structure when the USSR was established in 1924; the class unity of the new socialist state was nevertheless preserved by the unitary party's monopoly of power. The arrangement was described as "national in form and socialist in content." An early effort to educate new socialist cadres from among the minorities was reflected in Lenin's policy of "indigenization" (korenizatsiia). But, because new cadres proved to be as prone to "nationalist deviations" as their bourgeois predecessors, the policy was scrapped when Stalin won the struggle for succession and introduced collectivization and industrialization policies. Recurrent massive purges destroyed the so-called bourgeois nationalists among the communist cadres. Manifestations of minority nationalism disappeared, and the Russians, who dominated the apparat implementing Stalin's policies, reasserted their dominant role. The Russians' role as an "elder brother" in the "Soviet family of nations" was explicitly articulated in the wake of the Great Patriotic War (World War II), wherein the nationalist appeal to defend Mother Russia proved its superiority over appeals to internationalism and class loyalties.[2]

After World War II most Western observers assumed that, in line with official Soviet pronouncements, the "national problem" in the USSR was indeed solved, as reflected in the literature of the period. But the post-1953 struggle for the Soviet leadership released the nationalist genie from the Stalinist bottle. National self-assertion among the non-Russians became increasingly visible and necessitated adjustments to the nationalities policy, albeit in the context—still and always—of the dialectical progression envisaged by Lenin, that is, the ascendancy of the internationalist over the nationalist trend. In 1961 at the Twenty-second Congress of the CPSU N. S. Khrushchev introduced the new formula of "flowering—rapprochement—merger" (*rastsvet—sblizhenie—sliianie*), and in the 1970s General Secretary L. I. Brezhnev announced that a new entity, the Soviet nation, had been created as the country entered a period of "mature socialism." Loyalty to the Soviet nation was to transcend particular national loyalties. At the same time, the perception of the Russian elder brother, which was played down in the 1950s, was revived in the 1960s and the 1970s.[3]

Thus, under mature socialism, the dialectics of national relations in the Soviet Union are said to promote full national self-realization of each Soviet nation and nationality (flowering/*rastsvet*), while at the same time drawing them "ever closer together" (rapprochement/*sblizhenie*) through "mutual enrichment" and on the basis of a common socialist economy and social structure. These two aspects of ethnic processes, the second in the ascendant, mark the road toward eventual merger (*sliianie*). N. S. Khrushchev saw the future merger of Soviet national groups as just around the corner. But minorities' pressures and recognition of political realities have forced his successors to consign this expectation to the distant time when communism wins its final worldwide victory. According to Iu. V. Andropov's statement on the occasion of the sixtieth anniversary of the USSR, "national differences will continue much longer than class differences."[4] Consequently, major policy emphasis in the late 1970s and early 1980s has been placed on the rapprochement part of the formula. Nevertheless, there has been a growing recognition on the part of Soviet leaders that, contrary to expectations, an unprecedented explosion of ethnic nationalism has taken place among Soviet nations and nationalities. And a new search is on for policies that would indeed assure that it is internationalism rather than nationalism that triumphs in the dialectics of national processes in the Soviet Union.

IMPACT OF PAST POLICIES

The policies adopted by successive Soviet leaders in the implementation of their twin goals (the construction of communism and system mainte-nance) all had their impact on ethnic relations and minority nationalism. Ideological expectations have not been validated. The relationship be-tween the national and the international, between *rastsvet* and *sblizhenie,* has not followed the prescribed path: the common economic and social framework and a growing volume of mutual transactions have had the effect of stimulating rather than minimizing the self-awareness of particu-lar national groups. Many of the policies intended to foster integration have instead resulted in the growth of ethnic nationalism. As I have argued elsewhere:

> Five key policy decisions have had a direct impact on the growth of national self-assertion in the multi-ethnic Soviet society: the legitimiza-tion of the system in class-based internationalist ideology of Marxism-Leninism; the federal state–unitary party dichotomy; the policy of accelerated modernization and economic development; the cultural policy aimed at the development of "national forms" of all the Soviet ethnic groups; and the dynamic post–World War II expansionist foreign policy.[5]

Here I will repeat main lines of the argument and relate them to selected theoretical insights derived from the study of ethnic relations elsewhere. The Marxist-Leninist ideological framework consigns nationalism to the garbage heap of history. Yet the fulfillment of each group's national destiny and the development of its national self-awareness (*rastsvet*) is seen as an integral part of the dialectics of ethnic processes on the road toward internationalism. This aspect of the ideol-ogy has served to confer legitimacy on expressions of nationalism, as long as they appear in the guise of the obligatory double talk. This ideological loophole has served the articulation of national demands. In the post-Stalin period, the loophole has been opened up wider by the revival of the Lenin myth, with its emphasis on the equality of all Soviet nations and nationalities and its legacy of an indigenization policy. The legitimacy of "flowering" has been particularly useful for expressions of cultural nationalism in all its aspects. As students of Soviet national problems well know, the articulation of cultural demands has been the first and most visible sign of national self-assertion, with cultural battles waged over the content of national forms not only by major union-republic nations, but by smaller national groups as well.

The federal structure of the Soviet state has been of major importance to Soviet national groups for the retention and development of their separate national identity. Under the original "national in form and socialist in content" formula, only the state structure was supposed to accommodate the "vestigial" identity of the country's major nations. But because the structure of the party—which is by definition unitary and a purveyor of universal socialist values—is parallel to the state structure and is based on the same territorial-administrative divisions, in practice the party and the state bureaucracies in the republics act as one and serve as the channel for the articulation of demands by the ethnic elites. As noted by students of ethnicity and nationalism in India, Canada, and other multiethnic federal states, the convergence of ethnic and administrative boundaries results in politicization of ethnicity and in the emergence of nationalism. The identification of ethnic with political and socioeconomic structures sharpens the perception of each group's relative position in the competition for the allocation of social values. The demands are aggregated on ethnic rather than functional lines, for reasons of strategic efficacy as much as ethnicity's affective value.[6]

In the Soviet Union the politicization of ethnicity received additional stimuli. First, the absence of autonomous subsystems in the social and economic spheres has precluded aggregation of interests on functional lines. Second, paradoxically, state forms and relevant bureaucracies are identified with national groups and are the only channels available for interest aggregation and articulation. The centralized nature of the Soviet system and the principle of the party's monopoly of power forces many of the political battles undercover. But conflicts between the republics and the "feds" in many issue areas were increasingly visible in the 1960s and 1970s. Apart from the cultural sphere, nationalist demands have been noted in particular in the placement of personnel and in investment and resource allocation and distribution, as shown in a growing number of Western studies based on evidence derived from Soviet sources.

The cultural renaissance of Soviet minorities has been a by-product both of the retention of formal national state structure and of policies that favored national "flowering." As originally designed, the policies aimed primarily at the development of national form as the vehicle for socialization, the better to transmit the socialist message. But, as national cultural forms developed—language, arts, and literature—they increasingly became the symbols of each group's distinct ethnic and cultural identity. This was especially so because, as noted earlier, the purported universalistic socialist message marched in tandem with the diffusion of the Russian value system and cultural norms.

As national cultures developed, the early formula of "national in form and socialist in content" was in fact reversed. The uniformity enforced by Moscow resulted in the convergence of forms into a common socialist pattern, although their content has diversified on national lines.

Modernization policies in the Soviet Union had effects similar to those in other multiethnic developing societies. Expectations of both communist theorists and early Western modernization experts were that traditional societies would disintegrate under the impact of economic and social change and that their traditional, particular (ethnic) identities would be replaced by a common "modern" identity and value system that, in multiethnic societies, would be identical to the identity and value system of the dominant and most advanced group. In practice, however, the impact has been to reintegrate traditional ethnic identity on a modern basis. Broadly speaking, and notwithstanding efforts at equalization (if and when these were present), the impact of modernization in the first phase has been to perpetuate inequalities and, as contacts increase, to sharpen the perception of differences and to increase conflict between the groups affected. Equal expectations are awakened, but, because of their initial advantages, the more developed groups benefit more from economic development and the greatest benefits accrue to the dominant group. At the same time the competition increases and a sense of relative deprivation affects other groups. In the second phase of modernization, when the gap between the dominant group and the minorities begins to narrow, it is the dominant group that begins to feel deprived, as it is faced by new competition from formerly subordinate groups. At each stage ethnic conflict is aggravated, and antagonisms begin to affect the social and political fabric of society as they are increasingly articulated by new elites, themselves a key product of modernization.[7]

In the Soviet Union, modernization's first phase has indeed perpetuated inequalities in the relative standing of national groups and has heightened their perceptions of differences. With the exception of two small Baltic nations in the northwest (Estonia and Latvia), the Russians are the most advanced on the modernizing scale. At the same time expectations have been awakened, stimulating perceptions of relative deprivation vis-à-vis neighbors and the dominant group, and the resulting demands have increasingly been articulated. Recent evidence indicates that the Soviet Union is entering the second stage of modernization.

The gap in socioeconomic indicators has begun to close, and complaints of unequal treatment are increasingly being heard from Russians who live in minority areas.[8] Thus, contrary to Soviet ideologues' expectations, neither equalization nor ethnic mixing (internationalization) seem to have contributed to ethnic homogenization or ethnic peace.

The theory of internal colonialism, expressed in the relations between the core and the periphery, is also applicable to the Soviet experience.[9] In general the political, economic, and cultural core-periphery slopes all seem to converge, that is, the Russian core is not only politically dominant but also enjoys economic and cultural superiority. The slopes do, indeed, converge in the case of the Muslim republics, even though in the Muslims' perception (stimulated by their cultural revival), the culture of Islam is superior to that of the Russians. But the modernization patterns that affect the Muslims, if slowly, are Russian patterns. The slopes also converge in Moldavia and Belorussia, as well as for the autonomous-republic nationalities and for dispersed groups. But, in terms of culture, this is not true for Armenia and Georgia and is not entirely true for the Ukraine in either the economic or the cultural sphere. In the case of the Baltic nations, which surpass the Russians on the modernization scale and are culturally a part of Scandinavia and east-central Europe, political subordination (by right of a relatively recent conquest) to a people who are perceived as culturally inferior has been particularly galling. Their resentment has been a major factor contributing to nationalism and national demands, including separatism, in the western borderlands.

Ethnic resentments are also stimulated by the overtones of Russification in the Sovietization process. As noted above, the Russians' ethnic attributes (ethnic markers, in sociological terminology) have been equated with the culture of "modernity" and, as articulated in the "elder brother" theory, are assumed to be superior to minority cultures. In fact, the pattern of ethnic organization in the Soviet Union (a majority Russian core combined with an almost equally large aggregate of minority groups) appears to have been a major catalyst for the emergence of minority nationalism. This, in turn, seems to have catalyzed the resurgence of Russian nationalism and its new militancy.

To make a final point, Soviet foreign policy pursuits in the post–World War II period have also contributed to the growth of ethnic nationalism. One aspect of this has been the Soviet outreach into the Third World, which involves an emphasis on and support for the principle of national self-determination. The argument that class unity overrides national loyalties under socialism has not been entirely convincing, it seems, in the Soviet domestic context. Moreover, a symbiotic relationship exists between Soviet domestic nationalities policies and Soviet policies regarding "fraternal" states in the Soviet bloc and the worldwide converts to a "socialist orientation." Assumptions governing nationalities policy at home are considered by the CPSU to apply to the workings of the "socialist world system," and lessons derived from the domestic experience are deemed applicable in the relations between socialist states.[10]

At the same time, Soviet minorities' nationalism has been responsive to bloc events. The "Prague Spring" of 1968 and Poland's 1980–1981 Solidarity movement have had an impact on the Soviet western borderlands, and the reverberations may continue for a long time. Events outside the bloc have been of importance also. The potential long-term effects of the Iranian revolution and the Soviet invasion of Afghanistan on Soviet Muslims can only be surmised at present.

At times a treatment of a specific minority evokes an echo abroad and a reciprocal response at home. The best-known case has been that of the Soviet Jews and the Jewish diaspora; less known has been the trickle of Soviet Germans emigrating to West Germany. The Armenians are a potential case. There are also the border-divided minorities: Uygurs and Kazakhs, who have both been used as pawns in the Sino-Soviet rivalry; Tadzhiks and Uzbeks, who have been used in the Soviet occupation of Afghanistan; and others.

To conclude this review of the impact of policies, there is little doubt that the nationalism of major non-Russian groups has been stimulated and is growing. Primarily affected are the union-republic nations, but a case can be made for autonomous-republic nations, such as the Tatars (most of whom live outside the Tatar Autonomous Soviet Socialist Republic [ASSR]), the Yakuts, and perhaps some others, although too little is known on the subject of smaller nations to offer conclusions.

Minority nationalism adds a new and important dimension to Soviet politics. The length of time, for example, that was required for the revision of the USSR's constitution (two decades) can be attributed, in my opinion, to behind-the-scenes debates that raged over whether republics have become obsolete under mature socialism and whether regional economic considerations should take precedence over ethnic claims. Glimpses of the debates appeared in Soviet publications. Judging by the results, the republican bureaucracies' preference for the status quo won the day. The power indigenous elites enjoy in their republics has increased over the last twenty years (spectacularly so, in the case of Central Asia), and there has been an improvement in their representation at the all-union level, albeit conditioned by the size and importance of particular republics and subject to the ups and downs of succession crises.

THE CURRENT SCENE

The Theory Amended: Ethnos and Ethnic Trends

The Soviet theory of national relations had to be adapted to the recent explosion of ethnic nationalism. The main burden of the adjustment has fallen on the shoulders of Soviet ethnographers, though contributions have been made by other disciplines. The first adjustment required was an explanation that the Leninist dialectics of nationalism and internationalism applied in the socialist period as well as in the capitalist period. The second adjustment was the articulation of a new theory of the *ethnos*—a perception of national culture and identity—which survives all changes in socioeconomic historical formations. The third was an interpretation of Soviet ethnic processes that both explained ethnic realities in terms of Leninist dialectics and provided policy guidelines for directing them into the correct path. This last interpretation distinguishes three major trends currently shaping the development of Soviet ethnic relations: consolidation and assimilation which contribute to the nationalism portion of the dialectic, and rapprochement, which reflects the ongoing process of internationalization.[11]

The "consolidation of the ethnos" is the first of these trends; it is synonymous with the *rastsvet* part of the political formula. The second is a trend toward assimilation, the reverse side of the ethnos consolidation process; it also contributes to the integration of Soviet peoples. The third trend is toward a "brisk transfer" (*peremeshchenie*) of ethnic specificity from the traditional sphere of material culture to a new "spiritual and mainly professional" (that is, modern) culture, which is synonymous with the process of rapprochement (*sblizhenie*).[12] The rapprochement phenomenon in particular is the focus of attention and study.

An ethnos carries all the specific characteristics of a given national group. In addition to a perception of common origins and, in most cases, of a common territory of settlement, key attributes of an ethnos are: the language, the culture of daily life (which includes customs and rituals), modes of oral creative expression, and such specific aspects of "psychological makeup" as norms of conduct, value orientation, and, most important, the "self-awareness" that is regarded as "one of the unchanging forms of ethnic manifestations." In fact, self-awareness has come to be seen as the crucial attribute of the ethnos and the source of the "we-they" dichotomy that causes members of one national group to see all others through a prism of its own cultural values.[13] These perceptions have been newly articulated by Soviet ethnographers. They come close to Western perceptions, which generally accept the cultural attributes listed above as characteristic of national entities. Self-awareness in particular is regarded as the necessary and crucial variable that, when linked to ethnicity, results in nationalism and is a necessary precondition for the existence of a nation.[14]

But an admission that value systems, norms of behavior, and self-awareness are all a part of an immutable ethnos (which does not change in response to the dialectical progression of history) departs rather conspicuously from standard Marxist perceptions of the relationship between the economic basis and the superstructure. What is more, Soviet sources now also recognize that national self-awareness persists even among groups (elites?) that have become culturally assimilated into a dominant culture: "It is known . . . that ethnic self-awareness may be formed and crystallized independently of a degree to which traditional components of life culture are safeguarded, and may even [be formed] when such [traditional components] are lost."[15]

All of these perceptions underlie a new approach to the study of the national problem. A nation is now recognized as an "ethnosocial community," and national processes are considered divisible into two basic aspects: ethnic and socioeconomic. It is clear from the discussion that the importance of this distinction lies in the recognition that because an ethnos is immutable, the ethnic aspect is basically unresponsive to manipulation. But the socioeconomic aspect can be altered to promote desirable changes, a return to the traditional base-superstructure relationship after all. As Academician Iu. V. Bromlei points out, the professional (modern) culture has a much stronger influence on ethnic processes—because it has mass impact—than does the traditional-life culture, the parameters of which are gradually being eroded.[16] It will be seen below that study of the most minute aspects of socioeconomic conditions in the various regions has now been made an urgent task for scholars in the various social science disciplines. Findings and recommendations of immediate policy relevance are required. New disciplines have thus emerged on the borderlines of ethnography and other traditional disciplines: ethnosociology, ethnopsychology, ethnolinguistics, ethnodemography, and so on.[17]

According to Soviet sources, the trends toward consolidation and assimilation both peaked in the period between 1926 and 1959, as seen in the decline in the number of ethnic groups enumerated in population censuses: there were 194 groups in 1926 as compared to 109 in 1959 and 104 in 1970 and 1979. The crystallization of nations is said to have benefited from the abolition of antagonistic social classes. As stronger nations consolidated their "ethnoses," they absorbed kindred and/or weaker national groups.

One measure for assessing the direction of the trend has been analysis of the change in territorial compactness of a given group, that is, the proportion of its people still living in the traditional national area. The Russians have shown a consistent decline in this indicator, which, in their case, has meant the extension of Russian culture throughout the Soviet Union. In 1926, 93.4 percent of ethnic Russians lived in the RSFSR, but only 82.6 percent did so in 1979. A similar decline took place in the number of Belorussians living in their national area. Some national groups, such as Lithuanians, Estonians, and Armenians, are said to have shown a consistent increase in the proportion of the "stay-at-homes" since 1926. For some others, such as the Ukrainians, Moldavians, Latvians and Azerbaijanis, compactness is said to have increased in the 1926–1970 period but to have decreased in the 1970–1979 period. A significant decrease was noted in the case of some autonomous-republic nations, such as the Tatars and the Bashkirs.[18] On the whole, the Armenians have the lowest indicator of compactness (60 percent in 1970) and the Georgians the highest (97 percent in 1970). It should be noted, however, that the traditional settlement area of many union-republic nations spills across the republics' boundaries. Thus a relatively low level of compactness—as defined here—does not necessarily imply a low level of ethnic consolidation. This has been particularly true in the case of the Muslim and Caucasian nations.[19]

The trend toward assimilation in most cases meant Russification: especially for minorities in the huge Russian republic (the RSFSR) and in urban and industrial centers dominated by the Russian ethnic element. But, because the demographic dynamism of the Russians decreased in the 1960s and 1970s and the self-assertion of other major nations emerged, assimilation also came to mean an absorption of culturally weaker groups by surrounding stronger ones. Cultural affinity, linguistic changes (linguistic assimilation or bilingualism), and mixed marriages have been singled out as contributors to assimilation.[20]

The tempo of cultural assimilation has depended on the proximity of a given culture and language to those of the dominant group and on the settlement pattern and degree of cultural cohesion of the group subjected to assimilationist pressures. Dispersed and highly urbanized groups tend to assimilate more easily than rural groups in compact settlement configurations. Individuals and/or groups living outside their national territories assimilate most quickly. Linguistic assimilation is seen as a major step toward ethnic assimilation but does not necessarily mean a change in nationality; bilingualism is regarded as a necessary first step for interethnic contact. In mixed marriages, children can choose the nationality of either parent. It is noted that in the RSFSR children predominantly opt for the Russian nationality if one parent is Russian and the residence is urban. But in other republics the titular nationality appears to be preferable. The highest percentage of mixed marriages in the union republics was reported for the cities of Moldavia, the Ukraine, and Belorussia (one-third).[21] But the percentages were considerably higher in the ASSRs where the titular group was in the minority, as in the Mordvinian ASSR and the Khakass autonomous region. All Soviet as well as Western sources see urbanization, linguistic change, mixed marriages, and ethnic interaction as factors favoring assimilation.[22]

By all accounts, Ukrainians and Belorussians are most vulnerable to Russification among union-republic nations. In this context, the importance of national state forms and demographic environment is striking. Assimilation indicators for both groups are much higher for individuals who live outside their national area than for those who remain at home. Within the republics the incidence of assimilation has been much higher in the eastern regions than it has been in the newly incorporated (during World War II) western regions. Lowest assimilation indicators are found in Central Asia and the Caucasus, because of the strength and cohesion of the Muslim and the Georgian and Armenian cultures (although smaller Muslim groups tend to dissolve in the surrounding Muslim majorities). Wixman notes that, despite the historically long-term Russian settlement in Kazakhstan and a high saturation there with the Russian ethnic element, linguistic Russification is very low, as it is in Tashkent (the capital of Uzbekistan), even though Russians account for almost 40 percent of the city's population. Obviously, he concludes, Christian Slavs are more prone to Russify than are Islamic Turks.[23] Similar conclusions were reached earlier by Brian Silver and are supported by findings of other Western and Soviet scholars. According to Soviet scholars, national groups with high assimilation indicators include Mordvinians, Karelians, Poles, Jews, Finns, Vepsy, Komi-Permyak, Kalmyks, and Udmurts.[24] To find groups prone to assimilation it is helpful to check language indicators in population censuses. All groups that show a decline in adherence to their own language *and* in bilingualism (Russian as the second language) are clearly undergoing linguistic Russification.

Soviet sociological research data show that Russification is not the only type of linguistic assimilation present. Dispersed national groups in the Ukraine, for example (Poles and Jews, but also Russians), have been assimilating into the Ukrainian language; and a number of small indigenous groups in Uzbekistan have adopted Uzbek as their language and eventually also as their nationality, a phenomenon noted in other republics as well.[25]

The factors that are considered to favor assimilation also contribute to the rapprochement-internationalization trend. The Russian migration has been rapprochement's most powerful promoter and has fostered modernization and interethnic mixing, the very factors that have been at the source of socioeconomic change. And, since socioeconomic change is seen as a necessary precondition for the development of internationalization, the trend toward rapprochement has been identified with socioeconomic development. The very essence of rapprochement is the transfer of ethnic specificity in the sphere of material culture from the traditional to the modern realm. In its impact on culture it is defined as "interethnic integration," and in fact it provides the crucial "buckle" between the ethnic and socioeconomic aspects of ethnic processes. Rapprochement is seen as the dominant characteristic (*magistral'naia liniia*) of these processes today and as the basis for the formation of the "Soviet people," the qualitatively new entity whose existence was proclaimed by the late secretary general, L. I. Brezhnev, at the twenty-fourth congress of the CPSU in 1971. As Academician Bromlei put it: "The rapprochement of nations in the economic, social, and cultural spheres, which is accompanied by the rapprochement of their cultures, is the basic essence of the processes of interethnic integration."[26]

The Russians: Their Changing Role and Perceptions

The Russians have played the key role in the rapprochement process. By attracting others they have been the focus of assimilation; their migration into every corner of the Soviet Union has spearheaded urban development and industrialization. But, as their demographic vitality has declined and that of others has increased—notably in the case of Soviet Asians—the Russians' relative impact has lessened, their dominant role in the borderlands has begun to be eroded, and the rapprochement process has lost much of its impetus.

Recently, an interesting two-part study on the demography and migrations of the Russians shed important light on the subject.[27] Its authors, S. I. Bruk and V. M. Kabuzan, distinguish two major periods in the post-1917 ethnodemographic development of the Russians. The first, which started with the revolution and ended in the 1950s, was the period of growth and dynamism: the Russians' share of the population grew at a fast rate because of both high rates of natural increase and assimilation. The period was characterized also by high mobility and the transfer of a significant portion of the Russian population from the European to the Asian part of the Soviet Union. But much of the dynamism was spent by the late 1950s, and during the 1950s and 1960s a decline set in. The Russians' rate of natural increase fell disastrously (by some estimates they no longer reproduce themselves), and their impact on other groups weakened.[28] Western sources confirm both the demographic decline and the change in migratory patterns. Rowland reports that the traditional Russian outward migration was much reduced in the 1959–1979 inter-censal period. Fewer emigrants went to the southern belt and there was a substantial reverse migration from the south and the east. Migratory momentum was sustained only into the northwest and eastern Siberia.[29]

But the results of the Russian migrations since 1917 have been massive. One-half of the Russians now resident outside the RSFSR either migrated in the Soviet period or are the descendants of such emigrants. The emigration was urban in character. Bruk and Kabuzan note that in the RSFSR in 1979 the Russians formed an absolute majority in all of the regions (krai) and provinces (oblasti), in five of the sixteen autonomous republics (ASSRs), in four of the five autonomous provinces, and in eight of the ten autonomous districts (okrugi). They dominated the cities and industrial centers. In other union republics, the Russians were a plurality in Kazakhstan and constituted more than one-third of the population of Latvia, more than one-fourth of Estonia and Kirgizia, and more than one-fifth of the Ukraine. Only in the Caucasian republics and in Lithuania did they constitute less than 10 percent of the population.[30] These figures bring home the massive impact the Russians have had on the indigenous populations of most of the Soviet regions and assimilation trends therein. Suffice it to say, as Bruk and Kabuzan point out, that 31 percent (18.9 million), or almost one-third of the overall increase in the number of Russians in the Soviet Union in the period between 1917 and 1979, was due to assimilation.[31]

But, as the impact of the Russians' decline began to be felt, the trends that favored their leading position and promoted integration slowed down or went into reverse. The rate of assimilation into the Russian majority declined, as noted above. The population explosion among Soviet Muslims placed in jeopardy the Russians' majority in the Soviet population. Although successive Soviet censuses showed only a minimal decline in the Russians' absolute majority position (from 54 percent in 1959 to 52 percent in 1979), projections by Western demographers indicate that in fact the Russians may already have become only a plurality.[32] In the 1926–1959 period the weight of the Russian group in union-republic populations, relative to the weight of the titular nationalities, showed a continuous growth; this trend has now been reversed in all but the Baltic republics, the Ukraine, and Belorussia.

Accustomed to a dominant position in the RSFSR and elsewhere in the Soviet Union, the Russians are now beginning to see themselves in the role of a minority in the non-Russian republics, a situation that is aggravated by the growth of local nationalisms and, in reaction, an equally spectacular growth of Russian nationalist feelings. Observers note a new awakening of Russian nationalism that manifests itself across a broad social spectrum: from emigrés and dissidents through working people and the professional and creative intelligentsia to the members of the Soviet armed forces and the party apparat. The concern over the preservation of Russian traditional culture and values (including the Russian Orthodox religion) has been joined by a growing perception of a decline (demographically and in genetic terms). Some Russians feel they have been used by the regime.[33] It is in this context that the burdens of the "elder brother" position (supporting junior brethren with Russian resources and at a sacrifice) have become increasingly apparent and resented in relation not only to the Soviet minorities but also to the East European and Third World members of the "socialist community." For the Soviet future the crucial problem seems to be not only the growth of minority nationalism but also, and perhaps more important, the spread of a perception among Russians that a conflict exists between the interests and well-being of the Russian nation and the "internationalist" demands of the regime.

Rapprochement in Practice: Problem Areas

As Soviet sources acknowledge, the momentum toward integration has now slowed, both because of the Russians' loss of dynamism and because the "flowering" of national cultures among the USSR's major nations has produced national elites with their own socioeconomic and sociocultural milieus. The obvious and growing strength of ethnic nationalism has actually forced an admission from Soviet observers that, dialectically speaking, rapprochement is compatible with the continued development of national ethnoses—albeit on the higher stage of historical development—and need not lead to their liquidation.[34] This more realistic assessment has been accompanied by a more open discussion of the trends and phenomena that are seen as major problems for rapprochement.

Demographic trends are of major concern to Soviet policymakers. Differential growth rates of the Soviet population in the 1959–1979 period resulted in a shift in the relative weight of the Slavic and the Asian groups in the population total. The Slavs' share declined from 77.1 to 72.8 percent, and the Turkic-language group increased from 11.1 percent to 15.2 percent.[35] We are told that

one of the serious problems, the urgency of which has increased in the
last few years, is the demographic situation that exists in the majority of
the country's provinces, especially in the European part among the
Russians, Ukrainians, Belorussians, the Baltic nations and some others
. . . [This is] a change to a family of one or two children . . . [By
comparison] growth indicators among the indigenous nations of Central Asia, the Kazakhs, and the Azerbaijani [are] three times higher than
the all-Union average.[36]

For purposes of an effective distribution of manpower, the demographic explosion of that part of the population that is least modernized
and culturally most alienated (as other portions decline) has been nothing
short of a disaster. The repercussions have been severe for the Soviet
armed forces. The problem is augmented by the Muslims' low urbanization rates (in 1979 fewer than 30 percent of the Uzbeks and 20 percent of
the Kirgiz were urbanized) and their continuing refusal to move to the
cities. In the last two decades, rural dwellers in Central Asia increased by
70 percent, whereas the village population in European Russia declined
by 22 percent. The reasons, we are told, are cultural and directly related to
the Muslims' adherence to tradition and their ignorance of the Russian
language.[37] This perception has long been accepted by Western observers.
Economic aspects also contribute to the lopsided pattern of urban-rural
migration. Central Asian collectives produce primarily cotton, a com-
mercial crop, and their earnings are fairly high; moreover, the traditional
way of life in the villages and a warmer climate make rural life more
comfortable for the Muslims. Earnings in the collectives of the core
regions of European Russia are extremely low, and the European collectives suffer from harsh climate, poor soil, and nonspecialized crops. By all
accounts, depopulation there has reached staggering proportions: only
old people and women stay in the countryside.

Differentials in levels of education and in the knowledge of Russian
are repeatedly singled out as important factors in the maldistribution of
the labor force. Problems of the distribution of manpower and the low
mobility of indigenous populations in a number of union and autonomous republics were the subject of numerous papers at an all-union
conference on national relations (a follow-up to the directives of the
twenty-sixth congress of the CPSU), held in Baku, May 25–30, 1981.[38]
Bromlei points out that in areas where the proportion of educated and
qualified youth is high (the RSFSR and the Baltic republics) the industrial
plant is old, and obsolete economic structures make it difficult for many
qualified workers to find jobs. In Central Asia, however, where there is
modern industrial equipment, the local youth lack skills, and many of

them "lack general cultural and professional qualifications needed"; in short, they have no "urban culture."[39]

Knowledge of Russian (bilingualism) is crucial for participation in the socialist (industrial) sector of the economy as well as in social and political life. It is also essential for development of the rapprochement trend. In a reversal of a standard practice, the stress in the discussion is no longer on the increase in the numbers of non-Russians who learn Russian, but on the numbers who do not. Accordingly, it is repeated that 40 percent of the non-Russian Soviet population still cannot communicate in the language of "international communication." In some republics "more than half of the population does not speak Russian." Even worse, we learn also that "in some republics one encounters a curious phenomenon whereby the middle-aged people know the Russian language better than the young ones." This is said to be true in particular in rural areas of Central Asia, in the Caucasian republics, and in Moldavia—a remarkable testimony to the strength of traditional cultures and to the failure of Soviet educational efforts of decades.[40]

The impact of multiethnic contacts on integration and the whole question of the effects of an "internationalized" environment seem to have come under new and more critical scrutiny in the early 1980s. The standard assumption that internationalization (the creation of a multiethnic environment at work, in the armed forces, and in social life) ipso facto encourages integration and automatically creates a setting where rapprochement thrives is no longer valid. It is incorrect to assume, we are told, that an increase in ethnic contacts always has a positive effect on national attitudes. Although an internationalist setting is still the best milieu for "the nurturing of the internationalist spirit" (the citation is from Andropov's speech on the sixtieth anniversary of the USSR), sociological research shows that in a given multiethnic environment the positive impact of multiethnic exchanges depends on whether the community has had a "long-standing experience of friendly contacts." In "new" collectives, districts, and cities, where there is an active immigration of alien peoples, national differences tend to stand out most strongly; national groups notice differences in culture and life-style between themselves and others. In fact, the growth of ethnic contacts actually stimulates national self-awareness of the various groups that interact with each other. Thus "there is a need for major educational work and for a tactful cadre policy, and special care has to be taken to provide for the cultural needs of the members of the interacting nationalities."[41]

The conclusion is that a differentiated approach, taking account of educational levels, social structure, and variations in the traditional setting, is needed to inculcate internationalist values. People who are not well educated have national prejudices because of ignorance. But—and this is an important admission—an education in itself does not necessarily create a positive approach toward other nationalities. If there is a surplus of educated young people and a shortage of jobs available, as in Georgia and Moldavia, there emerges a "competitive situation that may affect national attitudes." In some cases "in concrete life situations," there may even arise "perceptions of unrealized professional expectations," which may then "be transplanted into the national soil" and thus feed ethnic antagonisms.[42] Further, research in the Baltic republics has shown that an increase in the multiethnic composition of the cities did not result in the "wiping out" of national differences; a scientist from Grozny (the site of a major oil field in the North Caucasus) reported at the Baku conference in May 1981 that extensive surveys carried out in multiethnic collectives indicated that even the most favorable conditions created for ethnic exchanges at work failed to stimulate an extension of ethnic contacts into the social realm.[43]

Thus it is not surprising that the number of mixed marriages is low. Nevertheless, they are seen as a major vehicle for rapprochement and a positive phenomenon in fostering internationalist attitudes. Not only are their numbers small, however (13.5 percent of all marriages in 1970 as compared with 2.5 percent in 1925), but most seem to be taking place between kindred national groups (Slavs marry Slavs and Muslims marry Muslims). In any case, some fail to create an "appropriate climate" for the growth of "internationalist values."[44]

The existence, since the late 1930s, of an internal passport system that lists the owner's nationality has had a negative impact on integration because, in the words of some Soviet scholars, it has created a "legal-psychological deterrent."[45] Under this system, a citizen's nationality is predetermined by the nationality of the parents and cannot be changed. An option exists only for the children of mixed marriages who, at age 16, may choose the nationality of either parent. As noted above, the predilection has been to opt for the titular nationality in a given area. The significant role that the passport system has played in the survival of national differences in the Soviet Union is the focus of an interesting article by Yuri Luryi and Viktor Zaslavsky, a Soviet-trained sociologist now in the West.[46] The mention of the problem is new in Soviet sources; heretofore it has also been ignored by Western observers.

The admission that an internationalist environment stimulates rather than minimizes ethnic conflict may well have been prompted by complaints received from the Russians (and other immigrants) who claim unequal treatment in the national republics. Certainly there have been repeated calls for a Soviet version of affirmative action on behalf of the "nonindigenous immigrant population." These were heard at the twenty-sixth congress of the CPSU and have also appeared in other sources.[47] This is a new and interesting development, given the Soviet past practice of granting cultural institutions only to indigenous inhabitants of national areas. (Cultural amenities for the Russians have generally been available in urban areas throughout the Soviet Union.) The call may have been occasioned as much by the Russians' resentment of the preferential treatment local indigenous elites extend to their own people as by the need to attract non-Russians (particularly Muslims) to urban and industrial centers that they consider culturally "alien."[48] In either case, it can only be interpreted as a concession to ethnic "flowering" and a setback to the promotion of rapprochement.

The discussion in Soviet sources clearly indicates that the family, and in particular the rural family, has been the source of traditional socialization. Its influence remains undiminished and indeed may even be on the increase. Bromlei says that the family is "the bearer of the ethnos," that it "creates the value system," and that in "substantial part" it "determines social conduct"—a striking admission in a country where a massive socialization effort is supposed to have resulted in the creation of a "new Soviet man" and a "Soviet people." Research shows, Bromlei continues, that the loosening of family ties among the Slavs and Balts favored migration, whereas the retention of archaic elements by Central Asians has prevented their mobility. Further, he says, although rural family life differs between the various ethnosystems, it has generally been characterized by low outside contacts, strong peer pressures that are very effective for purposes of social control, and a convergence of the interest of the family and the collective, which results in the safeguarding of the family's economic interests in the form of the private (subsidiary) economy (*podsobnoe khoziaistvo*). For all the shortcomings of the internationalist environment in the city, Bromlei writes, it is there that the "professional" (modern) forms of national cultures develop with their (presumably) internationalist features due to "enrichment" by other cultures. A village, however, tends to maximize its uninational characteristics and to remain the center of the traditional aspect of the ethnos. Thus, internationalization processes there, in the form of the introduction of professional material culture (one-third of the collectives have TV), need special study in order to properly manage the national process.[49]

Another startling admission is that the village-derived values tend to survive urbanization and even a decline in family life: "although family life has declined, particularly for the white-collar and highly skilled blue-collar workers . . . national differences persist." The reference here appears to be to the southern republics. But general references are also made to an increase in the prestige of village life and to a "veritable renaissance" of village folklore—folk songs, for example—which, "in some cases," have acquired the dimensions of "ethnic symbols." It is noted that the preservation of national (traditional) elements in family life has had important social consequences, such as regulating the size of the family, the number of children, and the extent to which women participate in social and political life.[50]

The Role of the Elites

The characteristics of the new indigenous elites and their role in the overlapping processes of national consolidation and rapprochement are obviously of key importance. Without an elite, or with an elite that has been co-opted by the dominant group, a national group has no cohesion and no means for articulating its national demands: there is no self-awareness. Soviet sources see indigenous elites as the bearers of the rapprochement process, since they have been educated under socialism, operate within a socialist social structure, and share common principles of "socialist morality." Initially, these were the "creative" and "administrative-managerial" elites. Lately, that is, in the period of mature socialism, these have been joined, in most republics, by the "industrial and scientific-technical" elites.[51]

The ambiguous role played by Soviet minority elites—do they represent their group's consolidation or do they serve the international interests of Moscow?—has been difficult to interpret. There is much evidence that many members of minority elites have been assimilated into the Russian ethnos in everything but name. But there is also important evidence that the same people have been the spokesmen for their nation's self-awareness and the articulators of national demands to the central authorities; they have also promoted policies within their republics that favor indigenous inhabitants over the immigrants. Minority elites are an integral part of the Soviet political system and have a stake in its maintenance; at the same time they strive for the maximum of power and autonomy available to them within systemic constraints, which they seek to loosen and to erode. Fighting for a particular advantage in competition with others, they are manipulable by a divide-and-rule strategy. Many, undoubtedly, have been co-opted; certainly those who serve outside their republics as members of the all-union bureaucracies are in this category.

But several reasons militate against the minority elites' permanent co-optation: reasons opportunistic, psychological, and political. There is the strategic efficacy argument, that is, their careers and self-preservation depend on identification with the success (if not necessarily the interests) of their constituencies. And even among those who are most assimilated, there still appear to be vestigial commitments to the group of their origin and to the traditional culture. Moreover, genuine assimilation, or "passing," has been made very difficult, particularly for the non-Slavs. There is, of course, the ubiquitous passport system. Also, even in their own republics, members of indigenous elites still take second place to the (mostly Russian) representatives of the central apparat. The "feds" in republican bureaucracies are now much reduced in numbers in comparison with the 1940s and 1950s, but they are still placed in key positions such as the second secretaryship of the national Communist Party—the post that traditionally controls the republic's nomenklatura (personnel policy) and is the link to Moscow. Except for a few, transfers to the hub of power in Moscow have not been easy. The perception of "once an ethnic, always an ethnic" ultimately leads—as seen in ethnic elites elsewhere—to a need to revalidate one's power position through the national heritage and the support of the national constituency.

Experience in other multiethnic societies indicates that a drastic reduction and/or loss of traditional cultural attributes does not correlate with a reduction of the instrumental relevance of the group's ethnic identity in the political arena. In fact, ethnic militancy frequently has been characteristic of elites with a high degree of acculturation to the dominant culture.[52] This perception has now been confirmed in the Soviet context, as demonstrated in earlier discussion. None of the assimilation/rapprochement indicators actually guarantees integration; many, in fact, presage greater militancy. And, finally, minority elites' perception of their position vis-à-vis the dominant state system is dynamic in nature and depends on the system's current strength and viability. In the Soviet multiethnic state, the loss by the Russians of their demographic and political dynamism has undoubtedly been a significant factor in the growth of minority nationalism and the acceleration of minority demands.

Policy Relevance

It appears that the magnitude of the national problem is recognized at the highest level. This was reflected in the discussions during the twenty-sixth congress of the CPSU and its follow-up. The speech by Andropov in December 1982 sounded a note of concern and of urgency, which not only stimulated a vigorous response but also introduced an unprecedented and remarkable degree of frankness into the discussion. This frankness was reflected in the treatment of the subject during 1982–1983. The June 1983 plenum of the Central Committee of the Communist

Party of the Soviet Union (CC CPSU), in addition to discussing ideology, also devoted a large part of its deliberations to the national problem—in particular to the need to study the subject further and in greater detail, so as to allow for the adoption of appropriate policy measures.[53]

As summarized by Bromlei, the results of the discussion and the ongoing research revealed that

> a substantially more complex picture of ethnic and national development [has emerged] than was previously assumed . . . The massive [research] material available shows, first of all, that along with the dominant tendency toward internationalization of the total picture of social life of the nations [*narodov*] of our country there evolved also a tendency that in some measure is getting stronger [*koe v chem usilivaiutsia*], toward differentiation in economic, sociocultural, demographic, and other spheres.[54]

The "new look" at the national problem envisaged a more sophisticated approach, a more highly differentiated policy, and a much greater degree of social control and social engineering. The keynote for the new approach to nationalities policy in the brief period of Andropov's leadership was sounded by the general secretary himself:

> It is important [to assure] that the current increase in national self-awareness does not become converted into national conceit and self-importance and does not breed a tendency toward separation and a negligent attitude toward other nations and nationalities. This [increase] cannot be explained by the survivals of the past only. It is also a result of incorrect approach to the work [on the problem]. There are no details that are unimportant here: [neither] attitudes toward the language and the historical monuments and the treatment of historical events [nor] how we convert villages into cities and how we influence the conditions of life and work of the people.[55]

Andropov's policy seems to have been characterized by a more genuinely "internationalist" approach than that followed by his predecessor. It remains to be seen whether the new general secretary of the CPSU, Mikhail Gorbachev (K. U. Chernenko was a transition figure), will follow the new line or return to the emphasis on Russification that was promoted by the late General Secretary L. I. Brezhnev. The problem, however, remains, and centrifugal pressures are increasing.

The June 1983 CC CPSU plenum outlined the tasks facing ethnographers and other social scientists in connection with the new approach.

They were directed to study the national problem in all of its ramifications—to analyze the "flowering" and "rapprochement" trends and "mutual enrichment" processes, as well as the accompanying problems and possible resolutions. They were told to pay special attention to the general tendencies and basic directions of ethnic processes and to the "concrete mechanisms" of dialectical interaction; to seek and to analyze specific conditions, actions, and factors that promote and/or hamper the linkages between the ethnic and the socioeconomic aspects of ethnic processes; to study specific dynamics of national relations in the various regions in the urban as well as rural settings; and to study conditions of development and problems in the languages, cultures, and life-styles of the nonindigenous groups.[56]

The policy relevance of the research done by social scientists was made explicit. They were told to prepare policy recommendations for concrete situations. Moreover, they were promised a new mechanism for the transfer of their recommendations upward (*mekhanism peredachi*). No details of the new mechanism were given. But it is likely that the intention of the decisionmakers was to provide the scholars with a direct-access channel to Moscow, which would safeguard them from interference by interested local authorities. The plenum did demand a better central coordination of the scholarly effort.[57]

Much of the need for these heroic efforts was attributed to imperialist interference and "an imperialist threat" to the Soviet Union, which was described by Andropov in his introductory remarks as "the worst since the Great Patriotic War [World War II]." The domestic reasons cited sounded a familiar note; it was necessary "to combat nationalism, localism, a nonclass approach to the evaluation of historical events, and efforts at idealization of the patriarchal way of life (*patriarkhal'shchina*), as well as to utilize the positive traditions in practical daily life."[58]

The emphasis on social (state) regulation of ethnic processes and on administrative methods emerged clearly in the three areas of major concern: manpower, linguistic policy, and family life-styles, traditional customs, and traditions.

The labor problem has loomed the largest. Its intractable character emerged clearly from a complaint by Chernenko (who, as a secretary for ideological matters, was the main rapporteur at the plenum) that "it has not been possible, in full measure, to direct labor resources to where they are needed."[59] The plenum (as well as the twenty-sixth congress) discussed a need "to study the possibilities of a transfer [resettlement of labor reserves] between particular regions, and of [directly] managing the demographic situation. It is well known how important are the ethnic aspects of the problem."[60]

The study of the ethnic aspects of the labor problem is to include not only an "in-depth" investigation of "work habits and traditions" of various national groups and of ethnosocial processes in villages but also an analysis of the crucial problem of the differentials in the size of the family.[61] Legislation was apparently introduced to reward second and third (but not subsequent) children with family allowances in order to stimulate births in low-fertility areas. But this is perceived as just a first step in the social management of the problem, because, as Bromlei notes candidly, family allowances are not really adequate to motivate the Slavs and the Balts to expand the size of their families.[62]

Demographer V. I. Perevedentsev, long a student of the labor problem, came out in favor of social management of human reproduction processes at the Baku conference in 1981. But he also argued that the utilization of manpower can be better managed by locally adopted measures that would motivate rural youth in Central Asia to move into the cities, rather than attempting to transfer manpower from labor-surplus to labor-deficit areas. Such measures should include better instruction in Russian, the teaching of "urban skills" in the villages, and situating new enterprises near the villages. It is reported that many of the conference's participants supported the latter proposal.[63] Perevedentsev has been advocating this type of solution for some years now, but so far neither the investment pattern nor the talk of resettlement indicate its likely adoption. Instead, there are reports of pilot projects training Central Asian youths in technical schools in the RSFSR in anticipation that they will settle there after graduation.

The linguistic policy and, in particular, the promotion of bilingualism (that is, the knowledge of Russian), has been closely linked to the labor problem. The report on the June 1983 plenum indicates that the CC CPSU and the USSR Council of Ministers adopted new legislation on the study of Russian in the non-Russian republics.[64] Local reports indicate that the primary reason for the new measures is not only the need for skilled labor but also, and primarily, the need for Russian-speaking military manpower. M. N. Guboglo, a leading Soviet linguist, proposed at the Baku conference that social control should apply not only to the promotion of bilingualism but also to its use in "various aspects of social life"; no details were given, but apparently the proposal evoked a vigorous debate in which views were expressed both for and against this suggestion.[65]

The need, finally, for the study of family life, customs, and rituals, and of the impact of social processes on family life and the ethnic factor, were also given prominence at the June plenum. Special emphasis was placed on the need to "Sovietize" customs and rituals ("we cannot close our eyes to the fact that, at times, the new rituals become deformed . . . by middle-class, petit-bourgeois, and other alien customs and traditions") and on the need to combat—hence study—the influence of religion ("not a small part of the population remains under religious influence, which is promoted by foreign ideological centers aiming to give religion an anti-Soviet nationalist coloration").[66]

CONCLUSIONS

A general study of the politics of ethnicity concludes that the current political strength of ethnicity is "the most keen and potent edge of intrastate and interstate conflicts, displacing class and ideological conflict . . . It asserts itself today, dialectically, as the leading legitimator or deligitimating challenger of political authority."[67] Certainly the ethnic variable has emerged as the key social and political reference point in the Soviet Union in the last decades. This has been the message in Soviet sources, and it is strongly confirmed by interviews and surveys conducted by Western scholars with Soviet emigrés. The most recent Soviet materials available on the subject of ethnosocial processes in the Soviet Union validate our past assumptions that ethnic nationalism there has been growing faster than integration.[68]

Assimilation trends and integrative mechanisms cannot be dismissed lightly, however. To really "solve" the national problem, the integration of the three major Slavic groups is crucial because, if unified, the Slavic majority would have an overwhelming weight in the country, notwithstanding the Muslim population explosion. Under Brezhnev, there was a campaign promoting the notion of a common ancestry for the three groups. Certainly Belorussians and Ukrainians are very vulnerable to assimilation, but there is a strong and growing Ukrainian nationalism. The three Baltic nations are the most openly and uncompromisingly nationalistic of all Soviet groups. But they are inundated by Russian immigrants, and Latvia and Estonia may be on the verge of demographic extinction. Smaller groups continue to Russify and, despite the decline, the Russians will still constitute a near majority in the Soviet population in the year 2000.

But the fissures along ethnic fault lines run deep, and nationalism is perhaps more of an Achilles heel for the Soviet Union than many of its better known and more celebrated problems. Its magnitude continues to increase. At present nationalism does not seem to be an immediate threat to the country's stability. But the emergence of such a threat depends very much on unpredictable variables. It can be triggered by a perceived shift in the internal balance of power or by any number of outside developments that may affect or destroy this balance. As militant nationalisms, Russian and non-Russian, link with and feed on other causes of social discontent—economic shortages and mismanagement, the deterioration in health standards, the crisis of faith and bankruptcy of ideology, the elites' conspicuous consumption and growing class differentials, or the monumental incompetence and corruption—an explosive mixture develops that may need only a spark for spontaneous combustion.

NOTES

1. See Richard Pipes, *The Formation of the Soviet Union: Communism and Nationalism, 1917–1923,* rev. ed. (Cambridge, Mass.: Harvard University Press, 1964); and E. H. Carr, *The Bolshevik Revolution, 1917–1923,* vol. 1, pt. 2, *Dispersal and Reunion* (Harmondsworth, England: Penguin Books, 1966).

2. See Hélène Carrère d'Encausse, *Decline of an Empire,* trans. Martin Sokolinsky and Henry A. LaFarge (New York: Newsweek Books, 1979), chap. 1.

3. Teresa Rakowska-Harmstone, "The Dialectics of Nationalism in the USSR," *Problems of Communism* (May–June 1974): 1–22.

4. Cited in Iu. V. Bromlei, "Etnograficheskoe izuchenie sovremennykh natsional'nykh protsessov v SSSR. K 50-letiiu ordena Druzhby Narodov Instituta Etnografii AN SSSR," *Sovetskaia etnografiia,* no. 2 (March–April 1983): 5.

5. Teresa Rakowska-Harmstone, "Ethnicity in the Soviet Union," *The Annals of the American Academy of Political and Social Science* 433 (September 1977): 78. See also Rakowska-Harmstone, "The Nationalities Question," in Robert Wesson, ed., *The Soviet Union: Looking to the 1980s* (Stanford: Hoover Institution Press; Millwood, N.Y.: Kraus International Publications, 1980), 129–53.

6. Joseph Rothschild, *Ethnopolitics: A Conceptual Framework* (New York: Columbia University Press, 1981), p. 5; and N. Glazer and D. P. Moynihan, eds., *Ethnicity: Theory and Experience* (Cambridge, Mass.: Harvard University Press, 1975), introduction.

7. Rothschild, *Ethnopolitics,* chap. 4.

8. In the mid-1970s 67 percent of young Uzbeks (in the 20–29 age group) had higher and secondary education (but in their own language, presumably) as compared to 57 percent of young Estonians in a comparable sample (Estonians have traditionally had the highest modernization indicators), according to a leading Soviet sociologist. He also reports that differences in skilled labor statistics have also been equalized: "Whereas the percentage of older Uzbeks employed in skilled labor is lower than the percentage of Russians or Estonians, these figures are virtually identical for the younger Soviet citizens regardless of nationality. Some 80 percent to 90 percent of young urban Uzbeks, Russians, and Estonians are skilled workers, while in the

countryside these figures range from 60 percent to 80 percent" (Iu. V. Arutiunian, "On Several Trends in the Narrowing of Cultural Differences Among the USSR Peoples at the Stage of Developed Socialism," *Istoriia SSSR*, no. 4 [1978], abstracted in the *Current Digest of the Soviet Press* 30, no. 51 [January 17, 1979], p. 10). These figures should be seen in the light of each nation's urban/rural distribution, however. Also, the high percentage of skilled workers among Central Asians seems doubtful in view of information available in most Soviet sources.

9. Rothschild, *Ethnopolitics*, chap. 2.

10. See Teresa Rakowska-Harmstone, "'Socialist Internationalism' in Eastern Europe—A New Stage," *Survey* 22 (Winter 1976) and (Spring 1976): 38–54, 81–86.

11. See Rakowska-Harmstone, "The Nationalities Question."

12. I. S. Gurvich, "Osobennosti sovremennogo etapa etnokul'turnogo razvitiia narodov Sovetskogo Soiuza," *Sovetskaia etnografiia*, no. 6 (November–December 1982): 16.

13. Bromlei, "Etnograficheskoe izuchenie," p. 5, and "O nekotorykh aktual'nykh zadachakh etnograficheskogo izucheniia sovremennosti," *Sovetskaia etnografiia*, no. 6 (November–December 1983): 21.

14. See, for example, Rupert Emerson, *From Empire to Nation: The Rise to Self-Assertion of Asian and African Peoples* (Cambridge, Mass.: Harvard University Press, 1960); Walker Connor, "Nationalism and Political Illegitimacy," *Canadian Review of Studies in Nationalism* 8, no. 2 (Fall 1981): 201–28; and Hugh Seton-Watson, "Unsatisfied Nationalism," *Journal of Contemporary History* 6, no. 1 (1971): 3–14.

15. Bromlei, "O nekotorykh," p. 12.

16. Bromlei, "Etnograficheskoe izuchenie," pp. 5–6, and "O nekotorykh," p. 12.

17. Philosophers, party historians, economists, lawyers, and others are also included in the effort. The work is being coordinated by the Council on the National Problems at the Presidium of the Academy of Sciences of the USSR and the Academy's Institute of Ethnography. Professor Bromlei heads both of these institutions. *Sovetskaia etnografiia*, no. 2 (1983), for example, includes five articles on ethnosociology, grouped under a general heading of "Discussion and Comments."

18. Bromlei, "Etnograficheskoe izuchenie," p. 9. Bromlei does not specify the boundaries in which given groups were considered; in 1926 the Baltic states were not a part of the USSR; the same applies to parts of Moldavia, the western Ukraine, and Belorussia.

19. See Rakowska-Harmstone, "Ethnicity," table 1, p. 77.

20. Bromlei, "Etnograficheskoe izuchenie"; and S. I. Bruk and V. M. Kabuzan, "Dinamika chislennosti i rasseleniia russkikh posle Velikoi Oktiabrskoi Revoliutsii," *Sovetskaia etnografiia*, no. 5 (September–October 1982): 3–21.

21. Bruk and Kabuzan, "Dinamika chislennosti i rasseleniia russkikh" pp. 14–15.

22. Gurvich, "Osobennosti"; and Ronald Wixman, "Territorial Russification and Linguistic Russianization in Some Soviet Republics," *Soviet Geography* 12, no. 10 (December 1981).

23. Wixman, "Territorial Russification," pp. 674–75; Gurvich, "Osobennosti"; and Bruk and Kabuzan, "Dinamika chislennosti i rasseleniia russkikh." Bruk and Kabuzan provide more information by reporting that the Russians' share in the population of the Donetsk-Dnieper basin in the eastern Ukraine in 1979 was one-third of the total, while in the newly incorporated southwestern provinces it constituted only 7.3 percent. The impact of these figures on the Russification of the Ukrainians is obvious. See also Roman Szporluk, "Western Ukraine and Western Belorussia: Historical Tradition, Social Communication, and Linguistic Assimilation," *Soviet Studies* 31 (January 1979): 76–98.

24. Brian Silver, "Social Mobilization and the Russification of Soviet Nationalities," *The APSR* 68, no. 1 (March 1974), and "Levels of Sociocultural Development Among Soviet Nationalities: A Partial Test of The Equalization Hypothesis," ibid., no. 4 (December 1974); and Bruk and Kabuzan, "Dinamika chislennosti i rasseleniia russkikh," p. 16.

25. Bruk and Kabuzan, "Dinamika chislennosti i rasseleniia russkikh," p. 17.

26. Bromlei, "Etnograficheskoe izuchenie," p. 11.

27. S. I. Bruk and V. M. Kabuzan, "Dinamika chislennosti i rasseleniia russkogo etnosa (1678–1917 gg)," *Sovetskaia etnografiia*, no. 4 (July–August 1982): 9–26; also S. I. Bruk and V. M. Kabuzan, "Dinamika chislennosti i rasseleniia russkikh posle Velikoi Oktiabrskoi sotsialisticheskoi revoliutsii," *Sovetskaia etnografiia*, no. 5 (September–October 1982): 3–21.

28. See chapter by Mikhail S. Bernstam in this volume.

29. Richard H. Rowland, "Regional Migration and Ethnic Russian Population Change in the USSR (1959–1979)," *Soviet Geography* 22, no. 8 (October 1982).

30. Bruk and Kabuzan, "Dinamika chislennosti i rasseleniia russkikh," *Sovetskaia etnografiia*, no. 5 (Sept.–Oct. 1982): 3–21, pp. 3–4.

31. Ibid., table 9, p. 13.

32. Murray Feshbach, oral communication, 1983.

33. See chapters by John B. Dunlop and Mikhail S. Bernstam in this volume.

34. Gurvich, "Osobennosti," pp. 26–27; and Bromlei, "Etnograficheskoe izuchenie."

35. Bromlei, "Etnograficheskoe izuchenie," p. 8. It is not indicated whether the Tadzhiks are included. Soviet Muslims are reported to have natural growth rates equal to the highest in the world: a 3 to 3.5 percent increase per year (ibid.). See also Bromlei, "O nekotorykh," p. 14.

36. Bromlei, "O nekotorykh," p. 14.

37. Ibid., and Bromlei, "Etnograficheskoe izuchenie," p. 8.

38. A. A. Susokolov, "Vsesoiuznaia Nauchnaia Sessiia 'XXVI S'ezd KPSS i zadachi izucheniia natsional'nykh otnoshenii v SSSR,'" pp. 111–15, *Sovetskaia etnografiia*, no. 2 (March–April 1982).

39. Bromlei, "O nekotorykh," pp. 16–17.

40. Bromlei, "O nekotorykh," pp. 20–21. In this context it is particularly deplor-

able, Bromlei says, that the weight of the Russian group in the southern republics has been declining. See also Bromlei, "Etnograficheskoe izuchenie," p. 12.

41. Bromlei, "Etnograficheskoe izuchenie," pp. 12–13.

42. Ibid., and Bromlei, "O nekotorykh," p. 22.

43. Susokolov, "Vsesoiuznaia Nauchnaia Sessiia," pp. 112–13. See the papers by V. I. Parol' (Tallin), K. S. Khallik (Tallin), I. K. Apine (Riga), and I. R. Loov (Grozny).

44. Ibid., p. 114, and papers by R. A. Achylova (Frunze) and A. G. Aliev (Baku); and Bromlei, "Etnograficheskoe izuchenie," p. 10. Highest incidence of ethnic intermarriage was reported for Latvia, Kirgizia, and the Ukraine: 18 to 20 percent of the total in 1970, as compared to 14 to 15 percent of the total in 1959.

45. Bruk and Kabuzan, "Dinamika chislennosti i rasseleniia russkikh," Sovetskaia etnografiia, no. 5 (Sept.–Oct. 1982)," p. 17. A similar view is expressed in Bromlei, "Etnograficheskoe izuchenie," p. 10.

46. Victor Zaslavsky and Yuri Luryi, "The Passport System in the USSR and Changes in Soviet Society," Soviet Union/Union Soviétique 6, pt. 2 (1979): 137–53.

47. Bromlei, "Etnograficheskoe izuchenie," p. 8. The nonindigenous population in the national republics numbered about 55 million people in 1979 (ca. 20 percent of the Soviet population).

48. Evidence for this exists in surveys done in the West among recent Soviet emigrés. See, for example, Rasma Karklins, "Nationality Power in Soviet Republics: Attitudes and Perceptions," Studies in Comparative Communism 14, no. 1 (Spring 1981): 70–93. See also V. Perevedentsev, Metody izucheniia migratsii naseleniia (Moscow: Nauka, 1975).

49. Bromlei, "O nekotorykh," pp. 15, 19. The study of the role of the family is now set up as a collective endeavor not only for the Soviet nations and nationalities, but also for the East European countries, members of the WTO-CMEA system.

50. Ibid., pp. 16, 20, and Bromlei, "Etnograficheskoe izuchenie," pp. 11–12.

51. Iu. V. Bromlei, "Osnovnye tendentsii natsional'nykh protsessov v SSSR (K 60-letiiu obrazovaniia SSSR)," Sovetskaia etnografiia, no. 6 (November–December 1982): 3–15.

52. Frederick Barth, ed., Ethnic Groups and Boundaries (Boston: Little, Brown, 1969), pp. 32–33.

53. The Andropov speech was printed in Pravda, December 22, 1982, and Kommunist, no. 1, 1983. On the plenum, see Bromlei, "O nekotorykh."

54. Bromlei, "O nekotorykh," p. 13.

55. Cited in Bromlei, "Etnograficheskoe izuchenie," p. 13.

56. "Iunskii Plenum TsK KPSS i zadachi sovetskikh etnografov," Sovetskaia etnografiia, no. 6 (November–December 1983): 5–6.

57. Ibid., pp. 6, 10.

58. Ibid., pp. 3, 6–7.

59. Cited in Bromlei, "O nekotorykh," p. 15.

60. "Iunskii Plenum," p. 7.

61. Ibid., pp. 7–8.

62. Bromlei, "Etnograficheskoe izuchenie," p. 8, and "O nekotorykh," p. 15. It is not clear how this legislation affects the standing legislation on family allowances, and whether or not it is applied differentially in the various regions.

63. Susokolov, "Vsesoiuznaia Nauchnaia Sessiia," p. 113.

64. "Iunskii Plenum," p. 8.

65. Susokolov, "Vsesoiuznaia Nauchnaia Sessiia," p. 114.

66. "Iunskii Plenum," pp. 7–8.

67. Rothschild, p. 31.

68. The interviews were carried out by, among others, Karklins, Zvi Gitelman, and Juozas Kazlas. See also Rakowska-Harmstone, "The Dialectics of Nationalism."

Language, Culture, Religion, and National Awareness

John B. Dunlop

On April 14, 1978, the main street of Tbilisi witnessed an unusual and stormy demonstration. A crowd some five thousand strong—mostly student youth—massed and then marched noisily from the university to the building of the Georgian Council of Ministers. Their purpose: to contest a new draft constitution for the republic of Georgia that omitted reference to Georgian as the state language. This deletion had touched a raw nerve among the demonstrators. The mood among the young people was so volatile that, according to an account published in the *New York Times*, the potential for bloodshed was "averted by a Russian general in charge of security who . . . reported that the situation was ugly, and suggested that it would be wise to yield on the language issue."[1] The next day the offensive clause was reformulated, and similar changes were hastily made in the draft constitutions for the republics of Armenia and Azerbaijan.

Three years later, on April 14, 1981, a date that by this time had come to symbolize Russification, several months of student unrest in Georgia reached their peak. Large numbers of young people attempted to assemble in Mtskheta, the ancient capital of Georgia, to engage in common prayer for their nation. Apprised of these plans, the KGB and militia sealed off the roads to the city, denying access even to pedestrians, and forbade trains to stop at Mtskheta station. Due to an oversight, however, some three hundred demonstrators nevertheless succeeded in reaching the ancient church of Svetitskhoveli in Mtskheta, where, after listening to taped recordings of ancient Georgian hymns, they knelt down, joined in the recitation of the Our Father, and prayed for Georgia. At the same time, in Tbilisi, a chain of militia and KGB men cordoned off the city's main cathedral, letting no one in. Over a hundred students subsequently signed a letter to First Secretary Shevardnadze of the Georgian Communist Party, deploring the actions of the authorities.[2]

The tumult in Georgia has involved more than merely students. In 1976, for example, at the Eighth Congress of Georgian Writers, Revaz Djaparidze excoriated Georgia's minister of education for suggesting that such subjects as history and geography be taught henceforth in Russian, that all textbooks be published in that language, and that dissertations and their defenses be translated into Russian. Djaparidze's speech was greeted by a quarter-hour of applause, and the audience refused to permit the minister to answer him. When First Secretary Shevardnadze spoke, he was interrupted by angry shouts as he sought to allay fears of Russification.[3]

As such incidents attest, language, culture, religion, and national identity are clearly and inextricably connected in the mind of contemporary Georgians. But recent evidence suggests that this also holds true for a number of other minority nationalities of the Soviet Union and, increasingly, for an important segment of ethnic Russians as well.

THE ISSUE OF LANGUAGE

Why, one might ask, is the Soviet government so obviously courting trouble by seeking to Russify such an ancient and nationally self-conscious people as the Georgians? To a large degree, the rationale can be traced to Marxist-Leninist ideology as it has been applied in the Soviet Union since 1917. From the very beginning, the Soviet state has been viewed by its leaders as a unitary body whose underlying principle, proletarian internationalism, allowed no room for national differences and aspirations. Despite numerous tactical zigzags, beginning with the NEP, this concept of nations as ultimately ephemeral has never been abandoned by the Soviet leadership. The twenty-second party congress under Khrushchev even advanced the radical term *sliianie* (fusion), implying a biological homogenization of the Soviet nationalities. Khrushchev's successors have been more cautious, preferring blander phrases such as *polnoe edinstvo* (full unity [of Soviet nationalities]), but, despite tactical fluctuations, the Brezhnev regime evidenced little real concern for the survival of nations. Hélène Carrère d'Encausse has pointed out that the Soviet leader most aware of the enduring and refractory quality of the

Soviet nationalities was Stalin, who made "Great Russian chauvinism" one of his tools.[4] Coercion—including, if necessary, the uprooting of whole peoples—was Stalin's equivalent of Khrushchev's naive belief in a future "fusion" of nationalities.

If one accepts the premise that nations are transitory entities, it follows that their means of communication, languages, are no less ephemeral. A unitary state grounded in an ideology containing the whole truth about man and society needs a single lingua franca to ensure mind control and internal security, and for administrative efficiency in general. Through this common language of the one state, citizens are molded and transformed by a single ideology, Marxism-Leninism. Commentators have noted that the utilization of Russian for such a purpose comes at a considerable price to the language itself. "Associatively," Jonathan Pool observes, "Russian belongs to the Russian people, but it is also the 'language of Lenin.'"[5] Lithuanian poet Tomas Venclova has formulated the problem well: "Russian to a growing degree is seen not as Russian, but as 'Soviet' and large groups of Russians themselves perceive it in just this way. The fact is that Russian is more connected with the official ideology than non-Russian languages of the Soviet Union." Serving as the language of politics and ideology, Russian "has experienced the retroactive and destructive influence of that secondary semiotic system."[6]

Ideology is thus a factor pushing the Soviet leadership to Russify the minority nationalities of the USSR. But economic and demographic considerations are perhaps even more important today. As is well known, the fertility rate of ethnic Russians and Eastern Slavs is not keeping pace with that of Central Asians and other non-Slavs. Serious manpower shortages are already being felt in Soviet industry and agriculture. Manpower-surplus areas, such as Central Asia, must thus become donors to manpower-deficit areas, such as Western Siberia, if Soviet military-industrial expansion is to continue. But if non-Russians are to be integrated successfully into the Soviet economy, they must be taught Russian and, optimally, be Russified. Yet the 1970 census offered disturbing evidence that certain Soviet nationalities, particularly Islamic peoples of Central Asia, were being recalcitrant even about learning Russian as a second language. This was almost a kind of sabotage and too dangerous—because of its possible links with "bourgeois nationalist" aspirations and even separatist inclinations—to be permitted to continue. As a result, the Soviet leadership decided in the 1970s to press ahead with, and speed up, the process of Russification.

The Soviet regime, of course, has long been encroaching upon the language rights of its minority peoples. In 1958, for example, Khrushchev's notorious Thesis 19 suggested that the study of local languages by aliens, that is, Russians, living in the non-Russian republics should be made optional. Thus asymmetric bilingualism was recommended as the desired norm. As Michael Rywkin has noted, this reform was one that even Stalin never attempted, since in his period Russians living outside the RSFSR were required to learn local languages.[7] In Latvia, Thesis 19 caused a tremendous stir and was heatedly debated in the republic's press. The Latvian Supreme Soviet, in a rebellious move, actually increased the number of compulsory hours for the study of Latvian in the republic's schools (March 1959).[8] After a purge of Latvian "national communists," however, Khrushchev's recommendation became policy in Latvia, as elsewhere in the USSR. The results of this asymmetry were demonstrated by the 1979 census: only 3.5 percent of ethnic Russians claimed to have fluency in the language of any other Soviet people.

By the late 1970s, the Brezhnev regime had apparently decided upon an even more intense policy of Russification. The removal of Podgorny, who may have been a Ukrainian Nationalist sympathizer, from the Politburo in 1977 perhaps removed the last obstacle to such initiatives. By a decree of the Council of Ministers of the USSR issued in October 1978, Russian was introduced into the lower grades of all elementary schools in the USSR. It is a measure of the perceived political sensitivity of this decree that it was promulgated in secret. (There was nothing novel in this procedure, of course: major new legislation on religion, introduced in 1962, was not published in the Soviet Union until 1975.)[9] According to one account, the October 1978 decree was delivered to educational officials by special courier, with instructions that it be read and memorized on the spot and then returned to the courier; party Central Committee bureaus in the republics were, in turn, to issue detailed confidential decrees embodying the new policy.[10] The decree of the Estonian Bureau was eventually leaked and published by Estonian emigrés in Sweden.

In May 1979, the regime went a step further, organizing a major theoretical conference in Tashkent on the topic "The Russian Language—The Language of Friendship and Cooperation of Peoples in the USSR." In this case, too, elaborate attempts were made to keep the agenda secret—it was mandated, for example, that the conference's draft documents be kept in safes. The recommendations (which, this time, were leaked by the Lithuanians) included the proposal that ministries of education introduce the teaching of Russian to five-year-olds in non-Russian kindergartens. The recommendations went beyond mere language instruction: Russian was to be used in play and various extracurricular activities at school, and parents were to be encouraged to make consistent use of Russian at home. School newspapers, excursions, and discussions of television programs and films were to be conducted in Russian.[11]

These extraordinary measures show that the regime was not as concerned as many Western analysts had thought it would be over the reaction to such bullying tactics by the republican elites. The Brezhnev leadership was clearly willing to take a calculated risk: to Russify aggressively in the hope of rejuvenating a stagnant economy and thwarting "bourgeois nationalism" and separatism in the future.

Understandably, the Tashkent recommendations created a stir in the minority republics. Five thousand Lithuanians protested the recommendations in a petition to the Central Committee, and an open letter by Estonian intellectuals scored, among other manifestations of Russification, "the hyperbolic and inept propaganda campaign pushing the teaching of Russian in schools and kindergartens."[12]

In the midst of this heavy-handed campaign of Russification, a minor tactical retreat on the language front was sounded by Brezhnev at the twenty-sixth party congress in 1981. On that occasion, he urged that the linguistic and cultural needs of migrant workers in the Soviet Union be cared for. From other statements in his address, it was clear that Brezhnev was seeking to encourage the migration of Central Asians and peoples of the Transcaucasus to Siberia and the Far East.[13] This unexpected solicitude for the linguistic and cultural needs of migrants should not be seen as blunting the thrust of Russification. Brezhnev was surely aware that migrants are more apt eventually to assimilate, linguistically and culturally, than "stay-at-homes," even though Islamic peoples have historically been less likely to assimilate than others.

During his brief tenure as general secretary, Andropov showed himself to be a believer in a Soviet melting pot in which the national distinctions of the peoples of the USSR would be submerged. In December 1982, he made his first major speech since becoming party leader. This statement was devoted to the sixtieth anniversary of the formation of the USSR, and in it Andropov advanced the highly controversial merger theory (*sliianie*), according to which the peoples of the Soviet Union will merge into one entity, *sovetskii chelovek* (Soviet man).[14] Brezhnev, it should be noted, had carefully avoided this term, no doubt because it had earlier caused considerable trouble for Khrushchev.

How successful has the Russification process been from the regime's point of view? Fragmentary data available from the 1979 census suggest mixed results. Actual linguistic assimilation of non-Russians has been proceeding very slowly. (Furthermore, as the case of the Jews demonstrates, linguistic assimilation does not necessarily betoken ethnic reidentification.) In 1959, 59.3 percent of Soviet citizens—54.5 percent of the population was ethnically Russian—gave Russian as their native tongue; hence 4.8 percent of the population had been linguistically assimilated; in 1970, this figure rose to 5.3 percent and in 1979 to 6.2 percent.[15] Due to fertility trends, however, the actual percentage of native speakers of Russian vis-à-vis the populace as a whole has declined slightly, from 59.3 percent in 1959 to 58.6 percent in 1979.

In a few important cases, linguistic assimilation seems to be proceeding quite rapidly. More than a quarter of Belorussians (25.8 percent in 1979) now do not speak Belorussian as their native language; in 1970, this figure was 19.4 percent. As for Ukrainians, 82.8 percent were native speakers of Ukrainian in 1979, as opposed to 85.7 percent in 1970—a decline of 2.9 percent. For obvious reasons, the Russification of Eastern Slavs enjoys a high priority with the regime. In the case of the Ukraine— where, as the Shelest incident showed, nationalist tendencies can manifest themselves among the top party elite—Russification is undoubtedly viewed as being engaged in a particularly important race with centrifugal forces.

Other Soviet peoples appear to be resisting linguistic assimilation with considerable success. In the 1979 census, Lithuanians showed no change from the 1970 census in the linguistic assimilation of their populace (97.9 percent were native speakers of Lithuanian). The number of native speakers of Estonian and Latvian dropped only 0.2 percent each (to 95.3 percent and 95 percent, respectively). In view of the regime's desire to Russify the Baltic—especially Latvia and Estonia, with their large numbers of Russian migrants—these census figures seem to show determined resistance on the part of the Balts.

The adoption of Russian as a second language cannot in itself be construed either as assimilation or ethnic reidentification. Nevertheless, from the regime's point of view, it is obviously a necessary first step in a desirable process, a step the leadership has been anxious to promote. One striking instance of growth in the knowledge of Russian as a second language is that of Uzbekistan. In 1970, a mere 14.9 percent of Uzbek respondents claimed fluency in Russian—in 1979, the figure stood at 49.3 percent, a jump of 34.4 percent. Michael Rywkin is correct in drawing our attention to the fact that the assessment of fluency in Russian depends on the respondent and that, as a result, "It is quite possible that demographically vigorous Uzbeks, feeling ethnically secure, tend to exaggerate their own knowledge of Russian."[16] It is nevertheless clear that a major effort must have been made over the period 1970–1979 in Uzbekistan to increase fluency in Russian. Uzbeks are the most populous Central Asian people, and Tashkent is the showplace capital of the Soviet Islamic world. It is symbolically important that, of all the Soviet peoples, Uzbeks should learn Russian, and quickly.

Contrary to what is often believed, even by specialists, Russian nationalists were not happy with the campaign of Russification that was pursued by the Brezhnev and Andropov regimes. Indeed, even such an ardent foe of Russification as Ivan Dziuba, author of the seminal study, *Russification or Internationalism?* (1965), singled out Russian nationalist writers Vladimir Soloukhin and Leonid Leonov for strong praise as principled opponents of Russification.[17]

Virtually all present-day Russian nationalist spokesmen are "polycentric" nationalists, that is, they regard all peoples and their cultures as of intrinsic worth. As official nationalist Ilya Glazunov puts it: "I believe that world culture has nothing to do with Esperanto but is a bouquet of different national cultures."[18] A contributor to *Veche*, the important samizdat journal that served as a forum for Russian nationalism in the early 1970s, assails the thoughtless policy of seeking to create a "Soviet nation" and attacks the "elemental Russification" taking place in the borderlands.[19] Such spokesmen insist that undue significance should not be ascribed to the fact that Russian is the language of state; that Russian language represents no more than a kind of emasculated and cliché-ridden Esperanto. Alexander Solzhenitsyn, among others, has frequently scored the decline and degeneration of the Russian language during the Soviet period.

Which are the elements in the party leadership who are seeking to Russify the minority nationalities? Marxist-Leninist ideologues of the Ponomarev orientation would seem to have few scruples about the process, and neither would devotees of the defense-heavy industrial complex. "The speedy urbanization of Central Russia," Mikhail Agursky notes perceptively, "is a question of life or death for the military industrial complex . . . They are not afraid of the Soviet melting pot for, even without traditional Russian culture, this melting pot is essentially Russian for them."[20] Groping for a term, Agursky calls this group "progressive" or "radical" Russian nationalists, but I would disagree. A *Russian* nationalist, I would contend, cannot be indifferent to the demographic, social, and spiritual well-being of ethnic Russians, to their language and culture. Let us rather call these elements "Soviet patriots," since their essential concern is expansion of the USSR's military and industrial might.[21]

One other ramification of the language issue deserves mention. Western broadcasts to the Soviet Union—by the Voice of America, Radio Liberty, the BBC, Deutsche Welle, and so on—serve as the Soviet populace's only reliable source of information concerning both domestic and foreign events, and they could serve, potentially, as a means for the West to help bring about desirable changes in Soviet politics. Russian-language broadcasts, however, present a particular problem. Since Russian is both the lingua franca of the Soviet federation and the native language of 137 million ethnic Russians, the directors of such broadcasts have been unable to decide whether they should design their programs for an ethnic Russian audience or for the Soviet populace as a whole. The temptation has been to opt for ethnically "neutral" programming, a tactic that ignores or downplays the cultural and religious needs of the dominant nationality of the Soviet Union. (A number of Russian nationalist dissenters, including Solzhenitsyn and Father Gleb Iakunin, the imprisoned cofounder of the Christian Committee for the Defense of Believers' Rights in the USSR, have commented on this paradox.)[22] It has been argued persuasively that the present practice runs counter to the real needs of the contemporary West.

THE SPHERE OF CULTURE

If nations and their languages are transient phenomena, their cultures and histories, too, can have only relative significance. Lenin himself elaborated the theory of two "streams" (*potoki*), according to which the prerevolutionary historical-cultural "stream" of a given people must be sharply distinguished from its postrevolutionary development. The year 1917, in this view, represents a leap into a higher and superior reality. Events in a nation's past thus take on significance only in reference to the Bolshevik revolution. In the case of Russia, the Decembrists and "revolutionary democrats"—Belinsky, Chernyshevsky, Herzen—are normally accorded value because they, at least indirectly, helped prepare the way for October. Dostoevsky, the Slavophiles, Andrei Rublev, and St. Sergius of Radonezh, however, should be shunned, since they belong to that part of the prerevolutionary "stream" that is best forgotten.

It is, however, precisely in the cultural sphere that the regime faces a real and growing predicament. In the terms of Kostas Papaioannou, as cited by Alain Besançon, Marxism-Leninism has become a cold ideology, "a cooled down ideology that has lost all power to arouse enthusiasm or even simple belief" among the populace of the USSR.[23] Of course, even a "cooled down" ideology, as Besançon and others point out, can still exert tremendous power. Nevertheless, in the area of cultural expression, it becomes almost worthless; devoid of élan, the ideology can no longer serve to stir or uplift the public. There is simply no longer a "market" in the Soviet Union for works embodying the message of *Mother, Chapaev,* or *How the Steel Was Tempered*, although some echoes can on occasion still be encountered in contemporary literature and art.

Finding no sustenance or inspiration in Marxist orthodoxy, present-day cultural expression tends to veer either toward introspection, experimentation, and Western-style avant-garde or toward nationalism and religion. In literature, the first direction is represented by the writings of Andrei Bitov and Yuri Trifonov (d. 1981). In other spheres, one could mention a recent rock opera staged in Moscow by Andrei Voznesensky and Aleksei Rybnikov or the staging of the 1981 "Moscow-Paris" exhibit of modern art.[24]

What seems to be the stronger tendency, however, involves an attempt to replace an increasingly irrelevant and "cold" ideology by an appeal to nationalism or a combination of nationalism and religion. In prose fiction, for example, the two writers who presently enjoy the greatest popularity in the Soviet Union, Siberian author Valentin Rasputin and Kirgiz writer and filmmaker Chingiz Aitmatov, both adhere to this tendency. In each case, we are light-years away from such socialist realist classics as *The Rout* and *Cement*.

Rasputin won a prestigious State Prize for his novel *Live and Remember* (1974), which was carried as part of the mass-edition *Roman-gazeta* series, but he earned the authorities' strong disapproval for his next work, *Farewell to Matera* (1976), a powerful, quasi-allegorical novel that seems to call into question the whole phenomenon of breakneck Soviet modernization.[25] *Farewell to Matera* recounts the fate of the inhabitants of an island, Matera, located in the midst of the Angara River in Siberia, during the last few summer months preceding their evacuation to the mainland. Matera and other nearby islands are due to be inundated by the construction downriver of a huge hydroelectric plant. The majority of the island dwellers whom we get to know are elderly peasants who have spent their entire lives on Matera. Their imminent removal to an urban-type sovkhoz settlement fills them with apprehension.

Farewell to Matera makes clear that Rasputin, though a relatively young author (b. 1937), has little sympathy for modern industrialized Russia, at least in its present incarnations. Rasputin's *porte-parole*, the elderly grandmother Darya, believes that modern man has sought to clamber out of his "human skin" and has uprooted himself from the earth, from nature, and from God. Modern cities remind Darya of the frenetic scurrying of ants and the swarming of midges. The flooding of Matera—a place name deriving from the word *mat'* (mother)—is symbolically akin to a process of national matricide. The Russian earth, family cemeteries, and venerable churches (Matera's church has been converted into a storehouse and its crosses knocked off) are all being sacrificed for electricity and the specious cult of progress touted by Soviet prometheans. Modern Russia, Rasputin believes, must be rooted in the mind and wisdom of centuries-old traditional Russia. If not, then fire and flood will inevitably ensue.

Chingiz Aitmatov (b. 1928) is at once a pillar of the Soviet literary and film establishments and a bold, completely original talent. If in his early writings he dealt with themes tangentially pertinent to Soviet ideological interests—for example, Islamic women in Kirgiz villages who break with an established pattern of life—his writings in the 1970s have become increasingly unorthodox. In perhaps his best known and most controversial work, *The White Steamboat* (1970)—a short novel proclaimed by Russian nationalist writer Vladimir Soloukhin to be the height of perfection—he describes a nameless boy, abandoned by his divorced parents, who lives in a remote mountain outpost with his grandfather, Momun.[26] The grandfather instills in the boy the values of his ancestors, telling him legends from the Kirgiz past. The evil in society is represented by Momun's son-in-law Orozkul, a Soviet official in charge of the outpost. Orozkul exhibits a predatory, destructive attitude toward nature and is thoroughly abhorrent in other ways. The juxtaposition of this character to the goodness embodied in traditional partriarchal values is striking.

Summarizing Aitmatov's writings of the 1970s, N. N. Shneidman observes: "The message of Aitmatov's latest work is unmistakable. It is primarily an ethical message which is not at all complimentary to our modern society. Technological and social progress have done little to change man for the better. On the contrary, they have prompted him to believe that he is the master of life, a delusion fraught with dangerous consequences."[27]

Despite the fact that Rasputin is a Russian from Siberia and Aitmatov is a Kirgiz, the remarkable thematic similarity of their writing is apparent. Mindless Soviet prometheanism is excoriated and Soviet officials are often shown to be crudely indifferent to nature and the future well-being of the planet. Religio-ethical concerns and a lyrical nationalism—a nation's history is seen as a life-giving continuum, a "single stream"—inform the writings of both authors. It is the grandparents, Darya and Momun, who have a message of immense value to pass on to their grandchildren. Such is the fare the Soviet public wants in its serious literature. The regime would appear to be in trouble.

The strong appeal of the religious and national tendency was also exemplified at the recent exhibits in Moscow and Leningrad by a Russian nationalist painter, Ilya Glazunov (b. 1930). The June 1978 and October 1979 showings of four hundred paintings by Glazunov, many of them on

Russian national themes, often with an undertone of Orthodox religiosity, were a cultural event of the first magnitude.[28] Six hundred thousand visitors braved extraordinarily long lines in order to see the 1978 Moscow exhibit, and the month-long Leningrad exhibit—held only after fierce opposition from the Leningrad *obkom* had been overcome—drew 746,000 viewers (when those who came on excursions are added, the total rises to approximately one million, a quarter of the city of Leningrad).

Two especially popular paintings were the programmatic *Return of the Prodigal Son*, based on a parable from the Gospel of St. Luke, and the polemical *To Your Health!*, which assails the scourge of Soviet alcoholism. The former canvas depicts a shirtless young man in blue jeans on his knees. He is being comforted by a Christ-like figure, behind whom stand holy men and cultural figures from Russia's past (St. Sergius of Radonezh, Dostoevsky, Gogol, and others). In the foreground, from which the young man has turned away, are scenes associated with wild debauch, Soviet prometheanism, and political terror.

Copies of the comment books of the two exhibits have reached the West, where they have been published. The reactions of viewers are overwhelmingly favorable:

Long live the Russian idea, risen up like a Phoenix!

Thank you for the festival of Russian culture.

Thank you for Rus'! For that which lives in us always and everywhere, which is impossible to kill in us, to which we shall return.

One senses a deep faith in Christ, the savior of our poor fatherland.

Thank you for your fiery love for much-suffering Russia.

I am thirty-five years old . . . for the first time I have come to understand the meaning of the phrase "national self-awareness." Thank you.[29]

The much-suffering Russia to which the respondents refer is not, of course, the new reality that came into existence in 1917 but rather "thousand-year-old Russia," the Russia of monastic sketes, Dostoevsky, and heroic battles for national survival, such as Kulikovo Field and Borodino. That there is a strong demand for this message is confirmed by the comment books for the Glazunov exhibit. But why, one wonders, were the showings permitted in the first place? And who overruled the objections of the powerful Leningrad *obkom*?[30]

In the area of film, whose importance was appreciated by Lenin and especially by that meddlesome cinema buff, Stalin, the situation resembles that of literature and painting. The films that, since the 1960s, have enjoyed great popularity generally eschew the "cooled down" official ideology and often serve out healthy morsels of nationalism and religion. Perhaps the most popular film of the early 1970s, for example, was Vasily Shukshin's *The Red Snowball Tree* (*Kalina krasnaia*), which featured an uprooted, semiurbanized peasant as its central protagonist. When Shukshin died at age 45 in 1974, one hundred and sixty thousand letters of commiseration poured in from fans.

During the period 1979–1980, two important films with a Russian nationalist orientation appeared: Andrei Mikhalkov-Konchalovsky's brilliant *Siberiade*, winner of a special prize at the Cannes film festival in 1979, and Vladimir Menshov's *Moscow Does Not Believe in Tears*, which won an Academy Award in 1980. These films contest Soviet prometheanism and headlong modernization (*Siberiade*) and investigate the social, demographic, and moral effects of urbanization and Westernization (*Moscow*). One might also note that *Moscow* (100 million viewers) and *Siberiade* (80 million) are the all-time domestic box-office hits of the Soviet film industry.

The Russian nineteenth-century classics have also served as useful vehicles for nationalist and religious ideas in the 1970s. One thinks, for example, of the films *Nest of Gentry* (1970), *Crime and Punishment* (1970), *An Unfinished Place for a Mechanical Piano* (a 1977 film based on several writings of Chekhov), and *Oblomov* (1980). (It might be objected that neither Turgenev, Goncharov, nor Chekhov were "nationalist" authors. *Nest of Gentry* is, however, Turgenev's most "Slavophile" work, and Chekhov and Goncharov's writings allow modern filmmakers to depict a milieu that, for all its failings, can be regarded as superior to the drab present.) It is noteworthy that the Mikhalkov brothers (Nikita and his older brother, Andrei Mikhalkov-Konchalovsky) have played a central role in this process of resurrecting the past. As sons of Sergei Mikhalkov, a writer and high-ranking functionary of the Writers' Union, they presumably enjoy relative immunity from petty harassment on the part of the authorities.

Other gifted films of a religious and national orientation have been made in recent years, either to be shelved or held up for years and then permitted only limited distribution. (In the West, however, their very high quality has been recognized, and they have been awarded numerous prizes at international film festivals.) One thinks particularly of Andrei Tarkovsky's controversial *Andrei Rublev* (1966), based on the life of Russia's greatest icon painter, and *The Mirror* (1974), among other things a meditation on Russia's national destiny, or Sergei Paradjanov's *Shadows of Forgotten Ancestors* (1964) and *Color of Pomegranates* (1969).

Paradjanov's case is particularly interesting (and appalling). An

Armenian from Tbilisi, Paradjanov chose to set his first film, the internationally acclaimed *Shadows of Forgotten Ancestors*, in an isolated Carpathian mountain district where the inhabitants speak Hutzul, a Ukrainian mountain dialect. The *Color of Pomegranates*, an expressionistic life of eighteenth-century Armenian poet Sayat Nova, was ordered shelved by the authorities. In 1974, Paradjanov was arrested on a trumped-up charge and given a five-year sentence in the camps. An actual reason for his arrest was probably his refusal to dub a Ukrainian film into Russian. In 1982, he was arrested for a second time. One suspects that it was Paradjanov's flirtation with Ukrainian nationalism that made this gifted filmmaker so odious to the authorities.[31]

Paradjanov's "polycentric" concern with national consciousness is widespread among contemporary Soviet filmmakers. Thus the late Larissa Shepitko, a gifted Ukrainian director, began her career by doing a film based on a story by Chingiz Aitmatov that touches on the role of Islam in Central Asia. She also made a fine film, *The Ascent* (1978), based on a story by Belorussian cultural nationalist Vasil Bykov. Shepitko's husband, Elem Klimov, has made a Russian nationalist and monarchist film, *Agony* (1975), which recounts the fall of the Russian monarchy. The film was released for general distribution only in 1985; it was first screened at the Moscow film festival in 1981.[32] An Uzbek director, Ravil Batyrov, has won acclaim for his *We'll Be Waiting for You, Lad* (1972), which was written by the Russian nationalist, Andrei Mikhalkov-Konchalovsky.

Although these films do not openly challenge Marxist-Leninist ideology, they tend to ignore it as irrelevant. With its direct appeal to mass audiences, Soviet film plays an important role in inculcating religious and national values. The journal *Kommunist* may still trumpet the dicta of Lenin, but Soviet filmgoers want, and often receive, a completely different diet.

Before leaving the cultural sphere, one should say something concerning the voluntary preservationist societies that have been springing up in the USSR since the 1960s. The All-Russian Society for the Preservation of Historical and Cultural Monuments (known by its Russian acronym, VOOPIK), which was founded in 1965, had 14.7 million members by 1982.[33] VOOPIK was established through the efforts of such widely known nationalist figures as Soloukhin and Glazunov. Its purpose is to halt, and reverse, the widespread destruction of ancient Russian monuments—monasteries, cathedrals, country churches—that had gained particular momentum during the Khrushchev antireligious campaign (ca. 1959–1964). VOOPIK funds restoration work, organizes volunteer student brigades to engage in such work, sponsors thousands of lectures on preservationist topics, and promotes indigenous tourism to the sites of historical monuments. Although the regime carefully controls the society—it is permitted no regular journal and has no publishing house—and has to some degree attempted to co-opt it, Soviet ideologues of the Ponomarev orientation can hardly be happy with the mass organization's orientation. Indeed, the antireligious monthly, *Nauka i religiia*, has more than once felt called upon to score the society's obvious sympathies for Russian Orthodoxy and a "single stream" view of history. According to Soloukhin, as well as other sources, the existence of voluntary preservationist societies in Georgia and the Baltic served as a catalyst for the formation of VOOPIK. Zviad Gamsakhurdia, an important Georgian nationalist and Orthodox religious dissenter, was, until his arrest in 1978 and subsequent partial recantation, active in the Georgian society for the preservation of monuments. (Gamsakhurdia was, incidentally, close to such "liberal" Russian nationalists as Father Gleb Iakunin and Igor Shafarevich.) The *Chronicle of the Lithuanian Catholic Church* has reported the arrests of Lithuanian *kraevedy* (students of local lore) on suspicion of Lithuanian nationalism. In both the RSFSR and the minority republics, therefore, preservation has emerged as an important nationalist issue. (It should be noted that mass ecological voluntary societies such as the All-Russian Society for the Preservation of Nature, which enjoyed a membership of 19 million in the early 1970s, also have a nationalist, antipromethean thrust to their activities.)

To sum up, cultural expression is the sphere of contemporary Soviet reality that most graphically illustrates the lack of appeal of Marxism-Leninism to the Soviet populace. Nationalism and religion are increasingly, if cautiously, being utilized by Soviet writers, artists, and filmmakers to fill an obvious void. The gradual but ineluctable transformation taking place in the cultural area may anticipate even more dramatic changes in the political arena.

RELIGION

If the Brezhnev and Andropov leaderships were unhappy with nationalism and nationalist cultural expression, words fail to convey their detestation of "religious survivals" 68 years after the Bolshevik revolution. Even more unsettling from the regime's point of view is the symbiosis of religion and nationalism that has been observable in Lithuania, Georgia, Armenia, the western Ukraine, and, recently, in Russia itself; the specter of such a fusion, or of a pan-Islamic movement in Central Asia, is also worrisome.

Official Soviet thinking on the role of religion in the USSR has always been clear: religion has no future in a communist state. As specialist Bohdan Bociurkiw recently testified before two House of Representatives subcommittees:

> Marxism-Leninism is the official state philosophy [of the USSR] and atheism of the militant Leninist kind, not the more agnostic atheism that is common in the West, is an integral part of Soviet official doctrine . . . it is inevitable that religious doctrines are treated by the regime as dissident, false, anti-scientific teachings, religious organizations are considered to be dispensers of these false teachings, and the believers are treated as deviants from the official Communist norms.[34]

At his 1980 trial, Vladimir Poresh (b. 1949), one of the founders of a dissident religio-philosophical seminar, put it this way: "In essence, I am condemned for my world-view. If our state is totalitarian, then I indeed break the law by having my own world-view . . . I simply do not understand how I could not have ended up in prison."[35] And, in a 1977 appeal to Brezhnev protesting the proposed draft constitution for the USSR, the founders of the Christian Committee for the Defense of Believers' Rights in the USSR stated:

> The building of communism is the fundamental and ultimate aim of the Communist Party and its sympathizers . . . The published program of the CPSU leaves no doubt that, as far as present-day party theoreticians understand the position of communism and religion . . . religion must be done away with. The Rules of the CPSU impose upon each member the duty: "to lead a resolute struggle against the survivals of religion." An anti-religious policy was and remains an integral part of the theory and practice of the CPSU.[36]

For tactical reasons, the regime has usually veiled its ultimate intentions with respect to religion. A secret document recently leaked to the West, however, exposes the regime's actual aims in this sphere with remarkable clarity. This is the 1974 report of Furov, deputy chairman of the Council for Religious Affairs of the Council of Ministers of the USSR, to the party Central Committee concerning the Russian Orthodox Church.[37] (Internal evidence suggests that the document was actually written in late 1975.)

The Furov report does not mince words in describing the degree of control exerted by the Council for Religious Affairs over the Moscow patriarchate. The ruling synod of bishops of the Russian church—the body that de jure makes all major decisions—is described as "under the control" of the council. The makeup and assignment of duties to its members is "entirely" (*vsetselo*) in the hands of the council. All questions for the agenda and all decisions to be made by the synod are agreed "in advance" with the council.

Despite this extraordinary degree of control, Furov believes that improvements can and should be made. Bishops of the Russian church are divided by him into three categories—what might be termed "good," "so-so," and "potentially dangerous." Good bishops are those who "are aware that our [Soviet] state is not interested in increasing the role of religion" in the USSR and draw appropriate conclusions, namely, they refrain from manifesting "any particular activity in extending the influence of Orthodoxy among the populace." Bishop Iona of Stavropol is a good bishop. He "does not exhibit any particular zeal" in carrying out his duties, gives short, uninspiring sermons that he concludes by "calling on believers to live in peace, to struggle for peace in the whole world, to contribute money to the Peace Fund, and to work well at their place of employment." In seven years, the report notes approvingly, Bishop Iona has not once visited the outlying parishes of his diocese.

So-so bishops, such as the late Metropolitan Nikodim of Leningrad, though "loyal to the state," try nevertheless to "activate servers of the cult and the church *aktiv*, and advocate increasing the role of the church in personal, family, and social life." Potentially dangerous bishops, such as Archbishop Nikolai of Vladimir and Suzdal, are those who attempt to "get around the laws concerning cults." The author of the Furov report expresses satisfaction that the number of clergy of the Moscow patriarchate has been steadily declining (8,252 priests in 1961 at the height of the Khrushchev persecution, and only 5,994 in 1974) and implies that the council will do what it can to ensure that this trend continues. He notes that 48.5 percent of Orthodox priests and deacons are over 60—a hopeful sign.

The astonishing degree of control exerted by the Soviet state over the church is repeatedly confirmed by the Furov report. In Nikolaev *oblast*, we learn, 21,590 Orthodox sermons were delivered in 1973; 23,350 in 1974—an unwelcome development. (Another source tells us that the authorities carefully count each candle and *prosfora* sold in Orthodox churches throughout the USSR.)[38] On several occasions Furov quotes from internal church documents, showing that the church can have no secrets from its overseers. (This practice led to a curious incident in 1976, when an anti-Catholic polemic by I. Iu. Bonchkovsky was published in Moscow; the book contained quotations from the personal correspondence of Miguel Arranz of the Oriental Institute in Rome and Metropolitan Nikodim of Leningrad. Arranz was furious, the Moscow patriarchate was embarrassed and compromised—the book also contained citations from internal church documents—and the ranking KGB officer in charge of church affairs, Titov, suffered a heart attack and died.)[39] In the samizdat *Chronicle of the Lithuanian Catholic Church*, one frequently encounters a fear that the authorities are seeking to make the Lithuanian church a replica of the Russian one.

Why, one might ask, does the regime not administer the coup de grace to organized religion? The sheer number of religious believers is one factor. According to specialist William C. Fletcher, "the religious sector of the population has declined only from 56 percent in 1937 to 45 percent today, and the absolute number of religious citizens in Soviet society has actually increased from an estimated 90 to 95 million to an estimated 115 million." In breaking down his figures, Fletcher estimates that 25 to 35 percent of the population in the Russian areas continues to be religious, and 60 percent in the non-Russian areas.[40] Another specialist, sociologist of religion Christel Lane, has calculated that between 20 and 25 percent of the Soviet populace continues to adhere to the Orthodox Church, that is, between 52.4 and 65.5 million persons, based on the population figures of the 1979 census.[41] Clearly, the religious segment of the populace is significant and must be dealt with gingerly by the regime.

In instances where religion fuses with nationalism, the results are especially alarming for Soviet officials. Lithuania, where a symbiosis of religion and nationalism rivals that in nearby Poland, is perhaps the extreme example. Despite prodigious efforts, the regime has so far been unable to cow the Lithuanian church. A samizdat memorandum from Lithuanian believers, dated December 1971, contained 17,054 signatures, an incredible number in a communist state; another such document is reported to have contained 148,000 signatures.[42] Special pressure is always placed by the authorities on clergy, yet, in 1979, we find 522 Lithuanian Catholic Priests signing protests against religious persecution—an unheard-of development. From the perspective of the regime, Lithuania must be seen as almost out of control. It is also noteworthy that the Lithuanians have of late shown an interest in the status of religion in other republics, particularly that of Catholicism in Belorussia, the Ukraine, Moldavia, and Siberia. Lithuanian religious dissenters worked closely with the liberal Russian nationalists constituting the Christian Committee before the latter were suppressed in 1979–1980. (As noted above, the Christian Committee also worked closely with Georgian Orthodox dissenters.)

In the RSFSR, Orthodox believers have also been active. Believers in the city of Gorki, for example, recently gathered first fifteen hundred, then three thousand signatures on petitions to open a new church. (Predictably, the efforts failed.) As dissident mathematician Igor Shafarevich commented to two Western correspondents: "Perhaps in your country these [1,500 and 3,000] are small numbers, but in our country they are enormous. Under no petition devoted to the rights of man did anyone succeed in collecting more than one-tenth that number of signatures."[43] Although the number of signatures is obviously lower than the number collected in Lithuania, Shafarevich is justified in terming them "enormous." Believers in the RSFSR run a significantly greater risk in signing such petitions than do believers in Lithuania. The Gorki instance is far from unique. In 1970, 1,432 Orthodox believers signed a petition in Naro-Fominsk requesting that a church be opened there—believers have been trying to attain that aim in Naro-Fominsk for the past 40 years. And in 1977, believers in Chkalovsk region collected 3,146 signatures seeking to obtain the opening of a church there; such efforts have been going on in Chkalovsk since 1952.[44]

The link between Russian Orthodoxy and Russian nationalism is as evident as that between Lithuanian nationalism and Catholicism. "Orthodoxy is indestructible," states a contributor to the nationalist samizdat journal *Veche*. "It is God's work, and a Russian can only be Orthodox." Glazunov puts it thus: "Dostoevskii said: 'He who is not Orthodox cannot be Russian.'"[45] All major dissenting Russian nationalists—Solzhenitsyn, Vladimir Osipov, Igor Ogurtsov, Shafarevich, Alexander Ogorodnikov, and others—are outspoken in their Orthodox religious views. Many "official nationalists," including a number of adherents of the leading school of Soviet letters, "village prose," also hold such views, though, understandably, they are more cautious in expressing them.

Especially noteworthy of late has been the struggle of Vladimir Soloukhin (a recognized nationalist writer since the publication of his *Vladimir By-Roads* [1957]) to obtain the restoration of Optina Pustyn' Monastery, whose famous *startsy* were visited by such writers as Dostoevsky, Tolstoy, and Gogol. His efforts to promote a sympathetic view of the Orthodox religion in his writings are unmistakable. In early 1982, Soloukhin was savaged by *Kommunist* for his "flirtation with goddie" (*zaigryvanie s bozhen'koi*) and his "religio-mystical ideas and moods," as expressed in a piece published in *Nash sovremennik*. During 1981, three issues of the antireligious monthly, *Nauka i religiia*, carried a lengthy article assailing Soloukhin and his attachment to the odious *startsy*. *Literaturnaia gazeta* has also attacked Soloukhin.[46] Amazingly, even after the attack by *Kommunist*, the journal *Nash sovremennik* was able to continue with the publication of Soloukhin's controversial "Pebbles in a Palm" (no. 3, 1982). Shortly afterward, however, *Kommunist* succeeded in extracting apologies from the editor and party committee of *Nash sov-remennik* and, secondhand, from Soloukhin himself.[47] Andropov's wide-ranging and brutal assault on the Russian nationalists during 1982 made itself felt in this episode.[48]

In Georgia, Armenia, and the western Ukraine (that is, that part of the Ukraine influenced by Uniate Catholicism), as in Lithuania and Russia, one frequently encounters a religio-national symbiosis. Religious ties are particularly important in this regard: during the 1970s, one saw increasing cooperation between Russian and Georgian Orthodox Christian nationalists and Lithuanian and Ukrainian Catholics. Protestants, however, though often very active in defense of their religious rights— witness the activities of dissident Baptists and Pentecostals—seem virtually uninterested in nationalist causes. The established Lutheran church of the Latvians, Estonians, and Volga Germans also seems relatively untroubled by nationalist concerns.

As for the Soviet Union's estimated 35 million Islamic believers,[49] appearances can be deceiving. Officially, there remain only 300 working mosques, as compared with 24,000 before 1917, and less than a thousand registered clerics. But, as Alexandre Bennigsen has pointed out in several recent articles, relying to a large degree on published Soviet sources, beneath the surface things may be different. Soviet specialists in Islam worry publicly, for example, about the existence of secret Sufi brotherhoods with great strength in Azerbaijan, the Chechen-Ingush and Dagestan areas, and in the Karakalpak region of Uzbekistan. In the northern Caucasus, according to Bennigsen, there may be more than half a million adepts of the brotherhoods, "a fantastic number for an underground society which is banned by Soviet law."[50] Although officially there are only thirteen mosques in Azerbaijan, it is reported that "many hundreds" of clandestine mosques are in existence there. Militant Islam, thus, remains strong in the Transcaucasus and Central Asia, a potent counterforce to Russification. Whether Islam eventually will combine with local nationalisms—the less dangerous alternative from the regime's point of view—or whether it should manifest itself in some form of pan-Islamic, pan-Turkic, or pan-Turanian sentiment, it seems clear that *Homo islamicus* is still a long way from becoming *Homo sovieticus*.

In addition to the sheer numbers of religious believers in the USSR and the dangers of activating a religio-national symbiosis through extreme persecution, there are several other obstacles and considerations restraining the regime in its war on religious survivals. First, to drive religion underground, beyond the control of the authorities—as in the case of the Sufi brotherhoods and "catacomb" True Orthodox Christians—can be counterproductive. Second, official church delegations can be an immensely valuable propaganda weapon in countering charges of religious persecution in the USSR and in advancing Soviet political aims at such forums as the Soviet-sponsored peace committee. Finally, in the case of the largest religious body, the Orthodox church, the Soviet leadership undoubtedly recalls Stalin's discovery in the war against Hitler—that the church provided valuable assistance in the patriotic revival that helped defeat the invaders. In a conflict, with, say, China, such support could prove useful once again. Religion could also, one suspects, prove helpful in coping with such rampant social ills as alcoholism, but the state has so far refrained—spurning the advice of dissident Orthodox priest Dimitrii Dudko, who was arrested in 1980—from asking for such assistance.

CONCLUSIONS

The subjects we have been examining—language, cultural expression, religion, and national consciousness in the contemporary Soviet Union—represent a web of major problems for the regime. In the short run, these difficulties seem manageable. Control of the mass media and a reasonably efficient security apparatus in tandem with a "cold" but still potent ideology should enable the regime to prevent nationalism and religio-nationalism from getting out of hand. (The foreign radio could play a destabilizing role here, but one suspects that Western governments are too timid—as well as genuinely ambivalent about the value of religion and of national self-awareness—to take any consistent steps in this regard.) It should be kept in mind that ethnic conflict in the Soviet Union is not just between Russians and "everyone else." In the Transcaucasus, for example, Abkhazians have recently tried to secede from Georgia and join the RSFSR, and both Georgians and Armenians have vigorously protested the treatment of their countrymen living in Muslim Azerbaijan.[51] Also, as we have seen, it would be a mistake to identify the regime with the interests of ethnic Russians; no "Russian nationalist" political leadership would have attempted, for example, to hinder and thwart the celebration of the 600th anniversary of the battle of Kulikovo Field in 1980.[52]

Having said that nationalism and religion should prove manageable for the regime in the short term, one should add that they cannot be kept at bay indefinitely. The continued "cooling down" of Marxist-Leninist ideology, combined with serious and growing problems in agriculture and the economy, as well as major demographic and social difficulties, make a policy of immobilism an unviable option for the future. The Gorbachev leadership will have to take resolute steps, and these steps will inevitably impinge on the subjects of discussion in this paper. If the future leaders should consist of Russian nationalists or Russian nationalist sympathizers, they will have to take energetic measures to improve the fortunes of ethnic Russians in the Soviet Union. A possible spin-off of this could well be the withdrawal of ethnic Russians from the borderlands and a loosening of controls on the non-Russian areas. Such concessions could release pressures that would result in a real federalism and even the secession of certain border republics from the union. "Official" as well as dissenting Russian nationalists openly discuss this eventuality and do not seem to be afraid of it.[53] The RSFSR, Belorussia, and that part of the population of the Ukraine that is Orthodox Christian (77 percent according to one estimate)[54] can, they believe, form the nucleus of a great federal state, to which various spokesmen would add heavily Russified or Orthodox Christian areas of the USSR—Kazakhstan, Kirgizia, Moldavia, and Georgia.

"Soviet patriots," however, with their links to the defense-heavy industrial complex, as well as neo-Ponomarev dogmaticians, would probably want to push ahead with maximal Russification in order to bring about the development of a Soviet nation. In this case, the infamous Tashkent recommendations could be harbingers of even harsher policies. Heavy-handed indifference to the linguistic, cultural, and religious needs of the component nationalities of the USSR could, especially in connection with a major shock such as a conflict with China or food riots, set off explosions that would cause the Soviet empire to unravel.

The unlikely but possible development of a "Moscow spring," along the lines recommended by Roy Medvedev, could—by loosening the viselike control exerted by the state—lead to a marked betterment of the condition of the peoples of the USSR. Such a loosening could also, however, lead to uncontrolled surges of national and religio-national sentiment that would swamp Medvedev's socialist democracy. It is instructive to recall that even Khrushchev's relatively timid democratization served to release such forces.

Whichever scenario actually occurs, the Soviet leadership and Western observers will be keeping a close watch on the development of nationalism and religio-nationalism during the last two decades of this century. The strength of the phenomena we have been discussing is so obvious and the appeal of Marxism-Leninism so weak we can expect important manifestations of these new forces before the conclusion of the 1980s.

NOTES

1. *New York Times*, December 21, 1979, p. 2.

2. *Russkaia mysl'*, September 3, 1981.

3. Ronald Grigor Suny, "Georgia and Soviet Nationality Policy," in Stephen F. Cohen, Alexander Rabinowitch, and Robert Sharlet, eds., *The Soviet Union Since Stalin* (Bloomington: Indiana University Press, 1980), p. 219.

4. On the Soviet concept of nations, see Hélène Carrère d'Encausse, "Determinants and Parameters of Soviet Nationality Policy," in Jeremy R. Azrael, ed., *Soviet Nationality Policies and Practices* (New York: Praeger, 1978), pp. 39–59.

5. Jonathan Pool, "Whose Russian Language?" in Edward Allworth, ed., *Ethnic Russia in the USSR* (New York: Pergamon, 1980), p. 239.

6. Tomas Venclova, "Two Russian Sub-Languages and Russian Ethnic Identity," in Allworth, *Ethnic Russia*, pp. 250–51.

7. Michael Rywkin, *Moscow's Muslim Challenge* (Armonk: M. E. Sharpe, 1982), pp. 95–96.

8. Juris Dreifelds, "Latvian National Demands and Group Consciousness Since 1959," in George W. Simmonds, ed., *Nationalism in the USSR and Eastern Europe* (Detroit: University of Detroit Press, 1977), p. 138.

9. Walter Sawatsky, "Secret Soviet Lawbook on Religion," *Religion in Communist Lands* (Winter 1976): 26.

10. Yaroslav Bilinsky, "Russian Nationalism and the Soviet Empire" (Paper prepared for the thirteenth national convention of the American Association for the Advancement of Slavic Studies, Asilomar, Calif., September 20–23, 1981), p. 20.

11. Kestutis Girnius, "The Draft Recommendations to the Tashkent Conference," Radio Liberty Research Paper (hereafter, RLRP) 189/79, June 19, 1979, pp. 3–5.

12. Bilinsky, "Russian Nationalism and the Soviet Empire," p. 40.

13. Roman Solchanyk, "New Turn in Soviet Nationalities Policy," *Soviet Analyst*, April 15, 1981, pp. 4–5. See also the discussion of this speech in Boris Meissner, "The 26th Party Congress and Soviet Domestic Politics," *Problems of Communism* (May–June 1981): 19–22.

14. Iu. V. Andropov, "Shest'desiat let SSSR," *Pravda*, December 22, 1982, pp. 1–2. Andropov's speech also appeared in a booklet edition of 3 million copies, published by Izdatel'stvo Politicheskoi Literatury in December 1982. For a discussion of the relationship of his speech to the nationalities issue, see Ann Sheehy, "Andropov Speaks on Nationalities Policy," RLRP 510/82, December 21, 1982, and "Andropov and the Merging of Nations," RLRP 516/82, December 22, 1982; and Roman Solchanyk, "Merger of Nations: Back in Style?", RLRP 84/83, February 18, 1983.

15. Bilinsky, "Russian Nationalism and the Soviet Empire," p. 9. For the results of the 1979 census, see *Naselenie SSSR po dannym vsesoiuznoi perepisi naseleniia 1979 goda* (Moscow: Politizdat, 1980).

16. Rywkin, *Moscow's Muslim Challenge*, p. 97.

17. Ivan Dziuba, *Internatsionalizm ili Rusifikatsiia?* (Amsterdam: Suchasnist', 1973), p. 234. This edition is a Russian translation of the Ukrainian original. For an English translation, see *Internationalism or Russification?* (London: Weidenfeld and Nicolson, 1968).

18. Interview with followers of Father Dimitrii Dudko, published in *Vol'noe slovo* 33 (1979).

19. "Russkoe reshenie natsional'nogo voprosa," *Veche*, no. 6, Arkhiv samizdata (AS) 1559, pp. 9–10.

20. Mikhail Agursky, "The New Russian Literature," Soviet and East European Research Center, Hebrew University of Jerusalem, Research Paper no. 40 (July 1980), p. 15.

21. Their relative lack of concern for the demographic, social, and moral plight of ethnic Russians would distinguish adherents of this tendency from present-day National Bolsheviks, whereas their lack of emphasis on ideology would set them apart from neo-Stalinists.

22. See Aleksandr Solzhenitsyn, "O rabote russkoi sektsii Bi-Bi-Si," *Kontinent* 9 (1976): 210–23, and "Zapadnoe radioveshchanie dolzhno zavoevat' doverie russkogo naroda," *Posev* 11 (1981): 16–24; Viktor Sokolov, "Zapiski radioslushatelia," *Kontinent* 12 (1977): 268–86; "Open Letter to the Directors of Radio Stations 'Voice of America,' BBC, and 'Deutsche Welle,'" *Documents of the Christian Committee for the Defense of Believers' Rights in the USSR* (1979), 3: 342–43; "Kolonka redaktora: Snova vserez o 'Svobode,'" *Kontinent* 29 (1981): 383–85.

23. See Alain Besançon, *The Soviet Syndrome* (New York: Harcourt Brace Jovanovich, 1978), p. 19.

24. "Commissars of Culture Don't Relax Very Often," *New York Times*, November 8, 1981, p. 8E.

25. See Valentin Rasputin, *Farewell to Matyora: A Novel* (New York: Macmillan, 1979). The text that follows represents a condensed version of my essay, "Valentin Rasputin's *Proshchanie s Materoi*," in Evelyn Bristol, ed., *Russian Literature and Criticism* (Berkeley, Calif.: Berkeley Slavic Specialties, 1982), pp. 63–68.

26. Published in *Novyi mir* 1 (1970): 31–100.

27. N. N. Shneidman, *Soviet Literature in the 1970s* (Toronto, Canada: University of Toronto Press, 1979), p. 42.

28. The following is a condensed version of an account appearing in my book, *The Faces of Contemporary Russian Nationalism* (Princeton, N.J.: Princeton University Press, 1983).

29. For the comment books of the two exhibits, see *Khudozhnik i Rossiia* (Düsseldorf: Grad Kitezh, 1980).

30. It is now known that Soviet ideological overseer Mikhail Suslov was Glazunov's protector. Indeed, it seems likely that, in the last years of his life, Suslov became a protector of all Russian nationalists willing to work within the Soviet system to achieve their ends. On this, see Roy Medvedev, "The Death of the 'Chief

Ideologue,'" *New Left Review* (November–December 1982); Semen Reznik, "Kto takoi Sergei Semanov," *Novaia gazeta* (New York), December 11–17, 1982, p. 10; and Mark Higgie, "From Brezhnev to Andropov," *Soviet Analyst*, August 17, 1983, p. 6.

31. On Paradjanov, see Richard Grenier, "A Soviet 'New Wave'?" *Commentary* (July 1981), p. 63. For a useful overview of postwar Soviet and East European film, see Mira Liehm and Antonin J. Liehm, *The Most Important Art* (Berkeley: University of California Press, 1977).

32. *New York Times*, November 8, 1981, p. 8E.

33. The following is a condensed version of an account appearing in my book, *The Faces of Contemporary Russian Nationalism*. See note 28 for reference. The figure of 14.7 million is mentioned in "Listok No. 24," *Izvestiia*, December 11, 1982.

34. *Hearings Before the Subcommittees on International Political and Military Affairs and on International Organizations of the Committee on International Relations, House of Representatives*, 94th Cong., 2d sess., June 24 and 30, 1976 (Washington: U.S. Government Printing Office, 1976), pp. 35–36.

35. In *Vol'noe slovo* 39 (1981): 99.

36. *Documents of the Christian Committee*, 3: 339.

37. "Iz otcheta Soveta po delam religii—Chlenam TsK KPSS," *Vestnik R.Kh.D.* 130 (1979): 275–344. The document is described as "over the signature" of V. Furov, i.e., he may not have been its actual author.

38. From a press conference held by Iakunin in April 1977. For the text, see *Vol'noe slovo* 28 (1977): 79–86.

39. On this, see the open letter of the Christian Committee to Pope John Paul II in *Vol'noe slovo* 35–36 (1979): 117–20.

40. William C. Fletcher, *Soviet Believers: The Religious Sector of the Population* (Lawrence: Regents Press of Kansas, 1981), p. 212.

41. Christel Lane, *Christian Religion in the Soviet Union: A Sociological Survey* (London: George Allen & Unwin, 1978), p. 46.

42. Michael Bourdeaux and Michael Rowe, eds., *May One Believe—In Russia?* (London: Darton, Longman & Todd, 1980), p. 78. For selected issues of the *Chronicle*, see *Khronika litovskoi katolicheskoi tserkvi* (New York: Khronika, 1979). English translations of the *Chronicle* are regularly published by the Lithuanian Roman Catholic Priests' League of America.

43. Igor' Shafarevich, "Tele-interv'iu radiokompanii Bi Bi Si," *Vestnik R.Kh.D.* 125 (1978): 209–10.

44. Bourdeaux and Rowe, *May One Believe—In Russia?*, p. 19; and *Documents of the Christian Committee* (1978), 4: 479.

45. Russkii khristianin [a Russian Christian], "Zametki russkogo khristianina," *Veche*, no. 1, AS 1013, p. 51. Glazunov's statement is from an interview in *Vol'noe slovo* 33 (1979): 93–96.

46. "Napadki na Vl. Soloukhina," *Posev* 4 (1982): 3–4.

47. "Pochta zhurnala," *Kommunist* 8 (1982): 128.

48. On this assault, see my essays, "Andropov and the Russian Nationalists" (Paper presented at the Kennan Institute for Advanced Russian Studies, January 11, 1984), and "The *Nash sovremennik* Affair, 1981–1982" (Paper Presented at Western Slavic Association Meeting, Hoover Institution, Stanford University, March 31, 1984). In 1985, these two pieces appeared in *The New Russian Nationalism*, a collection of my essays published in the Washington Papers Series (Praeger Publishers and The Georgetown Center for Strategic and International Studies).

49. *Hearings Before the Commission on Security and Cooperation in Europe*, vol. 2, 95th Cong., 1st sess., on implementation of the Helsinki Accords, April 27 and 28, 1977 (Washington: U.S. Government Printing Office, 1977), p. 88.

50. Alexandre Bennigsen and Chantal Lemercier-Quelquejay, "Muslim Religious Conservatism and Dissent in the USSR," *Religion in Communist Lands* (Autumn 1978): 156. See also Alexandre Bennigsen, "Muslim Conservative Opposition to the Soviet Regime," in Azrael, *Soviet Nationality Policies and Practices*, pp. 334–48.

51. See Suny, "Georgia and Soviet Nationality Policy," pp. 217, 220; Vahakn N. Dadrian, "Nationalism in Soviet Armenia," in Simmonds, *Nationalism in the USSR*, p. 210; and *Posev* 6 (1981): 7 and 5 (1982): 11. See also *Russkaia mysl'*, September 3, 1981.

52. N. Rutych, "Rossiia i ee problemy," *Posev* 1 (1982): 25–30.

53. See, for example, "Slovo natsii," in *Veche: Nezavisimyi russkii al'manakh*, no. 3 (1981): 106–31; and Oleg Dmitriev, "Ne nazyvaia imen (interv'iu)," *Sintaksis* 2 (1978): 37–48.

54. Walter Dushnyck, "Religious Situation in Ukraine," in *Hearings Before the Commission on Security and Cooperation in Europe*, 2: 96.

Social and Economic Aspects of the Nationality Problem

Gertrude E. Schroeder

POLICIES OF THE SOVIET STATE

Having established hegemony over a number of states with strong national identities, the Russian Bolshevik government needed both an ideology and some policies for managing its multinational empire. In the economic and social spheres, Lenin's much touted "nationalities policy" provided the framework. According to the rhetoric, the diverse peoples of the Soviet Union would simultaneously "flourish" and "come together" in all kinds of ways as the new socialist society made its way through socialism to communism. "Flourishing" (*prosvetanie*) meant that all national groups would participate in and reap the benefits of the drive for rapid industrialization and social modernization that became the keystone of Soviet development policy. Because the national states at the outset differed greatly in actual levels of economic and social development, "drawing together" (*sblizhenie*) supposedly entailed initial efforts to allocate resources in ways that would reduce those large gaps. Reduction of differences in development and standards of living among ethnic groups, in turn, became an integral part of a policy of narrowing societal differences in general—between the economic status of men and women, between city and village, and between mental and physical labor. This evolutionary process was to be carried out under the guidance of a strong centralized government and single political party, which would see to it that allegedly common goals and tasks were accomplished. In the process, feelings and expressions of distinct national identities, as survivals of a previous (capitalistic) era, were supposed to disappear gradually.

With regard to the economy, twin themes of general social and economic progress and of equalization (*vyravnivanie*) of levels of economic development among peoples—a facet of *sblizhenie*—appeared repeatedly in government policy statements until the early 1970s. These goals were explicitly stated in the directives for the several postwar five-year plans, including the plan for 1971–1975. Subsequently, the theme of equalization was dropped from the text of the five-year plan directives. The rhetoric on the subject altered greatly after Brezhnev's December 1972 speech in celebration of the fiftieth anniversary of the founding of the USSR; in this speech the general secretary stated, "Now that the problem of the leveling of the development of the national republics has on the whole been solved, we are able to approach economic questions from the point of view of the interests of the state as a whole, of raising the effectiveness of the national economy of the USSR, allowing, of course, for the special interests of the union and autonomous republics."[1] Doctrine on the nationalities question was integrated into the emerging ideology of "developed socialism," the term adopted by Soviet theorists of progress to characterize the present stage in the striving toward the ultimate goal of achieving communism. The doctrine is based on the stated conviction (or assertion) that a historically new people—the "Soviet people"—has now come into being and on the belief that the Soviet economy must now be managed as a single "national economic complex" to ensure economic progress and reap the benefits of the so-called scientific-technical revolution.

Writing in January 1982, Politburo member Shcherbitsky put the doctrine this way: "In carrying out the scientific direction of the developed socialist society the Party placed at the front of its nationalities policy an optimal combination of the interests of each nation and people of the USSR with the general interests of the entire Soviet people." In short, central economic planning henceforth evidently is supposed to aim at "rational" specialization and cooperation among the republics, with the goal of maximizing the total product. On this basis, social and economic progress is supposed to continue in all regions, with economic ties among them becoming ever closer and more varied. Thus, "flourishing" of all peoples supposedly is provided for in the doctrine, but what about "equalization"? Shcherbitsky states,

> Moreover, under present conditions the problem of equalizing development levels of the union republics takes on a new meaning. Whereas during the period of the construction of socialism the main task was elimination of the actual inequality of nations, . . .today . . . it is a matter of the further drawing together of levels, of the harmonious

development of national republics and oblasts, and of the rational specialization of production in the common interests of the entire Soviet people . . . The CPSU proceeds from the thesis that further drawing together of levels of economic development and the overall progress of each union republic also determines the increase in its contribution to the economic might of the Soviet Union.[2]

The CPSU resolution on the sixtieth anniversary of the founding of the Soviet Union, adopted in early 1982, declared the intent to "decide economic and social questions from a primarily general state approach" while resolutely combating all manifestations of "parochialism" and "nationalism" among the workers.[3] In his maiden speech dealing with nationality issues, newly elected General Secretary Andropov went even further, emphasizing that the party's ultimate goal was "not only the drawing together of nations, but their merger (sliianie)"; he also stressed the need for greater integration of the economies of the various republics and regions.[4]

As others have shown, assessing the economic and social results of the implementation of the stated Soviet nationalities policies is fraught with extraordinary difficulties.[5] They are, above all, defining the actual aims of policy in practice and expressing them in terms that can be measured quantitatively, however roughly. For instance, did the leaders aim at bringing about absolute regional equality in levels of economic development and in living standards? How should progress be gauged? By national per capita income? Level of industrial production? Per capita consumption? Opinions differ widely as to the operational content of stated policy objectives, the choice of yardsticks for assessing the degree of success achieved, and the interpretation of the significance of the results. I shall not enter here into this debate, which often becomes highly technical and focuses on the interpretation of various sets of data and their comparability among regions and over time. Rather, I propose to describe some of the quite obvious results of the Soviet government's policies over the years in managing social and economic development in its multinational state. Using the union republics and their titular nationalities as units of analysis and focusing on the period since World War II, we shall consider, in turn, trends in geographic location and urbanization of the major nationalities, language assimilation and education, economic development, and living standards. A concluding section considers the significance of these socio-economic policies and achievements as vehicles for fostering a major political objective—the withering away of nationalism as a potential threat to the purposes of the dominant Russian state—and speculates about the future.

LOCATION AND URBANIZATION

To an overwhelming extent, the fifteen titular nationalities, comprising over 90 percent of the total Soviet population, reside in their native republics. Moreover, the dominance of the titular nationality in each republic tends to be large and persistent.[6] In 1979, over 90 percent of all Georgians, Turkmen, Estonians, Latvians, and Lithuanians lived in their own republics, as was also the case in 1959. The shares were 80 to 88 percent for all others except the Armenians and Tadzhiks, whose respective shares were 66 and 77. The percentage of Russians living in the RSFSR and of the titular nationalities living in the three Western republics and Georgia were a little lower in 1979 than they had been twenty years earlier, whereas the shares of the other titular nationalities were somewhat higher. The proportion of Armenians living in Armenia, however, increased by 10 percentage points.

The titular nationalities also tend to be predominant in the total populations of their respective republics, in some cases by growing margins. In 1979, Russians made up nearly 83 percent of the total population of the RSFSR, only a little less than in 1959. The dominance of the Ukrainians, Belorussians, and Moldavians in their republic populations—74, 79, and 64 percent, respectively in 1979—also was reduced somewhat, but the percentage of Latvians and Estonians in their republic populations dropped substantially—from 62 to 54 percent for the former and from 75 to 65 percent for the latter. In the Transcaucasian, Central Asian, and Kazakh republics, in contrast, the share of the titular nationalities rose substantially; it also increased a little in Lithuania. In 1979, the titular nationalities made up well over half, and usually two-thirds or more, of the total population in their own republics everywhere except in Kazakhstan and Kirgizia. The share of each titular nationality in its republic population is important for evaluating the use of statistics for republics as proxies for the usually unavailable data on nationality groups per se.

Russians constitute the second most numerous ethnic group in most of the non-Russian republics. Between 1959 and 1979, however, the percentage of Russians in the republic populations dropped markedly in all Transcaucasian and Central Asian republics and in Kazakhstan. Their share rose substantially, however, in all other republics—by 6–7 percentage points in Latvia and Estonia.

Urbanization has proceeded everywhere under the impact of Soviet development policies, but at widely differing rates. According to official data, which may not be entirely comparable either among regions or over time, the proportion of urban dwellers in the total population did not exceed 37 percent in any republic in 1940 and was below 25 percent in five of them. At the beginning of 1982, the urban shares were over half in all republics except those of Central Asia and Moldavia. Between 1959 and 1982, by far the fastest rates of urbanization took place in Belorussia and Moldavia, where urban shares nearly doubled. In striking contrast, the urban population rose a mere 1 to 2 percentage points in Tadzhikistan and Turkmenistan over the period as a whole. In Tadzhikistan the share rose from 33 percent in 1959 to 37 percent in 1970, but by 1982 it had declined to 34 percent.

Titular nationalities in the non-Russian republics tend to live in rural areas. In 1970 (1979 data have not yet been published), the percentage of the titular nationality was substantially higher in the rural population than in the urban population for all non-Russian republics except Armenia. In most republics, the proportion of the titular nationality in the rural population ranged between 70 and 90 percent. The titular nationality was a conspicuous minority in the cities of Central Asia, Kazakhstan, and Moldavia, and Latvians made up somewhat less than half of the urban population in Latvia. Assuming that the data are reasonably reliable as to trends, we may conclude that there has been considerable convergence with respect to urbanization. But the differences are still large. In 1982, the urban share of the total population ranged from 34 percent in Tadzhikistan to 71 percent in the RSFSR and Estonia.

According to data published by a Soviet ethnographer, all of the titular nationalities, regardless of where they lived, became more urban between 1970 and 1979. Rates of urbanization differed greatly, ranging from a gain of only 1.3 percentage points for Turkmen to 11 percentage points for Belorussians.[7] But there were still enormous differences in 1979; for example, only 19.6 percent of all Kirgiz lived in cities, compared with 74.4 percent of all Russians.

LANGUAGE AND EDUCATION

From the outset, Soviet policy has vigorously promoted the acquisition of fluency in the Russian language for all non-Russian ethnic groups. Russian was to become "the common language of internationality discourse and cooperation." Although the goal of universal fluency in the Russian language has remained fixed, the vigor with which the goal has been pursued has waxed and waned over the years. Nonetheless, substantial progress has been made, and the convergence of nationalities on this measure has been notable. In fact, actual language assimilation was reported by 13 percent of the non-Russian population by 1979, that is, these people gave Russian as their native language. The corresponding proportion was 11 percent in 1959. Most of these non-Russians were Slavic peoples, mainly Ukrainians and Belorussians. Nonetheless, the vast bulk of the non-Russian population—85.6 percent in 1979—still regarded their own languages as their native tongues.

The drive for bilingualism, with Russian as the second language, has made considerable headway. In 1979, a little over 62 percent of the total non-Russian population claimed fluency in the Russian language, compared with 49 percent in 1970. The situation differs greatly among nationality groups, however, as in all probability, does the extent to which reported fluency actually reflects a real command of the language. In 1979, Russian-language fluency was reported by at least half of Ukrainians, Belorussians, Kazakhs, Latvians, and Lithuanians. Among the Central Asian titular nationalities, 49 percent of Uzbeks, but only 25 percent of Turkmen, claimed mastery of Russian. Percentages for the Transcaucasian groups ranged from 27 to 39. Lowest of all were the Estonians, with 24 percent, a decline from 29 percent in 1959. With that exception, sizable gains in acquisition of Russian-language fluency were registered by all of the titular nationalities. The census data claim an increase from 14 to 49 percent for Uzbeks during 1970–1979, reflecting a major campaign to push mastery of Russian in Uzbekistan during those years. The figure for 1979 evidently is considerably overstated. Moreover, in evaluating all of these data concerning fluency in Russian, one must keep in mind that individual notions of what constitutes fluency may differ widely. One would suspect that many non-Russians might tend to report themselves as fluent in Russian even with only a minimum command of the language.

Raising the level of education of the people has been a key part of Soviet policy from the outset, and large investments have been devoted to that task. According to official data, literacy in 1922 for people age 9 to 49 ranged from 3.8 percent in Tadzhikistan to 63.8 percent in the Ukraine; the rate was over 80 percent in Latvia and Estonia, not then a part of the USSR. In all republics, literacy among men was far higher than among women. By 1970, literacy was nearly universal for this age group. Inclusion of older persons, however, probably would reveal lower literacy rates as well as substantial differences among regions and between the sexes.

Levels of education have risen dramatically in all republics and among their titular nationalities. Although large differences in educational attainment still exist, they have narrowed greatly.[8] Between 1959 and 1979, the percentage of persons age 10 and over who have completed a higher education tripled in the USSR as a whole; it doubled in Georgia and Azerbaijan and quadrupled in Belorussia. In 1979, the percentage of college graduates among persons age 10 and over ranged from 4.9 percent in Tadzhikistan to 10.3 percent in Georgia. The range is narrower with respect to persons who have completed secondary school. In both cases, the differences decreased over the twenty-year period. In all republics, a larger share of men than of women were college graduates in 1979, but again interregional disparities were sizable. For men, the percentage of college graduates ranged among republics from 6.2 percent to 11.2 percent, but for women it ranged from 3.5 to 9.4 percent. The shares for women relative to those for men varied from 53 percent in Turkmenistan to 94 percent in Lithuania. Women's relative shares increased substantially during 1959–1979 everywhere except in Tadzhikistan and Turkmenistan, where they actually declined. In general, women scored better on this measure in the more urbanized republics.

Differences in average educational attainments of urban and rural residents, although narrowing, are still large, and there are substantial variations among republics. In Table 1, I assess these matters using data on the percentages of secondary school graduates among employed persons. In 1979, the percentage of employed persons in urban areas who had completed secondary school ranged from 56 percent in Lithuania to 81 percent in Georgia; in 1959, the corresponding percentages had been 24 and 46. In rural areas in 1979, the share of workers with at least a high school education varied from 29 percent in Lithuania to 62 percent in Uzbekistan; in 1959, the shares ranged from 4.5 percent in Lithuania to 58 percent in Kazakhstan. The census data show a large reduction in the educational gap between urban and rural areas over the twenty-year period (see Table 1). In 1979, rural workers in all Central Asian and Transcaucasian republics were better educated than in the rest of the republics, and generally by sizable margins. In all three census years, levels of education of urban workers in these republics exceeded the national average. Without a study in depth, it is hard to know what to make of these findings of relatively high educational attainments of employed persons in these seven lesser developed republics. The statistics may not be equally reliable, the quality of schooling may differ substantially by region, and differences in economic and occupational structures may be important explanatory variables. With regard to educational quality in general, there is much anecdotal evidence in the Soviet press suggesting that rural schools provide education much inferior in quality to that provided in cities.

Educational attainment data by nationality have not yet been published for 1979. Data from the two earlier postwar censuses show that differences in educational levels among the fifteen major nationalities are still large, but the gaps are being reduced. In 1970, for example, only 11 percent of Moldavians but 40 percent of Georgians had completed secondary school; in 1959, the respective percentages were 4 and 28. In both years, Georgians and Armenians were best educated, followed by Russians: that ordering prevailed for men and women as well as for urban and rural areas. Except in Georgia, Russians living in non-Russian republics were better educated than the titular nationality in every republic, usually by a wide margin. As shown in Table 1 for 1970, the relative educational levels of titular nationalities compared to republic populations as a whole varies widely. Among employed persons in 1970, secondary school graduates in four republics were more common among the titular nationality than in the republic population as a whole, but in the other

TABLE 1

PERCENTAGE OF SECONDARY SCHOOL GRADUATES
AMONG EMPLOYED PERSONS

	URBAN				RURAL			
	TOTAL POPULATION			TITULAR NATIONALITY	TOTAL POPULATION			TITULAR NATIONALITY
	1959	*1970*	*1979*	*1970*	*1959*	*1970*	*1979*	*1970*
USSR	26.1	42.9	61.8	—	9.5	20.1	39.9	—
RSFSR	24.8	40.1	58.7	40.0	9.7	18.1	34.2	18.4
Ukraine	28.2	49.0	67.7	46.6	8.2	19.6	38.5	19.4
Belorussia	28.4	47.9	67.7	42.9	7.3	16.7	33.4	16.0
Uzbekistan	28.5	46.1	67.3	47.3	11.3	30.2	61.8	30.4
Kazakhstan	23.3	39.4	60.1	48.8	15.8	24.4	47.0	29.7
Georgia	45.8	65.6	80.5	76.1	18.6	35.9	55.7	39.3
Azerbaijan	31.7	51.6	68.8	53.1	12.3	27.6	50.9	27.5
Lithuania	24.3	37.3	55.5	35.7	4.5	11.2	29.3	11.2
Moldavia	26.5	43.5	64.7	32.2	4.9	11.9	32.6	10.6
Latvia	29.8	44.0	60.8	44.0	9.3	18.3	34.4	20.2
Kirgizia	27.7	43.8	65.1	55.0	12.2	27.1	53.6	29.2
Tadzhikistan	25.4	40.3	60.1	39.4	8.5	22.9	48.4	22.4
Armenia	38.4	56.3	73.0	56.7	14.8	26.5	59.8	27.4
Turkmenistan	25.0	40.1	59.7	37.4	10.1	25.8	54.3	25.5
Estonia	29.3	42.1	58.3	43.0	10.4	20.4	35.3	20.1

SOURCES: Calculated from data given in *Vestnik statistiki*, no. 2, 1981, pp. 63–78; and *Itogi vsesoiuznoi perepisi naseleniia 1970 goda*, vol. 4, pp. 607–45.

republics the titular nationalities were less well educated than the general population. In most cases, however, the differences were not large. The picture differed between urban and rural areas and between men and women.

ECONOMIC DEVELOPMENT

Economic development, which meant primarily industrialization, was on the Bolsheviks' agenda from the beginning of their hegemony over the diverse peoples who made up the formal empire after 1922. Despite numerous problems with the statistics, it is clear that economic development has occurred in all union republics, but at widely varying rates and in diverse patterns. It is also evident that large development gaps still exist among them, however measured. When differing rates of population increase are taken into account, moreover, interrepublic differences have widened, at least in the past twenty years. Lacking economic data by nationality, I tentatively assume that trends for a given republic reflect reasonably well the experience of the titular nationality living in that republic. The validity of this assumption will be addressed later in this paper.

Judging from Soviet official production data for 1922–1940, regional development patterns appear thus: rapid industrial growth took place in all republics, but only in three republics did the rates exceed that of the RSFSR. In contrast, agricultural production rose much faster in the non-Russian republics (with one exception) than it did in the RSFSR. Investment increased at least twenty-fold in all republics and was directed toward developing an industrial sector and the required infrastructure. Urbanization was taking place everywhere, most rapidly in the RSFSR and Kazakhstan. Also, education and public health networks were being put in place in all republics. From the array of statistics for this period, it is clear that Soviet policy aimed at fostering modernization and economic development in each republic, and that resources were channeled to that end; but even though these policies were successful, it seems that the relative development gaps in 1940 probably were not greatly different from what they had been in 1922. What the diverse regions would have accomplished in the absence of strong direction and some resource transfers from a determined central government cannot be known. The results surely would have been different.

Similar conclusions emerge from a survey of postwar economic development among the republics. With high rates of investment and rapid industrialization still the central focus of development policy, industrial output increased rapidly everywhere during 1950–1980, but at widely differing rates—from an 8-fold increase in Turkmenistan to a 30-fold rise in Lithuania. Most of the non-Russian republics scored greater gains than did the RSFSR. Similar diversity prevailed with respect to the much slower growing agricultural sector; Central Asia, Transcaucasia, and Kazakhstan recorded faster growth than elsewhere. Rapid capital formation continued in all regions, again at widely varying rates. To give an idea of the diversity of the pace of progress, Table 2 provides officially published data on per capita growth rates of national income and industrial production in the fifteen republics during 1960–1980, along with other relevant data. Similar regional disparities in growth rates have characterized agricultural production.[9] In assessing these relative growth rates it is important to note that they are based on official Soviet measures of national income (net material product) and industrial production. Western research has shown that these measures considerably overstate real growth as measured by concepts and procedures used in Western countries.[10] Whether the degree of overstatement differs among republics has yet to be determined.

Insight into the objectives of Soviet investment policy concerning its national states is provided by examining trends in republic shares of total investment during 1950–1980. Although there has been some fluctuation, the shares have been quite stable. The RSFSR has obtained 59 to 65 percent of total investment in each five-year plan period since 1950, with its share declining in the 1950s and 1960s and rising in the 1970s. The Ukraine received 15 to 17 percent, on a generally declining trend. The share of Transcaucasia has remained at around 3.5 percent since 1955, but the share of Central Asia rose from 4 percent to 6 percent. Shares for Belorussia and Moldavia have increased steadily—from 3 to 4.5 percent—and the share of the Baltic republics also rose—from 2 percent to 3 percent. Kazakhstan's share has ranged between 5 and 7 percent. This investment allocation pattern suggests that Soviet policy proceeded from the premise of ensuring that at least some economic development continued in all republics, taking population growth into account, while simultaneously paying attention to the need to steer investment towards areas of highest economic return (for example, the Baltic republics) and more recently toward developing energy and raw material reserves in Siberia. No consistent effort to reduce regional development gaps, at least on a per capita basis, is discernible in the allocative results of investment policy. Thus, investment per capita rose two to five times during 1951–1980 in the Transcaucasian and Central Asian republics, five times in the RSFSR, and over 6 to 8 times in Latvia and Estonia, already the most developed regions.

TABLE 2
INDICATORS OF RATES AND LEVELS OF ECONOMIC DEVELOPMENT

	National Income[a]	Industrial Production[a]	Percentage of Agriculture in Total Employment 1975	National Income Per Capita (USSR = 100) 1980	Urban Population as Percentage of Total Population 1959	1981
USSR	4.9	6.1	28	100	48	63
RSFSR	5.2	6.0	22	116	52	71
Ukraine	4.5	6.1	36	90	46	63
Belorussia	6.6	9.2	38	111	31	57
Uzbekistan	3.3	3.7	42	55	34	42
Kazakhstan	4.0	5.4	32	74	44	55
Georgia	5.7	6.4	41	88	42	52
Azerbaijan	3.7	4.6	42	70	48	53
Lithuania	5.3	7.9	40	100	39	63
Moldavia	5.1	7.5	50	81	22	41
Latvia	4.8	6.3	28	132	56	69
Kirgizia	3.5	6.5	38	56	34	39
Tadzhikistan	3.0	4.0	55	47	33	34
Armenia	5.5	6.4	28	86	50	66
Turkmenistan	1.6	3.4	45	56	46	48
Estonia	5.1	6.4	25	135	56	71

SOURCES: Rates of growth of national income and industrial production were calculated from official indexes and population data given in *Narkhoz SSSR*, 1970 and 1980. Urban population shares were calculated from data in *Narkhoz SSSR*, 1980, pp. 10–11. Figures for 1959 relate to January 15; those for 1981 relate to January 1. Levels of national income per capita were obtained by extrapolating the totals published for 1970 in *Narkhoz Latviiskoi SSR*, 1971, p. 56, using indexes of population and national income. Percentages of agriculture in total employment were calculated from official data on employment in the public sector and my estimates of private-sector employment presented in "Regional Dimensions of the Legal Private Economy in the USSR," in Gregory Grossman, ed., *The Second Economy in the Soviet Union* (Berkeley and Los Angeles: University of California Press, forthcoming).

[a] Average annual growth rates per capita, 1960–1980.

Even though Brezhnev asserted in 1972 that levels of economic development had been essentially equalized, a large body of Soviet official data shows that substantial development gaps still exist among the republics. Table 2 provides one such indicator—relative levels of per capita national income (net material product) in 1980.[11] In that year, per capita national income in the most affluent republic—Estonia—was nearly triple that in the poorest one—Tadzhikistan. Interrepublic differences have widened since 1960.[12] Estonia, Latvia, and the RSFSR have ranked at the top throughout the period, and the Central Asian republics and Azerbaijan have occupied the lowest positions. Very rapid population growth in the latter republics has prevented a rise in their relative position, despite above-average growth in total national income in most of them. Belorussia, Georgia, and Armenia have managed to improve their relative positions considerably. Although present interregional disparities in the Soviet Union may not be unduly large by international comparison, they clearly are substantial and are not diminishing.

EMPLOYMENT AND STRUCTURAL CHANGE

Both by choice and by necessity, Soviet development policies have featured rapid mobilization of the adult population into the labor force. At present, labor force participation among adult men is nearly universal, and rates for women are uniquely high for a country at the Soviet level of development. These policies have been carried out in all republics, but not with uniform success. McAuley estimates that in 1975 labor force participation rates for women aged 16–54 years were 82 to 91 percent in the RSFSR and the western republics, compared with 60 to 67 percent in 1960. In contrast, rates in Transcaucasia were 64 percent in 1975 and 53 percent in 1960, but in Central Asia the corresponding figures were 65 and 60 percent.[13] Although participation rates are relatively low among adult women in Transcaucasia and Central Asia in comparison with other republics, the share of women in the state labor force there has increased steadily and substantially, although more slowly since 1970. In most cases it has also risen among collective farmers. Women in all republics tend to be concentrated in low-wage sectors and in less skilled occupations. Nonetheless, there is no doubt that Soviet policy has achieved a large measure of convergence among regions in women's access to employment, as it has in education.

As is characteristic, Soviet economic development has produced major changes in the structure of employment, reflecting the transition from a predominantly agricultural society to a moderately industrialized one.[14]

In 1950, over half of the labor force in the USSR was employed in agriculture; among the republics, the shares ranged from 46 percent in the RSFSR to 84 percent in Tadzhikistan. By 1975, the shares in these two republics had been reduced to 22 and 55 percent. Excepting Estonia, the percentage of agricultural workers in non-Russian republics was considerably higher than in the RSFSR in both years. The shares for 1975 are shown in Table 2. Within agriculture, the proportion of workers engaged in the private sector differs markedly among regions, and is generally larger in Transcaucasia and the Baltics than elsewhere. Although employment data are not available by nationality, the proportion of the titular nationality in each republic that is employed in agriculture probably is higher than the rate for the republic population as a whole. This conclusion would seem to follow from the fact that titular nationalities tend to live in rural areas in their republics. Also, the proportion of collective farmers tends to be higher among the titular nationalities.[15]

Reflecting the state's policy of fostering industrialization in all regions, the proportion of the labor force employed in industry and construction has increased considerably in all republics since 1950, but at greatly differing rates. In 1975, this sector's share in total employment ranged from 17 percent in Tadzhikistan to almost 40 percent in the RSFSR. In 1950, the respective shares for these republics were 29 and 6 percent. The share of the services sector also rose in all republics, ranging in 1975 from 27 percent in Moldavia to 40 percent in Kazakhstan. (The percentages were 14 and 23, respectively, in 1950.) The diverse trends in the sectoral distribution of the labor force and the present large regional differences in employment structures provide additional evidence for the thesis that Soviet nationality policies in the economic sphere, rhetoric notwithstanding, have been directed toward providing some economic progress for all republics, without any consistent attempt to bring them to the same level.

Economic development, along with a deliberate policy choice, however, has brought substantial convergence among republics in the class structure of society, that is, in the distribution between workers and employees (state labor force) and collective farmers, who for decades were treated in all respects as second-class citizens. According to census data, the percentage of collective farmers in the total gainfully employed population in 1959 varied from 21 percent in Estonia to 71 percent in Moldavia; in 1979 their shares ranged from 5 percent in Kazakhstan to 32 percent in Turkmenistan. Their shares dropped markedly in all republics, the result not only of decreases in the relative importance of agriculture, but also of a policy of setting up new farms as state farms and converting collective farms to state farms. Moreover, the social status of all collective farmers has been radically upgraded since 1965 by putting them under the state system of social security and giving them internal passports like other citizens. Their relative economic status has been greatly improved also as a consequence of the introduction of guaranteed wage payments and a concerted policy of gradually raising the wages of collective farmers to the level paid to state farmers. These processes have proceeded unevenly among the republics, but the data needed to sort it all out are not available. Nonetheless, it is clear that regional disparities in incomes of collective farmers are still large.[16]

LIVING STANDARDS

There is no way to measure relative standards of living for ethnic groups in the Soviet Union, since economic data are not published either on incomes or expenditures by ethnic group. With due qualifications, however, we can make some judgments about the matter from relevant data for the republics. Table 3 gives three indicators of trends and relative standards of living in the republics in 1960–1980. As background, we should note that almost no rise in per capita household consumption took place in the Soviet Union as a whole between 1928 and 1950, although education and health services improved greatly. Since then, Soviet living standards have risen quite rapidly—at an average annual rate of 3.5 percent as given by indexes of real per capita consumption constructed by Western scholars. This measure is the best overall indicator of changes in standards of living, for it includes all expenditures by households on goods and services, as well as government outlays on health and education. I have developed such a measure for the republics for the period 1960–1980.[17] The results are believed to be reasonably reliable despite the problems involved in making the estimates. According to these measures, real per capita consumption increased substantially in all republics, with average annual growth rates ranging from 2.5 percent in Tadzhikistan to 4.6 percent in Moldavia; the rate for the RSFSR was 3.3 percent, slightly above the national average. In most cases, faster improvements were made in the 1960s than in the 1970s.

Measures of relative levels of per capita consumption in the republics in 1960, 1970, and 1980 are shown in Table 3. They are based on estimates in current prices I have put together from a variety of data on personal incomes, including income in kind and government outlays for consumption. These estimates of relative levels of per capita consumption by region accord well with a variety of relevant data on incomes and expenditures. Despite their imperfection they are far better indicators of relative

TABLE 3
INDICATORS OF RELATIVE LIVING STANDARDS

	Consumption Per Capita (USSR = 100)			Urban Housing Stock (Square meters per capita)			Savings Deposits (Rubles per capita)		
	1960	1970	1980	1960	1970	1980	1960	1970	1980
USSR	100.0	100.0	100.0	8.8	11.0	13.0	51	192	589
RSFSR	106.6	107.1	109.5	8.6	11.0	13.2	61	216	644
Ukraine	94.3	96.6	91.7	9.8	11.9	14.0	46	193	685
Belorussia	84.4	95.0	98.9	8.6	10.7	13.0	31	161	658
Uzbekistan	80.4	78.1	77.6	7.8	8.2	9.3	23	78	212
Kazakhstan	95.6	91.2	90.6	7.9	9.8	11.6	32	138	402
Georgia	95.4	88.9	93.4	9.8	12.2	14.5	52	247	685
Azerbaijan	74.4	69.4	67.7	8.1	9.3	9.9	30	101	268
Lithuania	109.9	118.4	115.9	9.4	11.3	13.6	31	236	925
Moldavia	72.5	90.8	97.0	8.4	10.1	11.6	21	93	610
Latvia	127.3	126.3	114.9	12.2	13.9	15.8	51	239	677
Kirgizia	74.7	76.1	72.7	7.4	8.8	10.0	30	102	274
Tadzhikistan	70.5	66.7	62.1	7.9	8.8	9.8	22	86	194
Armenia	87.0	85.9	84.4	7.9	9.6	10.9	44	249	637
Turkmenistan	82.4	82.2	78.3	8.4	9.8	10.5	28	96	254
Estonia	130.2	132.9	131.1	11.5	13.7	16.3	59	295	759

Sources: Data for 1960 and 1970 are given in my "Regional Living Standards," in Gertrude E. Schroeder and I. S. Koropecky, eds., *Economics of Soviet Regions* (New York: Praeger, 1981), pp. 124–25, 129, 138–39. The sources and methodology are described there. Data for 1980 were obtained using similar sources and methodologies. The figures for consumption per capita are my estimates; the figures for urban housing stock per capita and savings deposits per capita were calculated from data regularly published in *Narkhoz SSSR*.

levels of incomes and of living standards in the republics than are the official data on per capita national income (NMP) given in Table 2. From these measures, it is clear that sizable differences in living standards exist among the republics. Except for the Baltics, living standards in all non-Russian republics in 1980 were below the RSFSR by substantial margins—by one-fourth or more in Central Asia and Azerbaijan. Republic rankings were quite stable during the period: the three Baltic republics ranked highest throughout, the RSFSR was fourth, and Tadzhikistan held the lowest place. Only Belorussia and Moldavia managed to improve their rankings significantly. As percentages of the RSFSR level, however, the relative positions of the other non-Russian republics generally have deteriorated during the period. Overall, regional differentiation increased sharply in the 1970s; the coefficient of variation was .105 in 1960, .107 in 1970, and .142 in 1980.[18]

These aggregate measures conceal some interesting diversities among republics. As indicated in Table 3, the Ukraine and Georgia had more urban housing space per capita in 1980 than did the RSFSR, which ranks well above them in overall per capita consumption. These two republics also had higher per capita savings deposits than the RSFSR. On both of these measures, however, the Baltics generally rank near the top and the Central Asian republics near the bottom, along with Azerbaijan, as is the case with respect to total per capita consumption. Other indicators—number of doctors per 10,000 people, for instance—show a similar pattern.

Our measures of regional living standards necessarily are based on data for the legal economy, both public and private. What about the ubiquitous "second" economy—illegal production of goods and services, black markets, corruption, and theft of state property? Are there not substantial regional differences in the incidence of the illegal economy? Some observers think that it is particularly rampant in Central Asia and Transcaucasia. We simply do not know. The available information is entirely anecdotal and therefore cannot be aggregated. Deep immersion in these materials has persuaded me that the presence of illegal economic activities does not seriously distort the perceptions of regional disparities in living standards as given by our measures of per capita quantities of goods and services provided in the legal public and private economy.[19] Aside from illegal production of *samogon*, largely a Russian pursuit, most illegal activities seem to involve redistribution of goods and incomes among groups in the populace, rather than production of additional goods and services. Moreover, an estimate of private services, which are substantial, has been included in our measures of per capita consumption.

To what extent can we infer that the disparities in living standards shown by data for republics reflect those for their titular nationalities? Clearly, the situation varies among republics. Probably the most important considerations are the titular nationality's proportion in the total population of its republic and the extent to which rural/urban proportions, educational levels, and occupational distributions of the titular nationality resemble those for the republic as a whole. In 1979, the titular nationality made up better than 54 percent of the total population in all republics except Kazakhstan and Kirgizia. It comprised 74 percent or more in the RSFSR, the Ukraine, Belorussia, Azerbaijan, Lithuania, and Armenia. In the four Central Asian republics (Uzbekistan, Kirgizia, Tadzhikistan, and Turkmenistan), members of the four titular nationalities (taken together) made up between 61 and 84 percent of the population of each republic. On the nationality proportion criterion, then, we might conclude that only for Kazakhstan may republic data not be roughly indicative of the position of its titular nationality.

Data from the 1970 census show, however, that the proportions of titular nationalities that live in rural areas in their republics are higher than the corresponding rural proportions for the republics as a whole; Armenians living in Armenia and Russians in the RSFSR provided the sole exceptions. The differences between the respective rural shares ranged from 4 percentage points for Lithuanians living in Lithuania to 24 percentage points for Kazakhs living in Kazakhstan. In the USSR as a whole, standards of living in rural areas are perhaps two-thirds to three-fourths of urban levels; qualitatively, the difference is much greater.[20] No doubt, such differentials vary among regions.[21] Since agriculture, however, is overwhelmingly the dominant rural pursuit and since farm incomes have been rising faster than nonfarm incomes since 1950, rural/urban gaps in living standards are being reduced. On the rural/urban count alone we may conclude that living standards of titular nationalities, except in Armenia and the RSFSR, probably are below those shown by republic data. The differences may not be large in Belorussia, Georgia, and Lithuania and may not exist at all in Estonia, where farm incomes tend to exceed nonfarm incomes. The differences could be sizable in Kazakhstan, Moldavia, and much of Central Asia.

We also know from 1970 census data that educational levels of the titular nationalities tend to be lower than those for their republics — except for Russians, Kazakhs, Georgians, and Armenians. Also, levels of educational attainment in rural areas are well below those in urban areas, both for titular nationalities and republics as a whole. In both urban and rural areas, however, attainments of the employed titular nationality in most cases equal or exceed those for all urban and rural residents in the republic. On this criterion, then, we may conclude that shares of titular

nationalities in total populations and disparities in rural/urban proportions are far more important than differing educational attainments in
assessing living standards of titular nationalities relative to the average in
their republics.

In summary, it seems safe to say that if we had the data to sort out all
these complex variables, we would be likely to find that the Baltic
nationalities and the Russians are best off economically, at least as conventionally measured, and that the Central Asians and Azerbaijanis are
worst off. That is the conclusion to be drawn from republic data. Also,
we would surely find substantial differences between the economic status
of men and women and between rural and urban living standards among
the various nationalities living in their own republics.

INTERREGIONAL INCOME TRANSFERS

The nature and extent of transfers of income (income produced in one
republic and used in other republics for consumption and investment) has
generated a great deal of interest and research. Although problems with
availability and interpretation of the data preclude definitive and precise
answers, the general picture seems fairly clear. Throughout the Soviet
period the Ukraine has transferred roughly 10 percent (or perhaps as
much as 14 percent in recent years) to other republics; that is, national
income produced in the Ukraine exceeded the income used for consumption and investment there by that amount.[22] Since 1960, Azerbaijan also
has transferred income out of the republic—by small amounts until 1975,
but by 1981 national income produced in Azerbaijan exceeded income
used there by 2.4 billion rubles, or 25 percent.[23] Although Georgia and
Armenia were net recipients of income transfers during most of the
1960s, they contributed income to the rest of the USSR in the most recent
years for which data are available, 1979 and 1975, respectively. Latvia also
has consistently transferred incomes elsewhere since 1960, generally
about 5 to 6 percent each year, the rate that also prevailed in 1980.
Lithuania and Estonia appear to have been recipients of transfers for the
most part. Inadequate data preclude valid generalizations for Belorussia
and Moldavia.

In contrast, the Central Asian republics seem to have been consistent
recipients of resource transfers from other republics since 1960 (and
probably in earlier decades also). For Uzbekistan, for example, income
used there exceeded income produced there during 1961–1975 by 2 to 18
percent; the ratio was 6 percent in 1978, the latest year for which data are
available. The ratios apparently have been consistently higher for the

other Central Asian republics throughout this period. Kazakhstan also may have been the beneficiary of income transfers, but we cannot be sure because of uncertainties about the data. On balance, the RSFSR seems not to have been a new recipient of income transfers, although this situation may have changed in the past few years as a result of the huge demands on resources to develop energy and raw materials sources in Siberia.

In sum, it appears that considerable redistributions of income among the republics has taken place in the Soviet period, with the Central Asian republics the principal gainers and also perhaps Georgia and Armenia (until recently). The resources transfers to recipient republics seem to have been directed toward investment rather than consumption, that is, investment rates were higher in those republics than probably would have been the case otherwise. Although the transfers may also have contributed to developing education and health care in those republics, they clearly have not added to consumption levels directly. As we have seen, the relative position of Central Asia and Transcaucasia with regard to per capita consumption has worsened over the past two decades.

CONCLUSIONS

In the social and economic spheres, proclaimed Soviet nationalities policies have been a mixture of successes and failures. Under the direction of a strong central government, the diverse ethnic groups were supposed to "flourish" and also to be "drawn together." This process, in turn, was supposed to bring a withering away of nationalism as a potentially divisive social and political force. The various national states clearly have "flourished," if that term is taken to mean that fairly rapid economic development, urbanization, and advances in education have taken place everywhere. "Drawing together," too, has occurred, if reference is to reducing disparities in levels of education, providing at least minimal public health care and social security coverage for all, and reducing the differences in economic and social opportunities between men and women and between urban and rural areas. If the term means equalizing levels of economic development and living standards among nationalities, as proclaimed repeatedly until a decade ago, then a great deal still remains to be done. As we have seen, a mass of evidence shows that gaps in economic development and standards of living among republics, and therefore among their titular nationalities, remain large and persistent. The development process, though, has brought one major political benefit to the Soviet state—an intricate web of mutual dependencies and a large degree of economic integration among the republics and their peoples.[24] Each republic is now both a major importer of goods from other republics and a major exporter to them; the smaller republics are far more trade-dependent than the large ones, particularly for investment goods. In the former, both exports and imports make up roughly one-fourth of total production and supplies. Defection from the union would be very costly, at least in the short run, unless the Soviet government sanctioned independence, hardly a likely scenario.

But economic and social modernization has not brought the desired eradication of national identities and aspirations as potentially divisive forces. The goal of Russification and assimilation has proved an impossible dream. Even though Soviet policy has helped the poorer republics in Central Asia to industrialize and has fostered mastery of the Russian language there, Central Asians have not become Russian clones in the process. Ethnic, cultural, and religious identities remain strong. Moreover, titular nationalities in the republics that provide the resource transfers, notably the Ukraine, no doubt resent being forced to help the less developed republics to industrialize. Baltic nationalism is alive and well, even though those republics are relatively affluent by Soviet standards. Rising standards of living and increased educational attainments in the non-Russian regions have not automatically caused their peoples to identify with the Soviet state. In a word, Soviet nationalities policies have not produced a melting pot. Nonetheless, the Soviet state, with its manifest willingness to resort to force, should be able to keep divisive nationalist displays within tolerable bounds.

Since one of the proclaimed goals of Soviet development policy in general has been to catch up with capitalist countries in standards of living, it seems appropriate to provide some perspective on what has been accomplished insofar as the diverse nationalities are concerned. A rough assessment of this matter can be made using our findings for the republics and the results of recent international comparisons of per capita consumption in the Soviet Union and a number of other countries at varying levels of development.[25] Tenuous though they are, these comparisons for the Soviet republics probably are in the ball park. They show that in 1980 per capita consumption in the RSFSR and the Baltic republics was below 1975 levels in all Western European countries investigated, including Spain and Ireland, and it was also below levels in Hungary and Poland. The Western republics, Kazakhstan, and Georgia were near the level in Yugoslavia, and Armenia was on the same level as Romania. Levels in Central Asia were near or a little below levels in such countries as Iran, Syria, and Brazil. In assessing the welfare implications of these findings, however, one must take account of the peculiarities of Soviet income and consumption policies. Peoples in all Soviet republics benefit from education and health care provided universally and with little or no direct charge. They do not have to fear unemployment, and state-run programs provide a variety of pensions and other benefits. Although we cannot be sure, personal incomes (earned in the legal economy) probably are distributed less unequally in Soviet republics than in comparable market economies. People in all republics, however, have to put up with the familiar deficiences of centrally planned socialism—random but perennial shortages of desired goods, black markets, queues, archaic retail distribution facilities, and poor quality goods and services. And the non-Russians are forced to submit to Russian hegemony.

The next decade or two surely will be a time of troubles for the Soviet state and for its diverse peoples. Economic progress is bound to slow to a crawl in the country as a whole due to (1) a demographically determined, drastic reduction in the growth of the labor force; (2) decreasing returns and raw materials shortages that constrain investment; and (3) the absence of the sources of an upsurge in productivity. With a much decreased rate of growth in the gross national product and a continued population growth, living standards can rise only modestly at best and could stagnate. These are Western assessments.[26] Soviet planners display a more optimistic outlook. The eleventh five-year plan (for 1981–1985) provides for a speedup in both industrial and agricultural growth. Real income per capita (the Soviet measure of living standards) is scheduled to increase only a little more slowly than in 1976–1980. As in past plans, varying rates of development are planned for the fifteen republics, and especially high growth rates are scheduled for Transcaucasia, Moldavia, and Belorussia. Economic performance during 1981–1984, however, indicates that these plans will not be met.

In the period of economic stringency that lies ahead, the competition for scarce investment resources will be severe. The Soviet government will be hard pressed to provide enough funds to ensure continued progress in all republics, taking population growth into account. The need for new funds will be particularly pressing in Central Asia and Transcaucasia, since the state must provide jobs for their rapidly growing labor force. Alternatively, ways may have to be found to transfer their workers to labor-deficit areas elsewhere. Such transfers have not proved easy in the past and are unlikely to be so in the future. Clearly, there is much potential for ethnic tension and conflict in such an environment of economic austerity. Although nationalistic manifestations may become more frequent and more disruptive, it is hard to believe that they could seriously threaten the existing political order in the absence of a major internal revolution or international conflict. Perhaps it was a nagging (if not acute) concern about the potential for ethnic turmoil, however, that made "cohesion" the watchword of the party resolution on the sixtieth anniversary of the founding of the USSR. But this emphasis was also an implicit recognition that a solid popular consensus on the legitimacy of the Soviet state and its purposes had not been achieved during those 60 years.

NOTES

1. *Pravda*, December 22, 1972.

2. *Voprosy istorii KPSS*, no. 1, 1982, pp. 10–11. Further elaboration of these themes is provided in Iu. V. Bromlei, ed., *Razvitiia natsional'nykh otnoshennii v SSSR v svete XXVI s'ezda KPSS* (Moscow, 1982), pp. 116–267.

3. *Pravda*, February 21, 1982.

4. *Pravda*, December 21, 1982.

5. The many problems and results of diverse approaches by scholars from various disciplines are summarized in Donna Bahry and Carol Nechemias, "Half Full or Half Empty? The Debate over Soviet Regional Equality," *Slavic Review* 40, no. 3 (1981): 366–83.

6. The discussion rests mainly on Soviet census data for 1959, 1970, and 1979. The limited data released thus far on nationality and language in 1979 are published in *Vestnik statistiki*, nos. 7–11, 1980.

7. V. I. Kozlov, *National'nosti SSSR: Etnodemograficheskii obzor* (Moscow, 1982), p. 100.

8. Data on educational attainment by republic are published in *Vestnik statistiki*, no. 6, 1980, and nos. 2 and 4, 1981.

9. See, for example, Alfred Evans, Jr., "Interrepublic Inequality in Agricultural Development in the USSR," *Slavic Review* 40, no. 4, (1981): 570–84.

10. For a discussion of these matters see U.S. Congress, Joint Economic Committee, *USSR: Measures of Economic Growth and Development, 1950–80* (Washington, 1982).

11. Net material product (NMP) differs from the concept of gross national product (GNP) used in the West in excluding personnel services in so-called nonproductive sectors (health, education, government administration, and other services). The relative positions of the republics change little when a measure of per capita GNP (rather than NMP) is employed. See I. S. Koropeckyj, "National Income of the Soviet Union Republics in 1970: Revision and Some Applications," in Zbigniew M. Fallenbuchl, ed., *Economic Development of the Soviet Union and Eastern Europe* (New York: Praeger, 1975), vol. 1, p. 316.

12. This conclusion is based on extrapolation of levels of national income in 1970 given in *Narkhoz Latviiskoi SSR v 1971 godu* (p. 56) using indexes for 1960–1980 published in *Narkhoz SSSR* (1970, p. 534 and 1980, p. 379). The results may not be very reliable.

13. Alastair McAuley, *Women's Work and Wages in the Soviet Union* (London: George Allen and Unwin, 1981), p. 37. For an excellent assessment of women's progress in Central Asia, see Nancy Lubin, "Women in Soviet Central Asia: Progress and Contradictions," *Soviet Studies* 33, no. 2 (April 1981): 182–203.

14. The data on changes in the structure of employment were derived from official statistics on employment in the state and cooperative sectors and on my estimates of employment in the private sector of agriculture. Official statistics for the USSR and republics have been compiled by Stephen Rapawy in "Regional Employment Trends in the U.S.S.R., 1950 to 1975," in U.S. Congress, Joint Economic Committee, *Soviet Economy in a Time of Change* (Washington, 1979), vol. 1, pp. 604–10. The derivation of the estimates of private agricultural employment is explained in Gertrude E. Schroeder, "Regional Dimensions of the Legal Private Economy in the USSR," in Gregory Grossman, ed., *The Second Economy in the Soviet Union* (Berkeley and Los Angeles: University of California Press, forthcoming).

15. This conclusion is based on a comparison of data on the class composition of republics and nationalities in 1970 and 1979 as given in *Narkhoz, 1922–1982*, pp. 31–32, and *Sotsiologicheskie issledovaniia*, no. 4, 1982, p. 23.

16. For some indications of the interrepublic differences in the incomes of various groups of farmers, see Gertrude E. Schroeder, "Regional Income Differences: Urban and Rural," in NATO, Economic Directorate, *Regional Development in the USSR: Trends and Prospects* (Newtonville, Mass.: Oriental Research Partners, 1979), pp. 24–40.

17. The derivation and limitations of these measures are explained in some detail in my "Regional Living Standards," in I. S. Koropeckyj and Gertrude E. Schroeder, eds., *The Economics of Soviet Regions* (New York: Praeger, 1981), pp. 118–56. A variety of related evidence is also presented there.

18. Using a variety of data, Carol Nechemias has found sizable declines in regional disparities within the RSFSR. See her paper "Regional Differentiations of Living Standards in the RSFSR: The Issue of Inequality," *Soviet Studies* 32, no. 3 (July 1980): 366–78.

19. For a discussion of these matters, see Gertrude E. Schroeder, *Regional Dimensions of the 'Second' Economy in the USSR*, Kennan Institute for Advanced Russian Studies, Occasional Paper 115 (Washington, D.C., 1980).

20. This conclusion is based on my "Rural Living Standards" in Robert Stuart, ed., *The Soviet Rural Economy* (Totowa, N.J.: Rowman and Allanheld, 1983), pp. 241–57.

21. The rather inconclusive results of my efforts to sort out these complex matters are given in Schroeder, "Regional Income Differentials," pp. 22–40.

22. The extent of resource transfers from the Ukraine to other republics is discussed in I. S. Koropeckyj, "A Century of Moscow-Ukraine Economic Relations: An Interpretation," *Harvard Ukrainian Studies* 5, no. 4 (December 1981): 467–96.

23. The data given in this section rest on a study by James W. Gillula, "The Economic Interdependence of Soviet Republics," in *Soviet Economy in a Time of Change*, 1: 621–35. Data for years after 1977, the concluding year of his study, were

taken from the most recent available annual statistical handbooks of the respective republics.

24. For details, see ibid., pp. 646–52.

25. The sources are U.S. Congress, Joint Economic Committee, *Consumption in the USSR: An International Comparison*, by Gertrude E. Schroeder and Imogene Edwards (Washington, D.C.: Government Printing Office, 1981); and Irving B. Kravis, Alan Heston, and Robert Summers, *World Product and Income: International Comparisons of Real Gross Product*, International Comparison Project Phase III (Baltimore, Md.: The Johns Hopkins Press, 1982).

26. See Schroeder, "Consumption," in Abram Bergson and Herbert S. Levine, eds., *The Soviet Economy Toward the Year 2000* (New York: George Allen and Unwin, 1983), pp. 311–49. Also see "An Overview" by Daniel L. Bond and Herbert S. Levine in ibid., pp. 1–33.

The Demography of Soviet Ethnic Groups in World Perspective

Mikhail S. Bernstam

NORTH AND SOUTH

The Soviet Union, with its population of 273.8 million (as of January 1, 1984), can serve as a demographic model of the world. The Soviets have their own North, represented by the developed Slavic, Baltic, and other European populations. These groups constituted 77.0 percent of the total population of the USSR in 1979, and their average natural increase in the 1970s was 0.56 percent a year. This growth, however, was due exclusively to population momentum, for fertility was below replacement level. Like all other developed populations of the world, Soviet Europeans have experienced a demographic depression and face the long-term possibility of eventual depopulation.

The Soviets also have their own South, represented mostly by populations of Turko-Muslim origin and located in Central Asia, the Caucasus, and some parts of the RSFSR. The South comprised 22.7 percent of the total population of the USSR in 1979, with an average annual natural increase in the 1970s of 2.14 percent—four times that of

Acknowledgments are due to Gary S. Becker, Ansley J. Coale, Paul A. David, Kingsley Davis, Murray Feshbach, Milton Friedman, Masanori Hashimoto, Dudley Kirk, Robert T. Michael, William Petersen, Rita Ricardo-Campbell, Sherwin Rosen, and Robert J. Willis, who provided very useful comments on various drafts of this paper. Peter R. Meffert provided invaluable assistance at various stages of this work. Naturally, all the responsibility for the content and remaining errors rests with the author.

the North. The rate of natural increase of the indigenous Central Asians was 3.29 percent a year—that is, 5.4 times that of the ethnic Russians.[1] The continuing demographic explosion of the Soviet South, which has proceeded despite a rapid and significant economic development, resembles the situation in many developing countries.

The simultaneousness of demographic depression in the North and demographic explosion in the South has created a Malthusian conflict of food and population, since the North is responsible for the bulk of industrial and agricultural production in the country. It is rather ironic that this Malthusian dilemma has become the chief problem of economic development for the major Marxist states in the 1970s and 1980s (the USSR and the People's Republic of China). The ethnodemographic balance of the Soviet Union is also at stake. The Soviets themselves are most concerned with the prospect of the eventual depopulation of the Northern ethnic groups, which will start between the years 2000 and 2010, according to their own estimates.[2]

Other explosive problems are declining social mobility and difficulties in financing the welfare state, especially its social security component. Thanks to the inefficiency of their employment system, the Soviets recognized a few years ago the same mathematical theorem that Americans and West Europeans currently are discussing in the social security debate: the dependency burden on working generations is high when fertility is high, but it is even higher when fertility is low. The demographic explosion of the South and the demographic depression of the North both lead to an increasing share of consumption in the national income, widening of capital, and a rise in the price of resources relative to the price of human inputs. These, in turn, impose new constraints on economic growth and technological advancement and eventually reduce the standard of living. Since, in addition to the internal problems of the North, the rapidly growing South is and will continue to be significantly dependent on the North, the situation may not be a question of who will overpower whom, but rather of a joint, long-term, economic decline.

DATA AND METHODOLOGY

A number of purely technical problems have to be solved before a historical and theoretical analysis of the demography of Soviet ethnic groups can be presented. The state of the data is such that statistics must be calculated or recalculated before meaningful questions can be asked. All territorial units of the USSR, that is, the union republics, autonomous republics, and so on, represent heterogeneous populations for which irregular series of vital data are available.[3] These data have to be recalculated into series for homogeneous populations, that is, ethnic groups. The Soviet censuses of 1959, 1970, and 1979 provide only erratic and inconsistent data on nationalities that are not comparable from one point in time to another. Regional life tables of the urban population only are available for 1974[4]—a year close to the peak in the trend of changing Soviet life expectancy.[5]

The new formula of computing expectancy for life at birth in any population, established by Preston and Coale, could not be used here because of the lack of relevant data on age distribution.[6] A regression model proposed by Mazur[7] was used in this article for calculating ethnic life expectancies. From these data, with the use of Coale and Demeny's Regional Model Life Tables and Stable Populations (Model East), survivorship ratios were derived for females at the mean age of childbearing (MEAN). (MEAN values for nationalities are calculated from the ethnic age-specific fertility schedules for 1975–76.) These ratios were adjusted in congruence with known survivorship ratios for the USSR as a whole (from the 1959, 1970, and 1979 censuses)[8] and interpolated for single interim years. Net reproduction rates were then calculated for ethnic groups.

Total fertility rates were transferred from the data on territorial units to ethnic groups by the simple method described by Coale, Anderson, and Harm,[9] with the use of their estimates of the underreporting of births in Muslim areas and with age-distribution adjustments from the 1970 census in accordance with Biraben's computations.[10] Since ethnic spatial distribution changes in the last two decades were not significant enough to affect ethnic/territorial fertility ratios, the 1969–70 ratios were assumed to be constant, with adjustment for the differences in Muslim birth underreporting for 1958–59, 1965–66, 1967–68, and from 1969–70 on. Surprisingly, it was found that the Soviets made no significant improvement in fertility registration in Central Asia through the 1970s if the estimates from Coale et al. for 1969–70 are compared with the 1970s fertility schedules and Feshbach's calculations on children aged 0 to 9 (from the 1979 census).[11]

Age-specific marital schedules for five-year female age groups for fifteen major nationalities were calculated from the 1970 census and used for the entire 1970s (due to the lack of data from the 1979 census), although the proportion of women currently married declined in the 15–19 and 20–24 age groups.[12] On the basis of (1) the 1970 schedules, (2) the ethnic/territorial fertility ratios, and (3) territorial age-specific fertility schedules calculated with the use of Bongaarts's index, the index of proportion of women married at ages 15–49 and the totals defined here as "age-specific marital fertility rates accumulated by age" (AMFR) were derived.[13] Then Coale and Trussell's Model Fertility Schedules techniques were applied to all these data.[14] Both marital and overall age-specific fertility rates by ethnic groups were computed so that three variables would fit: (1) total fertility rates of ethnic groups, (2) AMFR, and (3) median values of m, the index of the degree of departure from natural fertility. The fit was made by the least squares method.

A modified version of Bongaarts's model of fertility and birth control was applied to compute ethnic schedules of pregnancies terminated by births and averted by contraception, spontaneous abortions, induced abortions, and by pathological secondary infertility.[15] The results in this article are on the conservative side; the model used derives as its index of the proportion currently married the ratio of total fertility to the AMFR, and this provides for the minimum values of abortions, their aftereffects, and contraception. More realistic values could be derived if the index of marriage were converted into the index of the proportion of the total female population under stable hazardous conditions. This could be done by incorporating data on consensual unions and other arrangements, with the average coital frequency, into the age-specific marital rates. For this purpose, and for reconstructing the 1979 marital schedules from the available data, the Coale and Coale-McNeil model could be used.[16] This, however, remains a subject for further research.

Soviet censuses, like those in many other countries, provide data on ethnic groups based on the personal statements of the respondents. In a multiethnic country, significant nationality reidentification takes place, and all vital rates for ethnic groups are biased accordingly. (Whether this process is a genuine assimilation or a change on paper is of no concern here.)[7] A new method was developed to evaluate similarity and dissimilarity in the growth rates of different ethnic groups within given territorial units and to reconcile ethnic and territorial growth rates in an intercensal time span.[18] The method yielded satisfactory results (compared with those derived by using conventional techniques) in cases of low spatial redistribution of a given nationality. It failed otherwise (for Armenians, Chechens, and a few other minority cases), and it also failed in the case of a nationality that resides in a very heterogeneous territorial unit (the Kazakhs). In those cases conventional projections were used to approximate the adjustments for ethnic reidentification. Using earlier established fertility patterns and model life tables, control tests were made to compare the results of the new and conventional methods. For example, the number of ethnic Russians in 1979 calculated by the new method was 133,487,000 and the number calculated by conventional techniques was 132,964,000 (the census figure was 137,397,089, reflecting the fact that Russians are the main target of in-assimilation). The computed growth rates from 1959 to 1970 and from 1970 to 1979 yielded adjusted numbers for various Soviet populations on the dates of the different censuses. The total of the numbers for all ethnic groups did add up to the total USSR population according to the censuses.

The ethnic distribution of the USSR for 1970—the year of the smallest proportion of females of prime childbearing age in all Soviet populations—was adjusted for nationality reidentification and projected to the years 1984, 2000, 2050, and so on for high, medium, and low series. Various aspects of the issues and techniques of projections are developed in the works of Brass, Keyfitz, Coale, Bourgeois-Pichat, and Lee.[19] Some of the premises of these works, especially their discussion of fertility cycles, are implicitly incorporated in my work. The total Soviet population from the medium projection series (the only series presented in this article) is estimated at 299.0 million in the year 2000—only slightly higher than 297.5 million, the conventionally projected figure of the Foreign Demographic Analysis Division of the U.S. Bureau of the Census.[20]

ETHNODEMOGRAPHIC STRUCTURE

Background

In 1917 the former Russian empire, with a population of 174.6 million (excluding Finland and the net World War I losses), was a predominantly European country, with nationalities of Slavic, Baltic, and Ugro-Finnic origin constituting about 85 percent of the total (see Table 1). After several border changes, wars, domestic devastations, and famines, and decades of demographic transition, the balance sheet shows a relatively modest growth of nationalities of the North from about 140.2 million in 1927 (in the present borders) to 173.0 million in 1959. Some ethnic groups of the South, such as the Uzbeks, Azeris, Kirgiz, Turkmen, Tadzhiks, and Tatars, almost doubled in the aggregate from 1917 to 1959, increasing their share in the total population from 5.1 percent to 8.3 percent.

By the end of the 1950s the present ethnodemographic structure of the USSR was established. Northern growth started to decline very rapidly, and ethnic Russians moved from a solid to a bare majority of the total population (54.7 percent in 1959 and 50.9 percent in 1979 after adjustment for assimilation). The share of the South increased from 17.0 percent in 1959 to 22.7 percent in 1979, and that of the predominantly Muslim Southeast increased from 13.0 percent to 18.2 percent. (The

TABLE 1

SELECTED ETHNIC GROUPS AS PERCENTAGES OF THE TOTAL USSR POPULATION

	1917	1927	1937	1959 Reported	1970 Reported	1970 Adjusted	1979 Reported	1979 Adjusted	1984 Forecast	2000 Forecast	2050 Projected	2105 Projected	2200 Projected
NORTH	84.71	83.07	83.36	82.86	79.87	79.52	77.49	77.01	75.46	70.18	51.56	39.82	26.21
Slavs	74.51	77.98	78.53	77.11	74.62	74.07	72.68	71.94	70.54	65.63	47.79	36.22	22.79
Russians	45.38	52.91	58.41	54.65	53.37	52.28	52.35	50.86	49.94	46.42	32.22	22.00	10.55
Ukrainians	18.36	21.22	16.56	17.84	16.86	17.19	16.14	16.60	16.24	15.12	12.15	11.08	9.53
Belorussians	4.01	3.22	3.11	3.79	3.74	3.86	3.61	3.76	3.66	3.44	2.90	2.68	2.31
Baltic Peoples	2.71	.24	.18	2.26	2.11	2.18	2.02	2.11	2.07	1.97	1.74	1.71	1.72
Ugro–Finns	1.67	2.11	1.99	1.57	1.43	1.52	1.41	1.44	1.39	1.28	1.01	.89	.70
SOUTH	14.67	16.56	16.62	17.04	20.02	20.33	22.27	22.69	24.25	29.52	48.17	59.90	73.48
Southwest	3.23	2.83	3.13	4.08	4.32	4.36	4.46	4.53	4.64	4.97	5.74	6.41	7.24
Armenians	1.18	1.07	1.27	1.33	1.47	1.49	1.58	1.64	1.76	2.16	3.09	3.66	4.26
Southeast	11.44	13.74	13.49	12.96	15.69	15.97	17.81	18.16	19.61	24.55	42.43	53.49	66.25
Uzbeks	1.16	2.69	2.86	2.88	3.80	3.81	4.75	4.74	5.44	8.18	19.29	25.70	31.65
Tadzhiks	.29	.67	.72	.67	.88	.90	1.10	1.13	1.32	2.02	5.66	7.62	11.12
Kazakhs	2.78	2.70	1.83	1.73	2.19	2.22	2.50	2.51	2.66	2.96	3.31	3.59	3.94
Tatars	1.78	2.24	2.54	2.38	2.45	2.55	2.41	2.61	2.63	2.62	2.52	2.62	2.84

SOURCES: For 1917, see the 1917 census: *Istoriia SSSR*, no. 6 (1961), pp. 97–115, and no. 3 (1980), pp. 88–89. Ethnic distribution is proportionally adjusted according to net World War I losses. See also M. S. Bernstam in *Le Messager*, no. 128 (1979), pp. 323–26, 353–54. For 1927, see the 1926 census: *Vsesoiuznaia perepis' naseleniia 1926 g.*, vol. 17 (Moscow, 1929), pp. 8–14. For 1937, see the 1937 census (USSR total) and the 1939 census (ethnic distribution): *Naselenie SSSR 1973: Statisticheskii sbornik* (Moscow, 1975), p. 7; *Pravda*, 29 April 1940, p. 2; and *Sovremennye etnicheskie protsessy v SSSR* (Moscow, 1977), pp. 487–89. Since USSR and ethnic totals in the 1939 census are significantly inflated, the 1939 ethnic distribution was projected according to the USSR total from the 1937 census. For 1959, see the 1959 census, vol. *SSSR*, pp. 184–88. For 1970 and 1979, see Table 2. For projections, see n. 19.

population of Muslim origin, adjusted for assimilation, numbered 44,545,000 in 1979, that is, 17.0 percent of the total.) The seven major Muslim nationalities of Central Asia and Transcaucasia (Uzbeks, Tadzhiks, Kazakhs, Kirgiz, Turkmen, Azeris, and Karakalpaks) rose from 16.1 million in 1959 to 31.7 million in 1979, almost doubling in a twenty-year period.

Trends in Nationality Reidentification

Analysis of trends in ethnic reidentification, starting from 1959 and ignoring all previous assimilation, serves three purposes. First, adjustment for reidentification helps to establish true nationality numbers and growth rates and to predict trends in fertility more accurately, which in turn helps in population projections. Second, the figures for reidentification provide a critical test for the official Soviet policy of nationality "merging," which has been implemented in the last few decades. Third, analysis of the changing patterns of reidentification on the part of the Turko-Muslim minorities can help to illuminate the social framework for their decreasing, yet very high, fertility and can demonstrate several offsetting influences.

Computations show that the number and growth rates of ethnic Russians are inflated by the censuses of 1959, 1970, and 1979 due to the reidentification as Russians of various nationalities, especially Ukrainians, Belorussians, Poles, Tatars, Chuvash, Armenians, Mordvinians, other Ugro-Finns, Germans, Jews, and Baltic peoples (see Table 2). If reidentification occurring prior to 1959 is assumed a closed case, adjustment for the post-1959 period reveals that about 4 million people had included themselves in the number of ethnic Russians by 1979. In 1979 ethnic Russians thus amounted not to 137.4 million (52.4 percent of the USSR's population), as the census registered, but to 133.5 million (50.9 percent).

Actually, today the Russians have ceased to form the majority of the USSR's population and have become a plurality only. However, if one takes into account the large amount of assimilation that occurred in the 1950s, this politically important change occurred even earlier, and the Russians may not now exceed 48.5 percent of the Soviet population.

For a number of decades, assimilation was an important reservoir for the growth of the Russians, but in the 1970s the rate of assimilation declined to half that of the 1960s; in the 1980s this reservoir may dry up completely. Left with their natural growth only, the Russians will reach zero growth in the mid-1990s, to be followed by negative growth.

An especially interesting trend is the reverse identification of individuals (or their children) who claimed to be Russians in the 1970 census, but reidentified themselves with the Turkic peoples in the 1979 census. The change in the direction of the reidentification process, which some observers consider a manifestation of rising nationalism, was rather a matter of rational economic choice. Since in the Soviet Union various kinds of quotas and affirmative action exist with regard to education and career opportunities, reverse identification is actually subsidized, in spite of the apparent policy of "merging." Such appropriate, rational behavior children suggests that the high fertility of the Turko-Muslim minorities is also a rational choice, not merely obedience to tradition.

Due to these and other subsidies, rapid economic development in Soviet Central Asia did not launch the social changes that are usually congruent with a decline in marital fertility as experienced by other societies.[21] Reverse ethnic identification and other socioeconomic trends among Central Asian Turko-Muslims (resistance to out-migration, a zero or even negative rate of urbanization, a resistance to reducing the quantity of children as income increases, and a low rate of female participation in nonagricultural employment) provide no explanation for a decline in marital fertility. If marital fertility decline has started among Central Asian Turko-Muslims, other extremely powerful socioeconomic forces must be offsetting the gains from unlimited fertility.

Migration, Urbanization, and Spatial Distribution

Twelve to sixteen million people a year migrate in the USSR, and the net immigration into urban areas exceeded 1.9 million a year in the mid-1970s. The bulk of this amount was provided by Russian rural areas—about 1.1 million a year. In the South, especially in the Turko-Muslim republics, rural out-migration was insignificant.[22] Soviet sources are alarmed by "the process of the concentration of rural population in Central Asia."[23] The rural population of the Russian non-blacksoil area halved between 1959 and 1979; the rural population of Central Asia increased more than 1.75 times for the same period.[24] The absolute depopulation of rural areas of the Slavic and Baltic republics, along with low productivity in agriculture and the twofold increase of the major Turko-Muslim populations, were among the causes of a major Soviet problem—food production and distribution.[25]

One-half to two-thirds of the Slavic and Baltic ethnic groups were urbanized in 1970, whereas only one-fourth of Central Asians were urbanized. Despite strong official pressure on the Central Asian populations to transfer to the cities and the availability of urban jobs and higher urban wages, the rate of urbanization in the Central Asian republics

TABLE 2
USSR POPULATION BY SELECTED ETHNIC GROUPS, ADJUSTED FOR NATIONALITY REIDENTIFICATION (IN THOUSANDS)

	1959	1970	1979	1984	2000	2050	2105	2200
NORTH	173,033	192,222	202,106	206,642	209,872	171,566	117,417	57,120
Slavs	161,023	179,054	188,793	193,185	196,273	159,021	106,810	49,680
Russians	114,113	126,363	133,487	136,749	138,828	107,233	64,881	23,001
Ukrainians	37,252	41,541	43,564	44,470	45,215	40,417	32,669	20,775
Belorussians	7,913	9,328	9,855	10,040	10,287	9,651	7,890	5,037
Poles	1,380	1,428	1,483	1,517	1,533	1,363	1,086	687
Other Slavs	363	391	403	407	407	354	282	179
Baltic Peoples	4,714	5,259	5,531	5,667	5,901	5,775	5,057	3,748
Lithuanians	2,326	2,728	2,947	3,063	3,257	3,338	3,043	2,430
Latvians	1,399	1,481	1,498	1,497	1,492	1,299	1,028	649
Estonians	988	1,048	1,085	1,107	1,151	1,137	985	669
Ugro-Finns	3,277	3,683	3,791	3,817	3,815	3,351	2,633	1,535
Mordvinians	1,285	1,305	1,310	1,310	1,290	1,088	785	356
Mari	504	669	712	725	736	667	557	358
Udmurts	624	778	818	829	836	743	611	391
Komi	430	488	498	496	495	450	360	228
Karelians, Finns	259	265	272	271	269	233	184	116
Other Europeans	3,887	4,072	3,830	3,812	3,714	3,251	2,765	2,035
Jews	2,267	2,150	1,810	1,765	1,624	1,250	949	586
Germans	1,619	1,921	2,019	2,047	2,089	2,000	1,816	1,449

SOUTH	35,583	49,132	59,549	66,400	88,284	160,294	176,636	160,159
Southwest	8,521	10,536	11,885	12,696	14,866	19,091	18,909	15,770
Moldavians	2,214	2,734	3,007	3,139	3,343	3,498	3,217	2,575
Georgians	2,691	3,244	3,541	3,680	3,910	4,044	3,703	2,961
Armenians	2,786	3,607	4,314	4,813	6,446	10,286	10,805	9,295
Southeast	27,062	38,596	47,663	53,704	73,418	141,202	157,727	144,388
Uzbeks	6,015	9,212	12,452	14,908	24,464	64,198	75,784	68,970
Tadzhiks	1,396	2,181	2,972	3,605	6,043	18,831	22,473	24,245
Kazakhs	3,621	5,372	6,583	7,294	8,850	11,020	10,597	8,584
Azeris	2,939	4,368	5,385	5,963	7,284	9,128	8,785	7,118
Kirgiz	968	1,502	1,939	2,248	3,239	5,588	6,253	5,495
Turkmen	1,001	1,530	2,029	2,389	3,629	7,683	9,573	9,630
Karakalpaks	172	248	324	390	662	3,110	4,078	4,128
Dagestani	944	1,352	1,630	1,781	2,231	2,797	2,667	2,156
Chechen	418	612	755	840	1,046	1,324	1,273	1,031
Tatars	4,967	6,171	6,838	7,211	7,848	8,371	7,724	6,188
Bashkirs	989	1,238	1,378	1,446	1,566	1,668	1,540	1,233
Chuvash	1,469	1,785	1,889	1,926	2,090	2,166	1,970	1,572
TOTAL:	208,826	241,720	262,436	273,854	299,041	332,780	294,892	217,948

SOURCES: For 1959, see the 1959 census. For 1970 and 1979, data are derived from the 1970 and 1979 censuses (ethnic distribution by all territorial units) and adjusted for assimilation. Data for 1984, 2000, etc., are forecast and projected from the 1970 ethnic distribution (adjusted series). Medium series of projections.

sharply declined in the 1970s in comparison with the 1960s. The percentage of the urban population has actually declined in the Tadzhik and Turkmen republics in recent years. This development is particularly significant in view of the beginnings of a marital fertility decline in the same areas in the same years.

Although Soviet industry is in need of migration from the West to the East, and both industry and agriculture need migration from the South to the North, all migration trends are precisely the opposite.[26] The Soviets call them "nonrational flows" and openly blame the stubbornness of the Central Asians, who just do not wish to migrate.[27] Some official sources, though, admit that there is a rationale for this trend, namely, the preferential distribution of taxes, agricultural wages, prices, and other benefits and subsidies for the Southern tier at the expense of European Russia—a phenomenon known in the West as welfare colonialism.[28]

All the Turko-Muslim nationalities of Central Asia, as well as the Kazakhs and Armenians, increased their relative shares in the population of their home republics in the 1970s. Most reduced their already insignificant shares in the population of the RSFSR. Since the mid-1970s, the Russians and other Europeans have begun to move back to the RSFSR from Kazakhstan and Kirgizia with significant acceleration.[29] For the first time since the advent of the Virgin Lands program in the 1950s, the RSFSR had a positive migration balance of about 287,000.[30] The Russian exodus from rural Kazakhstan to the central industrial cities contributed to the acuteness of the food problem.

DIFFERENTIAL GROWTH

The Soviet population increased from 208.8 million in 1959 to 262.4 million in 1979, that is, it grew by 25.7 percent. The population of the Soviet North increased in the same twenty years from 173.0 million to 202.1 million (16.8 percent), and the Southern quarter of the USSR's population rose from 35.6 to 59.5 million (an increase of 67.3 percent). The nationalities of the predominantly Muslim Southeast rose from 27.1 to 47.7 million (up 76.1 percent). The seven Central Asian and Transcaucasian nationalities nearly doubled between 1959 and 1979, from 16.1 million to 31.7 million. The Russians increased from 114.1 million in 1959 to 133.5 million in 1979, an increase of 17.0 percent (see Table 2).

The momentum for natural increase is still very high in Central Asia. The growth rate will be 3.1 percent a year for Uzbeks and 3.2 percent a year for Tadzhiks until the end of the century, which spells a continuous explosion and another twofold increase between 1979 and 2000—a twelvefold increase since 1917. The explosion will continue through the next century, since population momentum and net growth potential will be there. Russians, all other Slavic nationalities, Latvians, the Ugro-Finnic group, Germans, and Jews (that is, the majority of the North) are projected to have negative growth from the second half of the 1990s on.

DIFFERENTIAL DEMOGRAPHIC TRANSITION

The differential growth of Soviet ethnic groups was and still is mostly dependent on varying causes of mortality decline and different types of relationships between mortality and fertility trends. Some of the trends and relations are typical for world populations; others are peculiar to Soviet populations.[31]

The dimensional or quantitative ends of demographic transition, particularly the decline of fertility to a very low level, were achieved by the Soviet North much more rapidly than by other Western populations. Qualitative ends of transition, such as the dissemination of contraception and the replacement of abortion as the major means of birth control, have not been achieved at all. Emergence of a market economy, with its competition, appreciation for the value of human life as an indivisible commodity, establishment of the simple one-family household as the main economic unit, improved nutrition, and development of medical and child care, brought a gradual increase in life expectancy and a gradual decline in fertility in the West. The emergence of a socialized economy witnessed the waste of millions of human lives, the deterioration of nutrition, the elimination of the economic independence of the family, and rapid social mobility. This first brought an advanced mortality, then a very rapid increase in the life expectancy of the decimated cohorts of survivors (due to the adoption of medical care), and finally a drastic fertility decline among Soviet Northern ethnic groups.

One has to emphasize that parity-specific fertility control (that is, control exercised by parents to stop reproduction after achieving the desired number of offspring) was not widespread when induced abortions were legal during 1920–1936. In fact, contrary to one of the basic assumptions of conventional demographic transition theory, the return to natural fertility from controlled fertility had occurred in the 1920s among the rural Northern populations of the USSR. In the Ukraine, available age-specific fertility and marital schedules suggest that the degree of departure from natural fertility was virtually zero in the mid-1920s, whereas it was moderately high in the beginning of the twentieth century.[32] We attribute this reversal to the restoration of the rural commune after the 1917 revolution. Fertility started to decline rapidly in the mid-1930s, when the redistribution of land allotments was replaced by collectivized agriculture and abortions were illegal (1936–1955).

The emergence of the transfer society with its crucial social security and public education components historically coincided in the West and in the USSR, although in the latter only the social framework of the welfare state was implemented, not its economic base. This development impersonalized intergenerational transfers, inflated aspirations of parents with regard to the quality of children, eliminated some fundamental functions of the family as a private institution and economic unit, transformed children into public goods, and thus engendered a second wave of fertility decline that began in the mid-1960s, this time dropping to a level below replacement.

Other components of the recent trend were an increase in the dependency ratio (the ratio of children and pensioners taken together, to the working-age population), a decline in age-specific marital proportions, rising divorce rates, and the establishment of cohabitance as an institution. In the Northern Soviet populations, especially among Slavic ethnic groups, induced abortions, the Soviet feature in this demographic depression, reached the highest historical rate in the world (except for Romania in the 1960s). Uncontrolled pregnancies were limited only by the extent of pathological secondary infertility. Regardless of differing trends in life expectancy at birth for the Soviet North and Western developed populations, both continued a drive toward steady negative intrinsic growth (not a transitional course toward a stationary population). When, in the 1950s, mortality excesses were suspended by the Soviet state, Northern fertility was only slightly higher than replacement level and certainly could not provide for population explosion.

A population explosion did take place in the Soviet South, especially among the populations of Muslim origin. An increase in the duration of life began there in the second half of the 1930s and infant mortality has declined since the 1950s.[33] The prerequisite for the explosion was provided by the 2 to 4 percent difference between the high crude birthrates under natural fertility conditions and the low crude death rates of young populations. Mortality decline in the Soviet South, as in the Southern world in general, was brought by already modernized and medically advanced external forces. It coincided historically with the invention of antibiotics. Increase in the duration of life occurred rapidly, almost instantaneously.

Having been induced by outside forces, the population explosion was not preceded by a behavioral change based on new attitudes about the value of individual human life. In fact, the relative generational quality of children increased without additional costs for the parents. Nutrition level, health care, and social hygiene improved dramatically. Female participation in the nonagricultural work force was also induced into Muslim populations. The combination of these factors shortened birth intervals from 36 to 30 months, and natural fertility has actually increased. The level of natural fertility prior to the mid-century mark can be estimated as 9.000 for the Georgians and 9.144 for the Central Asians (Uzbeks, Tadzhiks, Kirgiz, and Turkmen).[34] In the mid-1970s this level increased to 10.023.

The emergence of a fertility increase at an early stage of demographic transition has been characteristic for historical and modern world populations. For example, it was observed in Zaire and in several Latin American countries.[35] However, behavioral change with regard to fertility did not coincide with the induced decline of mortality in the majority of less developed countries from the 1940s through the mid-1970s.[36] As in the Soviet Southeast, subsidies and intergenerational transfers provided little or no incentive to exchange quality for quantity of children. Foreign aid and welfare colonialism contributed to the world population explosion, hunger, and sustained poverty. To what extent the USSR will face a declining standard of living and a new dimension of food and population conflict is uncertain, but the momentum for those is building.

DIFFERENTIAL LIFE EXPECTANCY AND MORTALITY

In the late 1960s and 1970s the effect of the advanced mortality of previous decades started to wither away. Expectancy of life at birth has been returning to its proper lower values to correspond with conditions of Soviet life (Table 3). Several factors also contributed to a mortality increase at various ages, especially among males. Since the mid-1960s the combination of these two trends has resulted in an unprecedented peacetime decline of life expectancy at birth among all major Soviet ethnic groups except the Armenians (see Table 3). This same conclusion can be reached from an observation of the data on crude death rates and standardized death rates per 1,000.[37]

Duration of life between the North and the South has converged within the last quarter-century, due mostly to the significant rise of life expectancy among Uzbeks, Tadzhiks, Kazakhs, Turkmen, and other Turko-Muslim nationalities. On the other hand, by the end of the 1970s, the duration of life among Russians, Latvians, Estonians, and Moldavians had fallen below their respective values at the end of the 1950s. In 1958–1960 the lowest expectancy of life was observed among Central

TABLE 3

EXPECTANCY OF LIFE AT BIRTH BY NATIONALITIES

	1958–60	1969–70	1978–79
Russians	67.50	68.64	65.90
Ukrainians	68.40	70.16	68.57
Belorussians	69.10	71.35	69.94
Lithuanians	70.30	70.65	70.20
Latvians	73.10	71.20	71.41
Estonians	72.80	70.73	71.14
Moldavians	67.90	68.88	64.68
Georgians	71.20	70.98	70.85
Armenians	69.40	72.74	72.80
Uzbeks	62.40	71.22	69.94
Tadzhiks	63.30	69.67	67.07
Kazakhs	63.70	71.35	69.51
Azeris	64.80	67.90	67.70
Kirgiz	65.20	68.36	68.06
Turkmen	61.90	67.73	66.44
USSR averages	68.59	69.50	67.80

SOURCES: For 1958–59, see Census 1959. For 1969–70, see *Vestnik Statistiki*, no. 2 (1974), p. 94. For 1978–79, see Jean Bourgeois-Pichat, "Levels and Trends of Mortality Since 1950," *Population and Development Review* 9, no. 2 (June 1983), pp. 362–63. On the nationalities, see D. Peter Mazur, "Expectancy of Life at Birth in 36 Nationalities of the Soviet Union: 1958–60," *Population Studies* 23, no. 2 (July 1969), p. 244. Data for the nationalities, 1969–70 and 1978–79, are calculated on the base of methodology derived from D. Peter Mazur, "Using Regression Models to Estimate the Expectation of Life for the USSR," *Journal of the American Statistical Association* 67, no. 337 (March 1972), pp. 31–36. Data on crude death rates for respective republics were used with application to nationalities.

Asians (61.9 among Turkmen, 62.4 among Uzbeks, 63.3 among Tadzhiks, and 63.7 among Kazakhs). In 1978–79 all Central Asians except Turkmen were at the average USSR level in this respect, while Russians and Moldavians experienced the lowest duration of life in the USSR (65.9 and 64.7, respectively). It appears that since the late 1960s the Turko-Muslims have converged with typical Western populations, whereas the Russians have departed from such a convergency.

In the Soviet Union male expectancy of life at birth declined from 64.8 in 1969–1971 to 61.9 in 1980.[38] In Central Russia and Siberia in the 1960s and 1970s, male expectancy of life at birth was some three years below the average Soviet level.[39] The female/male difference in expectancy of life at birth in the USSR has widened from 9.8 years in 1970 to

11.6 years in 1980; the gap was already that size in 1970 in Central Russia.[40] Russian male expectancy of life at birth now may not exceed 60.0. A continuous aging of the population has contributed to a significant increase of crude death rates in all Northern territorial units. A genuine mortality increase among adult males, a rise in infant mortality, and especially a mortality increase at old ages in both sexes (among all nationalities except Armenians) have fueled the soaring crude death rates. This increase in age-specific mortality rates in the late 1960s and 1970s was most rapid in the RSFSR, a trend that, in addition to the aging of the population, appears to be the main factor in the rise of Russian crude death rates.[41]

The aging of the population, therefore, has not yet realized its full effect on Russian mortality. When it reaches full swing in the next decade, the crude death rate will approach a life-table level of about 15 per 1,000 against 11 per 1,000 at present. Negative growth will emerge by the mid-1990s.[42]

FACTORS OF MORTALITY DIFFERENCE

Four major factors account for the mortality differences among Soviet nationalities. The first is age distribution: Northern ethnic groups are getting older, whereas the Turko-Muslim ethnic groups are getting younger. In 1979 people aged 60 and older constituted 12.9 percent of the Russian population, but among Uzbeks they made up only 6.9 percent.

A second factor, health care, cannot be meaningfully evaluated in time series or along ethnoterritorial lines. The number of physicians and hospital beds per capita is still increasing across the board, with a higher sustained provision in the North and a higher acceleration in the South, leading toward convergency.[43] The correlation between health care and mortality level, however, is very weak, which is not a peculiar Soviet phenomenon. Armenia has one of the lowest levels of medical personnel and the lowest number of hospital beds per capita, but enjoys the highest duration of life and the lowest mortality schedule in the USSR. The RSFSR's experience is just the opposite.

The third factor, chronic alcoholism, has increased among working men in the USSR from 3.5 percent in 1925 to 37 percent in the late 1970s.[44] This factor has produced a significant increase in advanced mortality, since alcoholics die earlier than others in a normal mortality schedule: one-third of a cohort of Soviet alcoholics will die of direct alcohol abuse and poisoning, and 17 percent of the cohort will die of alcohol-related work and traffic accidents.[45] Mortality from cardiovascular diseases increased in the USSR from 3.8 per 1,000 in 1970 to 5.4 in 1980–81, and Soviet sources attribute one-third of those deaths to alcohol abuse.[46] Among males aged 20–24, mortality from alcohol-caused cardiovascular disease, alcohol poisoning, and alcohol-related accidents was responsible for up to 80 percent of the entire age-specific death rate.[47] According to studies by Treml, Dutton, and Feshbach, the bulk of alcoholism and related mortality is heavily concentrated in the Soviet North, especially among the Russians and, to a lesser extent, the Latvians and Estonians.[48]

Differences in diet also contribute to mortality differentials. Official Soviet sources report that the daily caloric intake per capita reached 2,700 in 1965, 2,944 in 1975, and about 3,000 in 1979 (it was 3,380 in the United States in 1977, but most experts find that level too high).[49] Caloric intake has fallen in the 1980s, since the food supply is rationed in a number of localities. A significant deficiency in protein and vitamins characterizes the Soviet diet. Even the amount of vegetable protein in bread products, which still constitute 40 percent of Soviet caloric intake, has drastically decreased in recent years.[50] The evidence suggests, moreover, that official data on food production and per capita consumption are significantly inflated. Consumption is usually reported as the product output divided by the number of people; industrial and agricultural uses of crops are actually included in human consumption. Both the output and consumption of animal husbandry products are significantly exaggerated, by an estimated 27 percent.[51]

Regional and ethnic differences in the consumption of protein-rich and vitamin-rich products are very sharp. In the Baltic area, meat consumption per capita is 40–45 percent above the USSR average, milk and butter consumption is 30–50 percent above average, and egg consumption is 15–30 percent above average. In most Turko-Muslim areas, these products are consumed at levels 30–45 percent below the USSR average, but the Central Asian and Transcaucasian populations consume more vitamin-rich products, especially fruits.[52] In terms of a combination of animal protein and vitamins, the population of the RSFSR appears to be the most disadvantaged of Soviet republics. This may have contributed to its high mortality schedules.

DIFFERENTIAL FERTILITY

The total fertility of Soviet Northern ethnic groups is one of the lowest in the world and in the history of human populations. The total fertility of the Soviet Southeast, especially that of its Turko-Muslim absolute majority, is one of the highest in the world and in history. In the 1970s crude birthrates per 1,000 ranged from 11.4 among Latvians to 42.8 among Tadzhiks, and in the mid-1970s total fertility rates ranged from 1.9 among Russians to 8.2 among Tadzhiks (see Table 4).[53] In both cases the respective ratio was approximately 1 to 4. By the late 1950s the ratio of lowest to highest fertility in the USSR was 1 to 3.5. Fertility differentials, therefore, have widened through the 1960s and early 1970s, due both to the fertility increase among Central Asians and the continuous fertility decline in Northern populations.

The entire North, with its given expectancy of life, now has net reproduction rates below the level of replacement (with the exception of the Estonians, who stand on the edge of replacement). The Latvian and Estonian populations were almost unique among developed countries of the world in that their low fertility tended to stabilize rather than decline further. This was probably the result of an expansion of private plots, which caused income to increase relative to the cost of children.

The common assumption that the Baltic peoples, and the Latvians in particular, have the lowest fertility in the USSR is true in terms of crude birthrates only. In terms of intrinsic fertility rates, the Slavic nationalities, especially the Russians, experience the lowest fertility and the highest birth control in the country. This was corroborated by a special study of the difference between republican and ethnic rates in the Baltic area and by the 1979 census data on the difference between republican and ethnic numbers of children ever born per average living woman aged 15 and over.[54]

In the last two decades the Belorussians and Lithuanians have experienced a rapid fertility decline to below the replacement level. Belorussian fertility in terms of intrinsic rates is now the second lowest in the country. Ukrainian and Russian fertility has had a rapid and steady decline, experiencing nonreplacement net reproduction rates continuously through the 1960s, the 1970s, and the early 1980s (Table 4).

The Georgians have passed from a moderate fertility level to bare replacement. The Moldavians and Armenians still have moderate fertility, but for Armenians recent decades have been a time of rapid decline, from almost 5.0 children born per woman to 2.4. Their reproduction halved within twenty years, and in relative terms of age-specific marital fertility rates they have the highest index of birth control in the country.

In the late 1950s the Kazakhs had the highest level of natural fertility in the USSR—7.4 children born per woman of a synthetic cohort. After two decades of rapid and steady decline, their total fertility reached 4.8 and net reproduction reached 2.2—still high and more than two times higher than rates in the North. The Azeris have also experienced a steady, albeit more gradual, decline from 6.0 to 3.8 in total fertility. The rate of

TABLE 4
TOTAL FERTILITY RATES (F) AND NET REPRODUCTION RATES (R) BY NATIONALITIES

	1958–59		1967–68		1976–77		1980–81	
	F	R	F	R	F	R	F	R
Russians	2.522	1.130	1.918	0.883	1.889	0.860	1.820	0.821
Ukrainians	2.343	1.059	2.059	0.956	2.029	0.938	1.975	0.909
Belorussians	2.706	1.235	2.155	1.009	2.038	0.948	1.959	0.906
Lithuanians	2.750	1.265	2.346	1.100	2.262	1.052	2.068	0.957
Latvians	2.117	0.988	1.985	0.933	2.086	0.975	2.062	0.960
Estonians	2.069	0.965	2.111	0.992	2.228	1.041	2.157	1.004
Moldavians	3.904	1.765	2.978	1.373	2.686	1.206	2.625	1.163
Georgians	2.545	1.181	2.494	1.171	2.410	1.126	2.214	1.031
Armenians	4.876	2.225	3.656	1.720	2.800	1.336	2.411	1.154
Uzbeks	7.275	3.102	7.642	3.478	7.379	3.432	6.467	2.992
Tadzhiks	6.044	2.611	7.592	3.496	7.972	3.638	7.282	3.290
Kazakhs	7.350	3.175	5.451	2.527	5.293	2.451	4.795	2.204
Azeris	5.965	2.610	5.875	2.693	4.555	2.102	3.846	1.771
Kirgiz	6.950	3.077	6.809	3.128	6.980	3.200	5.967	2.723
Turkmen	6.533	2.785	7.645	3.463	7.228	3.285	6.274	2.840
USSR (adjusted)	2.848	1.288	2.416	1.122	2.394	1.099	2.278	1.039

SOURCES: Total fertility rates for republics were calculated from age-specific fertility data derived from *Vestnik statistiki* and adjusted for birth underreporting. The data were then translated into ethnic rates according to the methodology described in the text. The total fertility rate for the USSR was adjusted for birth underreporting in Central Asia.

NOTE: Total fertility rate is the number of children born per woman within her fertile life in a synthetic cohort.

decline in both cases has slowed, and this may signal the future trend for the Kirgiz, Turkmen, Uzbeks, and other highly fertile Turko-Muslims.

The Central Asian four (Uzbeks, Tadzhiks, Kirgiz, and Turkmen) have steadily increased their degree of birth control since the mid-1960s. From the early 1970s and especially since the mid-1970s this has been strongly expressed in a decline of the total fertility rates. The latter, however, are still very high, in the range of 6.0 to 7.3, with corresponding net reproduction rates in a range from 2.7 to 3.3. The crude birthrates of the entire Turko-Muslim group are still 2 to 2.5 times higher than they would have been if the existing mortality level had been accompanied by the corresponding fertility level of the European, American, or Russian patterns.

DEMOGRAPHIC VARIABLES OF FERTILITY DIFFERENCES

Sex Structure

The excessive male mortality that steadily increased in the 1970s, particularly among the Northern nationalities, has imposed serious constraints on Soviet fertility. In the USSR as a whole there was a rough sex parity at ages 0 to 50 in 1979, but this was unevenly distributed by nationalities. In 1981 there were 860 males per 1,000 females in the RSFSR and 966 in Central Asia at all ages.[55] Since the bulk of the gap in Central Asia must be attributed to the older ages, and since males exceed females at younger ages, sex parity at fertile ages in Central Asia means a shortage of males for fertile females in the Soviet North.[56]

In addition, fertility in the predominantly Russian areas suffers from an uneven sex distribution imposed by what the Soviets call "economically advantageous development." They have established a number of "male towns" and "female towns," highly specialized in particular industries (construction, mining, metallurgy, on the one hand; textile works, on the other). Since one worker cannot make a living for an entire family in the USSR, people seldom bring mates or establish families in these places. In the 1970s one-sex residential areas expanded into some agricultural parts of the RSFSR as well. In places with highly mechanized agricultural labor young males cannot find a girl; local girls are concentrated in small towns where they are employed in various workshops.[57] This development has to be taken into account in trying to evaluate the apparently pronatalist Soviet demographic policy.

Age Structure

The percentage of females aged 15 to 49 is relatively higher among the Northern ethnic groups (due to the large share of children in the South-eastern populations), but the percentage of females aged 20 to 29 is higher in the South. Due to the first factor, the Northern decline in crude birthrates appeared to be slower than the decline in total fertility. As population aging continues, however, the second factor will become especially significant. The numerous cohorts of Turko-Muslim women born in 1960–1975 will enter their prime fertile ages, and the relative share of women of fertile ages will increase. This factor builds in significant momentum for high growth among these nationalities. According to one Soviet forecast, in the year 2000 only about 45 percent of all Soviet females at fertile ages will be Russian, and Russian women will account for only 30 percent of total Soviet births.[58]

Nuptiality and the Family

A new pattern of marriage has recently emerged among advanced welfare state populations. A rapidly declining demand for marriage has followed a decline in the number of children per household. Consensual unions and other such arrangements as a substitute for marriage are major institutional features. In the United States, the proportion of women ever-married at ages 20–24 was 71.6 percent in 1960, 64.2 percent in 1970, 59.7 percent in 1975, and 44.5 percent in 1983; in Sweden, it was 44.0 percent in 1959, 40.0 percent in 1970, 28.1 percent in 1980; and in Latvia, it was 42.4 percent in 1959, 50.8 percent in 1970, and about 46.7 percent in 1979.[59] Data for Soviet republics for 1979 are lacking, but assuming the trend in Latvia to be typical for the RSFSR as well, one can estimate from the 1970 marital schedule that the proportion of Russian females ever-married at ages 20–24 declined from 55.5 percent in 1970 to 52.0 percent in 1979.

In a parallel development, together with the decline in marriages, a rapid increase in illegitimacy has emerged in the last two decades among the Northern Soviet populations. In Belorussia, the illegitimate fertility rate per 1,000 unmarried women at ages 15–49 was 14.4 in 1959 and 32.3 in 1970. The illegitimacy ratio (the ratio of illegitimate births to all births) increased from 7.3 percent in 1959 to 18.2 percent in 1970.[60] The current illegitimacy ratio among the Slavic and Baltic populations can be estimated as more than 20 percent, that is, higher than that of the United

States. Among other things, this rapidly rising illegitimacy rate among nearly universally working women must have been an unappreciated factor but, in my view, it is the most significant cause of the infant mortality increase in the USSR.

The non-European or traditional pattern of marriage (75 percent to 95 percent of women are ever-married at ages 20–24; 1 to 3 percent are still unmarried at ages 45–49) was typical for Central Asians, Kazakhs, Azeris, Armenians, and Southeastern minorities of the USSR prior to the 1950s. Convergence toward a unified European pattern has since occurred in all these populations, but among the Central Asian four the change was markedly slower than among the Armenians, Azeris, Kazakhs, or such outside populations as those of Taiwan, Korea, Morocco, and Kuwait.[61]

Delay of very early marriage and an increase of two years in singulate mean age at first marriage (to 19.8) actually contributed to an increase in natural fertility among Central Asians in the 1960s and early 1970s (previously, marriages at ages of 13–16 were responsible for weak fecundability and prolonged birth intervals).[62] Aggregate nuptiality data from the 1979 census and a recent analysis of early marriages by cohorts indicate that the trend toward later marriages slowly continues among the Turko-Muslim populations.[63]

Divorce rates in the USSR as a whole have tripled within the last two decades, which is the highest rate of increase of family disintegration in the world.[64] As a result, divorce has become a substantial factor of fertility in the USSR. One-third of all Soviet divorces reportedly occur, mostly in the form of separations, within the first year of marriage. Another one-third take place one to five years after marriage. An estimated 2.9 years elapse between separations and legal divorces.[65] This span is usually truncated from women's prime fertile period, ages 20–29, during which more than one-half of all divorces apparently occur.

Latvian divorce rates are now the second highest in the world, following the United States. The RSFSR is rapidly catching up, having already surpassed Estonia. In terms of average divorce rates per 1,000 marriages, the Slavic and Baltic republics have far exceeded any West European country. Unlike Western Europe and the United States, the rate of remarriage is reported to be very low in the USSR, but this requires further research. Soviet explanations of this divorce pandemic blame alcoholism and infidelity.[66] This reasoning overlooks such fundamental causes as declining gains from marriage (due to female employment and the reduction of private benefits derived from children) and increasing demand for nonmarriage relationships as more congruent with impersonalized intergenerational transfers.[67] The family as a private institution has been supplanted by the "cell of state," as the Soviets themselves call it, various profamily policies notwithstanding.

Fertility Schedules and Birth Control

Prior to the mid-1970s, the extent of birth control among the Central Asian populations was low and developing slowly. A comparative evaluation of ethnic and republican trends in age-specific fertility rates and in the growth of the index of the departure from natural fertility demonstrates a rapid increase in the extent of birth control among the Kirgiz and Turkmen in the late 1970s and a significant, albeit slower, increase among the Uzbeks and Tadzhiks.[68] Fertility decline at ages 20–24 has also taken place since the mid-1970s, and this factor has been responsible for a certain underestimate of the real extent of departure from natural fertility among Turko-Muslims within recent years.

During the same period, all the nationalities of the Southwest (Armenians, Georgians, Moldavians, and so on) and, to a lesser extent, the Kazakhs and Azeris, experienced a rapid decline of marital fertility at mature ages and an increase in the degree of birth control. Since marital fertility at ages 20–24 continues to be relatively high among these ethnic groups, the calculated values for the index of the degree of departure from natural fertility in Georgia and Armenia recently exceeded even those of the Baltic republics.

Slavic marital fertility rates at ages over 30 are, on the average, half of those of Baltic ethnic groups. Correspondingly, the extent of control is significantly higher among the Slavs. Slavic marital and overall fertility rates at ages 35–39 are currently the lowest in the world, especially in terms of marital fertility rates: 19.9 per 1,000 among the Russians, 22.0 among the Ukrainians, 25.5 in West Germany, and 32.5 in Sweden. This specific Russian and Slavic feature may be caused not by parity-specific control per se but by excessive secondary infertility at ages over 30, due to multiple abortions performed by the dilation and curettage method. After an average of 5.95 abortions per Russian woman in the mid- and late 1970s (computed on the basis of a conservative assumption), only 52.9 percent of the entire cohort remains effectively fecundable or fertile. One Soviet source reported as early as 1968 that in the Northwestern provinces of the Russian republic an estimated 95.8 percent of all women actually ceased childbearing by age 33.[69] This part of the country at exactly that period experienced the highest reported rate of induced abortions in the USSR.[70]

The new fertility pattern that has emerged among the Soviet Northern (and other advanced) populations features an actual shortening of the active fertile age span. In standard natural fertility, only 42.4 percent of total births take place within the prime fertile period of the mother (ages 20–29). In the new fertility pattern, from two-thirds to three-fourths of total births occur within the ten prime fertile years: 62.5 percent in the United States, 65.4 percent in Germany, 67.0 percent in Sweden, 67.9 percent among the Latvians, and 71.1 percent among the Russians.

Birth Control: Abortions versus Contraception

A specific feature of demographic transition in all Marxian states, regardless of national traditions and degree of development, is that the transition from high to low fertility is made without a fundamental transition from abortion to contraception at later stages of the fertility decline.[71] Therefore, parity-specific control consists mostly of an expansion of induced abortions, constrained only by pathological secondary infertility. The absence of family planning on an institutional level is more than compensated for by adoption of socioeconomic policies that make the family a "cell of state" and implicitly control human reproductive behavior to an extent unachievable by birth control agencies. Soviet demographic policy denies any conflict between economic growth and population growth, and, therefore, has a strong negative attitude toward birth control. At the same time, the policy is aimed at total human, including total female, participation in the work force, the elimination of male / female demographic inequality (that is, childbearing), and domination over the social freedom of individuals, especially women.[72]

As a result, birth control is neither offered nor prohibited. The demand for birth control, however, consists of two qualitatively different variables: a demand for a means to prevent pregnancies, and a demand for a means to avert already established pregnancies. The latter demand seems more controllable and reversible to the state ideologues (who tend to discount the market forces that offer illegal abortions). Hence, liberalization of abortions under conditions of state-controlled medical services is actually nonliberal and inhuman relative to the free-market offering of contraception, abortions, and information about the competing commodities.

Under socialism, the demand for birth control can be met in the form of goods (contraceptives) or in the form of services (abortions). Both are scarce and of poor quality in an economy targeted at the preferential development of heavy industry, but services require mostly labor and reusable goods (surgical tools) and constitute a demand more easily met than the design, production, advertisement, and dissemination of non-reusable goods (all contraceptives except sterilization). Abortions performed within a system of socialized medical care are also more congruent with Marxist ideology than is contraception, which is an individual family's action. In fact, this system of birth control, dominated by abortions, is extremely expensive for the state. Female working days are lost and individuals are not charged for the service, whereas use of contraceptives, arbitrarily priced by the state, could provide a pecuniary surplus. This is a pure case of ideological and political preferences overriding any practical considerations.

The popular ignorance of contraceptives in the USSR, one of the most developed countries in the world, stands in contrast to the majority of less developed countries. According to the continuous World Fertility Survey of the 1970s, contraceptive knowledge among ever-married women at ages 15–49 was 100 percent in Fiji and Costa Rica, 95 percent in the Philippines, and 90 percent in Syria and Turkey.[73] In Moscow in 1976, a survey of married women (40 percent college graduates and 58 percent paraprofessionals) revealed that 80 to 90 percent did not have any clear knowledge of contraceptive methods and 80 percent were not aware of the existence of any contraceptives in the retail sales system.[74]

All Soviet data available for the 1960s and 1970s on contraception use, contraception effectiveness, and abortions are inconsistent. In Latvia, for instance, where 78.8 to 79.8 percent of all married couples reportedly use contraceptives, with an average theoretical effectiveness of 82.4 percent, abortions per woman ranged from 3.0 to 4.3 within her fertile life.[75] If, however, the total contraceptive use and effectiveness were as high as reported, the total abortion rate could not have exceeded 1.0 in a conservative series or 2.4 in a less conservative series of computations. The same incompatibility of data is presented in the case of the RSFSR, where more than 60 percent of women reportedly use contraceptives of some 70–80 percent effectiveness, but the crude pregnancy rate was over 5.5 percent a year, about 90 percent of women had abortions, and between 6 and 16 percent had repeat abortions within one calendar year.[76] Since about 2.5 abortions are needed within 2.25 years to avert one birth, the true impact of contraception was nearly zero. Among urban Uzbek women with at least a junior college education, about 25 percent are said to have used contraception, but within less than ten years of marriage an average woman had borne four children and had 3.3 induced abortions.[77] This, too, implies an index of contraception of about zero.

In fact, then, less than half of Soviet users of contraception used it regularly or properly. Nonregularity doubled contraception failure (halved the proportion of real users) and improper use did the same (halved the real effectiveness). What actually happened was that whichever method (condoms, chemical means, diaphragms, withdrawal, and so on) was employed, it was not used as such, but in combination with biological rhythm. For example, the withdrawal method is not used throughout the cycle, but only on the days believed to be hazardous. The biological rhythm method is used in an abridged form based not on personal scientific estimates but rather on taking the mean of the cycle. Even for the few days variance around the mean, people do not abstain, as biological rhythm requires, but use other means of contraception, mostly withdrawal. This common Soviet procedure is based on complete ignorance of sexual realities. Various official Soviet statistics on the relative share of contraceptive methods, which are not adjusted for their sporadic use and the compound probability of failure, must be dismissed as completely invalid and irrelevant.

In sum, in the USSR the eventual index of contraception (the proportion of users multiplied by regularity, multiplied by the theoretical effectiveness, multiplied by the proportion of proper use) is extremely low. This outcome is only natural, for people cannot demand information about effective contraceptives and their use when they lack the initial information that such goods even exist. This constraint of knowledge prevents the expression of a preference for contraception and makes induced abortions a perfect substitute.

From the numerous bits of reported Soviet data it is certain that induced abortions have spread in recent years even among the indigenous Turko-Muslims in Central Asia, but most sources underestimate their extent. This is probably due to the proliferation of illegal abortions in the USSR, owing to a scarcity of medical services, the poor quality of legal abortions, and desire to keep the matter secret (especially important in the case of young Turko-Muslim women). In urban areas of the USSR, according to some unverifiable sources, 70 percent of induced abortions terminating a woman's first pregnancy were illegally performed (90 percent in rural areas).[78] In the 1960s in the RSFSR, illegal abortions accounted for 16 percent of all induced abortions; in the 1970s the rate varied from 18 to 79 percent, depending on locale.[79] Much of the official Soviet data on induced abortions, therefore, must be dismissed.

The results of our independent mathematical exercise, based on various Soviet data on fertility, contraception, and medical factors, are presented in Table 5. The detailed data and the methods of derivation are published elsewhere.[80] The ratio of induced abortions to births in the 1970s ranged from 0.137 among Tadzhiks and 0.201 among Uzbeks to 1.220 among Estonians, 1.404 among Latvians, 2.481 among Ukrainians, and 3.206 among Russians. The USSR average was 2.044. The total number of induced abortions per woman (the total abortion rate) was 1.076 among Tadzhiks, 1.486 among Uzbeks, 1.920 among Turkmen, 3.033 among Kazakhs, 4.083 among Azeris, 4.273 among Georgians, 5.195 among Armenians, 2.759 among Estonians, 3.021 among Latvians, 3.518 among Lithuanians, 5.056 among Byelorussians, 5.118 among Ukrainians, and 5.950 among Russians.

Biological Aftereffects

The commonly used (or abused) ad hoc combination of biological rhythm and withdrawal has an unfortunate biological consequence. In cases of contraception failure, the unintended conceptions are more likely to take place with overripe gametes. This, in turn, produces at least a 25 percent increase in the rate of spontaneous abortion and an extremely significant incidence of embryonic chromosome abnormalities, especially mental deficiencies, in the children eventually born.[81] In the early 1970s, Soviet studies found an increase in newborns with first-generation and inherited chromosome abnormalities, particularly in the Ukraine. This factor contributed to an overall child mortality increase (53 percent of children born with chromosome abnormalities die within the first year of life).[82] This genetic damage has a particular effect on ethnic groups with a relatively high proportion of contraception users but with a relatively low proportion of regular and proper use, namely, the Slavic nationalities. In addition, the rising rate of spontaneous abortion contributes to pathological secondary infertility and limits human reproductive potential.

Soviet studies report that work overload and work hazards imposed on Soviet women also contribute to the above-normal levels of primary and secondary sterility. An excessive rate of primary sterility is typical for women employed in manual labor, chemical production, and other unskilled industrial work. An excessive rate of secondary sterility characterizes women who work manually in construction, manufacturing, processing and finishing metals, and in the timber and textile industries.[83] Yet the trend in the USSR is toward still higher female participation in arduous and hazardous occupations. While men shift to more mechanized jobs, women replace them as manual workers. In January 1981 women were barred from 460 heavy and hazardous occupations, but it takes more than a decade to implement such a decree. Again, most of the women involved in such occupations are Slavic and Baltic women.

The excessive demand for abortions overstrains Soviet medical facilities. Given the three days' care for an induced abortion provided by Soviet hospitals and the RSFSR's rate of induced abortions in the mid-1970s, some 305,000 hospital beds were needed for abortions alone.

TABLE 5
FERTILITY AND BIRTH CONTROL AMONG SOVIET ETHNIC GROUPS, 1969–1980

	Years	Total Fertility Rate	Proportion Married	Marital Fertility	Index of Contraception	Proportion of Secondary Infertility	Total Abortion Rate	Abortions to Births Ratio
Russians	1975–79	1.856	0.571	3.250	0.125	0.207	5.950	3.206
Ukrainians	1969–79	2.063	0.594	3.473	0.210	0.174	5.118	2.481
Belorussians	1969–79	2.107	0.575	3.664	0.190	0.172	5.056	2.400
Lithuanians	1969–79	2.301	0.539	4.269	0.298	0.115	3.518	1.529
Latvians	1969–79	2.152	0.516	4.171	0.352	0.097	3.021	1.404
Estonians	1969–79	2.261	0.504	4.486	0.360	0.088	2.759	1.220
Moldavians	1969–79	2.743	0.601	4.564	0.105	0.186	5.420	1.976
Georgians	1969–79	2.437	0.563	4.329	0.220	0.143	4.273	1.753
Armenians	1969–79	2.898	0.625	4.637	0.140	0.178	5.195	1.793
Uzbeks	1969–79	7.381	0.804	9.180	0.050	0.045	1.486	0.201
Tadzhiks	1969–79	7.866	0.832	9.454	0.040	0.032	1.076	0.137
Kazakhs	1969–79	5.298	0.689	7.689	0.093	0.097	3.033	0.572
Azeris	1969–79	4.677	0.696	6.720	0.100	0.136	4.083	0.875
Kirgiz	1969–79	6.858	0.779	8.804	0.080	0.059	1.920	0.280
Turkmen	1969–79	7.228	0.808	8.946	0.060	0.057	1.843	0.255
USSR	1969–79	2.399	0.570	4.209	0.164	0.167	4.903	2.044

SOURCE: See text and references in the sections on contraception and abortions.

There were, however, only 213,000 gynecological beds for all purposes, including childbearing, abortions, complications, and various diseases.[84] Hospitals in the RSFSR had only half the necessary facilities, services, and presumably, equipment. Complaints concerning these shortages were officially reported as one of the major causes of illegal abortions.[85] Accordingly, the modern methods of performing induced abortions that are used in the United States and other Western countries, and which impose virtually no risk to the future fertile life of women, have not been adopted in Marxist states. In Soviet reports, vacuum aspiration (VA), harmless in terms of secondary infertility, is seldom mentioned, and most induced abortions are evidently performed by D&C.[86]

In addition to causing sterility, the aftereffects of multiple induced abortions performed by D&C combine with venereal diseases, work hazards, and malnutrition to increase the rate of spontaneous abortion and the incidence of intrauterine adhesion and extrauterine pregnancies. These complications do not necessarily make women sterile, but they do not allow women to realize fertility, either. The entire complex of factors that avert birth, over and above the average rates of natural sterility and fetal wastage, is defined as pathological secondary infertility. Table 5 presents the results of my calculations of this measure for various nationalities. In the 1970s, 20.7 percent of all ethnic Russian women at fertile ages were pathologically secondarily infertile; among other nationalities, the rates were 18.6 percent of Moldavian women, 17.8 percent of Armenian women, 17.4 percent of Ukrainian women, 17.2 percent of Belorussian women, 13.6 percent of Azeri women, 9.7 percent of Latvian and Kazakh women, 8.8 percent of Estonian women, 5.9 percent of Kirgiz women, 4.5 percent of Uzbek women, and 3.2 percent of Tadzhik women.

Although the reproductive potential of the Turko-Muslims may gradually decline, increasing Russian reproductive potential would require a significant replacement of induced abortions by contraception, or of D&C by other methods, and a reduction in female employment. Such a change cannot be reasonably expected. This would require another state, another ideology, and another economic system.

ECONOMIC CHANGE AND FERTILITY DECLINE

Urban / Rural Fertility Differences

During the last quarter-century, in all Soviet territorial units except the traditional ethnic Russian areas of the northern and central RSFSR, the differential between urban and rural fertility was smaller among the more highly fertile populations and larger among the less fertile populations. This pattern is characteristic of a number of populations, including those of the United States (with minorities), the United Kingdom, France, Mexico, India, Syria, Ghana, and the East European countries.[87] In the 1970s a convergence in terms of overall fertility has occurred between urban and rural areas in Japan, England and Wales, Finland, France, Luxembourg, Norway, and Belorussia. In fact, in the mid-1970s, rural fertility was lower than urban fertility in Japan and Belorussia: 63.4 versus 65.4 and 54.6 versus 62.3, respectively.[88]

A large sample study of induced abortions in the RSFSR in the late 1950s and early 1960s found basically the same extent of abortions per woman in urban and rural areas (1.16 induced abortions a year for urban women and 1.15 abortions a year for rural women).[89] In this sense, the Soviets are justified in claiming that the Marxist goal of eliminating urban/rural differences has been realized, although thus far only among the Russians and Belorussians.

Income Distribution

The relationship between income, standard of living, taxes, public welfare, and redistribution of wealth, on the one hand, and reproductive preferences and fertility, on the other, is one of the most complex in modern economic demography.[90] Whether income has a negative or positive effect on fertility is an issue that has produced a long-lasting disarray in Soviet economic and demographic literature since the 1930s. In fact, most of the current Soviet doubts about the effectiveness of their pronatalist policies are caused by their lack of a microeconomic utility theory of the household.

The problem, however, is not confined to the Soviets. Incremental income apparently produces different effects among the developed, low-fertility populations of the North (pure income effect) and the developing, high-fertility populations of the South (substitution effect). But even this general observation is challenged by recent experience in some countries (for example, the People's Republic of China).

Earnings and family incomes have significantly increased in the last two decades in all areas of the USSR. This has not, however, prevented a steady fertility decline among all low-fertility nationalities during the same period. Income increments did not alter the declining fertility, and there definitely were other powerful factors that overruled the positive impact of income increase on fertility trends. This was also true for the Turko-Muslim republics of Central Asia and Transcaucasia. However, among Central Asians, various development subsidies, especially for education and social mobility, became a factor as important as changes in nominal income. On the one hand, these subsidies kept the expected quality of children high relative to the conventional standard of living, and fertility remained high. On the other hand, various interfamily transfer programs within the community of Central Asians, such as social security for the collective farm population, produced an opposite effect, and reduction in the number of children per family occurred. I shall discuss these issues in a later section.

Housing

There is a strong positive correlation between housing size per capita and fertility with respect to Soviet Northern populations with low fertility. The provision of housing over the past quarter-century has steadily, albeit slowly, increased in all Soviet republics. Correspondingly, this trend should have contributed to a fertility increase among the Northern population. However, the gap between desired and available housing space works as an important fertility suppressor.[91] This gap contributes to the increase in the costs of children relative to the expected standard of living. The Soviets themselves in 1922 set the "biological sufficient level" of living space per capita at 9.0 square meters, a target that had not been achieved for the country as a whole in 1981.[92] The differences in urban living space per capita among the Slavic and Baltic republics correspond to the differences in their fertility levels and the speed of their fertility declines (Table 4).

Among the highly fertile Turko-Muslim populations of the USSR, housing space has no apparent effect on fertility. This can be observed from data available on the Kazakhs and extrapolated for other Central Asians. Type of housing is, however, a more important factor. In the Turko-Muslim republics, 30 to 40 percent of urban living space and practically all rural living quarters were privately owned in the 1970s.[93] This ownership was, to a significant extent, subsidized by high prices for Central Asian agricultural products.

The process of closing the housing gap in the North and maintaining subsidized private housing in the South could have worked as an incentive for higher fertility. The continued fertility decline among all Soviet populations again points out that other powerful factors have overridden the impact of housing on the quality and quantity of children.

Female Employment

Increasing female participation in gainful employment may reveal at least two different behavioral preferences. One is a desire for higher household income, which could have a positive fertility effect by increasing the household's ability to bear the costs of children. The second preference is for financial and social independence, which implies a declining reliance on the family and children and has a negative fertility effect. Theoretically, the net fertility effect of increasing female employment can be either positive or negative, but historically only the negative net effect has so far been observed in various populations.

One of the most important socioeconomic features of Soviet Northern populations is nearly universal female participation in the labor force. Total gainful employment of women aged 16 to 54 (inclusive) increased in the RSFSR from 66.7 percent in 1960 to 86.1 percent in 1975.[94] Most data on female employment are available by republics only and do not fully reflect the differential ethnic participation of women in the labor force. For example, in 1970 in the Turkmen republic, the female participation rate in the nonagricultural labor force was 44.8 percent at ages 16 to 54. The respective rate for indigenous Turkmen women, however, can be calculated as only 21.5 percent.[95] In general, one can conclude that the full-time participation rate of women of working age in non–collective farm employment is about 25 percent among Turko-Muslim populations and about 85 percent among Slavic and Baltic populations. The latter rate implies that nearly all Northern women of childbearing age are employed in kinds of work that separate women from traditional wifehood and motherhood.

The relationship between female employment and fertility trends in the 1970s and 1980s is very complex. A rapid increase in female participation in the labor force in the Soviet North in the 1960s and early 1970s evidently contributed to a fertility decline. On the other hand, continued fertility decline among Slavic and Baltic populations in the 1970s and early 1980s (to a level below replacement) could no longer be attributed to the impact of female employment, since nearly universal participation had already been achieved. Certain side effects of excessive female participation, however, such as fundamental changes in the family as an institution, have had deep, long-term effects.

Central Asian populations represent a particularly interesting case with regard to female employment trends. Female participation rates in the non–collective farm labor force increased rapidly in the republics of Central Asia in the 1960s (in Uzbekistan, for example, it rose from 29.8 percent in 1959 to 43.6 percent in 1970). The trend ceased, however, in the 1970s.[96] Despite a nearly unlimited supply of women of working ages and a rising aggregate demand for labor, in the 1970s these rates increased by only two to three percentage points in the Central Asian republics. In fact, even this modest increment, as well as part of the previous rise, must be attributed to an increased participation of nonindigenous residents and to a decline in female work in collective farms.

The demographic effect of the rapid increase of female participation in non–collective farm employment in the 1960s in Central Asia was positive. Shortening of birth intervals due to earlier weaning among newly employed women aged 20–29 produced significant increases in the age-specific fertility at prime fertile ages. These increments were higher than the corresponding parity-specific reductions in fertility at ages 35–49. As a result, total fertility rates actually increased, to one of the world's highest levels. In the 1970s, however, fertility decline and an expansion of birth control surfaced despite a decline in female labor participation.

PRESENT TRENDS AND HYPOTHETICAL PROJECTIONS

The main purpose of long-term hypothetical projections is to demonstrate the numerical results of certain theoretical assumptions and technical procedures. These assumptions, in turn, are based on our understanding (or misunderstanding) of present trends and their causes. The usefulness of long-term projections is often disputed, yet there is much demand for them, especially from financial institutions and governments. My projections are based on a technical approach and a projection model I have established and applied to Soviet ethnic data.[97]

Application of the model indicates eventual negative growth (albeit in the remote future and after a continuing explosion through the twenty-first century) of the highly fertile Turko-Muslim populations of the USSR. This conclusion is justified by the present trends toward increasing birth control, declining age-specific fertility rates, decreasing expectancy of life, and, therefore, significantly declining net reproduction rates (Table 4). However, for the foreseeable future the Turko-Muslim populations will show only a steady decline in positive growth and population momentum, not an actual negative growth. More important, the theoretical justification for projecting declining growth lies in an analysis of the impact of the expansion of the welfare state and its social security component on Turko-Muslim populations.

A second controversial projection is rapid depopulation of Slavic ethnic groups, especially the Russians, at a speed much higher than that of the Latvians and Estonians. Life expectancy is significantly declining among Slavic nationalities relative to the Latvians and Estonians. The momentum for positive growth is fading away. Age distribution has not yet realized its full impact on the rise in crude death rates and the decline in crude birthrates among Slavic populations, especially the Russians, but it will be rapidly realized in the not too distant future.

Fertility decline in the rural areas, to such an extent as to eliminate the urban/rural fertility differential, is a particular Russian and Belorussian phenomenon within the USSR, which brings the Russians and Belorussians into the same category as the most advanced welfare-state populations. Total fertility rates at a level around or slightly below replacement level is a characteristic feature of Baltic populations. The Slavs, especially the Russians, are experiencing a rapid decline in total fertility and an even more rapid decline in net reproduction rates, to a level significantly below replacement.

In an environment of rapid fertility decline, the Soviet system of birth control, which I regard as another long-lasting factor, will not substantially reduce the present high level of induced abortions and pathological secondary infertility among Slavic populations, especially the Russians. No improvement has been made over the decades with regard to abortive methods or the introduction of effective contraception. Within the framework of Marxist demographic policy, no changes in this area can be expected in the future as a part of governmental policy. Certain progress has been made by the Baltic populations through their individual demand for the use of safe birth control methods. The Russians, however, have not made any significant progress in terms of the index of secondary infertility, and the ratio of abortions to births is steadily rising.

The decline of the Russian and other Northern Soviet populations is expected to assume a more rapid pace than that of the Western welfare societies, primarily because of the more comprehensive fertility-depressing impact of state involvement in family matters. In addition, structural demographic factors within the fertility schedule will influence the trend. Mathematically, when the rate of natural increase is negative, later childbearing, which has now become an important structural factor of the age-specific fertility schedule in the United States and Western Europe, actually slows the acceleration of the negative growth rate. In Arthur's formulation, "the reason for this seemingly paradoxical result is that a delay in childbearing means that the next generation arrives later. Since this new generation is smaller than the last and the decline in numbers is spread over a longer time, the rate of decline is therefore not so rapid."[98] Northern Soviet populations, especially the Russians, are characterized by a steady and rather rapid decline of age-specific fertility rates at later ages, partially due to the pathological secondary infertility following induced abortions performed by D&C. Under these conditions, an acceleration in the negative growth rate can be expected.

Western scholars and the media have rendered certain attention to recent measures intended to increase fertility in the Soviet North by paying modest lump sums for first, second, and third births (50, 100, and 100 rubles, respectively). Another measure introduced in 1981 was a partially paid one-year maternity leave for working mothers. As already argued by McIntyre, these measures cannot change the trend toward further fertility decline in the North.[99] The small payment, only 20 percent of average earnings, does not take into account the higher costs of living in the North and various subsidies in the South. Most of the cash flow, therefore, will be concentrated in the Southern tier, where fertility is high without such payments (a two-year postponement of maternity payments in the Southern tier expired in the fall of 1983).

At the same time, state budgetary payoffs for child-care facilities are still distributed to the substantial disadvantage of the Russians. In 1979 the Soviet state annually expended an average of 328 rubles per child in the child-care system: 228 rubles in the Uzbek republic, 219 rubles in the Ukrainian republic, and 182 rubles in the RSFSR.[100] This policy works as an additional fertility suppressant for the ethnic Russian population.

For the short term, modest pronatalist subsidies and employment concessions can produce marginal benefits for some segments of the Northern populations. For those families that have stopped just short of having an additional child, these marginal benefits may exceed marginal costs in the familial economy of scale. This will contribute to producing a second child in families that, economically speaking, were already willing to have 1.9. But in most cases, these pronatalist measures will only reduce a postponement of births. This will increase total fertility rates in the short run, but will not alter the cohort's cumulative fertility. Another predictable effect of pronatalist grants and employment concessions will be an increase in illegitimacy. Single women with a strong demand for at least one child will benefit most from the new policies. When income begins to lag relative to the cost of children, these minor fertility changes will fade away.

All demographic, economic, and policy indications suggest that the ethnic composition of the Soviet Union will change dramatically within the next hundred years. By the year 2080, the seven main Turko-Muslim populations (Uzbeks, Tadzhiks, Kazakhs, Azeris, Kirgiz, Turkmen, and Karakalpaks) will reach 132.9 million or 41.8 percent of the USSR's population, and the three main Slavic populations will decline to 130.2 million or 41.0 percent of the total. By the year 2050, the combined Slavic populations will have ceased to constitute a majority of the USSR, and the North as a whole will form only a bare majority. Ethnic Russians lost their majority in 1984; in 1995 they will begin negative growth. By the year 2025 the Uzbeks will overtake the Ukrainians as the second most numerous Soviet nationality, and by the beginning of the twenty-second century the Uzbeks will be the most numerous Soviet nationality, with the Russians second (75.8 million and 64.9 million, respectively). By the year 2080 the USSR will be a predominantly Turko-Muslim country. The Russians will decline from 138.8 million in 1984 to 136.7 million in 2000, 128.3 million in 2025, 107.2 million in 2050, 84.8 million in 2080, and to 64.9 million by 2100 (that is, they will cease to be a major world population group within some 100–120 years). If the trend continues, there will be only 23.0 million ethnic Russians by 2200.

These conclusions are valid, of course, only so long as the assumptions on which they are based hold up. One might recall Oswald Spengler's prediction that the communist revolution would turn out to be for the Russians what the barbarian conquest had been for the ancient Romans. In the twenty-second century, said Spengler, there will be no Russians, just as in the seventh century there were no more Romans.

DISCUSSION

For Soviet policymakers, the major demographic and economic issues concern the differential growth of the Northern and Southern population clusters. For an economic demographer, however, the challenge is to explain the fertility decline below replacement level in the North and the parity-specific limitation of births among indigeneous Central Asians.

Demographic Inflation in Central Asia

As discussed earlier, the Central Asian demographic transition has not been conventional. Central Asians did not adopt those social and cultural behavioral patterns that have usually been considered prerequisites for, or concomitant with, the parity-specific limitation of births. Nor did they experience the endogenous social and institutional changes thought to be congruent with demographic transition. The onset of birth control, combined with still high net reproduction rates, resulted in Central Asia from the offsetting impact of development subsidies and interfamily transfers (mainly in the form of public education and social security).

Variations on this combination influenced different fertility trends among the Central Asian nationalities. In Kazakhstan, where state farms expanded as a side effect of the Virgin Lands program in the 1950s, many indigenous households found themselves within the system of intergenerational social security payments to state farm workers. As a result, demographic transition started among the Kazakhs as early as the late 1950s, although it took another fifteen years to commence among the Uzbeks, Tadzhiks, Turkmen, and Kirgiz. On the other hand, the importance of private plots in Central Asia helped to keep fertility high. This did not happen, however, among the Azeris, where private plot agricultural production is only about half as high as among Kazakhs.[101]

For the Uzbeks, Tadzhiks, Kirgiz, and Turkmen, an estimated 60 percent of whom belonged to the collective farm population in the 1970s, the single most important socioeconomic change was the extension of social security pensions to collective farmers. The first law on pensions for collective farm members was introduced in the USSR in 1964. It specified that collective farmers were to receive a pension equal to 50 percent of their previous earnings. These pensions were to range from 12 to 102 rubles a month. As late as 1970, however, the pension of an average Soviet collective farmer amounted to 22 rubles a month, less in Central Asia (in nominal monetary terms). The minimum subsistence level per capita in the Soviet Union was 51.4 to 59.4 rubles a month.[102] The main source of income for collective farmers in the USSR, especially in Central Asia, remained their private plots. The 1964 law did not change the economic and demographic variables in Central Asia, nor did it have a substantial impact on fertility trends.

In 1971, the minimum pension for collective farmers was raised to 20 rubles a month. In addition, pensions were to be calculated on the same sliding scale that was used for state employees. By 1974 an average old-age pension for a collective farmer amounted to 33 rubles a month. This was still some 36 to 44 percent short of the subsistence level per capita, but the 1974 change was rather significant for the Central Asian population since the nominal personal income per capita in the Central Asian republics had always been below the Soviet average, due mostly to large household size. (It amounted to 30 rubles a month in 1960 and 45–49 rubles a month in 1970.)[103] Therefore, pensions in the mid-1970s provided retired collective farmers with at least the average income of 1960. With the help of private plots, they could accumulate monetary and nonmonetary assets above the average standard of living in their area in the 1970s. This development directly coincided with the beginning of the fertility decline among Central Asians.

At the same time, the reliance of rural households on their private plots increased. On these plots, family members, including children, are the main source of labor (wage labor is virtually nonexistent and is forbidden by law). The shortages of the Soviet economy produced high agricultural prices for privately marketed output. Given differential constraints on private production in the European and Asian areas, there emerged an implicit subsidy for the segment of the population involved in private agricultural production in Central Asia. Since the costs of children were also reduced in developing areas of the USSR by education and medical care subsidies from the national budget, the marginal benefits from children exceeded personal marginal costs at a very high parity. This kept the fertility level high and slowed the pace of fertility control.

This Central Asian transition provides a numerically significant case for the critique of the now famous Ryder-Caldwell hypothesis of fertility limitation due to change in the direction of net intergenerational transfers from positive to negative.[104] The cause of this change is assumed to be the exogenously rising costs of children due to the termination of child labor in the market economy and the proliferation of a costly modern life-style, including education. In the Central Asian case, however, after social security and public education started to affect the quality of children for their parents and the cycle of intergenerational transfers, fertility began to decline *notwithstanding* an expansion of the private plots with their highly profitable child labor, and despite health care and educational subsidies that reduced the costs of childrearing.

Nonreplacement Fertility in the Soviet North

The convergence of Soviet Northern fertility since the late 1960s with the nonreplacement fertility of other developed countries compels us to develop an explanation that can address persistent below-replacement fertility in both Soviet and non-Soviet populations. Various hypotheses that attribute fertility decline to specific Soviet developments, such as relative housing shortages, relatively low levels of income, early legalization of induced abortions, excessive female employment, rising alcoholism, and so on, must be dismissed. These factors can explain some differences in fertility trends between Soviet ethnic groups, but none can explain the trend itself, that is, nonreplacement fertility.

A comprehensive explanation is difficult to develop due to fundamental differences between the USSR and other developed countries in terms of economic foundations, standard of living, social structure, political system, and the relationship of the micro-units (household and family) to macro-entities (market and institutions). At the same time, one can see an advantage in covering the Soviet North simultaneously with other low-fertility populations. A comparison of some Soviet and non-Soviet socioeconomic variables at least helps to clarify what factors have not caused the current demographic depression in the developed world. For example, declining life expectancy and rising age-specific mortality among the Soviet Northern populations suggests that nonreplacement fertility in other developed countries is not related to further improvements in these statistics.

Some of the frequently discussed Western factors of very low fertility are not relevant in the Soviet case. These include the contraceptive revolution and the increase in female wages relative to those of males. The latter factor, which is one of the cornerstones in the Beckerian economics of household behavior, can, however, be re-emphasized, if the trend in female wages is related not to that of male wages, but to the trend in the value of female domestic activities. If this value declines or does not increase relative to female wages, and the value of women's marginal product in household production becomes smaller than the market wage, the opportunity costs of childbearing can exceed the benefits of female reproductive activities.

Other Western factors important in having caused nonreplacement fertility were persistently present during decades of above-replacement fertility (1930s through mid-1960s) among the Northern populations of the USSR. This includes high female participation in the labor force (from two-thirds to three-fourths of all women of reproductive age, which is higher than the current rate in any developed country with nonreplacement fertility, except very recently in Denmark, Finland, and Sweden). The same can be said about egalitarian sex roles. An increasing cost of education was also present in the USSR at a time of high fertility, for Soviet high schools and higher education required tuition payments in the 1930s.

This is not to say that such factors are not important in their relation to the current worldwide fertility trend. They are not primary causes but simultaneous choice variables, caused, along with nonreplacement fertility, by the truly exogenous variables.

It may be useful to reiterate the factors by which populations with below-replacement fertility differ—and which, therefore, cannot be primary causes of the current demographic depression. Fertility decline is not primarily due to (1) further declines in mortality, (2) the contraceptive revolution, (3) increasing urbanization, (4) equalization of sex roles and rising female status, (5) women's self-promotion, (6) an increase in women's wages relative to those of men, (7) increasing female employment, (8) increasing female educational attainment, (9) rising costs of education, (10) capitalism and abundance, (11) socialism and shortages, (12) individualist social culture, or (13) collectivist social culture. Nor is the decline due to (14) the rising cost of time, a factor that is not relevant in the Soviet economy or among the Japanese rural population. Nonreplacement fertility cannot be attributed to (15) total or relative secularization and decline of religious life, a factor that does not apply for Poland,

Hungary, Lithuania, Estonia, or Latvia. The same can be said about (16) the decline of traditional values and life-style changes in general. In the Japanese case, nonreplacement fertility coexists with the extended patriarchal family and joint household.

Both the Soviet and Japanese experiences testify that the current demographic depression is not (17) merely the trough of an endogenous fertility cycle (a "baby bust"). Endogenous fertility cycles operate as self-generating mechanisms within general fertility trends, and the shape of the cycles (their timing, length, height, and direction, as well as the shape of their peaks relative to their troughs) is subject both to general trends and exogenous changes. In the 1970s and early 1980s developed countries with previously very different fertility cycles showed a remarkable convergence in the downward fertility trend. The recent demographic depression common to the developed world must have an explanation different from specific national endogenous cycles, although the latter will continue to be an intrinsic part of the general downward trend.

The cyclic hypothesis (the Easterlin hypothesis) of current below-replacement fertility levels gave a special explanatory significance to (18) reduced relative income. This explanation assumed that the income of the current generation of young parents was low relative to the standard of living they experienced while dependents of their families of origin. Therefore, the current generation of young parents should opt for having fewer children than the previous generation. While the Easterlin hypothesis provided a persuasive explanation for the baby boom, the empirical evidence suggests that relative income did not in reality decline in the United States in the 1970s. In the case of the Soviet Northern populations, per capita income adjusted for inflation actually increased almost 1.6 times between 1960 and 1983.[105]

A final factor that is widely argued to account for the current demographic depression is (19) the momentum and irreversibility of fertility decline itself, or an unlimited demographic transition. In earlier versions of demographic theory, transition was interpreted as an equilibrating self-adjustment of net reproduction rates. This theory implied not an unlimited fertility decline toward zero reproduction, but a reproductive adjustment toward a low fertility/low mortality regime. It was a self-contained demographic model, in which mortality decline could be either exogenous or endogenous, but fertility control was definitely endogenous. This version was congruent with the economic theory of fertility, which assumed stable preferences and a demand for children in which the quality of children substituted for their quantity.

Recent versions of the transition theory, however, assume a demographically independent fertility decline with exogenous birth control technology. This was probably in view of the difficulties of explaining the early French and American fertility declines, which both began before the decline in mortality. In these versions, fertility decline is independent of any socioeconomic changes except contraceptive knowledge. These versions, then, are no different in explaining the current demographic depression than the contraceptive revolution theory. The historical Soviet experience with abortions and contraception, discussed above, does not corroborate this theory.

On a more general level, the new model of demographic transition with exogenous technology may imply that there is no demand for children at all and that unlimited fertility decline is simply a given. In Caldwell's phrase, "no fertility is rational." Schultz stressed that this extreme version of the transition theory not only rejects a possibility of an optimum equilibrium level in the demand for children, but also dismisses human choice entirely.[106]

The Transfer Society and Demographic Depression

An explanation for nonreplacement fertility should be sought in primary independent factors that are common to all the populations affected and that at the same time exogenously affect the optimum equilibrium between the quality and quantity of children as determined by parental choice. The only such factor I find is the new socioeconomic order in which the state provides for individual or household welfare via compulsory interfamily and intertemporal transfers.

I would argue that a number of elements of the transfer society, such as social security, public health care, and public education, tend to reduce fertility. I should emphasize that the effect produced by interfamily and intertemporal transfers is not a continuation of secular fertility transition. The effect is marginal, and fertility decline below replacement proceeds gradually over generations, because each of the transfers has a partially offsetting mechanism of intergenerational reimbursement.

The factor of compulsory interfamily and intertemporal transfers is more general than a mere aggregation of various welfare-state programs, some of which may not exist among all populations experiencing nonreplacement fertility. In the USSR, for example, there is virtually no general welfare program in the Western sense, that is, direct income supplements for nonworking or low-income households. In Japan, old-age support is not exclusively based on public pensions, and the social security system is funded from mandatory taxation of individual wages. Public education in the USSR is financed not from local property taxes, but from federal income and sales taxes (including turnover and other hidden taxes). Small children's consumption in the majority of households is thus reduced in order to finance the higher education of young adults in a minority of households.

Public investment in human capital is not, therefore, a positive fertility factor that can offset the divergency between the private and social marginal costs of children, as in Willis's model. In addition, the funded social security system in Japan stands against this model's argument that negative fertility effect is produced not by general impersonalization of intergenerational transfers, but only by its pay-as-you-go structure.[107] In every social security arrangement, private marginal costs of children exceed private marginal benefits to parents. The birth of additional children does not add significantly to parents' public pensions. At the same time, children's ability to privately support their elderly parents is significantly constrained by mandatory intertemporal transfers (payroll taxes, hidden taxes, or compulsory saving for their own pensions).

The most important transfer effect occurs because, due to mandatory social security taxes levied on young adults (whether to finance their future pensions or to support the current cohort of retirees), their parents have to increase personal downward transfers and extend the part of the life cycle in which they make transfers to children. Parents do this in order to help their children to bear and raise the grandchildren. Thus, for each consecutive generation, private marginal costs of children increase and equal the private marginal benefits at a relatively lower level of parity.

In the same manner, in a system of public education, young adults who are the parents of small children have to finance education of older children from other families. Since small children's consumption of goods and services should normally be less expensive than that of older children, public education can be considered as income transfer from younger to older parents. Even those households that are eventually reimbursed in the form of their own children's public education can be considered as having exercised involuntary transfer over the life cycle at the least opportune time. Social security and public education may also undermine parental control over the allocation of costs and the quality of children (unless individual preferences in education and the like are identical with those of the government).

Although the investment function of children has faded in the market economy, the implicit intergenerational contract of reciprocal support remains. Thus, the investment function of children as an emergency insurance, a source of security and personal care at old age, remains. With the emergence of compulsory intertemporal and interfamily transfers, these relations are debilitated.

Intergenerational reciprocity has a value beyond economic exchange over the life cycle. Reproductively, parents assess the prospects for a continuity of personality, not only of biology, in children and grandchildren. Social security and public upbringing of children reduce this factor and require parents to increase costs to retain the expected quality of children. An additional substitution of quality for quantity of children thus occurs. This division of children between family and society may lead to their exchange for other utilities that can embody a higher individual value from the standpoint of personal maximization (education, career, and so on). This substitution away from children follows not from a selfish but from an implicitly altruistic behavior: parents refuse to produce children of (from their perspective) suboptimal quality. Parents respond to various involuntary intertemporal and interfamily transfers by stopping fertility at a low parity level in order to retain the relative quality of already existing children. When the expected opportunities for children and expected benefits to children do not increase relative to their expected needs, additional costs per child must be incurred to compensate for this change.

In a transfer society, children are public goods that are still produced privately in the household. The production level under these conditions is always suboptimal from the societal standpoint.[108] If production is subsidized, it will be much over the optimum societal level (for example, the Central Asian case or the numbers of illegitimate children among welfare recipients in the United States). If it is subject to net taxation, fertility will be below replacement.

The dependency ratio, defined as the ratio of net consumers (conditionally, children below 15 years of age and the elderly over 60 years of age, according to Soviet economic distribution) to net producers (population of the working ages, 15–59), increases at an accelerating rate as fertility declines below replacement. The lower fertility is below replacement, the greater the increase in the total dependency of the population with each additional fertility reduction. And the greater this increase, the more compulsory interfamily transfers will be imposed on the household, thus placing further limitations on reproduction.

In the presence of social security and public education, young adults simultaneously support the previous generation (or themselves as future retirees, in the Japanese case), invest in the human capital of other young adults, and incur the private costs of childbearing and childrearing. This is a perversion of the natural cycle of intergenerational transfers hitherto unnoticed in the literature. Under natural conditions, people at age 40 to 65, who have the highest earnings profile, incur the total costs of old-age insurance on the microlevel, in terms of both support of their parents and saving for their own retirement. Around the same age, people incur the most expensive part of the costs of their children's education. In the modern transfer society, a significant proportion of these costs is placed on young parents and, by extension, on the consumption of their small children.

Provided the continuation of reciprocal intergenerational altruism, however, the phenomenon of floating transfers will occur. Middle-aged and elderly parents reimburse their young adult children, thus producing a self-offsetting mechanism to social security[109] and public education. The problem, though, is that grandparents must partially offset the costs of about five grandchildren if the replacement level of the population is to be maintained.

The time shift of costs (from small children to students, from young adults to middle-aged adults) means only partial reimbursement will occur via floating transfers. In this chain-letter model of involuntary transfers and partial reimbursements, younger households are worse off relative to older households. Each successive generation is worse off relative to each previous generation. The expected quality of children declines in each successive generation due to this shift in expenditures. This in turn leads young parents to reduce the quantity of children to compensate for their declining quality. Thus, although floating transfers may partially offset the counterreproductive effect of compulsory interhousehold and intertemporal transfers, young parents will gradually reduce their fertility over generations.

NOTES

1. Calculated from the values in Table 2.

2. N. P. Fedorenko, ed., *Vosproizvodstvo naseleniia i trudovykh resursov* (Moscow, 1976), pp. 32–33; D. Valentei and A. Kvasha, "Sotsial'no-ekonomicheskie problemy narodonaseleniia SSSR," in *Demograficheskaia situatsiia v SSSR* (Moscow, 1976), pp. 7–8; A. G. Volkov, "O neobkhodimosti vozdeistviia na rozhdaemost'," in *Rozhdaemost': Problemy izucheniia* (Moscow, 1976), pp. 36–39; G. A. Bondarskaia, *Rozhdaemost' v SSSR: Etno-demograficheskii aspekt* (Moscow, 1977), pp. 90–94; V. S. Steshenko et al., *Demograficheskoe razvitie Ukrainskoi SSR, 1959–70* (Kiev, 1977), pp. 150–54; A. I. Antonov, *Sotsiologiia rozhdaemosti* (Moscow, 1980), pp. 76–79, 264–65; M. B. Tatimov, *Razvitie narodonaseleniia i demograficheskaia politika* (Alma-Ata, 1978), pp. 40, 47, 120–21; A. Ia. Kvasha, *Demograficheskaia politika v SSSR* (Moscow, 1981), pp. 83, 90–91, 115, 168, 184; G. I. Litvinova, *Pravo i demograficheskie protsessy v SSSR* (Moscow, 1981), pp. 38–39, 49; K. Katus, "Naselenie Estonii v protsesse stabilizatsii," in *Nashe budushchee glazami demografa* (Moscow, 1979), p. 109;

and V. I. Perevedentsev, "Vosproizvodstvo naseleniia i sem'ia," *Sotsiologicheskie issledovaniia* (hereafter, *SI*), no. 2 (April–June 1982): 87–88.

3. Barbara A. Anderson, "Data Sources in Russian and Soviet Demography," in *Demographic Developments in Eastern Europe* (New York: Praeger, 1977), pp. 23–63; Murray Feshbach, "Development of the Soviet Census," in *Soviet Population Policy: Conflicts and Constraints*, ed. Helen Desfosses (New York: Pergamon, 1981), pp. 3–15; and *Vestnik statistiki* (hereafter, *VS*).

4. S. Soboleva, *Migration and Settlement: Soviet Union* (Laxenburg, Austria: International Institute for Applied Systems Analysis, 1982), pp. 108–12.

5. Murray Feshbach, "The Soviet Union: Population Trends and Dilemmas," *Population Bulletin* 37 (August 1982): 34.

6. Samuel H. Preston and Ansley J. Coale, "Age Structure, Growth, Attrition and Accession: A New Synthesis," *Population Index* 48 (Summer 1982): 217–59.

7. D. Peter Mazur, "Using Regression Models to Estimate the Expectation of Life for the USSR," *Journal of the American Statistical Association* 67 (March 1972): 31–36; and Ansley J. Coale and Paul Demeny, *Regional Model Life Tables and Stable Populations* (Princeton, N.J.: Princeton University Press, 1966).

8. *Itogi Vsesoiuznoi perepisi naseleniia 1959 gods* (hereafter, *1959 Census*), vol. SSSR (Moscow, 1962), p. 266; *VS*, no. 2 (1974): 95; USSR TsSU, *Zhenshchiny v SSSR: Statisticheskii sbornik* (Moscow, 1975), p. 22; V. I. Perevedentsev, "Narodo-naselenie i demograficheskaia politika partii," *Politicheskoe samoobrazovanie*, no. 8 (1981): 50; and V. Nauduzhas, "Aktual'nye demograficheskie problemy v Litovskoi SSR," in *Naselenie SSSR segodnia* (Moscow, 1982), p. 59.

9. Ansley J. Coale, Barbara A. Anderson, and Erna Harm, *Human Fertility in Russia Since the Nineteenth Century* (Princeton, N.J.: Princeton University Press, 1979), pp. 241, 266–67.

10. *Itogi Vsesoiuznoi perepisi naseleniia 1970 goda* (hereafter, *1970 Census*), vol. 2 (Moscow, 1972), pp. 12–75, vol. 4 (Moscow, 1973), pp. 360–64; and Jean-Noel Biraben, "Naissances et Repartition par Age dans l'Empire Russe et en Union Sovietique," *Population* 31 (March–April 1976): 476–77.

11. Murray Feshbach, "Between the Lines of the 1979 Soviet Census," *Problems of Communism* 31 (1982): 32.

12. *1970 Census*, vol. 2, pp. 263–68, and vol. 4, p. 383; "Vsesoiuznaia perepis' naseleniia" (hereafter, *1979 Census*); *VS*, 1980–1983, esp. no. 2 (1980): 58; "Is Induced Abortion Murder by Experts?" *Nauka i Tekhnika*, no. 9 (Riga, 1980): 27–30, printed in English in *The Current Digest of the Soviet Press* 33 (1981): 11.

13. John Bongaarts, "A Framework for Analyzing the Proximate Determinants of Fertility," *Population and Development Review* 4 (March 1978): 105–32.

14. Ansley J. Coale and T. James Trussell, "Model Fertility Schedules: Variations in the Age Structure of Childbearing in Human Populations," *Population Index* 40 (April 1974): 185–258, and 41 (October 1975): 572; George W. Barclay et al., "A Reassessment of the Demography of Traditional Rural China," *Population Index* 42 (October 1976): 606–35.

15. For the latest presentation of the initial Bongaarts model, see John Bongaarts and Robert G. Potter, *Fertility, Biology, and Behavior: An Analysis of the Proximate Determinants* (New York: Academic Press, 1983), pp. 78–126. For my modification of the Bongaarts model, see M. S. Bernstam, "Marksizm i kontrol' rozhdaemosti v SSSR," *Novyi zhurnal* 153 (December 1983): 234–41.

16. Ansley J. Coale, "Age Pattern of Marriage," *Population Studies* 25 (1971): 193–214; and Ansley J. Coale and Donald R. McNeil, "The Distribution by Age of the Frequency of First Marriage in a Female Cohort," *Journal of the American Statistical Association* 67 (1972): 743–49.

17. Coale, Anderson, and Harm, *Human Fertility*, pp. 247–50; Barbara A. Anderson, "Some Factors Related to Ethnic Reidentification in the Russian Republic," *Soviet Nationality Policies and Practices*, ed. Jeremy R. Azrael (New York: Praeger, 1978), pp. 309–33; and Robert A. Lewis, Richard H. Rowland, and Ralph S. Clem, *Nationality and Population Change in Russia and the USSR: An Evaluation of Census Data, 1897–1970* (New York: Praeger, 1976), pp. 44–45, 92–93, 215–307.

18. For a new technique of estimating ethnic reidentification, see M. S. Bernstam, "Demography of Soviet Ethnic Groups in World Perspective" (Paper delivered at the Hoover Institution conference on Nationalities and the Soviet Future, Stanford, California, 1983).

19. William Brass, "The Distribution of Births in Human Populations," *Population Studies* 12 (1958): 51–72, "Perspectives on Population Prediction," *Journal of Royal Statistical Society* A-137, no. 4 (1974): 532–83, and "On the Scale of Mortality," in *Biological Aspects of Demography*, ed. William Brass (London: Taylor and Francis, 1971), pp. 69–110; Ansley J. Coale, "The Use of Fourier Analysis to Express the Relation Between Time Variations in Fertility and the Time Sequence of Births in a Closed Human Population," *Demography* 7 (February 1970): 93–120; Nathan Keyfitz, *Introduction to the Mathematics of Population* (Reading, Mass.: Addison-Wesley, 1968), and "On the Momentum of Population Growth," *Demography* 8 (February 1971): 72–80; Jean Bourgeois-Pichat, "Stable, Semi-Stable Populations and Growth Potential," *Population Studies* 25 (July 1971), pp. 235–54; Keyfitz, "On Future Population," *Journal of the American Statistical Association* 67 (1972): 347–63; Louis Henry, "Passe, Present et Avenir en Demographie," *Population* 27 (1972): 383–95; Ronald D. Lee, "New Methods for Forecasting Fertility: An Overview," *Population Bulletin of the United Nations* 11 (1978): 6–11, "Demographic Forecasting and the Easterlin Hypothesis," *Population and Development Review* 2 (1976): 459–68, and "Forecasting Births in Post-Transition Populations: Stochastic Renewal with Serially Correlated Fertility," *Journal of the American Statistical Association* 69 (1974): 607–17; Paul A. Samuelson, "An Economist's Non-Linear Model of Self-Generated Fertility Waves," *Population Studies* 30 (July 1976): 243–47; Keyfitz, "Population Waves," in *Population Dynamics*, ed. T. N. E. Greville (New York: Academic Press, 1972): 3–38.

20. Feshbach, "The Soviet Union," p. 38.

21. Kingsley Davis, "The Theory of Change and Response in Modern Demographic History," *Population Index* 29 (November 1963): 345–66; *Migration: A Com-*

parative Perspective, ed. A. Brown and E. Neuberger (New York, 1976), pp. 150–51; A. J. Coale, "The Decline of Fertility in Europe from the French Revolution to World War II," in *Fertility and Family Planning: A World View*, ed. S. J. Behrman et al. (Ann Arbor: University of Michigan Press, 1969).

22. L. L. Rybakovskii, *Regional'nyi analiz migratsii* (Moscow, 1973), p. 17; V. I. Perevedentsev, "Migratsiia naseleniia SSSR," in *Narodonaselenie stran mira* (Moscow, 1978), pp. 457–63; and A. V. Topilin, *Territorial'noe pereraspredelenie trudovykh resursov v SSSR* (Moscow, 1975), pp. 34–35.

23. Perevedentsev, "Migratsiia naseleniia SSSR," p. 463; see also Murray Feshbach, "Prospects for Outmigration from Central Asia and Kazakhstan in the Next Decade," in *Soviet Economy in a Time of Change* (Washington, D.C.: Joint Economic Committee of the U.S. Congress, 1979), vol. 1, pp. 670–71; and R. Mirzoev and N. Khonaliev, "Voprosy ispol'zovannia trudovykh resursov v Tadzhikistane," *VS*, no. 5 (1982), pp. 22–28.

24. *1959 Census*; *1970 Census*; Soboleva, *Migration and Settlement*, pp. 3, 22–32, 44–45; Perevedentsev, "Narodonaselenie," pp. 47–48.

25. Feshbach, "The Soviet Union," p. 13.

26. Valentei and Kvasha, "Sotsial'no-ekonomicheskie problemy," p. 3; Feshbach, "Prospects," pp. 668–71; *Problemy demografii i narodnogo blagosostoianiia* (Moscow, 1976), pp. 32–38.

27. Topilin, *Territorial'noe pereraspredelenie*, pp. 46–47; Litvinova, *Pravo*, pp. 147–48; David M. Heer, "Soviet Population Policy: Four Model Futures," in *Soviet Population Policy*, pp. 137–38; Bondarskaia, *Rozhdaemost'*, pp. 10–11; Feshbach, "Prospects," pp. 669–70.

28. G. I. Litvinova and B. Ts. Urlanis, "Demograficheskaia politika Sovetskogo Soiuza," *Sovetskoe gosudarstvo i pravo*, no. 3 (March 1982), pp. 38–46; Litvinova, *Pravo*, p. 153.

29. O. Ata-Mirzaev and B. Goldfarb, "Perspektivy vosproizvodstva naseleniia Srednei Azii," in *Nashe budushchee*, pp. 115–18; Feshbach, "Prospects," pp. 671–72; Feshbach, "The Soviet Union," p. 37; Heer, "Soviet Population," p. 138; the author's unpublished calculations prepared for the present article.

30. Calculated from *Narkhoz*, various issues (e.g., 1964, 1972, 1980).

31. See note 21 above; see also J. C. Caldwell, "The Mechanisms of Demographic Change in Historical Perspective," *Population Studies* 35 (March 1981): 5–27; Frank Lorimer, *The Population of the Soviet Union: History and Prospects* (Geneva: League of Nations, 1946); Jean-Noel Biraben, "Essai sur l'Evolution Demographique de l'URSS," *Population* 13, no. 2 (1958): 29–62; and David M. Heer, "The Demographic Transition in the Russian Empire and the Soviet Union," *Journal of Social History* 1 (1968): 193–240.

32. Calculated from M. V. Ptukha, *Ocherki po statistike naseleniia* (Moscow, 1960), p. 447; and USSR State Planning Commission, *Vsesoiuznaia perepis' naseleniia 1926 goda*, vol. 51 (Moscow, 1931), p. 6.

33. Tatimov, *Razvitie*, p. 117; M. Burieva, "Formirovanie sem'i v sel'skoi

mestnosti Uzbeksoi SSR," in *Liudi v gorode i na sele* (Moscow, 1978), p. 98; and N. Deriaev, "Iz istorii materinstva i detstva v Turkmenskoi SSR," *Zdravookhranenie Turkmenistana*, no. 6 (1980): 33–35.

34. Coale, Anderson, Harm, *Human Fertility*, pp. 85–121, 179–206; Burieva, "Formirovanie sem'i," pp. 96–101; R. I. Sifman, *Dinamika rozhdaemosti v SSSR* (Moscow, 1974), pp. 77–85. Data on the natural fertility level is calculated from D. R. Tsitsishvili, *Besplodnyi brak* (Tbilisi, 1967), vol. 1, p. 44; and Burieva, "Formirovanie sem'i," p. 101.

35. A. Romaniuc, "Increase in Natural Fertility During the Early Stages of Modernization: Evidence from the African Case Study, Zaire," *Population Studies* 34 (1980): 302–9; Eduardo E. Arriaga, *Mortality Decline and Its Demographic Effects in Latin America* (Berkeley: University of California, 1970), pp. 148–65; Joycelin Burne, *Levels of Fertility in Commonwealth Caribbean, 1921–1965* (Kingston, Jamaica: Institute of Social and Economic Research, 1972); U.N., *Levels and Trends of Fertility Throughout the World* (New York, 1977); Jean Bourgeois-Pichat, "Recent Demographic Change in Western Europe: An Assessment," *Population and Development Review* 7 (March 1981): 20, 23; C. Mosk, "The Evolution of the Pre-Modern Demographic Regime in Japan," *Population Studies* 35 (March 1981): 28–40.

36. W. Parker Mauldin, "Patterns of Fertility: Decline in Developing Countries, 1950–1975," *Studies in Family Planning* 9 (April 1978): 75–84; and William D. Mosher, "The Theory of Change and Response: An Application to Puerto Rico, 1940 to 1970," *Population Studies* 34 (1980): 45–58.

37. Soviet crude death rates are drawn from *Narodnoe khoziaistvo*. On England and Wales, see U.N., *Demographic Yearbook*. On standardized death rates for 1958–59, 1965–66, and 1969–70, see John Dutton, Jr., "Changes in Soviet Mortality Patterns, 1959–1977," *Population and Development Review* 5 (1979): 286; for 1974–75, see I. Rylkova, "Prodolzhitel'nost' zhizni naseleniia SSSR," *Vozobnovlenie pokolenii nashei strany* (Moscow, 1978), p. 82; for 1978, see *Osobennosti demograficheskogo razvitiia v SSSR*, ed. R. S. Rotova (Moscow, 1982), p. 94; and for 1980, see *Narodonaselenie SSSR i mira* (Moscow, 1983), p. 77.

38. Dutton, "Changes in Soviet Mortality Patterns," pp. 267–91, and "Causes of Soviet Adult Mortality Increases," *Soviet Studies* 33 (October 1981): 548–59; and Feshbach, "The Soviet Union," p. 34.

39. M. S. Bednyi, *Prodolzhitel'nost' zhizni v gorodakh i selakh* (Moscow, 1976), pp. 61–62; E. M. Levitskii, *Ekonomiko-matematicheskoe issledovanie vosproizvodstva naseleniia Sibiri i Dal'nego Vostoka na osnove tablits prodolzhitel'nosti zhizni* (Novosibirsk, 1962), pp. 113–15.

40. Feshbach, "The Soviet Union," p. 34; Bednyi, *Prodolzhitel'nost'*, pp. 61–62.

41. Dutton, "Changes in Soviet Mortality Patterns," p. 288.

42. Calculated from the *1959*, *1970*, and *1979 Censuses*.

43. *VS*, no. 11 (1982): 57–62.

44. Iu. P. Lisitsyn and N. Ia. Kopyt, *Alkogolizm: Sotsial'no-gigienicheskie aspekty* (Moscow, 1978), p. 95; and *Molodoi kommunist*, no. 2 (1980): 65.

45. *Sovetskoe gosudarstvo i pravo*, no. 12 (1980): 118; and Vladimir G. Treml, "Fatal Poisoning in the USSR," Radio Free Europe/Radio Liberty, *Research Bulletin* RL 490/82, pp. 1–12.

46. *VS*, no. 12 (1971): 81, and no. 11 (1982): 65; Lisitsyn and Kopyt, *Alkogolizm*, Litvinova, *Pravo*, p. 114.

47. Fedorenko, *Vosproizvodstvo*, p. 62.

48. Vladimir G. Treml, *Alcohol in the USSR: A Statistical Study* (Durham, N.C.: Duke University Press, 1982), pp. 70–75; Dutton, "Changes in Soviet Mortality Patterns," pp. 280–81, 283–85, and "Causes of Soviet Adult Mortality Increases," pp. 549–58.

49. *Effektivnost' narodnogo khoziaistva* (Moscow, 1981), p. 230; *Voprosy ekonomiki*, no. 12 (1981): 105; and *Ekonomika sel'skogo khoziaistva*, no. 10 (1982): 72.

50. M. Elizabeth Denton, "Soviet Consumer Policy: Trends and Prospects," in *Soviet Economy in a Time of Change*, vol. 1, p. 771; *Zaria Vostoka* 26 (November 1981); *Voprosy ekonomiki*, no. 12, (1981): 105, and no. 1 (1982): 126–27; *Ekonomika sel'skogo khoziaistva*, no. 10 (1982): 72; and R. A. Lokshin, *Spros, proizvodstvo, torgovlia* (Moscow, 1975), pp. 82, 89.

51. M. S. Bernstam, "Behind US Grain Sales to the USSR: Re-Examining Soviet Grain Balances and Strategic Grain Reserves, 1971/72–1981/82," *Defense and Foreign Affairs*, no. 9 (September 1982): 22–24; Lokshin, *Spros*, p. 94; *Planovoe khoziaistvo*, no. 10 (1982): 48, 51; and D. Gale Johnson, "The Soviet Livestock Sector: Problems and Prospects," *ACES Bulletin* 26 (Fall 1974): 47–50.

52. *Problemy raspredeleniia i rost narodnogo blagosostoianiia* (Moscow, 1979), pp. 198–99; Lokshin, *Spros*, pp. 94–95, 126–31; and *Narkhoz*, various republic issues.

53. Method of estimating crude birthrates from crude natural growth rates and child/women ratios is derived from D. Peter Mazur, "Using Regression Models to Estimate the Expectation of Life for the USSR," *Journal of the American Statistical Association* 67 (March 1972): 34–35. The hypothetical crude birthrates are those that a given population would have had if it had had the same birthrates as European and North American countries or the RSFSR at the same respective mortality level. The definition, concept, and approach have been introduced by Kingsley Davis.

54. *VS*, no. 1 (1982): 64–66; *Sovremennye problemy vosproizvodstva naseleniia* (Riga, 1980), pp. 12–21; I. Kaliniuk and I. Veselkova, "Demograficheskie protsessy v SSSR," *Naselenie SSSR segodnia*, pp. 10–11.

55. *VS*, no. 2 (1980): 20, and no. 11 (1981): 70.

56. Mirzoev and Khonaliev, "Voprosy," p. 23; and V. I. Kozlov, *Natsional'nosti SSSR* (Moscow, 1975), p. 177.

57. Kvasha, "Demograficheskaia politika," p. 120; *Osobennosti demograficheskogo razvitiia v SSSR* (Moscow, 1982), p. 229; *Rainonnye osobennosti vosproizvodstva naseleniia SSSR* (Cheboksary, 1972), pp. 29–30; and *Neva*, no. 2 (1981): 153–57.

58. Bondarskaia, *Rozhdaemost'*, p. 101.

59. U.S. Bureau of the Census, *Statistical Abstract of the United States: 1985* (Washington, D.C.: GPO, 1984), p. 39; U.N., *Demographic Yearbook, 1979: Special*

Issue; Historical Supplement, pp. 893, 898, 903; *Statistik Arsbok for Sverige 1980* (Stockholm: Sveriges Officiella Statistik, 1980), pp. 41–42. On Latvia, see *1970 Census*, vol. 2, p. 266; and "Is Induced Abortion Murder by Experts?", p. 11. For procedure, see Coale, Anderson, and Harm, *Human Fertility*, pp. 269–70.

60. Calculated from *1970 Census*, vol. 2, pp. 24–25, 264; *Naselenie SSSR 1973*, p. 72; and N. G. Iurkevich and G. V. Iakovleva, "K voprosu o vnebrachnoi rozhdaemosti," *Vzaimootnosheniia pokolenii v sem'e* (Moscow, 1977), p. 186.

61. Coale, Anderson, and Harm, *Human Fertility*, pp. 141–46.

62. M. A. Bukzhanova, *Sem'ia v kolkhozakh Uzbekistana* (Tashkent, 1959), pp. 26–29; Burieva, "Formirovanie sem'i," pp. 96–99.

63. *VS*, no. 12 (1980): 58; I. Il'ina, "Differentsiatsiia brachnosti v neskol'kikh pokoleniiakh zhenshchin v SSSR," *Demograficheskaia situatsiia v SSSR* (Moscow, 1976), pp. 70–78.

64. For Western populations, see U.N., *Demographic Yearbook* for 1976 and 1980 and *Demographic Yearbook, 1979: Special Issue*. For the USSR and Soviet republics, see *1959 Census, 1979 Census*, and the *Narkhoz* statistical yearbooks for various republics. In the USSR all marriages are declared by census respondents regardless of legal status and they are used as a denominator to calculate the ratio of divorces per number of married couples (average divorce rate). Since cohabitance is included in the denominator, the average divorce rate is underestimated. To avoid this error, I have calculated the number of married males on each census date and used it as a denominator. Biraben's single-year age distribution was employed here (Biraben, "Naissances et Repartition par Age dans l'Empire Russe et en Union Sovietique," pp. 441–78). Since age distribution in 1979 was not published, the following procedure was applied: the ratio 0.9874 was regarded as the number of legal marriages per number of reported marriages (U.N., *Demographic Yearbook, 1979: Special Issue*, p. 1136), and the ratio 0.9245 was regarded as the number of reported marriages per number of registered families of all types, which included single-parent families, grandparent/grandchildren families, etc. (*VS*, no. 2 [1980]: 20, and no. 12 [1980]: 59, and no. 11 [1981]: 60). Note that the Soviets misreported their average divorce rate to the United Nations: they apparently divided the number of legal divorces by the number of individuals (not couples) who reported being married. Thus an average divorce rate of 5.9 (in 1970) instead of 11.9 was published by the U.N. for the USSR (U.N., *Demographic Yearbook, Special Issue*, p. 906). One must divide 5.9 by 0.9874 and then multiply by two in order to derive a true figure.

65. V. I. Perevedentsev, "Vosproizvodstvo naseleniia i sem'ia," *SI*, no. 2 (1982): 87; *VS*, various issues; V. A. Sysenko, *Ustoichivost' braka: Problemy, faktory, usloviia* (Moscow, 1981), p. 138, and "Razvody: Dinamika, motivy, posledstviia," *SI*, no. 2 (1982): 99.

66. A. B. Sinel'nikov, "Prodolzhitel'nost' sushchestvovaniia sovremennykh brakov," in *Vozobnovlenie pokolenii nashei strany*, p. 111; Sysenko, "Razvody," pp. 99–102; and *Komsomol'skaia pravda*, 14 July 1982, p. 4.

67. Alastair McAuley, *Women's Work and Wages in the Soviet Union* (London: George Allen and Unwin, 1981), pp. 32–47, 190–205.

68. *VS*, various issues (e.g., 1971, no. 12; 1977, no. 12; 1981, no. 11).

69. U.N., *Demographic Yearbook, 1979: Special Issue*, pp. 264–65, 1072–73; *Statistik Arsbok*, pp. 41–42, 84; N. V. Dogle, "Territorial'nye osobennosti rozhdaemosti Severo-Zapadnogo ekonomicheskogo raiona RSFSR," *Izuchenie vosproizvodstva naseleniia* (Moscow, 1968), p. 260; R. I. Sifman, "Dinamika plodovitosti kogort zhenshchin v SSSR," *Voprosy demografii* (Moscow, 1970): 151.

70. N. S. Sokolova, "Statisticheskii analiz iskhodov beremennosti," *Zdravookhranenie Rossiiskoi Federatsii* (hereafter, *ZRF*), no. 3 (1970): 38–40; and "Voprosy izucheniia iskhodov beremennosti u zhenshchin," *ZRF*, no. 3 (1980): 13–14; Henry P. David, ed., *Abortion Research: International Experience* (Lexington, Mass.: D.C. Heath, Lexington Books, 1974), pp. 211–12; Malcolm Potts, Peter Diggory, and John Peel, *Abortion* (Cambridge: Cambridge University Press, 1977), pp. 67–68; and Henry P. David and Robert J. McIntyre, *Reproductive Behavior: Central and Eastern European Experience* (New York: Springer Publishing Co., 1981), pp. 109–17.

71. J. A. Ross et al., "Findings from Family Planning Research," *Reports on Population / Family Planning*, no. 12 (October 1972): 36; David, *Abortion Research*, pp. 39–41; Kathleen Ford, *Abortion and Family Building: Fertility Limitation in Hungary and Japan* (Ph.D. diss., Brown University, 1976); Christopher Tietze and John Bongaarts, "The Demographic Effect of Induced Abortion," *Obstetrical and Gynecological Survey* 31 (1976): 699–709; C. Tietze and Anrudh K. Jain, "The Mathematics of Repeat Abortion: Explaining the Increase," *Studies in Family Planning* 9 (1978): 294–99; and Tietze, *Induced Abortion: 1979*, 3d ed. (New York: The Population Council, 1979).

72. H. P. David, "Abortion and Family Planning in the Soviet Union: Public Policy and Private Behavior," *Journal of Biosocial Science* 6 (October 1974): 417–26; Helen Desfosses, "Pro-Natalism in Soviet Law and Propaganda," in *Soviet Population Policy*, pp. 96–103; and Friedrich Engels, *The Origin of the Family, Private Property, and the State* (New York: Pathfinder Press, 1972), pp. 81–82.

73. James W. Brackett, R. T. Revenholt, and John C. Chao, "The Role of Family Planning in Recent Rapid Fertility Decline in Developing Countries," *Studies in Family Planning* 9, no. 12 (1978): 318. M. Vaessen, "Knowledge of Contraceptives: An Assessment of World Fertility Survey Data Collection Procedures," *Population Studies* 35 (1981): 357–73; and Robert Lightbourne, Susheela Singh, and Cynthia P. Green, "The World Fertility Survey: Charting Global Childbearing," *Population Bulletin* 37 (March 1982): 30–39.

74. Antonov, *Sotsiologiia rozhdaemosti*, pp. 126, 130–31.

75. Sh. Shlindman and P. Zvidrin'sh, *Izuchenie rozhdaemosti: Po materialam spetsial'nogo issledovaniia v Latviiskoi SSR* (Moscow, 1973), pp. 134–35, 144–46; Coale, Anderson, and Harm, *Human Fertility*, p. 136; David, "Abortion and Family Planning," pp. 420–21.

76. O. E. Chernetskii, "Organizatsiia raboty po snizheniiu abortov," *Sovetskoe zdravookhranenie* (hereafter, *SZ*), no. 6 (1961): 21; Karl-Heinz Mehlan, "Abortion in Eastern Europe," *Abortion in a Changing World*, ed. Robert E. Hall (New York: Columbia University Press, 1970), vol. 1, p. 313; I. Katkova, "Osobennosti demo-

graficheskogo povedeniia semei v pervye gody braka," *Molodaia sem'ia* (Moscow, 1977), pp. 84–95; *ZRF*, no. 2 (1971): 23–24, no. 6 (1972): 27, and no. 9 (1980): 29–30; David and McIntyre, *Reproductive Behavior*, pp. 108–9; *SZ*, no. 5 (1972): 17, no. 5 (1973): 22, and no. 12 (1976): 17. Other Soviet data as cited in Richard Johnson, "Abortion in the Soviet Union," Radio Free Europe / Radio Liberty, *Research Bulletin*, no. 25 (June 1982): 8–9; Ellen Jones and Fred W. Grupp, "Value Change and Political Stability in the Soviet Multinational State" (Defense Intelligence Agency and the CIA, unpublished paper, 1982), p. 24; Sokolova, "Statisticheskii," pp. 39–40. On the 93 percent rate in Latvia, see David, "Abortion and Family Planning," pp. 420–21; E. A. Sadvokasova, "Nekotorye sotsial'no-gigienicheskie aspekty izucheniia aborta," *SZ*, no. 3 (1963), and *Sotsial'no-gigienicheskie aspekty regulirovaniia razmerov sem'i* (Moscow, 1969), p. 149.

77. I. Katkova and A. Mamatokhunova, "Nekotorye aspekty formirovaniia sovremennykh mnogodetnykh semei," in *Demograficheskaia situatsiia v SSSR* (Moscow, 1976), pp. 84–85.

78. A. A. Popov, "Mediko-demograficheskie i sotsial'no gigienicheskie prichiny i faktory iskusstvennogo aborta," *ZRF*, no. 9 (1980): 28.

79. Sadvokasova, "Rol' aborta v osushchestvlenii soznatel'nogo materinstva v SSSR," *Izuchenie vosproizvodstva*, pp. 220–21; A. M. Lekhter, "Opyt izucheniia posledstvii abortov," *SZ*, no. 9 (1966), p. 23; and Popov, "Mediko-demograficheskie prichiny," p. 28.

80. Bernstam, "Marksizm i kontrol' rozhdaemosti," pp. 234–61.

81. J. T. Lanman, "Delays During Reproduction and Their Effects on the Embryo and Fetus," *The New England Journal of Medicine* 278 (1968): 993–99, 1047–54; R. Guerrero and O. I. Rojas, "Spontaneous Abortion and Aging of Human Ova and Spermatozoa," *The New England Journal of Medicine* 293 (1975): 573–75; D. Schwarts, P. D. M. MacDonald, and V. Huechel, "Fecundability, Coital Frequency and the Viability of Ova," *Population Studies* 34 (1980): 400; Eva Alberman and M. R. Creasy, "Factors Affecting Chromosome Abnormalities in Human Conceptions," *Chromosome Variation in Human Evolution*, ed. A. J. Boyce (London, 1975), p. 83; R. L. Butcher and N. W. Fugo, "Delayed Ovulation and Chromosome Anomalies," *Fertility and Sterility* 18 (1967): 297; C. Iffy and M. B. Wingate, "Risks of Rhythm Method of Birth Control," *Journal of Reproductive Medicine* 5 (1970): 96; and R. Guerrero, "Possible Effects of the Periodic Abstinence Method," *Proceedings of a Research Conference on Natural Family Planning* (Washington, D.C.: Human Life Foundation, 1973), p. 96.

82. L. A. Chirkova, *Genetika i selektsiia na Ukraine* (Kiev, 1971), vol. 2, pp. 125–26; A. F. Tur and E. F. Davidenkova in *Spravochnik po klinicheskoi genetike* (Moscow, 1970), p. 90; Fedorenko, *Vosproizvodstvo*, pp. 65–67.

83. Shlindman and Zvidrin'sh, *Izuchenie rozhdaemosti*, pp. 92, 96–97; *Demograficheskaia politika: Osushchestvlenie i sovershenstvovanie v usloviiakh razvitogo sotsializma* (Kiev, 1982), pp. 134, 160–67.

84. Calculated from *Zhenshchiny v SSSR*, p. 125; and VS, no. 7 (1974): 92. See also Godfrey S. Baldwin, *Population Projections by Age and Sex: For the Republics and*

Major Economic Regions of the USSR, 1970 to 2000 (U.S. Department of Commerce, Bureau of Census, Washington, D.C., 1979), pp. 92, 117.

85. Sadvokasova, "Rol' aborta," pp. 220–21.

86. Lekhter, "Opyt izucheniia," p. 25; Johnson, "Abortion in the Soviet Union," pp. 11–12, 14–16.

87. Coale, Anderson, and Harm, *Human Fertility*, pp. 30–40, 103; D. Peter Mazur, "Fertility Among Ethnic Groups in the USSR," *Demography* 4, no. 1 (1967): pp. 184–89; *Zhurnalist*, no. 5 (1978): 20–21.

88. Calculated from U.N., *Demographic Yearbook*, various issues; and *1970 Census*, vol. 2, p. 27.

89. Sadvokasova, "Rol' aborta," p. 212.

90. Gary S. Becker, *A Treatise on the Family* (Cambridge: Harvard University Press, 1981); Richard A. Easterlin, *Population, Labor Force and Long Swings in Economic Growth* (New York, 1968), and "Towards a Socio-Economic Theory of Fertility," in *Fertility and Family Planning: A World Review*, ed. S. J. Behrman, L. Corsa, and R. Freedman (Ann Arbor: University of Michigan, 1969), pp. 127–56; and Deborah S. Freedman and Arland Thornton, "Income and Fertility: The Elusive Relationship," *Demography* 19 (February 1982): 65–78.

91. Heer, "The Demographic Transition," pp. 236–38; K. H. Mehland, "Combatting Illegal Abortion in Socialist Countries in Europe," *World Medical Journal* 13 (1966): 87; Fedorenko, *Vosproizvodstvo*, p. 25; L. Chuiko, *Braki i razvody* (Moscow, 1975), tables 56–58; Heer, "Fertility and Female Work Status in the USSR," *Soviet Population Policy*, pp. 77–79; Cynthia Weber and Ann Goodman, "The Demographic Policy Debate in the USSR," *Population and Development Review* 7 (June 1981): 288; *Demograficheskie problemy sem'i* (Moscow, 1978), pp. 121–22, 176–78; and Henry W. Morton, "The Soviet Quest for Better Housing—An Impossible Dream?" in *Soviet Economy in a Time of Change*, vol. 1, pp. 795–800.

92. *Demograficheskie problemy sem'i*, pp. 118–20.

93. *Naselenie i trudovye resursy Kazakhstana* (Alma-Ata, 1979), pp. 60–61; Michal Rywkin, "Housing in Central Asia: The Uzbek Example," in *Soviet Housing and Urban Design* (Washington, D.C.: U.S. Department of Housing and Urban Development, 1980), pp. 39–42.

94. J. A. Newth, "Demographic Developments," in *The Soviet Union Since the Fall of Khrushchev* (New York: The Free Press, 1975), pp. 92–94; and Heer, "Fertility and Female Work," pp. 32–47, 190–205.

95. Heer, "Fertility and Female Work," p. 84. Calculated from *1970 Census*, vol. 2, p. 69, and vol. 4, p. 364; *Zhenshchiny v SSSR*, pp. 36–37; *Zhenshchiny Sovetskogo Turkmenistana* (Ashkhabad, 1976), pp. 70, 78–81.

96. Jones and Grupp, "Value Change," table 6.

97. The model is presented in Bernstam, "Demography of Soviet Ethnic Groups in World Perspective."

98. W. Brian Arthur, *The Analysis of Causal Linkages in Demographic Theory*

(Laxenburg, Austria: International Institute for Applied Systems Analysis, 1981), p. 18.

99. *Ekonomicheskaia gazeta*, no. 14 (April 1981): 4, no. 37 (September 1981): 3, and no. 36 (September 1982): 3, 9; *Pravda*, 26 August 1982; Weber and Goodman, "The Demographic Policy Debate," pp. 279–95; Robert J. McIntyre, "On Demographic Policy Debates in the USSR," *Population and Development Review* 8 (June 1982): 363–64.

100. A. Tkachek, "Zabota o zdorov'e naseleniia," *Naselenie i trudovye resursy RSFSR* (Moscow, 1982), p. 74.

101. Republican *Narkhoz*, various issues.

102. *Sotsial'noe strakhovanie i pensionnoe obespechenie v kolkhozakh*, ed. M. L. Zakharov (Moscow, 1966), p. 7; Alastair McAuley, *Economic Welfare in the Soviet Union: Poverty, Living Standards, and Inequality* (Madison: University of Wisconsin Press, 1979), pp. 18, 275

103. M. L. Zakharov and V. M. Piskov, *Sotsial'noe obespechenie i strakhovanie v SSSR* (Moscow, 1972), p. 270; and McAuley, *Economic Welfare*, pp. 109–10, 275.

104. W. Brian Arthur and Geoffrey McNicoll, "Samuelson, Population and Intergenerational Transfers," *International Economic Review* 19 (February 1978): 241–46; Mead Cain, "Perspectives on Family and Fertility in Developing Countries," *Population Studies* 36 (July 1982): 159–75, and "Fertility as Adjustment to Risk," *Population and Development Review* 9 (December 1983): 688–702; Norman B. Ryder, "The Character of Modern Fertility," *Annals of the American Academy of Political and Social Science*, no. 369 (January 1967): 26–36, and "Fertility and Family Structure," *Population Bulletin of the United States* 15 (1983), pp. 15–34; and John C. Caldwell, "The Mechanisms of Demographic Change in Historical Perspective," *Population Studies* 35 (March 1981): 1–27. The core of the Ryder-Caldwell hypothesis was assumed to be a commonplace in economic demography by the mid-1960s. See A. J. Coale, "Factors Associated with the Development of Low Fertility: A Historic Summary," in U.N., *World Population Conference, 1965* (New York: United Nations, 1967), vol. 2, pp. 205–9.

105. Valerie K. Oppenheimer, "The Easterlin Hypothesis: Another Aspect of the Echo to Consider," *Population and Development Review* 2 (September/December 1976): 433–57; *Narkhoz 1972*, pp. 516–17, 559–63; *Narkhoz 1983*, pp. 393–94, 409, 444.

106. John C. Caldwell, "Toward a Restatement of Demographic Transition Theory," *Population and Development Review* 2 (September/December 1976): 345; T. Paul Schultz, "Review of John C. Caldwell, *Theory of Fertility Decline*," *Population and Development Review* 9 (March 1983): 163.

107. Robert J. Willis, "Life Cycles, Institutions, and Population Growth: A Theory of the Equilibrium Interest Rate in an Overlapping Generations Model," Hoover Institution, Domestic Studies Program, *Working Papers in Economics* no. E-83-15, August 1983, pp. 84–88; see also Laurence J. Kotlikoff and Avia Spivak, "The Family as an Incomplete Annuities Market," *Journal of Political Economy* 89

(April 1981): 372–91; Donald O. Parsons, "On the Economics of Intergenerational Control," *Population and Development Review* 10 (March 1984): 41–54; Robert J. Willis, "The Old Age Security Hypothesis and Population Growth," *Demographic Behavior: Interdisciplinary Perspectives on Decision Making*, ed. T. Burch (Boulder, Colo.: Westview Press, 1980): 43–68; Victor R. Fuchs, *How We Live* (Cambridge, Mass.: Harvard University Press, 1983).

108. For a theoretical framework, see Paul A. Samuelson, "Pure Theory of Public Expenditure and Taxation," *Public Economics*, ed. J. Margolis and H. Guitton (New York: American Elsevier, 1969); and William H. Oakland, "Public Goods, Perfect Competition, and Underproduction," *Journal of Political Economy* 82 (September–October 1974): 927–39

109. Robert J. Barro, "Are Government Bonds Net Wealth?" *Journal of Political Economy* 82 (November–December 1974): 1095–1117.

Eastern Europe
Within the Soviet Empire

Milovan Djilas

When Stalin was "liberating" East European countries, he well knew that he was enlarging the Soviet empire. This was clearly visible not only in the manner in which some actual problems were solved but also in Stalin's manner of talking about it, despite attempts to play down both. This helped to calm the "socialist consciousness" of Stalin and his followers by reassuring them that they were dealing with a socialist and not a capitalist empire.

Even then, in 1945 or 1946, when dealing with Romania, the unscrupulous Vishinsky slipped when explaining the real relationship that was to exist between the Soviet Union and the "liberated" countries. In his talk with a Yugoslav diplomat, Ales Bebler, Vishinsky said, "What do the Western great powers want? They dominated long enough. It is our turn now."

Vishinsky distorted history in arguing that the Western powers had reigned over Eastern Europe. It is more correct to state that they exerted lesser or greater influence on certain East European countries, depending upon particular circumstances at specific times. Soon after the Soviet liberation of Eastern Europe, however, the real Soviet reign was felt not only by the "bourgeois nationalists" but also by many Communists who were the victims of "brotherly aid" from the "fatherland of socialism."

What really happened?

The lordship over Eastern Europe is organically related to the internal metamorphosis of the Soviet Union under Stalin and to Soviet foreign policy, which was already crystallized at the beginning of World War II. Although it is true that internal changes and certain modifications in foreign policy originated in Lenin's time, the final, qualitative changes took place under Stalin. These changes were characterized internally by the establishment of the party monopoly and externally by an expansionist foreign policy (division of Poland with Hitler in 1939; the occupation of the Baltic states; the attack on Finland).

The term *Stalinism* really means the merger of party monopoly and military imperialism. Stalin only rationalized and organized the spontaneous development of the "socialist revolution" toward a monopolistic structure and expansionism. To survive with its inheritance, the multinational and socially backward structure of the Russian empire, the revolution adopted, through Stalin's policies, the traditional tsarist political and bureaucratic centralism coupled with bureaucratic Great Russian chauvinism. This was greeted with even more enthusiasm because it took place along with the industrial transformation, which announced the arrival of happy days and greater global power for the Soviet Union. All these developments enabled the ruling strata to appropriate more enduring or, one can say, more permanent sources for their existence. Thus Soviet expansionism acquired its material and social foundation as well as its national inspiration.

The creation of Soviet Eastern Europe was in essence the continuation of these internal changes and foreign ambitions of the Soviet system. Stalin and the Soviet leadership conceived of the "liberation" of Eastern Europe not only as the expansion of their influence but also as the extension of controls by the Soviet party and policy apparatus. Most of the communist parties carried out their assigned functions more or less competently—with the exception of the Yugoslav Communist Party, which had created its own self-conscious strata through years of revolutionary struggle. I remember that, during the visit of the Yugoslav delegation to Moscow in the beginning of 1948, the Soviet leadership considered the idea of the formal unification of the East European countries with the Soviet Union. This was to take place after the reorganization of the USSR itself, thus enabling the unification of various East European countries with the Russian, Belorussian, and Ukrainian republics. This in turn led the Soviet Union to demand the "unification" of Yugoslavia, Bulgaria, and Albania.

In this process of submission for Eastern Europe, a specific role was ascribed—and still belongs—to Leninism as the ideology uniting Eastern Europe with the Soviet Union. But such a "spiritual tie" would have been fruitless if it had not been nurtured by the vital interests of national bureaucracies or, more precisely stated, by the totalitarian currents within those bureaucracies. Such elements are aware that they owe their existence, and the survival of their "socialism," to the Soviet Union.

Soviet domination in Eastern Europe is, therefore, the merger of the great Soviet state's expansionism and the monopolistic power of the national parties' bureaucracies. A formal merger of East European countries with the Soviet Union did not take place, because it might have caused worldwide protests in addition to the resistance that it would have aroused in particular countries. This was already clear in the increasing defiance of Stalin's overlordship by the Yugoslav party, not only by the "bourgeois" forces in Yugoslavia.

Under Stalin, relations between the Soviet Union and the East European states were similar to relations in oriental empires, if we assume that the Soviet system is a contemporary variant of "Oriental despotism." The common denominators of such systems are a godlike monarch or leader and the abolition of laws regulating relations between states, including commodity exchange.

Eastern Europe's indirect political dependence and its economic exploitation through political pressure, characteristic of the Stalin period, became senseless and unbearable the moment Stalin's personality cult was condemned in the Soviet Union itself. This forced the Soviet system, due to its own needs, to open itself to the outside world. The Soviet bureaucracy, however, was willing to change its relations with East European countries only after their uprisings and protests, the bloodiest and the most "educational" of which was the Hungarian uprising of 1956. But, even then, Khrushchev's leadership did not renounce the imperial hegemony. Instead, the hegemony was adapted to changing circumstances, including the transformation of Stalinist tyranny into Khrushchevian oligarchy. With the passing of Stalin the period of "telephone ordering" ended and the period of "consultations" of the Soviet center with subordinate East European governments began. Market prices between the Soviet state and subordinate East European governments gradually shifted to an approximation of world market prices. East European states evolved under Khrushchev and Brezhnev from the form of vassal satellites into individual but dependent members of a "community" subservient to the imperial center.

Thus began the process of differentiation of the East European countries. At the end of the 1960s, the economic and social structures of East European countries began more visibly to differ from one another, although all of them rigidly retain essential monolithic characteristics. Each in its own way—according to past heritage and the possibilities of its "own" party bureaucracy—develops the economy and rediscovers more efficient forms, but at the same time each retains the one-party system and control over the specific trends of national life.

The preservation of that monopolistic power of the Communist Party is the exact limit of the autonomy of each of those countries. Wherever tendencies emerged, even within some Communist parties, to cross over that magic border of weakening the party monopoly of power, the Soviet government intervened, if necessary by armed force (as in Hungary in 1956 and Czechoslovakia in 1968). Soviet interventions, of course, satisfied the wishes and interests of totalitarian forces within national Communist parties: "socialist solidarity" is mutual, as the term "limited sovereignty" is not only forced upon those countries but is also "voluntarily" accepted.

The Soviet Union allows—typical for a military empire—administrative and cultural autonomy. It allows East European countries economic and other sorts of initiatives in their relations with other countries. But all those initiatives have their limit: there must not be any overstepping that could threaten the character of party supremacy, that is, the unbreakable adherence to the Soviet bloc.

It should be mentioned that countries outside the Warsaw Pact, like Cuba and Vietnam, enjoy even greater autonomy: the leadership and Communist parties of those countries are dependent upon the Soviet Union mostly because of their own economic and strategic weaknesses. They make up for it by the spreading of their own and pro-Soviet "revolutionary" influence, which they cannot manage independently. This reveals, by the way, the very great flexibility and variability in an otherwise rigid and monolithic Soviet empire when engaged in spreading and strengthening its influence in the world.

Differences between East European countries over a period of time have become so great that they are not just superficial differences, visible at first glance. Their degree of dependence upon the Soviet Union is also quite different, despite the limitations imposed on all of them.

Romania is the most independent. This does not mean that it is more democratic than other East European states: on the contrary. The evolution of the party monopoly toward the personal and family dictatorship of Ceauşescu made Romania more independent. That independence was more easily possible because the system in Romania is a more rigid copy of the Soviet model: agriculture is collectivized, industrialization is based upon heavy industry, political-ideological control is total. Worried about his regime's survival, Ceauşescu refused to participate in the Warsaw Pact intervention in Czechoslovakia in 1968. But he was more rigorous in criticism of Solidarity and "antisocialist" forces in Poland. Ceauşescu has often demonstrated his independence—in order quickly to reconfirm his loyalty to the Warsaw Pact and Marxism-Leninism. He took a stand against atomic weapons in Europe, but soon expressed his understanding for the emplacement of Soviet SS-20 missiles directed at European cities. Romanian foreign policy seesaws between demagogy and fear, between promise and advantage. The Soviet Union cannot be pleased with such Romanian policy. But the Soviet leadership has realistically calculated that there are no reasons for military intervention in Romania. The oppressive internal order is a sufficient guarantee that Romania will remain within the imperial and ideological framework of the Soviet Union.

Bulgaria is the most faithful ally and most consistent pupil of the Soviet Union. The Bulgarian leadership works toward more complete integration of its country within the Soviet empire, beyond even the wishes of the Soviet leadership. The Bulgarian leadership sees such integration with the USSR as the basis for the realization of its hegemonistic pretensions. Bulgaria is independent only in its claims toward its neighbors—primarily Yugoslavia. This is similar to the role that Vietnam in Southeast Asia and Cuba in Latin America play for the Soviet Union. Bulgaria, with its national claims, enables the Soviet Union to penetrate the Balkans and subvert peace and stability there. In Bulgaria almost everything is more or less nationalized. Bulgaria is the most complete copy of the Soviet model. This is confirmed even by the sophisticated suppression of the cultural spirit of this proud and stubborn people. There are no Soviet troops in Bulgaria—one may say that Bulgaria is self-occupied. Bulgarian party leader Todor Zhivkov is the creator of the so-called East European thesis of "realistic socialism" as the only possible (and already realized) model. But one can observe in Bulgaria during the past few years noticeable tendencies toward economic changes and national affirmation. The tendency to carry out reform is an expression of economic difficulties; to lessen the impact of nationalist reawakening, the party tries to redirect nationalist feeling toward the glorious past and toward the Soviet Union as the "double liberator" (from the Turks in 1877 and from the monarchy and bourgeoisie in 1944) and the protector of Bulgarian territorial pretensions.

Czechoslovak relations with the USSR, as well as conditions in Czechoslovakia, are too well known to need detailed comment. After the Soviet military intervention in 1968, Czechoslovakia returned to total satellite dependence. The Czechoslovak theorists went furthest among satellite states to prove their vassalage to the Soviet Union. They invented a theory about the emergence of a common "socialist nation" following the Soviet intervention of 1968. They also forgot it quickly, since Soviet Russian expansionists did not show an inclination to renounce their ideological-national advantages. Still, Czechoslovakia became the loud-speaker for Soviet intentions and Soviet threats. Czechoslovakia failed in the long run to escape into "goulash socialism"; even Czechoslovakia, despite its highly developed technology, has fallen back into ineffectiveness and wastefulness. There is no doubt, however, that the Czech and Slovak intelligentsia, political and cultural, has preserved the spirit of independence and democracy.

East Germany is probably the country that the Soviet Union controls most completely, because it was occupied by Soviet troops after World War II. It also has great strategic importance for the USSR. East Germany, however, is also the country with the most orderly economy of the Soviet type. This advanced stage was achieved through some cooperation between East Germany and West Germany, as well as through an inherent sense for high-quality productivity and organization. East Germany became—probably because it is the most subservient—the most active assistant of Soviet expansionism in arms supply and the provision of "advisers" to revolutionary pro-Soviet regimes in Africa and the Middle East. East German ideologues developed an absurd theory about two German nations—socialist and capitalist. That theory was soon abandoned, since it became impractical during more active cooperation with the capitalist West German nation.

Hungary and Poland are the countries that attained the greatest autonomy within the Soviet bloc. That autonomy is the consequence of people's uprisings and spiritual resistance. But Hungarian autonomy and Polish autonomy—I refer to Polish autonomy before the introduction of martial law in December 1981—are different. Hungarian autonomy is primarily expressed in the emergence of national and intellectual independence. By the introduction of a partial market economy, that is, giving managers greater independence and encouraging the private "small economy," Hungary succeeded in circumventing the "gray planning economy" to achieve relative prosperity and to open itself to the world market. Contrary to such policy, Poland mindlessly incurred debts while continuing industrialization and preserving bureaucratic management. This led to the economic collapse in which the bureaucracy has been enmeshed. This also happened because the communist theorists believed that such a crisis, natural for capitalism, is impossible in socialism. Differences between Hungarian and Polish foreign policies are less visible. Poland did express greater initiative in expanding its ties with countries outside the Soviet bloc, but was careful not to overstep the borders of the Soviet sphere of interest.

Poland is the only East European country that succeeded in giving birth to an authentic and independent labor movement. At the same time solidarity became a point around which national and political activities could rally. Polish workers cast away all Leninist values and teachings. The corrupt and inefficient ruling Communist Party disintegrated under the onslaught of the working class. The perspective of an independent Polish state emerged. That new Polish state would base its relations with the Soviet Union upon geopolitical realities, not upon ideological or state subordination to the Soviet Union. But—under Soviet pressure and with active Soviet participation—that national and democratic process was halted in Poland. The party junta introduced martial law—a substitute for Soviet intervention. The stifling of the democratic movement in Poland meant at the same time the stifling of Polish desire for equality between states. This act led to the extinguishing of hopes, scattering illusions of détente that aimed at opening the Soviet system into a "rational," gradual, Soviet retreat from its imperial domination in Eastern Europe. This development created a new situation in Poland as well as in Europe. Poles have been thrown into a long-lasting struggle for liberation, and Europe into instability and rearmament.

Rebellions and resistance in East European countries can be traced to many sources: history, culture, economics, religion, nationality, and level of development. The last two sources of dissatisfaction—nationality and level of development—seem to me the most important at present, especially because they are impossible to dismiss. I do not separate these two forces from the others, neither do I underestimate the others; under specific conditions, the other sources can play even more important roles.

Communists, and especially the Soviet imperial Communists, simply are not capable of understanding the essence of the term *nation* and are thus unable to comprehend the determination and firmness of national movements. That spiritual blindness stems from an ideological prejudice: the belief that with the disappearance of capitalism and capitalists—that is, with the vanishing of "material causes"—national rivalries also vanish.

But peoples and nations are spontaneous creations, older than capitalism. And because of that they possess particularness—in spiritual, ethnic, historic, economic, and other characteristics. Nations also constantly gravitate toward a specific place in the world to preserve and strengthen their particularness. The Soviet leaders know from personal experience that "national prejudices" are hardy and long-lasting. But from such an experience—the tsarist and multinational state—they know that, through a combination of concessions and repression, those prejudices can also be curbed. But such methods are neither fruitful nor do they provide stability in Eastern Europe, because East European nations already possess ancient national consciousnesses. East European nations already had their place in Europe. The Soviet Union attempts to limit them, turn them back, by incorporating them into the Soviet imperial sphere. East European nations cannot accept that for a simple reason—it allows the Soviets to control their lives. Thus unrest and resistance are inevitable—and, if not possible from other sources, then at least in the ranks of East European national Communists themselves.

An irremovable misfortune faces Soviet leaders, making it impossible for them to control Eastern Europe: namely, the fact that East European countries were and are culturally and economically more developed than the Soviet Union. Even Romania and Bulgaria—not to mention others—were closer than Russia to the European standard of living, and Czechoslovakia was even above it. Western states' imperialism and colonialism were directed toward undeveloped areas, and exploitation also brought technical progress. In Eastern Europe today one finds the opposite case: there ideology—that is, naked force—complements the weakness and backwardness of the conqueror.

The economic relations of the Soviet Union and Eastern Europe passed through two phases—Stalinist and post-Stalinist. The first, Stalinist phase was characterized—as I have already stated—by Soviet attempts to exploit and integrate subservient states into the empire through brutal political pressure. In that period there was created, at Soviet initiative, the Council for Mutual Economic Cooperation (Comecon), which, in contrast to the European Economic Community (EEC), was not founded upon the free market but upon bureaucratic consultation.

In the Stalin era, the Soviet Union dictated conditions of trade as it pleased. But rebellions and resistance in Eastern Europe, coupled with Soviet economic weaknesses during and after Stalin's passing, changed those relations in many ways. The second phase began with Khrushchev's ascent to power. Economic factors began to play a greater role. But the political pressure did not cease; nor did the laws of supply and demand become prevalent. Political pressure is now expressed by giving priority to the Soviet Union's needs, that is, by demanding ideological, Leninist unity with the Soviet economy. Supply and demand are modified by the dominant role of bureaucratic mechanisms.

Because of unrest in Eastern Europe, the Soviet Union was forced to allow a certain autonomy to East European governments and, in economic life, to satisfy certain demands of those countries and to allow them a certain amount of intercourse with the outside world, primarily the West.

But the initial Stalinist goal of the Soviet Union did not change. The maneuvering toward fulfilling that goal simply became more realistic, plotted over a longer period of time. Thus, one may conclude that the Soviet Union failed to integrate East European economies into its own economic mechanism but succeeded in making those economies dependent on its own significant measure, especially in regard to raw materials.

Such relations, and such results, are doubtless the consequence of the current Soviet orientation, but are also the consequence of internal, political, and economic conditions in the East European countries. European regimes, one-party Leninist states in nature, are dependent upon the Soviet Union for their survival. Their economies, like industrial feudalism, are doomed to low productivity and poor quality.

On top of that, East European countries, to greater or lesser degrees, have fallen into crisis and huge debts to the West and the Soviet Union. These present crises illustrate most clearly the economic relations between the Soviet Union and East European countries. The Soviet government utilizes the difficulties of those countries in order to deepen and strengthen their dependence upon the USSR.

Romanian debts in 1980—according to *Le Monde diplomatique* of February 1982—increased to $11–12 billion, while its production increased only 2.5 percent instead of the planned 8.8 percent. These and other economic difficulties forced Romania not only toward closer cooperation with Comecon, but also toward a less independent foreign policy. According to Belgrade *NIN* (December 13, 1981), in the past, Romania was the East European country that was least involved in cooperation with Comecon. Its trade with Comecon had declined from 70 percent to 46 percent. But now Romania belongs to the Joint Investment Bank and participates in joint planning to develop exploitation of raw materials. After the outbreak of the war between Iran and Iraq, Romania had to find another source to satisfy 60 percent of its oil imports. Romania asked the USSR for help; it received a special shipment of 1.4 million tons of oil from the USSR in 1979. Ceauşescu complained in vain on November 27, 1981: "I proposed the meeting of the heads of the [Soviet bloc] parties . . . but was told that fraternal parties are prevented from doing so, since they have other important preoccupations. But in our view, there could be no more important problems for the communist parties than cooperation in COMECON."

According to Frank Lipsius (*International Herald Tribune*, February 17, 1982), in 1980 the East European countries borrowed $3.7 billion from the West and $23 billion from the USSR. The Czech premier complained about the Soviet oil price increase. Hungary was forced to decrease its export of goods to the West to supply Soviet needs, thus paying for the import of raw materials from the Soviet Union. It is true that Hungary applied for admission to the International Monetary Fund (IMF) and the World Bank. According to Lipsius, this was done as a fall-back position in case the "Soviet economic umbrella begins to leak." Now, after the declaration of martial law in Poland, Hungary is also reorienting itself toward strengthening trade with the USSR.

Sanctions against Poland after the reimposition of martial law also weakened efforts to achieve greater economic independence from the Soviet Union, according to Lipsius. No doubt those difficulties are also the result of other factors, such as overindebtedness to the West and lack of the monetary means to purchase raw materials. But the Soviet Union itself gave Poland, by means of special shipments, badly needed raw materials that made it even more dependent upon the USSR. According to Hedrick Smith (*International Herald Tribune*, March 18, 1982), the Soviets granted Poland around $1 billion worth of import credits in 1981. Smith cites Vanous, who calculated that in 1981 Poland received around $4 billion in imports from the Soviet Union, on top of another $4 billion surplus that the USSR had in trade with Poland that year. (Soviet exports to Poland were $6 billion; Polish exports to the USSR, $2 billion.)

East European members of Comecon attempted to increase the prices of their consumer goods in trade exchanges with the USSR, but they failed to accomplish that goal. Soviet price increases for raw materials sold to Eastern Europe are proportionally greater than the East European price increases for consumer goods sold to the Soviet Union. This is the result of the low quality of East European consumer goods as well as the Soviet "lack of understanding." Marie Lavigne stated in *Le Monde diplomatique* in January 1982 that East European states were forced to set aside part of their investment funds (normally used for production) for the acquisition of raw materials from the Soviet Union. In addition, the Soviet Union pays for its purchases from East European states in nonconvertible rubles, but sells significant amounts of its raw materials for hard currency—dollars. Thus the Soviet Union holds those countries economic hostage and stifles their trade with the West.

The dependence of the East European countries upon Soviet raw materials and markets is rising sharply. And, despite Comecon dif-ficulties—failure to increase productive cooperation or to create a common market, inability to realize convertibility of the ruble as a common currency—one can conclude that the strategic Stalinist plan for the economic subservience and economic dependence of East European countries has succeeded to a significant degree. But that success of Soviet hegemonists is pregnant with troubles: in some ways, it slowed down, and in other fields it almost stopped, development of the internal potential of the East European peoples.

One can draw the following conclusion about the future of the East European countries: it is uncertain for the simple reason that it is tied to and dependent upon internal developments in the Soviet Union. More precisely stated, as long as the monopolistic and expansionistic domination by the party bureaucracy in the Soviet Union exists, the East European countries will have no chance to break away from the Soviet imperial sphere—that is, to achieve genuine independence.

This is all true. But it is not so simple as it sounds.

The Soviet bureaucracy long ago ceased caring or worrying about whether persecution in the USSR or interventions in East European countries would cause a rift in the world communist movement. But precisely because imperial interests prevailed over ideological ones, the Soviet leadership must be sensitive, calculating, and mindful of the reaction of the other superpower, the United States, and of Western Europe and other nations. Soviet doubts are not the ideological but the calculating kind—pragmatic ones. They calculate which step pays more than the other, what reactions will be caused by this or that intervention, whether the strengths or weaknesses of eventual adversaries are precisely measured. And all this means that resistance and unrest in Eastern Europe depend not only on internal conditions in the USSR but also on Soviet global relations, primarily Soviet relations with the West and China. In other words, if all those global relations suddenly became unfavorable for the Soviet Union—which does not seem to be the case today—and if the Soviets were to find that their domination and intervention in Eastern Europe "does not pay," the likelihood of the East European countries freeing themselves from Soviet dominance would become more realistic. The chances of East European countries would become even more realistic if radical internal changes began to take place within the Soviet Union—this also does not seem possible—and if those changes brought to the surface democratic forces that would be aware that continuation of expansionism does not pay.

Unfortunately, the fact remains that the future of the East European countries is dependent upon global developments and, even more so, on developments within the Soviet Union. This is true not only of the East European countries that belong to Comecon but also of those other East European countries that—like Yugoslavia and Albania—succeeded in breaking from the Soviet imperial sphere.

Thus the future appears to be dark, because there are no forces within the Soviet Union capable of changing the course of internal development in the direction of a democratic system, nor is the external world sufficiently united and strong to force the Soviet bureaucracy to renounce domination over Eastern Europe. Moreover, recently, despite the economic inefficiency of the Soviet system, chances for change in the Soviet Union have declined rather than increased. Also, Soviet global expansionism and domination over Eastern Europe have increased. The interventions in Afghanistan and Poland are the most drastic examples. This only reconfirms that the ideological Marxist-Leninist bureaucracy, because of its closed social structure, is immune to any more fundamental changes and is a fertile ground for schemes that encourage external expansionism.

But, despite all this, not everything is so gloomy in Eastern Europe.

East European countries—as has already been pointed out—differ more and more: they acquire their natural forms, their real specificity. Life in those countries—in some more slowly than others, but no doubt in all of them—conquers new areas and undermines the vassalage due to monopolistic bureaucracy. These countries, their national and democratic forces, are getting ready, if they are not yet ready, for the day when they will "find their soul." Past rebellions and unrest were not in vain. They influenced consciences enormously and paved the way for better conditions, more conducive to change. East European nations are not only capable of surviving; they are already living their own lives, even if they are a bit suppressed.

Although pressured by the bureaucratic military empire, East European countries remain part of Europe and the contemporary world. This is a world that is problematic, uncertain, and dangerous. But this present world is in many ways better than the previous one. If in this world East European countries cannot soon win complete victory, they still can struggle in the direction of the final goal of independence with more or less success.

Nationalism in the USSR and Its Implications for the World

Donald W. Treadgold

The problems of Soviet nationalism are of immense importance for Soviet relations with other nations, for several ideological movements of worldwide scope, and for the policy of the United States and its West European allies vis-à-vis the Soviet Union. Unfortunately there is a good deal of confusion about the subject and much argument, some of it bitter indeed. This paper will endeavor to disentangle certain aspects of the problem and draw cautious conclusions.

Nationalism, however defined, looms as a factor in international relations that is quite different for the Russians and for the Soviet minorities (bearing in mind that the Russians or, more precisely, Great Russians, are on the verge of ceasing to be the majority). A number of authorities refuse to distinguish in any clear manner or with any great emphasis between Russian nationalism and the interests of the Soviet regime. But all, or almost all, find it easy to perceive the nationalism of the minorities and to analyze it as a danger to the regime.

Thus Seweryn Bialer, when he declares that "the crucial characteristic of the Soviet Union today is the deeply conservative and actively nationalistic nature of state and society," aside from suggesting an uneasy match of presumably passive conservatism and "active" nationalism, seems to dismiss the possibility that nationalism in the USSR today might be mainly a threat to the system rather than the chief characteristic of it.[1]

Perhaps the best way to approach the issue is by way of the minorities. And within the lengthy roster of minorities, perhaps the least known in the West (at any rate among the sizable groups) is the Muslims, most of whom are Turkic-speaking—or let us boldly call them simply ethnically Turkish. In 1971 Alexandre Bennigsen declared that, if current trends continued, by the year 2000 the USSR would have a Turkic and Muslim majority.[2] Since then the prospect has become better known in the West and is certainly very much on the minds of the Soviet rulers.

The American preparation for understanding events in Soviet Muslim regions is not extensive, as it was not adequate for understanding the recent Iranian events, before or after they happened. We know that at the highest levels of the federal government the rise to power of the Ayatollah Khomeini and his mullahs led to the unabashed posing of the question, "What is this Islam *thing?*"[3] There was an assumption that secularization, once under way, could not be reversed; and, if the inextricable closeness of religion and ethnicity in Islam was understood, it was thought that such attitudes were fast receding. There was, in the words of Leonard Schapiro, a belief in a "Manichean world of progress versus reaction, of light and darkness, in which progress will win."[4] Even elementary knowledge was apt to be confined to the so-called titular nationalities of the fifteen republics—that is, to the ethnic groups that give their names to the official designation of those regions—with one or two exceptions, such as the Jews.

Even the names are problematical. Uzbek, Kirgiz, Turkmen, Kazakh, and Tadzhik are not designations of ancient, continuous ethnic entities. For example, Tadzhik was at first the term used by pagan Turks for Muslims, irrespective of whether they were Arabs or Iranians, and later it was confined to Iranians who retained their language, while the Iranians of Turkestan came to be called Sarts as they became Turkicized. The term Sart was first used only for Iranians, then for Iranians and Turks, and finally only for Turks. The Uzbeks took their name from the Mongol potentate of the Golden Horde in the mid-fourteenth century. The Kazakhs detached themselves from the Uzbeks but for a time were called Kirgiz, and the people today called Kirgiz were once termed Kara-Kirgiz.[5]

Of course the makers of Soviet nationalities policy could not have created ethnic continuity where none existed. The point is that the identity of the Central Asians was above all linked with their Muslim religion and was secondarily discernible linguistically as Turkic or Iranian. At first Moscow wished to reduce sharply both elements in their consciousness, since the state was more concerned about the impact of religious and linguistic kinship with peoples across the border than the possibility of imparting socialism to those same peoples. It is not difficult to indict the establishment of the five republics for perverseness and absurdity; however, it is not easy to say what ought to have been done instead. The best students of Soviet Islam seem to paint a picture somewhat as follows: most Soviet Muslims are Sunnis, almost all of whom are of the Hanafi rite (except for the Dagestanis who follow the Shafi'i rite); but of the 50 million or so Muslims in the USSR about 3 million are Shi'ites, mainly the Azeris. The Sunni-Shi'ite antagonism, in our day deepened and embittered by the course of the Iranian revolution, is one factor. A second is the difference between those among whom Islam was most ancient and deep, especially the Turkestanis, the Volga Tatars, and the Azeris, and those converted within the last two centuries and only lightly Islamicized, such as the nomad Kazakhs and Kirgiz and some Caucasian mountain peoples.

The Russians tried to exploit such differences in the nineteenth century, especially by attempts to set the Kazakhs against their settled neighbors to the south (or, at a minimum, the tsarist state tried to separate the two and to draw the nomads of the north closer to the Russians). In this the Russians found some support among such indigenous leaders as Chokan Velikhanov and Ibray Altynsaryn. The religious differences overlapped with those between the settled and nomadic peoples (the Sarts versus the northern Central Asians). Doubtless it is true that only a few intellectuals thought of themselves as belonging to a common culture that was ethnically Arab-Turkic-Iranian and religiously Islamic.[6] It is probably also true that most thought in terms of loyalties to the clan or tribe on the one hand and religion on the other, without worrying overmuch about their ethnic identity, let alone their degree of kinship with the distant Arabs or the closer Persians and Turks.

This complex network of feelings and facts is simplicity itself, however, beside the ethnic composition of some of the particular regions. Foremost in startling heterogeneity is the North Caucasus, containing some 50 out of the somewhat over 200 nationalities (by a common reckoning) of the Soviet Union. Here tribes cut across nationalities, so that, for example, a Kazakh from the Nayman tribe considered himself a kinsman of a Nogay from the Nayman tribe but not of a Kazakh from a different tribe.[7] A linguistic classification yields something like the following: the Caucasic group has the Kartvelian (mainly Georgian), Abasgo-Kerketian, and Checheno-Dagestani subdivisions; there are several Turkic peoples (Azeri and others); and Indo-European speakers include scattered (though of course influential) Russians and other Eastern Slavs, some small Iranian groups, and the Armenian nucleus. Before the revolution the notion of a distinct nationality was, according to a recent student of the area, alien to many of these peoples, having been imported by Russian and other European outsiders. Self-description was apt to start with geography—the valley or village of the family, clan, or tribe concerned.[8] (Such modes of identification have been observed, to be sure, in premodern European peasants and other traditional types who distinguished themselves from those who lived over the hill, and beyond that were unable to classify neighbors and uninterested in doing so.) There was, however, a sense of being a Caucasian and mountaineer, and all peoples of the North Caucasus possessed the same male costume. Five or six of them were Christian (Abkhaz, Mingrelians, Svanetians, Udi, South Ossetians, Batsbi); the remainder were Muslim, and Wixman declares that a Muslim North Caucasian nationality was emerging.[9] South of the Caucasian ridge were the Muslim Azeris and two Christian nationalities, the Georgians and Armenians, that at the same time must be considered nations—indeed, were nations, and civilized ones, roughly seven centuries before the Russians were such.

Moving to the Soviets' western border, one finds, from south to north, six peoples. First come the Romanians of the Moldavian republic, whose date for the acceptance of Christianity and civilization is much in dispute, but whose refusal to acknowledge that Russians are more civilized than they is clear. Next are the Ukrainians and Belorussians, who constitute a quarter of the Soviet population and share the same religious and cultural heritage as the Russians, although they make valid claims to have differing political and social backgrounds. Finally, there are the three Baltic peoples, and again things are not simple. The Lithuanians were partners in history with the Poles since the fourteenth century and are linked with the West through their Roman Catholic religion. The Latvians lived for seven centuries under the rule of Germans who did not necessarily think in ethnic terms (they were Christian Crusaders who became landowners), finally in the Russian empire; the Latvians adopted the Protestant religion of their German lords. The Latvians spoke a tongue belonging to the Baltic family (as did the Lithuanians). The Estonians lived under Germans and became Protestants as did the Latvians, but Estonians spoke a Uralic language related to that of the Finns across the gulf but not to that of any of their neighbors. In this survey one ends with the capital of Estonia, Tallinn, the most advanced and the most Western of all Soviet cities.

It is not enough, to be sure, to state the present circumstances. The Soviet authorities no doubt know them well, though the choice may have been made to acknowledge them only in part, in sharply distorted form, or not at all. The regime, however, is committed to the belief that history is on its side. It can even point to evidence that seems to support the view: take simply the fact of the spread of communism from the USSR to include many other countries—without losing a single one. Therefore the trends are carefully studied. Some of them indicate that problems occasioned by the nationalities will diminish, others that they will increase.

To reverse the order just followed, the prospects for the Baltic nationalities do not seem bright. The 1979 census reported that Estonians made up 65 percent of the population of their republic, Latvians 54 percent of theirs. Both figures had fallen substantially since 1959. In contrast, the Lithuanians constitute 80 percent of the Lithuanian Soviet Socialist Republic (SSR), a figure that has held steady within a percentage point since 1959. But all three have few fellow countrymen abroad, no ethnically related neighbors interested in their fate (except for Estonia, which has had direct ferry service to Finland since 1965; but Finland is firmly committed not to disturb the USSR), and no particular sign of concern on the part of coreligionists abroad. Roman Catholics outside Lithuania may have some leverage regarding Soviet treatment of the church there, but Rome is presently preoccupied with Poland, constrained by developments in many other parts of the world to be cautious, and, as an authoritative recent statement puts it, the bolder Lithuanian Catholics "may be expecting more than the Vatican can deliver."[10] In Lithuania guerrillas continued operating until about the time of Stalin's death; there are none today. There is, accordingly, little that one can hope for by way of lessening pressure on the Baltic states.

Next to nothing has been heard of in the West from Belorussian particularists; in the Ukraine the same alternation of carrot and stick has prevailed for several years and seems to continue in matters affecting the use of the Ukrainian language or articulation of Ukrainian identity. The few dissidents to raise such issues, like Ivan Dziuba and Viacheslav Chornovil, were arrested or silenced in the late 1960s. Possibly the rise of persons whose names are identifiably Ukrainian into the higher ranks of Soviet officialdom has assuaged some feelings. Gradually the existence of Ukrainian communities of some size has become known to the rest of the population of the United States and, even more, of Canada. But if foreign pressure influenced any of the swings toward less repression noted during the last few years, it is scarcely discernible.

Little need be said here about Moldavians, Georgians, or Armenians. Of the first two Americans know next to nothing. The Romanians across the Soviet frontier are much interested in the contrived and unhappy situation of the Moldavian SSR, but their independent course in foreign policy is about the most they can be expected to do to make things uncomfortable for Moscow. No people outside the USSR is related to the Georgians in any way known to scholars, and most Christians in North

America know Georgia only as the home state of men such as Jimmy Carter. The Armenians have a somewhat higher profile—alas, some of that resulting from the reputation being acquired by Armenian terrorists who systematically murder Turkish officials. U.S. policy has paid no discernible attention to Armenia since Woodrow Wilson fleetingly interested himself in its welfare at the end of World War I, and it is unlikely to do so in the foreseeable future.

When we reach (once again) the Muslims, however, the picture becomes brighter for the minority (or minorities), darker for Moscow. There are some 50 million Soviet Muslims. Beyond Soviet borders there are more than 100 million Turco-Iranians, that is to say, peoples of the Muslim world who have ethnic brethren inside the USSR. And there are over 700 million Muslims worldwide, according to a recent attempt at estimating religious believers. Can Soviet Muslims be used to penetrate the regions of their fellow ethnics or coreligionists? Or instead will the latter be more likely to sway the Uzbeks and Tadzhiks?

Plainly the question concerns Soviet leaders and authoritative spokesmen. The issue of the revival of Islam and its possible tendency to oppose communism along with other secularizing movements—or above all others—is frequently mentioned.[11] The Soviets are patiently awaiting the collapse of the rule of the Ayatollah Khomeini's picked reactionary mullahs in Iran; they count on being able to exploit the resulting crisis. Their patience may yet be rewarded, but it is possible that the clerical regime in Teheran might first turn to systematically wiping out the far left. And whatever happens in Iran, there is Saudi Arabia, whose royal family seems irretrievably anti-Soviet, and Libya, whose dictator is quite pro-Soviet—both very rich, serious about religion, and far from simply following the enlightened self-interest of Western manuals of government. Will some modernizing or sharply antimodernizing current of Islam break through the dike that the Soviet frontier is supposed to provide? Despite an often cool reception, Moscow sends Central Asian mullahs traveling constantly among Muslim capitals with their message of peace and religious freedom for Islam, Soviet style. Propaganda does what propaganda can do by way of depicting Soviet achievements in Muslim-majority areas. And yet all this may not provide reliable insurance.

Soviet Muslims may cross the frontier from north to south, but the continuing experience of the war in Afghanistan leaves some doubt about the results, actual and potential. Army units that included substantial numbers of Central Asians were sent in with the invasion of December 1979. As early as February 1980, however, the Soviet command started to pull out units that were partly or wholly Central Asian and replaced them with partly Slavic ones.[12] At the same time Central Asian civilians employed in Afghan governmental posts were replaced by Russians or East Germans. Evidently contact between the Afghans and Soviet Muslims was regarded as a dangerous or pernicious influence, on one or the other or perhaps both; each group might learn facts or be exposed to attitudes that could not advance the purposes of the invasion. To be sure, not all Afghans reacted similarly to their northern neighbors. Pushtuns despised the Soviet Turks, whereas the non-Pushtuns (Tadzhiks, Turks, and Hazaras) of Afghanistan were apt to be overly friendly. Whether the Soviet commanders understood all these differences before the invasion or even after the fighting had gone on for a time remains unclear. That they soon wished to take no further chances is plain enough.

The degree of intellectual freedom enjoyed during any period in Afghanistan, Iran, Pakistan, India, or this or that Arab country may not be radically greater than in the USSR. But, in sharp contrast to all those states (except Afghanistan since the imposition of communist rule), the Soviet Union has one significant characteristic of interest to Muslims: its government is on record as committed to hastening the end of all religion and certainly of Islam in Central Asia, and it has followed a number of policies calculated to hamper Islam, reduce its influence, and prevent its growth. Soviet Muslims abroad can falsely argue or imply that there is freedom of religion in their republics and may accurately describe certain Soviet achievements. Muslims from abroad who visit the USSR can be misled, but ultimately not deceived, about both sides of the matter. According to Alexandre Bennigsen, the rule is that only Slavs are used to put down Muslim unrest in the USSR, and he may well be right; but, since the formation of the Soviet Union, there had been no occasion to deal with Muslim risings *outside* the USSR's borders until the Afghan affair. It is striking that Russian officers reportedly told their Muslim soldiers that the people they were fighting in Afghanistan were pagans, not Muslims.[13] The effectiveness of that lie is difficult to establish.

All of this suggests that the problems of Soviet Islam are by no means resolved, contained, or likely to diminish. Whatever the religious and political forces at work in the Middle East north or south of the Soviet border, demography implacably proceeds to make matters worse for Moscow. Let us take the single figure of the child-woman ratio, whose relation to population growth needs no lengthy explanation. Here are a few cases of that figure among certain national groups:[14]

	Children Per *Thousand Women*
Russians	863
Ukrainians	710
Belorussians	836

United States	1,114
Turkmen	1,809
Uzbeks	1,878
Kirgiz	1,885
Kazakhs	1,896
Chechens	2,204

The Russian ratio is the same as French, one of the lowest in the world; the Chechens have the highest in the world. No exhortations, family planning policies, or five-year plans are likely to alter appreciably the inexorable prospect sketched by these few numbers.

When Seweryn Bialer speaks of the "nationalistic nature" of the Soviet Union, he must have in mind some variety or modification of Russian nationalism. The question then arises, can Soviet "nationalism" (if nationalism can exist without ethnicity) and Russian nationalism be equated, harmonized, or in some way harnessed in tandem? A nationalism must be based on a nationality. Stalin's four criteria for a nationality were territorial unity, language, history, and psychological makeup. They will do. Of course, the Russians have characteristics corresponding to all four. The question is not whether the Russians have or have had a nationality and nationalism, but whether that Russian nationalism is the same as Soviet consciousness. The answer to the last question does not seem difficult: no. The two cannot be the same. From the tenth century or earlier, the historically formed Russian nationality was shaped by the religious forces of Orthodox Christianity. Its literature and its thought, its ethical outlook and its proverbs, are suffused with religion. Lenin and Stalin could not afford to make peace, historically speaking, with Saints Boris and Gleb, Stephen of Perm, Nil of the Sora, Sergius of Radonezh, Tikhon Zadonsky, Serafim of Sarov, or Father John of Kronstadt—not to mention Dostoevsky, Tiutchev, Leskov, and Vladimir Soloviev. Neither could Brezhnev, Andropov, Chernenko, or their successors. There is religion in the background of all peoples, but not necessarily in equal measure in both high and low culture; the Chinese seem to have less and the Russians more than many others. There is a Russian national tradition that leads much more in the direction of Pasternak and Solzhenitsyn than of Suslov and Brezhnev. The honest Communist will lament the fact but will not deny it. That tradition need not be labeled nationalist, and certainly for many centuries it predated anything that could be called nationalism outside or inside Russia. It underlies what Alexander Solzhenitsyn has recently called the "religious and national [not nationalist!] renaissance" now under way in Russia.[15] That awakening, which perhaps affects only a fraction of intellectuals today, but potentially has a sounding board among ordinary Russians of all walks of life, endangers the communist ethos at its root. The national tradition ultimately cannot be compatible with communism despite efforts of the regime to co-opt it—for example, by preserving or restoring ancient monuments. The specter of Russian nationalists, hiding their views successfully behind the mask of Politburo membership and about to take over the country, remains without supporting evidence.

The role of nationalism in the last few years can be followed only partially and through various distorting prisms. There have been samizdat and underground writings and even occasional meetings, most of which should not be described as revolutionary but internal-émigré—not that the difference is very reassuring to Soviet authorities. But the clearest reflection is probably in tensions that reach into the arena of highest leadership, into which only the Kremlinologist ventures.

There seem to have been three post-Stalin instances in which the national issue was in the forefront of Politburo maneuvering. In March 1953, Lavrenty Beria apparently took up the cudgel against harsh treatment of Ukrainian sensibilities (some would put it positively and say he opposed exaggerated Russian nationalism); the chief figure then pursuing such policies was Leonid Melnikov, first secretary of the Ukrainian Communist Party. When Melnikov was dismissed in June, the second secretary, Alexei Kirichenko, succeeded him. In several other cases the republic party's second secretaryship, hitherto invariably held by a Russian, was transferred to a national of the republic in question. But after his fall, Beria was attacked for fostering bourgeois nationalist elements in the Ukraine and elsewhere.

Kirichenko, possibly a symbol of Beria's opposition to Melnikov's denationalizing policies, nevertheless survived. But not for long. In 1960 he was dropped from his post in charge of cadres. One of the charges against the so-called antiparty group, presented by Nuritdin Mukhitdinov at the twenty-first party congress, was "chauvinism," that is, harsh Russian treatment of minorities.[16] But it is always possible to inveigh and act against both dangers, Russian and local, either simultaneously or one at a time. Michel Tatu suggests that the fall of Kirichenko, previously a wholehearted supporter of Khrushchev, "opened a new phase in Khrushchev's reign"—that is to say, it was a severe blow for the aspiring Nikita Sergeevich, who needed but could not again find as reliable a colleague on the Presidium. Whether the policy of gentler treatment of the minorities brought down Kirichenko or vice versa, the border territories suffered. Perhaps Latvia bore the brunt of the shift; hard-liner Arvid Pelshe symbolized the crackdown and was brought to the level of CPSU Presidium membership—where he remained at the time of his death in May 1983.

The third instance involves Piotr (Petro) Shelest. Once again the general issues of nationalism, autonomism, or opposition to Great Russian chauvinism (in descending order of intensity) seem to have assumed special sharpness in relation to the Ukraine. A decisive turn of events provoked the dismissal of a member of the highest authority, the Politburo (as the Presidium was renamed in 1966). A recent investigator declares that Shelest was not a nationalist but an autonomist: in his efforts "to protect his decisional autonomy from encroachments from Moscow, he built a power base in the Ukraine," which included many who leaned toward Ukrainian nationalism. The attack on Shelest began in 1973 with criticisms of his book, *Ukraino nasha radians'ka* (*O Ukraine, Our Soviet Land* [Kiev, 1970]), for excessive enthusiasm about its subject. Nevertheless, Farmer concludes that the main cause of Shelest's fall was a power struggle in which Vladimir Shcherbitsky was victor.[17]

Some Ukrainian emigrés exaggerated Shelest's nationalist tendencies after the fact to suggest that their values were shared in high places; other emigrés scoffed at such suggestions, because they implied that Ukrainian dissent was created by or dependent on the KGB or party authorities. Drawing firm conclusions is hazardous. One may risk noting, however, that ideology and power are often inextricably tangled; what is begun for the sake of principle may later be sought as a base of strength to protect the principle and then simply for itself; the power one strives to seize may take the shape of an ideological position. Whether one deeply believes in the ideology may not be of first importance. Joseph Schumpeter used to say that he did not credit the concept of insincerity in public affairs, for one invariably comes to believe what one incessantly professes. And it is so—perhaps not always but certainly from time to time. Human motives are often mixed, and fortunate is the man who understands and can describe his own motivation clearly.

The West, and in particular the United States, faces in the USSR a phenomenon unfamiliar in several respects. It is a multinational empire nearly unique in the world—an empire in the sense that a metropolitan people and several colonial peoples coexist, though several such peoples may be more advanced than the Russians.[18] Regardless of what Soviet or Western policies may be, certain attractions and pressures exist. The experience of Soviet minorities impinges on Soviet neighbors; this is especially true in the areas south of Azerbaijan and the Central Asian republics. Russian experience also influences Russian emigrés wherever they are today, especially in the United States and Western Europe, and

Russian Jewish experience influences many Israelis. Most resulting attitudes are ones of hostility, though that fact should not deceive us into thinking that positive feelings or impulses to praise, imitate, and repeat are entirely absent.

Here we may confine ourselves to pressures in the other direction. Regardless of governmental practices, American fashions in popular music, clothes, books and magazines, and even drugs find their way into the USSR. Official or unofficial U.S. radio has accelerated such trends and spreads news regarding events abroad and also, emphatically, inside the Soviet Union itself. It is hard to argue that U.S. foreign policy, however, has ever formed a clear pattern with respect to the issue of Soviet nationalities, Russian or non-Russian. Evidently affirming Russian tradition in the face of Soviet efforts to weaken or exterminate it has seemed too risky to the policymakers of Washington, D.C. Regarding the minorities, Western governments have seldom been in a position to arrive at any intelligent decision about what it would be desirable or sensible to expect or promote. Specialists on Georgia, for example, are almost nonexistent in the United States, let alone in its government. There are very few specialists on the Turks of the USSR; one might go quite a distance without finding an American official who knows what a Pshav or a Batsbi is or could locate their homelands within several hundred miles.[19] Therefore the instruments needed to promote policies or merely to articulate ideal states regarding the relation between Russians and minorities are lacking. But more fundamentally, the policies do not exist and there is no consensus (or even informed individual effort to state them) regarding ideal situations.[20]

A few lines cannot adequately sketch either the necessary policies or the ideal goals. Remarks under two or three headings, however, may indicate possible directions for such labors.

Language. "Political linguistics," writes a recent author, "represent Moscow's most successful accomplishment."[21] By the early 1930s, about 130 languages existed in the USSR, a result of official Soviet encouragement of small local dialects, the creation of new written languages, and the incorporation of new tongues into the educational system. Today there are fewer than 70 (or as many as 70, depending on what one finds surprising and whether one wishes to stress the change over the decades). It should not be concluded, however, that the number will soon diminish further. The proportion of Russian speakers has changed very little, and the remaining minority languages have held their own well. The chief development is bilingualism—the ability to speak Russian as well as a minority language or even substitution of it for one's primary tongue.

But change cuts both ways: in the Ukraine and Moldavia, Russian is gaining on the native tongues; among most Soviet Muslims, Russian is losing ground—but not among the Kazakhs, a minority in their own republic. Among culturally advanced groups, many Balts use Russian as a second language, but few Georgians do.[22] No particular social process or factor can be isolated, incidentally, as reliably predictive of such change.

When the West looks at the area of language, it sees a number of small languages that had no written literature before the revolution and perhaps have little oral literature that has not been more or less successfully adopted and co-opted by Soviet literary authorities. Larger and older minority languages have literatures that may hold dangers for the communist ethos no matter now *narodnyi* or Russophile the literature may be. Finally, there is the Russian language; many Westerners do not realize how much Russian literature and how many gifted Russian writers are anathema to the Soviets and virtually unknown to the present Russian generation. There is ample room for publication programs that would right imbalances and reawaken interest in the undeservedly neglected or forgotten, without raising any questions of a political sort.

Self-consciousness. The disappearance of the language of a tiny minority people may mean the de facto disappearance of that people. That may not happen on Soviet initiative; indeed, the contrary may be true, and much official money and effort may have been wasted in trying to give small groups real nationality status. But again, no sociological laws help much here. Take the Jews: in 1897 96.9 percent considered Yiddish their native language; in 1970 the figure was 17.7 percent.[23] Most Soviet Jews (72.8 percent) now say their mother tongue is Russian. Does the decline in the importance of Yiddish and the rise of Russian mean the disappearance of Soviet Jews? Clearly not. Germans and Tatars retain their own language to a greater extent, but they also are increasingly bilingual and make the Jews seem less unique. Again, there appears no easy correlation with other factors. The Jewish religion, for example, is in dire straits; but the sense of ethnic identity is very much alive.

For the West to offer a strong lead in this area is hazardous. The plight of the Jews is quite well known. Well-meaning efforts to help have actually hurt, or so it may be argued. But it is a continuing story that deserves continual reminders. That there ever were Soviet Germans in any number is known to relatively few in the West. The position of the Crimean Tatars, who for several Soviet official purposes are simply grouped with the Kazan Tatars, needs recalling, and even a modest amount of publicity might yield some Soviet concessions on the issue of allowing them to return home or reclaim property.

Religion. For close to 3 million Soviet Jews, 60 to 90 synagogues may actually be functioning; no schools for training rabbis exist in the USSR, though there is one in Budapest. In general, Soviet Judaism is hanging in the balance. For over 50 million Muslims, fewer than 200 mosques are open, and they are very unevenly distributed among the Islamic peoples; but here the numbers are even less revealing than for Jews or Christians. The state of the Russian Orthodox Church and other Russian Christians is lamentable in comparison to the prerevolutionary period but impressive when bearing in mind the long Russian campaign for atheism. Measurement is immensely difficult in the religious field. For example, during the early 1970s an American reporter asked some Uzbeks, just before the annual commemoration of the October Revolution, to name the most important holiday in the USSR. The invariable reply: the end of Ramadan.[24]

The religious past of the peoples of the USSR is part of their national heritage in every case, and it is invariably slighted in Soviet education and the mass media. There is a very broad field for outsiders to study, encourage, and publicize. No present danger exists that Judaism can be turned against the West anywhere. Although there cannot be fundamental compatibility between communism on the one hand and either Christianity or Islam on the other, the Soviets have a well-demonstrated ability to affect both religions by the assault certain leading clerics have mounted on Western positions, principles, or values. Roman Catholics in Brazil or El Salvador much more easily gain access to the U.S. press than those in Lithuania; "liberation theology" may be found in the former, but not in the latter. Soviet mullahs tour the Middle East, and Soviet officials are welcomed in South Yemen and Syria today, perhaps in Iran tomorrow. Muslim friends of the West—that is, identifiably religious persons and groups who are Muslim, rather than governmental figures who come from Muslim countries—are few; Western specialists on Islamic countries are a small, rather defensive, and embattled community. Within the last generation some Orthodox Christians in the West, especially via the newly named Orthodox Church in America, have made great efforts to enter fully into the life of the Western nations. There is still a long way to go. Many American Christians—Catholic and Protestant—are preoccupied with the shortcomings of their own government and society as they see them. Paradoxically, it is the refusal of many American Orthodox to take up antiestablishment positions that mainly impedes their assimilation into American religious culture. Some Orthodox groups are violently anticommunist and royalist, and proclaim canonization of the last tsar and many of his supporters; whatever its merits, such an ethos is far removed from other, moderate Orthodox groups—not to mention ordinary Americans.

Scholars, students, and publicists might take note, officially or un-officially, on the basis of public or private funds and concerns, of some of the circumstances here outlined. In addition, Western governments ought to be aware of them, with several kinds of consequences. First, in propaganda or informational activities, the existence and nature of the languages, religions, and national traditions ought to be understood and sympathetic efforts ought to be made to reach the peoples concerned, at least the larger nations, on a regular basis if possible. It is not necessary to incite all Soviet nationalities (Russians included) to revolution or to promote ethnic hostility. It is wise to indicate external concern and respect; the result may be to enhance internal concern, at least marginally, here and there. Second, in diplomatic interchange with the Soviets or other forms of exchange, cultural but also political and economic, West-ern representatives ought not to allow taunts about Western imperialism to go by without mention of Soviet imperialism; attacks on past Western colonies should not pass without mention of Soviet colonies of the present; and criticism of racial, ethnic, or other discrimination in the West should merit mention of Soviet racial discrimination. Although greater patience with Third World diplomats and intellectuals may be prudent, it would also be desirable to deliver occasional reminders that their ideolog-ical delusions may be challenged and threatened by both facts and alterna-tive interpretations. Above all, in its intercourse with the rest of the world, the West should exhibit for all cultures, not merely those of the Soviet peoples (lest a politically motivated selectivity be suspected instead of the universal attitudes we wish to foster), the kind of respect that is based on knowledge. Persons who are for one reason or other unable to do so, or are simply awkward and maladroit at it, should be employed in other capacities, not in international relations.

In our age it is common to find rational discourse replaced by the screeching of secular dogmatists, who are convinced that right and morality lie wholly on their side (not necessarily their *country's* side, indeed, often the contrary). At the United Nations, in international conferences and organizations of all kinds, in the media of several coun-tries, popular dogmas include nationalism and self-determination. It is characteristic of such doctrines, writes Elie Kedourie, "to disregard the limits imposed by nature and history, and to believe that a good will alone can accomplish miracles."[25] But if one is realistic and sensible, one may hope to give heart to suffering peoples, to show regard for their contribu-tions to the story of mankind, and to impel oppressive governments to lighten burdens, if ever so slightly, in the USSR and elsewhere.

NOTES

1. Seweryn Bialer, *Stalin's Successors* (Cambridge, England: Cambridge University Press, 1980), p. 54.

2. Alexandre Bennigsen, "Islamic or Local Consciousness Among Soviet Nationalities?" in Edward Allworth, ed., *Soviet Nationality Problems* (New York: Columbia University Press, 1971).

3. No doubt that is only one aspect of official failure to understand the profound political implications of religious (and atheist) influences in various corners of the world in our time, even in the West, where religion and politics are more separable.

4. Leonard Schapiro, "Some Afterthoughts on Solzhenitsyn," *Russian Review* 33 (October 1974): 417.

5. V. V. Barthold, *Four Studies on the History of Central Asia*, 3 vols. (Leiden: E. J. Brill, 1956), 1:15, 63–66.

6. Alexandre Bennigsen and Chantal Lemercier-Quelquejay, *Islam in the Soviet Union* (New York: Praeger, 1967), p. 5.

7. Ronald Wixman, *Language Aspects of Ethnic Patterns and Processes in the North Caucasus* (Chicago: University of Chicago, Department of Geography, 1980), p. 15.

8. Ibid., p. 101.

9. Ibid., p. 107.

10. V. Stanley Vardys, *The Catholic Church: Dissent and Nationality in Soviet Lithuania* (Boulder, Colo.: East European Quarterly; distributed by Columbia University Press, 1978), 226.

11. See the article in *Sovetskaia Kirgiziia*, December 27, 1981.

12. Alexandre Bennigsen, "Soviet Muslims and the World of Islam," *Problems of Communism* (March–April 1980), p. 47.

13. Ibid., p. 41.

14. Bennigsen, "Islamic or Local Consciousness?" p. 174.

15. Solzhenitsyn, "Misconceptions About Russia Are a Threat to America," *Foreign Affairs* 58 (Spring 1980): 832.

16. Robert Conquest (*Power and Policy in the U.S.S.R.: The Study of Soviet Dynasties* [New York: St. Martin's Press, 1961]) has studied these two episodes carefully. On Kirichenko, see also Michel Tatu, *Power in the Kremlin: From Khrushchev to Kosygin* (London: Collins, 1970), pp. 33–37.

17. Kenneth C. Farmer, *Ukrainian Nationalism in the Post-Stalin Era* (The Hague and Boston: Martinus Nijhoff, 1980), p. 214.

18. The People's Republic of China may seem closest, though only about 7 percent of its population is non-Chinese (non-Han) as against the USSR's half non-Russians; India certainly lacks ethnic homogeneity, but the colonial category is scarcely applicable except to the heritage or memory of British-Indian relations.

19. The Pshavs are a Georgian people who had no higher religion as of 1917; the Batsbi are a small North Caucasian Christian people.

20. An additional word may be in order about the difference between policies and ideal states. Policies are official stances or efforts to do what is judged politically feasible or wise under the circumstances; ideal states are what might be considered the best possible conditions but not necessarily those realizable in the near or even foreseeable future.

21. Hélène Carrère d'Encausse, *Decline of an Empire* (New York: Newsweek Books, 1979), p. 165.

22. Forty-five percent of Latvians, 35 percent of Lithuanians, 27 percent of Estonians, 20 percent of Georgians. Ibid., pp. 172–73.

23. Ibid., p. 203.

24. Ibid., p. 257.

25. Elie Kedourie, *Nationalism*, 2nd ed. (London: Hutchinson University Library, 1961), p. 109.

Index